Lecture Notes in Artificial Inte!

Edited by J. G. Carbonell and J. Siekmann

Subseries of Lecture Notes in Computer Science

Anssi Yli-Jyrä   Lauri Karttunen
Juhani Karhumäki (Eds.)

Finite-State Methods and Natural Language Processing

5th International Workshop, FSMNLP 2005
Helsinki, Finland, September 1-2, 2005
Revised Papers

 Springer

Series Editors

Jaime G. Carbonell, Carnegie Mellon University, Pittsburgh, PA, USA
Jörg Siekmann, University of Saarland, Saarbrücken, Germany

Volume Editors

Anssi Yli-Jyrä
Scientific Computing Ltd.
P.O. Box 405, 02101 Espoo, Finland
E-mail: ylijyra@csc.fi

Lauri Karttunen
Palo Alto Research Center
3333 Coyote Hill Rd, Palo Alto, CA 94304, USA
E-mail: karttunen@parc.com

Juhani Karhumäki
University of Turku
Department of Mathematics
20014 Turku, Finland
E-mail: karhumak@utu.fi

Library of Congress Control Number: 2006937535

CR Subject Classification (1998): I.2.6-7, I.2, F.1.1, F.4.2-3, F.2

LNCS Sublibrary: SL 7 – Artificial Intelligence

ISSN   0302-9743
ISBN-10   3-540-35467-0 Springer Berlin Heidelberg New York
ISBN-13   978-3-540-35467-3 Springer Berlin Heidelberg New York

This work is subject to copyright. All rights are reserved, whether the whole or part of the material is concerned, specifically the rights of translation, reprinting, re-use of illustrations, recitation, broadcasting, reproduction on microfilms or in any other way, and storage in data banks. Duplication of this publication or parts thereof is permitted only under the provisions of the German Copyright Law of September 9, 1965, in its current version, and permission for use must always be obtained from Springer. Violations are liable to prosecution under the German Copyright Law.

Springer is a part of Springer Science+Business Media

springer.com

© Springer-Verlag Berlin Heidelberg 2006

Preface

These proceedings contain the revised versions of the papers presented at the 5th International Workshop of Finite-State Methods and Natural Language Processing, FSMNLP 2005. The book includes also the extended abstracts of a number of poster papers and software demos accepted to this conference-like workshop.

FSMNLP 2005 was held in Helsinki, Finland, on September 1–2, 2005. The event was the fifth instance in the series of FSMNLP workshops, and the first that was arranged as a stand-alone event, with two satellite events of its own: the Two-Level Morphology Day (TWOLDAY) and a national workshop on Automata, Words and Logic (AWL). The earlier FSMNLP workshops have been mainly arranged in conjunction with a bigger event such as an ECAI, ESSLLI or EACL workshop, and this practice may still be favored in the future.

The collocation of the three events promoted a multidisciplinary atmosphere. For this reason, the focus of FSMNLP 2005 covered a variety of topics related but not restricted to finite-state methods in natural language processing.

The 24 regular papers and 7 poster papers were selected from 50 submissions to the workshop. Each submitted regular paper was evaluated by at least three Program Committee members, with the help of external referees. In addition to the submitted papers and two invited lectures, six software demos were presented. The authors of the papers and extended abstracts come from Canada, Denmark, Finland, France, Germany, India, Ireland, Israel, Japan, The Netherlands, Norway, Spain, South Africa, Sweden, Turkey, and the USA.

It is a pleasure to thank the members of the Program Committee and the external referees for reviewing the papers and maintaining the high standard of the FSMNLP workshops. Naturally, we owe many thanks to every single conference participant for his or her contributions to the conference and for making FSMNLP 2005 a successful scientific event.

FSMNLP 2005 was co-organized by the Department of General Linguistics at the University of Helsinki (host) and CSC, the Finnish IT center for science (co-ordination). We thank the members of the Steering Committees for their kind support in the early stage of the project and Antti Arppe, Sari Hyvärinen and Hanna Westerlund for helping with the local arrangements. Last but not least, we thank the conference sponsors for their financial support.

August 2005

A. Yli-Jyrä
L. Karttunen
J. Karhumäki

Organization

FSMNLP 2005 was organized by the Department of General Linguistics, University of Helsinki in cooperation with CSC, the Finnish IT center for science.

Invited Speakers

Tero Harju	University of Turku, Finland
Lauri Karttunen	Palo Alto Research Center, Stanford University, USA

Program Committee

Steven Bird	University of Melbourne, Australia
Francisco Casacuberta	Universitat Politècnica de València, Spain
Jean-Marc Champarnaud	Université de Rouen, France
Jan Daciuk	Gdansk University of Technology, Poland
Jason Eisner	Johns Hopkins University, USA
Tero Harju	University of Turku, Finland
Arvi Hurskainen	IAAS, University of Helsinki, Finland
Juhani Karhumäki, *Co-chair*	University of Turku, Finland
Lauri Karttunen, *Co-chair*	PARC and Stanford University, USA
André Kempe	Xerox Research Centre Europe, France
George Anton Kiraz	Beth Mardutho: The Syriac Institute, USA
András Kornai	Budapest Institute of Technology, Hungary
D. Terence Langendoen	University of Arizona, USA
Eric Laporte	Université de Marne-la-Vallée, France
Mike Maxwell	Linguistic Data Consortium, USA
Mark-Jan Nederhof	University of Groningen, The Netherlands
Gertjan van Noord	University of Groningen, The Netherlands
Kemal Oflazer	Sabanci University, Turkey
Jean-Eric Pin	CNRS/University Paris 7, France
James Rogers	Earlham College, USA
Giorgio Satta	University of Padua, Italy
Jacques Sakarovitch	CNRS/ENST, France
Richard Sproat	University of Illinois at Urbana-Champaign, USA
Nathan Vaillette	University of Tübingen, Germany
Atro Voutilainen	Connexor Oy, Finland
Bruce W. Watson	University of Pretoria, South Africa
Shuly Wintner	University of Haifa, Israel

Sheng Yu   University of Western Ontario, Canada
Lynette van Zijl   Stellenbosch University, South Africa

Organizing Committee

Anssi Yli-Jyrä, *Chair*   University of Helsinki and CSC, Finland
Hanna-Maria Westerlund   University of Helsinki, Finland
Sari Hyvärinen   University of Helsinki, Finland
Antti Arppe   University of Helsinki, Finland

Steering Committee I (FSMNLP Traditions)

Lauri Karttunen   PARC and Stanford University, USA
Kimmo Koskenniemi   University of Helsinki, Finland
Gertjan van Noord   University of Groningen, The Netherlands
Kemal Oflazer   Sabanci University, Turkey

Steering Committee II (Local Advisory Group)

Lauri Carlson   University of Helsinki, Finland
Tero Harju   University of Turku, Finland
Lauri Hella   University of Tampere, Finland
Arvi Hurskainen   University of Helsinki, Finland
Fred Karlsson   University of Helsinki, Finland
Krista Lagus   Helsinki University of Technology,
                                   Finland
Kerkko Luosto   University of Helsinki, Finland
Matti Nykänen   University of Helsinki, Finland

Additional Referees

Rafael C. Carrasco   Universitat d'Alacant, Spain
Loek Cleophas   Technische Universiteit Eindhoven,
                                   The Netherlands
Yvon Francois   GET/ENST and LTCI, France
Ernest Ketcha Ngassam   University of South Africa and
                                   University of Pretoria, South Africa
Ines Klimann   Universite Paris 7, France
Sylvain Lombardy   Universite Paris 7, France
David Picó-Vila   Universidad Politécnica de Valencia, Spain
Enrique Vidal   Universidad Politécnica de Valencia, Spain
Juan Miguel Vilar   Universitat Jaume I, Spain
M. Inés Torres   Universidad País Vasco, Spain
Anssi Yli-Jyrä   University of Helsinki and CSC, Finland

Sponsoring Institutions

CSC - Scientific Computing Ltd., Finland
University of Helsinki, Finland
The KIT Network, Finland
Academy of Finland
Connexor Ltd., Finland
Lingsoft Ltd., Finland

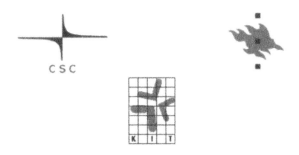

Table of Contents

Abstracts of Interactive Presentations

Abstracts of Software Demos

Characterizations of Regularity

Tero Harju

Department of Mathematics, University of Turku, Finland

Abstract. Regular languages have many different characterizations in terms of automata, congruences, semigroups *etc.* We have a look at some more recent results, obtained mostly during the last two decades, namely characterizations using morphic compositions, equality sets and well orderings.

1 Introduction

We do not intend to give a full survey on regular languages but rather a short overview of some of the topics that have surfaced during the last two decades.

Customarily regular languages are defined either as languages accepted by finite automata, represented by regular expressions, or generated by right linear grammars. The most common approach is by acceptance using deterministic finite automata, or a *DFA* for short. A DFA can be described as a 'concrete machine' with a read-only input tape from which the head of the automaton reads one square at a time from the left end to the right end. A DFA $\mathcal{A}$ can be conveniently presented as a 5-tuple

$$\mathcal{A} = (Q, A, \delta, q_0, F),$$

where Q is the set of initial states, A is the alphabet of the inputs, and the *transition function* $\delta \colon Q \times A \to Q$ describes the *action* of $\mathcal{A}$ such that $\delta(q, a) = p$ means that while reading the symbol a in state q, the automaton changes to state p and starts consuming the next input symbol. The state q_0 is the initial state of $\mathcal{A}$, and $F \subseteq Q$ is the set of its final states. The action of the automaton $\mathcal{A}$ is often written in the form $qa = p$ instead of $\delta(q, a) = p$. The transition function δ extends to words by setting $\delta(q, wa) = \delta(\delta(q, w), a)$. Thus for each word w, $\delta(q, w)$ is the state where the automaton enters when started in the state q and after exhausting w. If $w = \varepsilon$, the empty word, then $\delta(q, \varepsilon) = q$ for all states q.

More pictorially a finite automaton can be described as a directed *graph*, where nodes represent the states of the automaton and each labelled edge $q \xrightarrow{a} p$ corresponds to the transition $\delta(q, a) = p$. Then $\delta(q, w)$ is the state that is reached from q by traversing the edges labelled by the letters of w.

A language $L \subseteq A$ is *regular* if it is accepted by a DFA, $L = L(\mathcal{A})$, where

$$L(\mathcal{A}) = \{w \in A^* \mid \delta(q_0, w) \in F\}.$$

A. Yli-Jyrä, L. Karttunen, and J. Karhumäki (Eds.): FSMNLP 2005, LNAI 4002, pp. 1–8, 2006.
© Springer-Verlag Berlin Heidelberg 2006

The family of regular languages is a neat family in the sense that it is closed under many natural operations of languages: if L and K are regular languages, then so are

- $L \cup K$, $L \cap K$, $L \setminus K$, catenation $L \cdot K$, Kleene closures L^* and L^+, shuffle $K \text{s} L$, quotients $L^{-1}K$ and LK^{-1}, complement $A^* \setminus L$, morphic (and the inverse morphic) images $h(L)$ (and $h^{-1}(L)$), as well as the reversal L^R (mirror image).

This list could be continued much further.

Instead of deterministic finite automata one can also employ other finite models of automata for regular languages. For instance, a language L is regular if it is accepted by a *nondeterministic* FA where the transitions are given by a relation instead of a function.

We can extend the transition function (or relation) in several ways, say by attaching conditions to the transitions that change the design of the states. As an example, each state can have a sign, $+$ or $-$, and the transitions can depend on the signs and change them.

Also, one can expand the way how finite automata accept words. An *alternating* finite automaton is a nondeterministic FA where the states are divided into existential and universal states, and acceptance depends on the global tree of behaviour.

By allowing finite automata to read the input word both to the left and right does not influence the family of accepted languages, i.e., a 2-way FA accepts only regular languages.

Decision problems for regular languages are, as a rule, decidable. However, many algorithmic problems are hard for them. For instance, one can prove that the problem of finding a nondeterministic finite automaton with the smallest number of states accepting a regular language L is truly hard. The problem is PSPACE-complete.

The syntactic characterizations of regular languages are originally due to Myhill [1] and Nerode [2] as well as to Rabin and Scott [3] at the end of the 1950s. These characterizations follow from analyzing the behaviour and structures of finite automata.

For a language $L \subseteq A^*$ define the relation $\sim_L$ by

$$u \sim_L v \iff u^{-1}L = v^{-1}L,$$

where $u^{-1}L = \{w \mid uw \in L\}$. This relation is an equivalence relation on A^*, and thus A^* is divided into equivalence classes w.r.t. $\sim_L$.

Theorem 1. *A language L is regular if and only if $\sim_L$ is of finite index, i.e., there are only finitely many equivalence classes w.r.t. $\sim_L$.*

The idea behind Theorem 1 is that the set $u^{-1}L$ corresponds to the state $\delta(q_0, u)$ of the DFA accepting L. As an example, consider the language $L = \{a^n b^n \mid n \geq 0\}$ which is well known to be nonregular. We notice that the sets $u_i^{-1}L$ are all different for the words $u_i = a^i$, $i \geq 1$. Since there are infinitely many sets $u^{-1}L$, we deduce that, indeed, the language L is not regular.

Let

$$u \cong_L v : \quad xuy \in L \iff xvy \in L$$

be the *syntactic congruence* of $L \subseteq A^*$.

Theorem 2. *A language L is regular if and only if the syntactic congruence of L has finite index.*

Using syntactic congruences one can study the fine structure of regular languages more deeply. This approach leads to *algebraic theory* of regular languages. For instance, Schützenberger [4] showed that a language L is star-free if and only if its syntactic monoid is aperiodic, i.e., contains only trivial subgroups. Here we say that L is *star-free* if it can be represented by a generalized regular expression allowing complementation L^c but disallowing stars $*$. For instance, $A^* = \emptyset^c$, and

$$(ab)^* = 1 + a\emptyset^c \cap \emptyset^c b \cap (\emptyset^c aa\emptyset^c)^c \cap (\emptyset^c bb\emptyset^c)^c.$$

We also state an algebraic characterization of regular languages that is related to syntactic congruences.

Theorem 3. *A language L is regular if and only if it is recognized by a finite monoid M, i.e., there is a finite monoid M such that $F \subseteq M$ and*

$$L = \varphi^{-1}(F)$$

for a monoid morphism $\varphi \colon A^* \to M$ onto M.

We can restate this theorem as follows:

Theorem 4. *A language L is regular if and only if there exists a finite monoid M such that*

$$L = \varphi^{-1}\varphi(L)$$

for a monoid morphism $\varphi \colon A^* \to M$.

Regular languages can also be described by matrices. The following theorem is due to Schützenberger.

Theorem 5. *For each regular language L, there are $0, 1$-vectors u and v, and a matrix M (of finite sets) such that*

$$L = u^T M^* v.$$

Regular languages have had connections to logic since the studied made by Büchi [6], Elgot [7], and McNaughton and Papert [5].

Theorem 6. *A language L is regular if and only if L definable in the monadic second order logic (which allows comparisons of positions of letters in words and quantifiers over sets of positions).*

2   Morphic Characterizations

The topic of morphic characterizations of regular languages was was initiated by Culik, Fich, and Salomaa [8] in 1982, and it was continued by several people during the following years.

Recall that a mapping $h\colon A^* \to B^*$ is a *morphism* if

$$h(uv) = h(u)h(v)$$

for all words u, v. The *inverse morphism* is the many-valued mapping

$$h^{-1}(v) = \{u \mid h(u) = v\}\,.$$

In the theorems that follow the morphisms h_i, for $i = 1, 2, \ldots$, are between suitable alphabets. Culik, Fich, and Salomaa [8] proved that

Theorem 7. *A language L is regular if and only if there are morphisms h_i such that*

$$L = h_4 h_3^{-1} h_2 h_1^{-1}(a^*b).$$

This result was improved by Latteux and Leguy[9] in 1983:

Theorem 8. *A language L is regular if and only if there are morphisms h_i such that*

$$L = h_3 h_2^{-1} h_1(a^*b).$$

We shall sketch the idea behind the proof of this theorem.

In the other direction the claim follows from the fact that regular languages are closed under taking morphic images and inverse morphic images, and the starting language a^*b in Theorem 8 is certainly regular.

Let then L be a regular language and let $\mathcal{A}$ be a DFA accepting L. Assume that the states of $\mathcal{A}$ are

$$Q = \{q_0, q_1, \ldots, q_m\},$$

where q_0 is the initial state. Let

$$\varGamma = \{[q_i, x, q_j] \mid \delta(q_i, x) = q_j\}$$

be an alphabet that encodes the transitions of $\mathcal{A}$, and let a, b and d be three special symbols. Define our first morphism $h_1\colon \{a, b\} \to \{a, b, d\}^*$ by

$$h_1(a) = ad^m \quad \text{and} \quad h_1(b) = bd^m\,,$$

Hence $h_1(a^nb) = (ad^m)^n \cdot bd^m$ for each power n.

Let then $h_2\colon \varGamma^* \to \{a, b, d\}^*$ be defined by

$$h_2([q_i, x, q_j]) = \begin{cases} d^i ad^{m-j} & \text{if } j \neq m\,, \\ d^i bd^m & \text{if } j = m\,. \end{cases}$$

Hence

$$u \in h_2^{-1}h_1(a^n b) \iff u \text{ codes the accepting computation of } \mathcal{A} \text{ of } a_1 a_2 \dots a_n.$$

Finally, let $h_3 \colon \Gamma^* \to A^*$ be defined by

$$h_3([q, x, p]) = x.$$

Then $L(A) = h_3 h_2^{-1} h_1(a^* b)$.

Even a simpler variant was shown to hold by Latteux and Leguy [9]:

Theorem 9. *A language L is regular if and only if there are morphisms h_i such that*

$$L = h_3^{-1} h_2 h_1^{-1}(b).$$

The special case of regular star languages has especially appealing characterization.

Theorem 10. *For any language L, the language L^* is regular if and only if there exists a (uniform) morphism h and a finite set F of words such that*

$$L^* = h^{-1}(F^*).$$

The morphic characterizations of regular languages extend partly to transductions, i.e., to many-valued mappings $\tau \colon A^* \to B^*$ computed by finite transducers. The following is due to Turakainen [10], Karhumäki and Linna [11].

Theorem 11. *Let R be a given regular language. Then for all languages L,*

$$L \cap R = h_3 h_2^{-1} h_1 \mu(L),$$

where $\mu \colon A^* \to A^* d$ is a marking defined by $\mu(w) = wd$ for a special symbol d.

Latteux, Leguy, and Turakainen [9, 12] showed

Theorem 12. *Each rational transductions has the forms*

$$h_4 h_3^{-1} h_2 h_1^{-1} \mu \quad \text{and} \quad h_4^{-1} h_3 h_2^{-1} h_1 \mu,$$

where μ is a marking.

The following theorem of Harju and Kleijn [13] shows that there is no algorithm to decide whether the marking μ is needed.

Theorem 13. *Iy is undecidable whether or not a transduction has a representation without endmarker μ.*

3   Equality Sets

In the Post Correspondence Problem, *PCP* for short, the problem instances are pairs (g, h) of morphisms $g, h \colon A^* \to B^*$, and the problem asks to determine whether there exists a nonempty word w such that $g(w) = h(w)$. It was shown by Post in 1947 that the PCP is undecidable in general, that is, there does not exist an algorithm for its solution.

The set of all solutions of an instance $g, h \colon A^* \to B^*$ is called the *equality set* of g and h. It is the set

$$E(g, h) = \{w \in A^* \mid g(w) = h(w)\}.$$

Choffrut and Karhumäki [14] have shown that the equality set $E(g, h)$ is regular for a special class of morphisms, called bounded delay morphisms. However, for these morphisms the problem whether or not $E(h, g)$ contains a nonempty word remains undecidable! This means that there is no effective construction of a finite automaton $\mathcal{A}$ accepting the regular language $E(g, h)$ when the instance g, h consisting of bounded delay morphisms is given.

A morphism $h \colon A^* \to B^*$ is called a *prefix morphism*, if for all different letters $a, b \in A$, the image $h(a)$ is not a prefix of the image $h(b)$.

If A and B are alphabets such that $A \subseteq B$, then the morphism $\pi_A \colon B^* \to A^*$, defined by

$$\pi_A(a) = \begin{cases} a & \text{if } a \in A, \\ \varepsilon & \text{if } a \in B \setminus A, \end{cases}$$

is the *projection* of B^* onto A^*.

The next result is due to Halava, Harju, and Latteux [15, 16].

Theorem 14. *A star language $L = L^* \subseteq A^*$ is regular if and only if*

$$L = \pi_A(E(g, h))$$

for prefix morphisms g, h and the projection π_A onto A^*.

A morphism $f \colon A^* \to B^*$ is a *coding*, if it maps letters to letters.

Theorem 15. *A star language $L = L^* \subseteq A^*$ is regular if and only if*

$$L = f(E(g, h))$$

for prefix morphisms g, h and a coding f.

4   Well Quasi-orders

A *quasi-order* $\rho \subseteq X \times X$ on a set X is a reflexive and transitive order relation:

$$\left. \begin{array}{c} x\rho x \quad \text{and} \quad \begin{array}{c} x\rho y \\ y\rho z \end{array} \right\} \Longrightarrow x\rho z.$$

Moreover, ρ is a *well quasi-order*, *wqo* for short, if every nonempty subset $Y \subseteq X$ has at least one minimal element but only finite number of (non-equivalent) minimal elements. In the below instead of ρ we use $\leq$ for an order relation.

Lemma 1. *The following are equivalent for a relation $\leq$ to be a wqo:*

(1) Every infinite sequence of elements of S has an infinite ascending subsequence.

(2) If $x_1, x_2, \ldots$ is an infinite sequence of elements, then $x_i \leq x_j$ for some $i < j$.

(3) There are no infinite strictly descending sequences, nor infinite sets of pairwise incomparable elements.

The following result is a special case of Higman's [17] theorem:

Theorem 16. *The set of words A^* is well quasi-ordered by the subsequence order defined by*

$$\left. \begin{array}{l} x = x_1 x_2 \ldots x_n \\ y = y_1 x_1 y_2 x_2 \ldots y_n x_n y_{n+1} \end{array} \right\} \implies x \leq y.$$

The idea behind the proof of this theorem is gratifying: Let $w_1, w_2, \ldots$ be an infinite sequence of words such that $w_i \not\leq w_j$ for all $i < j$, and that the sequence is 'length minimal' in the sense that the length of w_k is as short as possible so that $w_1, w_2, \ldots, w_k$ satisfies $w_i \not\leq w_j$ for all $i < j \leq k$. There is a letter a that starts infinitely many w_i, say

$$w_{i_1} = av_1, \ w_{i_2} = av_2, \ldots$$

Now, $w_1, w_2, \ldots, w_{i_1-1}, v_1, v_2, \ldots$ is a 'smaller' sequence satisfying the requirements; a contradiction.

For the theorem of Ehrenfeucht, Haussler, Rozenberg [18] we say that a quasi-order $\leq$ is *monotone* if

$$\left. \begin{array}{l} x_1 \leq y_1 \\ x_2 \leq y_2 \end{array} \right\} \implies x_1 x_2 \leq y_1 y_2.$$

A language L is *upwards closed* closed w.r.t. the ordering $\leq$, if for all $w \in L$, $w \leq v$ implies that also $v \in L$.

Theorem 17. *A language L is regular if and only if it is upwards closed w.r.t. some monotone wqo on A^*.*

The proof in the direction ($\implies$) uses the Myhill–Nerode characterization of regularity: a language L is regular if and only if L is a union of equivalence classes of some congruence of finite index. Note that a monotone equivalence relation is a congruence.

References

1. Myhill, J.: Finite automata and the representation of events. Technical Report WADD TR-57-624, Wright Patterson Air Force Base, Ohio (1957)
2. Nerode, A.: Linear automaton transformations. Proc. Amer. Math. Soc. **9** (1958) 541–544

3. Rabin, M.O., Scott, D.: Finite automata and their decision problems. IBM Journal **3** (1959) 115–125

4. Schützenberger, M.P.: On finite monoids having only trivial subgroups. Inf. Control **8** (1965) 190–194

5. McNaughton, R., Papert, S.: Counter-free automata. The M.I.T. Press, Cambridge, Mass.-London (1971) With an appendix by William Henneman, M.I.T. Research Monograph, No. 65.

6. Büchi, J.R.: Weak second-order arithmetic and finite automata. Z. Math. Logik Grundlagen Math. **6** (1960) 66–92

7. Elgot, C.C.: Decision problems of finite automata design and related arithmetics. Trans. Amer. Math. Soc. **98** (1961) 21–51

8. Culik II, K., Fich, F., Salomaa, A.: A homomorphic characterization of regular languages. Discrete Appl. Math. **4** (1982) 149–152

9. Latteux, M., Leguy, J.: On the composition of morphisms and inverse morphisms. In: Lecture Notes in Comput. Sci. Volume 154. (1983) 420–432

10. Turakainen, P.: A machine-oriented approach to composition of morphisms and inverse morphisms. Bulletin of the EATCS **20** (1983) 162–166

11. Karhumäki, J., Linna, M.: A note on morphic characterization of languages. Discrete Appl. Math. **5** (1983) 243–246

12. Latteux, M., Turakainen, P.: A new normal form for the compositions of morphisms and inverse morphisms. Math. Systems Theory **20** (1987) 261–271

13. Harju, T., Kleijn, H.C.M.: Decidability problems for unary output sequential transducers. Discrete Appl. Math. **32** (1991) 131–140

14. Choffrut, C., Karhumäki, J.: Test sets for morphisms with bounded delay. Discrete Appl. Math. **12** (1985) 93–101

15. Halava, V., Harju, T., Latteux, M.: Representation of regular languages by equality sets. Bulletin of the EATCS **86** (2005) 224–228

16. Halava, V., Harju, T., Latteux, M.: Equality sets of prefix morphisms and regular star languages. Inf. Process. Lett. **94** (2005) 151–154

17. Higman, G.: Ordering by divisibility in abstract algebras. Proc. London Math. Soc. **3** (1952)

18. Ehrenfeucht, A., Haussler, D., Rozenberg, G.: On regularity of context-free languages. Theoret. Comput. Sci. **27** (1983) 311–332

Finnish Optimality-Theoretic Prosody

Lauri Karttunen

Palo Alto Research Center, Stanford University, USA

A well-known phenomenon in Finnish prosody is the alternation of binary and ternary feet. In native Finnish words, the primary stress falls on the first syllable. Secondary stress generally falls on every second syllable: (vói.mis).(tè.li).(jòi.ta) 'gymnasts' creating a sequence of trochaic binary feet. However, secondary stress skips a light syllable that is followed by a heavy syllable. In (vói.mis.te).(lèm.me) 'we are doing gymnastics', the first foot is ternary, a dactyl.

Within the context of Optimality Theory (OT, [5]), it has been argued that prosodic phenomena are best explained in terms of universal metric constraints. OT constraints can be violated; no word can satisfy all of them. A language-specific ranking of the constraints makes some violations less important than others. In her 1999 dissertation [2], A unified account of binary and ternary stress, Nine Elenbaas gives an analysis of Finnish in which the alternation between binary and ternary feet follows as a side effect of the ordering of two particular constraints, *Lapse and *(L'. H) The *Lapse constraint stipulates that an unstressed syllable must be adjacent to a stressed syllable or to word edge. The *(L'. H) constraint prohibits feet such as (tè.lem) where a light stressed syllable is followed by a heavy unstressed syllable. The latter constraint of course is outranked by the constraint that requires initial stress on the first syllable in Finnish regardless of the its weight. In his 2003 article on Finnish Noun Inflection [4], Paul Kiparsky gives essentially the same account of the binary/ternary alternation except that he replaces the *(L'.H) rule by a more general StressToWeight constraint.

Although OT constraints themselves can be expressed in finite-state terms, Optimality Theory as a whole is not a finite-state model if it involves unbounded counting of constraint violations [3]. With that limitation OT analyses can be modelled with finite-state tools. In this paper we will give a full computational implementation of the Elenbaas and Kiparsky analyses using the extended regular expression calculus from the 2003 Beesley & Karttunen book on Finite State Morphology [1]. Surprisingly, it turns out that Elenbaas and Kiparsky both make some incorrect predictions. For example, according to their accounts a word such as kalasteleminen 'fishing' should begin with a ternary foot: (ká.las.te).(lè.mi).nen. The correct footing is (ká.las).(tè.le).(mì.nen). There may of course be some ranking of OT constraints under which the binary/ternary alternation in Finnish comes "for free". It does not emerge from the Elenbaas and Kiparsky analyses.

This case study illustrates a more general point: Optimality Theory is computationally difficult and OT theorists are much in the need of computational help.

A. Yli-Jyrä, L. Karttunen, and J. Karhumäki (Eds.): FSMNLP 2005, LNAI 4002, pp. 9–10, 2006.
© Springer-Verlag Berlin Heidelberg 2006

References

1. K. R. Beesley and L. Karttunen. *Finite State Morphology*. CSLI Studies in Computational Linguistics. CSLI Publications, Stanford, CA, 2003.
2. N. Elenbaas. *A unified account of binary and ternary stress: considerations from Sentani and Finnish.* PhD thesis, Utrecht University, the Netherlands, 1999.
3. R. Frank and G. Satta. Optimality theory and the generative complexity of constraint violability. *Computational Linguistics*, 24:307–315, 1998.
4. P. Kiparsky. Finnish noun inflection. In D. Nelson and S. Manninen, editors, *Generative Approaches to Finnic Linguistics*. CSLI Publications, Stanford, CA, 2003.
5. A. Prince and P. Smolensky. Optimality theory: Constraint interaction in generative grammar. Technical Report RuCCS TR-2, Rutgers University Center for Cognitive Science, New Brunswick, NJ, 1993.

Partitioning Multitape Transducers

François Barthélemy

CNAM-Cédric, 292 rue Saint-Martin, F-75003 Paris, France
and INRIA, domaine de Voluceau, F-78153 Rocquencourt cedex, France
barthe@cnam.fr

Abstract. In this paper, we define a class of transducers closed under intersection and complementation, which are the operations used for contextual rule compilation. This class of transducers is not theoretically more powerful than the Epsilon-Free Letter Transducers most commonly used. But they are more convenient for morphological description whenever the correspondence between lexical and surface forms is not a symbol-to-symbol matching.

A complete set of operations on transducers is defined, including some operations (projection and join) which change the number of tapes of the transducers.

1 Introduction

Finite State morphology use contextual rules (rewrite rules or two-level rules) which are compiled into finite-state transducers. The key idea of compilation, due to Kaplan and Kay [3] is subtractive: first, compute a superset of the specified language, namely the concatenation closure of the rule centers; then retract what is not allowed by the contexts specified in the rules. At the operational level, the fundamental operations are complementation and subtraction.

Finite State Transducers are not closed under complementation and subtraction in general. The subclass of transducers where the transitions are labeled by exactly one symbol on each tape is closed under complementation, subtraction and intersection. It is called *Epsilon-Free Letter Transducer* [5]. This subclass is used for Finite State morphology. A special symbol 0 is artificially introduced to represent the empty string using an ordinary symbol. Introduction and removal of 0s are done as pre and post-processing when executing a transducer.

In this paper, we present another subclass of transducers that are closed under complementation, intersection and subtraction, called the Partitioning Multitape Transducers (PMTs). The relations defined are not necessarily same-length relations. The transitions are labeled by an independent regular expression for each tape. The same-length constraint does not apply on symbols but on partition components, which are possibly empty symbol sequences (i.e. strings). Each transition defines a partition.

PMTs have the same expressive power as Epsilon-Free Letter Transducer and regular languages. We give a compilation algorithm which compiles a PMT into a Finite State Automaton. We also define a computation framework with operations which change the number of tapes of the transducers.

A. Yli-Jyrä, L. Karttunen, and J. Karhumäki (Eds.): FSMNLP 2005, LNAI 4002, pp. 11–20, 2006.
© Springer-Verlag Berlin Heidelberg 2006

PMTs are convenient for defining correspondences between strings which symbols are not related. For example a feature structure associated to a morpheme although there is no symbol-to-symbol relation between them. Another example: words and their graphical representation in an ideographic writing system.

We first define the Partition Multitape Transducers and then, we propose a compilation algorithm for one of the most sophisticated two-level formalisms: the Partition-Based Two-Level Grammars by Grimley-Evans and al. [2].

2   Partitioning Multitape Transducers

2.1   Introducing the Concept

Epsilon-Free Letter Transducers generated by two-level compilers are two tape transducers whose transitions are labeled by exactly one symbol on each tape. We would like to extend the formalism in two ways:

- allowing the use of more than two tapes, with operations on transducers that increase or decrease the number of tapes.
- labeling transitions with a string, or even a regular set of strings on each tape.

We know that such transducers are not closed under intersection with respect to the usual semantics of n-relations, where such a n-tape transducer defines a set of string n-tuples.

Instead, we propose a new semantics based on the notion of partition. Any success path in the transducer is labeled by a sequence of transition labels, i.e. a sequence of regular expressions tuples. N-relations semantics assumes that the concatenation operation is distributive with respect to the tuple construction. The partition-based semantics does not.

For instance, the two paths $(aaa, \epsilon)(a, bb)$ and $(aa, b)(aa, b)$ are two ways of denoting the relation $(aaaa, bb)$ with the usual relation semantics. They are different elements for the partition based semantics. The transducer intersection has different meanings in the two semantics. Transducers are closed under intersection using the second kind of semantics.

2.2   Formal Definition

Definition 1. *Partitioning Multitape Transducer (PMT)*
A Partitioning n-Tape Transducer is a 5-tuple $A = (\Sigma, Q, i, F, T)$ where:

- *Σ is a finite set of symbols called the alphabet.*
- *Q is a finite set of states*
- *$i \in Q$ is the initial state*
- *$F \subseteq Q$ is the set of final states*
- *$T \subseteq \{(q_1, e_1, \ldots, e_n, q_2) | q_1 \in Q, q_2 \in Q, e_1, \ldots e_n$ are regular sets over $\Sigma^*\}$.*

We call n the arity of the transducer.

This is a standard definition of transducers, very similar to the one in [5], except that it does not distinguish a separate alphabet for each tape, with no loss of generality. The specificity of Partitioning Multitape Transducers lies in their semantics.

Definition 2. *N-tuple sequences defined by a n-tape transducer*
Let $s = (w_1^1, \ldots, w_1^n) \ldots (w_k^1, \ldots, w_k^n)$ a possibly empty sequence of string n-tuples where $w_i^j \in \Sigma^*$, and $A = (\Sigma, Q, i, F, T)$ a n-tape transducer. The sequence s belongs to A if there exists in A a success path $i \xrightarrow{t_1} q_1 \xrightarrow{t_2} \ldots \xrightarrow{t_k} q_k$ with $q_k \in F$ such that $\forall i, 1 \leq i \leq k, t_i = (q_{i-1}, e_i^1, \ldots e_i^n, q_i)$ and $w_i^1 \in e_i^1, \ldots w_i^n \in e_i^n$.

We call *partitioned n-relation* a set of string n-tuples. A *regular partitioned n-relation* is a partitioned n-relation defined by a Partitioning Multitape Transducer. An example of transducer with some of the n-tuple sequences it defines is given in figure 1.

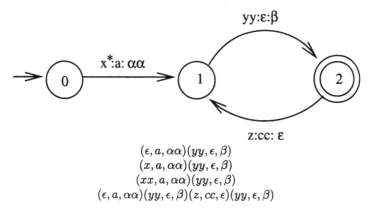

$$(\epsilon, a, \alpha\alpha)(yy, \epsilon, \beta)$$
$$(x, a, \alpha\alpha)(yy, \epsilon, \beta)$$
$$(xx, a, \alpha\alpha)(yy, \epsilon, \beta)$$
$$(\epsilon, a, \alpha\alpha)(yy, \epsilon, \beta)(z, cc, \epsilon)(yy, \epsilon, \beta)$$

Fig. 1. An example of PMT and some of its n-tuple sequences

Definition 3. *String recognized by an n-tape transducer*
Let w be a string of Σ^* and $A = (\Sigma, Q, i, F, T)$ a n-tape transducer. The string w is recognized by A on tape j if there exists an n-tuple sequence $s = (w_1^1, \ldots, w_1^n) \ldots (w_k^1, \ldots, w_k^1)$ of A such that $w = w_1^j . \ldots . w_k^j$.

We now briefly present a few operations on Partitioning Multitape Transducers. The formal definitions are straightforward, so we do not detail them.

- tape reordering: changes the order of the tapes in the transitions. The operation is defined given a transducer and a permutation upon tapes ranks. Notation: $reorder_{2,1,3}(A)$.
- projection: keeps the specified tapes and removes the others. Notations: $project_{\{1,3\}}(A)$ which keeps tapes 1 and 3, and $project_{\{\overline{2}\}}(A)$ which removes tape 2 and keeps all the other tapes.
- union, concatenation, with the usual notations.

Definition 4. *Join*

The join on k tapes of two regular partitioned relations r_1 and r_2 having respectively arity n and m is noted $r_1 \bowtie_k r_2$ and defined as follows:

$$r_1 \bowtie_k r_2 = \{ (s_1^1, \ldots s_1^{n+m-k}) \ldots (s_p^1, \ldots s_p^{n+m-k})|$$
$$(s_1^1, \ldots s_1^n) \ldots (s_p^1, \ldots, s_p^n) \subseteq r_1,$$
$$(s_1^{n-k+1}, \ldots, s_1^{n+m-k}) \ldots (s_p^{n-k+1}, \ldots, s_p^{n+m-k}) \subseteq r_2\}$$

This operation is very general. It combines two transducers having possibly different arities. We restrict here to joins where the last k tapes of the first operand are identified with the k first tapes of the second operand. This restriction is made only to simplify the definition. Thanks to the *reorder* operation, however there is no loss of generality.

The intersection is a join of two n-tapes PMT on all the tapes ($r_1 \cap r_2 = r_1 \bowtie_n r_2$). This is a direct consequence of the join definition.

Relation composition may be described as the sequence of a join and a projection which forgets the tapes on which the join operates.

This join operation was described in [4] for n-relations. Here we adapt the definition to partitioned n-relations. The name was chosen by analogy with the join operation of relational databases.

Definition 5. *Transducers join*

Let $A_1 = (\Sigma, Q_1, i_1, F_1, T_1)$ and
$A_2 = (\Sigma, Q_2, i_2, F_2, T_2)$ be two transducers defining the partitioned relations r_1 and r_2. The following transducer A defines $r_1 \bowtie_k r_2$.
$A = (\Sigma, Q_1 \times Q_2, (i_1, i_2), F_1 \times F_2, T)$ where
$T = \{ ((q_{i1}, q_{i2}), e_1, \ldots e_n, e_{n+1} \ldots e_{n+m-k}, (q_{f1}, q_{f2}))|$
$\quad \exists (q_{i1}, e_1^1, \ldots e_n^1, q_{f1}) \in T_1, \exists (q_{i2}, e_1^2, \ldots e_m^2, q_{f2}) \in T_2$ and
$\quad e_1 = e_1^1, \ldots e_{n-k} = e_{n-k}^1, \; e_{n-k+1} = e_{n-k+1}^1 \cap e_1^2, \ldots, e_n = e_n^1 \cap e_k^2,$
$\quad e_{n+1} = e_{k+1}^2, \ldots, e_{n+m-k} = e_m^2\}$

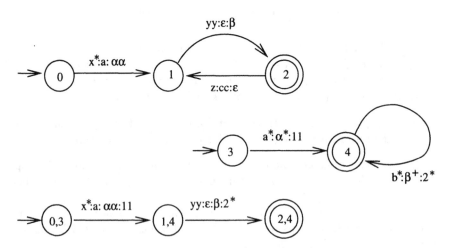

Fig. 2. An example of transducer join

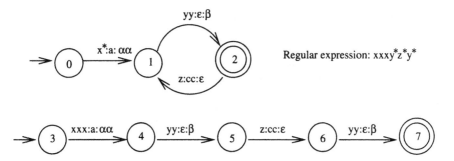

Fig. 3. An example of partitioning composition

Definition 6. *Partitioning Composition*
Let partition(α) be the partitioned relation $\{(a_1, \ldots, a_k)$ such that
$a_1 \ldots a_k \in \alpha\}$. The partitioning composition on tape i of a regular expression α
and a PMT t is defined by:
$$\alpha \circ_i t = \mathrm{reorder}_{2,\ldots i-1,1,i\ldots n}(partition(\alpha) \bowtie_1 \mathrm{reorder}_{i,1,\ldots i-1,i+1,\ldots n}(t))$$

The partitioning composition is the operation of recognition of a regular expression on a tape. An example of partitioning composition is given in figure 3.

3   Compiling Partitioning Multitape Transducers

Partitioning Multitape transducers are not convenient operational devices because the application of their transition is rather complex. It involves regular expression matching, which may be achieved by finite state automata execution.

We propose a translation into a finite state automaton.

Conceptually, all the tapes are read in parallel with no synchronization within a given partition. For instance, in the string 2-tuple sequence $(xx, a)(y, bc)(\epsilon, cc)$,

- there is a total order within each tape (we write as a subscript the occurrence of symbols): $x_1 < x_2 < y$ and $a < b < c_1 < c_2 < c_3$
- there is a partial order between symbols of different tapes: $x_2 < b$, $a < y$, $y_2 < c_2$
- there is no order between symbols in the same partition: for instance, a is not *before* or *after* x_1 or x_2

Any letter n-tape transducer will encode a stronger partial order relation, since at most one symbol of each tape is read at once. For instance, if a and x_1 are read by the same transition, then a is read before x_2. There are several ways of encoding the significant partial order using an epsilon-free letter transducer. For instance, the first partition of the sequence namely (xx, a) may be recognized by any of the following transition sequences:

$$\xrightarrow{x:\epsilon} \xrightarrow{x:\epsilon} \xrightarrow{\epsilon:a} \qquad \xrightarrow{x:\epsilon} \xrightarrow{\epsilon:a} \xrightarrow{x:\epsilon} \qquad \xrightarrow{\epsilon:a} \xrightarrow{x:\epsilon} \xrightarrow{x:\epsilon} \qquad \xrightarrow{x:a} \xrightarrow{x:\epsilon} \qquad \xrightarrow{x:\epsilon} \xrightarrow{x:a}$$

We propose to choose an arbitrary canonical representation. The basic idea of the compilation is to read on the tapes sequentially, one after the other, following the rank order. Each transition reads one symbol on one tape and nothing on the other tapes.

Now, one can flatten all the tapes in just one tape, the limits of tape being marked by two special symbols $<$ and $>$ not in Σ^1. Similarly, the partitions limits are marked by two special symbols $\ll$ and $\gg$, not in Σ.

Definition 7. *Compilation algorithm*
Let $A = (\Sigma, Q, i, F, T)$ be a partitioning n-tape transducer. For each transition $t = (q_0, w_1, \ldots, w_n, q_1)$ in T, compile the regular expression $\ll< w_1 > \cdots < w_n >\gg$ into a finite state automaton and insert it between states q_0 and q_1.

Note that it is always possible to compile the given regular expression in a finite state automaton having exactly one final state, thanks to the final transition on $\gg$.

Property 1. Property of the compiled automaton
We note $nbocc_s(p)$ the number of occurrences of the symbol s in the path p.

1. For all path p starting in the initial state, $(nbocc_\ll(p) - 1) * n \le nbocc_\gg(p) * n \le nbocc_>(p) \le nbocc_<(p) \le nbocc_\ll(p) * n$
2. All the strings recognized by the automaton begin with $\ll$ and end by an occurrence of $\gg$.

The property is obtained by construction, because each transition inserts one occurrence of $\ll$ and $\gg$ and n occurrences of $<$ and $>$.

Corollary. On each loop l in the automaton, $nbocc_<(l) = nbocc_>(l) = n * nbocc_\ll(l) = n * nbocc_\gg(l)$.

Lemma 1. *Every finite state automaton fulfilling the property 1 encodes a Partitioning Multitape Transducer.*

To retrieve the PMT from an automaton, one has to replace each path from a $\ll$ to a $\gg$ by a single transition labeled by a regular expression n-tuple. The only difficulty is that there must be a finite number of such paths to ensure the termination of the process and the finiteness of the transducer.

The most import property of the automata fulfilling the property 1 is that either a loop has no $<$ or $>$ symbol, or it traverses one or several partitions. In the first case, the loop concerns only one tape, it is translated with a star in the regular expression recognized on this tape. In the second case, the star comes at the partition level. It never happens that a loop contains a $<$ or a $>$ within a given partition. Therefore, the number of transitions of the transducer is finite.

In the following, we call *Partitioning Automaton* and we write $comp(t)$ a Finite State Automaton encoding a Partitioning Multitape Transducer t.

We have now to implement transducer operations on the compiled form. For this purpose, we use a few operations on finite state machines defined in [3] and [2].

---

[1] A single symbol marking the separation between tapes would be sufficient, but some definitions are made simpler with two surrounding symbols.

- The identity *id* is a 2-tape transducer which maps any symbol to itself.
- *insert* freely inserts a regular expression *e* into a given automaton. It is a 2-tape transducer where the empty string maps the inserted regular expression *e*.
- *replace* is an operation which replaces all the occurrences of a given regular expression by another one in a regular expression.
- *project* is the projection on the first ($project_1$) or the second ($project_2$) tape of the transducer.

The union (resp. the intersection, the concatenation) of two partitioning n-tape transducers is performed using the union (resp. intersection, concatenation) of the two corresponding compiled automata.

The proof is straightforward using property 1.

The complementation is slightly more difficult: the property 1 does not hold for the standard finite state automaton complement of a Partitioning Automaton. In order to except all the strings in the complement which are not string n-tuple sequences, the complement has to be intersected with the set of all the valid string n-tuple sequences, which is the compiled counterpart of $(\Sigma^*, \ldots, \Sigma^*)^*$, namely $(\ll< \Sigma^* > \cdots < \Sigma^* >\gg)^*$:

$$comp(\bar{t}) = \overline{comp(t)} \cap (\ll< \Sigma^* > \cdots < \Sigma^* >\gg)^*$$

The join operation of two PMT t_1 (arity n) and t_2 (arity m) on k tapes is performed as follows:

$$a_1 = project_{\{1\}}(replace_{>\gg,>(<\Sigma^*>)^{m-k}\gg}(comp(t_1)))$$
$$a_2 = project_{\{2\}}(replace_{\ll<,\ll(<\Sigma^*>)^{n-k}<}(comp(t_2)))$$
$$comp(t1 \bowtie_k t_2) = a_1 \cap a_2$$

The *replace* operations are used to insert new tapes at the end of the first automaton and at the beginning of the second one in order to obtain two automata having n+m-k tapes. The inserted tapes recognize the free language Σ^*.

The partitioning composition on tape k of a PMT t and a regular expression e is obtained by the following:

$$pbnd = (< \Sigma^* >)^{n-k+1} \gg\ll (< \Sigma^* >)^{k-1}$$
$$prefix = \ll (< \Sigma^* >)^{k-1}$$
$$suffix = (< \Sigma^* >)^{n-k+1} \gg$$
$$comp(e \circ_k t) = comp(t) \cap (prefix\ insert_{pbnd}(e)\ suffix)$$

The left-hand part of the intersection is the union of all the PMTs which recognize e on tape k and Σ^* on the other tapes. It is obtained by inserting freely partition boundaries surrounded by the irrelevant tapes, i.e. all but the tape k. The expressions *prefix* and *suffix* take care respectively of the first and last partition boundaries, the only ones which are not surrounded on both sides by tape boundaries > and <.

In the special case where the multitape transducer is a letter transducer, that is, in any partition, at most one symbol is read on each tape, a more efficient compilation algorithm may be used. The tape boundaries < and > are no more needed. A new symbol 0, not in Σ, is inserted to represent the empty string on tapes which read no symbols. Then, one knows that the ith symbol after a partition limit $\ll$ is on tape i. This kind of compilation for letter transducers is proposed by Ganchev and al. [1].

4   Using Partitioning Multitape Transducers for Two-Level Morphology

In this section, we show how a partition-based two-level formalism may be compiled into Partitioning Multitape Transducers. This formalism was defined by Grimley-Evans, Kiraz and Pulman [2]. We first recall the definition and then describe the compilation.

4.1   Partition-Based Two-Level Formalism

Let Σ be a finite alphabet of symbols.

Definition 8. *A Context Restriction Rule is a triple (l, c, r) where l, c and r are three n-tuples of regular expressions over Σ. Furthermore, the regular expressions of c are finite.*

The three n-tuples are called respectively the left context, the center and the right context of the rule.

Definition 9. *A Surface Coercion rule is a 4-tuple (l, cl, cs, r) where l and r are n-tuples of regular expressions over Σ, cl and cs are respectively a k-tuple and an m-tuple of regular expressions such that $k + m = n$.*

Here again, l and r are called the contexts, cl and cs are the lexical and surface centers. A Two-Level Grammar is a set of Context Restriction and Surface Coercion rules.

Definition 10. *A Two-Level Grammar accepts a string tuple P partitioned as $P_1, \ldots, P_q$ if and only if:*

1. *$\forall i, \exists (l, c, r)$ a CR rule such that $P_1 \ldots P_{i-1} \in l, P_i \in c, P_{i+1} \ldots P_q \in r$.*
2. *$\forall i, j, i \leq j$, there is no SC rule (l, cl, cs, r) such that $P_1 \ldots P_{i-1} \in l$, $P_j \ldots P_q \in r, \mathrm{project}_{\{1 \ldots k\}}(P_i \ldots P_{j-1}) \in cl$ and $\mathrm{project}_{\{k+1 \ldots n\}}(P_i \ldots P_{j-1}) \notin ls$.*

Note that in this definition, the center of a SC rule applies on a possibly empty sequence of consecutive partitions whereas centers of CR rules match exactly one partition. This strange definition is designed to handle adequately epenthetic SC rules, where the lexical center is a cross product of empty string ϵ^k.

4.2   Compilation into Partitioning Multitape Transducer

Partitioning Multitape Transducers are a natural operational device to compile a partition-based formalism since they have the same notion of partition.

Compiling the center of a CR rule is straightforward: the center is the description of exactly one partition. A two-state transducer with a transition labeled by the center implements it. Compiling contexts is slightly more difficult because the contexts may match a number of partitions. A different regular expression is given for each tape, but all the tapes must be divided in the same number of partitions. Inserting freely partition boundaries everywhere would not ensure that the result fulfills the property 1. The solution consists in cascading application of the partitioning composition of $\Sigma^*, \ldots, \Sigma^*$ (n occurrences) on each regular expression in the context.

The same idea works also for Surface Coercion rule lexical and surface centers which also match a sequence of partitions. Furthermore, the lexical and surface centers must match the same number of partitions: they have to be partitioning composed to the same free partition sequence.

$$comp((c_1, \ldots, c_n)) = ((((\underbrace{\Sigma^*, \ldots, \Sigma^*}_{n \text{ occurrences}})^* \circ_1 c_1) \ldots) \circ_n c_n)$$

Each part of a rule being compiled, we adapt the algorithm of [3] to the semantics of the partition-based formalism. This algorithm is subtractive: we first compute the closure under concatenation π^* of the set of CR rules centers π. Then we remove from this language the partitioned strings which violate at least one of the rules of the grammar G.

$$\pi = \bigcup_{(l,c,r) \in G} c$$
$$violate_{(l,c,r)} = \overline{(\overline{comp(l)} c \pi^*)} \cup (\pi^* c \overline{comp(r)})$$
$$violate_{(l,cl,cs,r)} = comp(l)comp(cl \times \overline{cs})comp(r)$$
$$system = \pi^* - \bigcup_{(l,c,r) \in G} violate_{(l,c,r)} - \bigcup_{(l,cl,cs,r) \in G} violate_{(l,cl,cs,r)}$$

4.3   Improving the Formalism

There is a restriction in the Two-Level Grammar definition which is related to the compilation algorithm given by Grimley-Evans and al.: the centers of Context Restriction Rules are compiled into letter n-tape transducers, by padding ends of strings with 0s. Combined with the condition of independence of the tapes within a given partition, it is a restriction to finite languages. In general, for a given relation R, there is no same-length regular relation such that the elements are the ones of R possibly lengthened with 0s at the end of strings.

Using the compilation into Partitioning Multitape Transducers, one can relax the restriction. The center of a CR rule may be any regular expression n-tuple.

The contexts of two-level rules are specified separately on each tape. No synchronization between tapes is expressible using the formalism. It is possible to change this and allow for synchronization at partition boundaries.

For instance, $(\Sigma^*, \Sigma^*)(C, C)$ is a valid context since it may be rewritten $(\Sigma^* C, \Sigma^* C)$, but $(\Sigma^*, \Sigma^*)(C, C)^*$ is not a valid context because no pair of independent regular expressions denotes the same language. There is a strong synchronization between the two tapes: there are the same number of Cs on both tapes. The definition by Grimley-Evans and al. does not allow such a synchronization. Compilation into PMT is possible if and only if the loops begin and end on a partition frontier. Contexts would be similar to the ones of Koskeniemi's original formalism: they would be regular expression over feasible pairs, the pairs being now pairs of regular expressions.

5   Conclusion

Partitioning Multitape Transducers are the right operational device to implement a partition-based two-level formalism. There is still work to make such formalism really attractive. First, the use of the notion of partition for morphology and phonology is not completely clear. We believe that some phenomena are well described in terms of partition whereas others are better described using single symbols. So the two degrees of granularity have to coexist. Secondly, the conflicts between two-level rules is a major difficulty in practice.

We are not aware of any attempt to define a partition-based formalism with rewrite rules and we are not sure if the idea is pertinent at all, since the one-to-one correspondence between pre and post rule application does not seem essential to this approach.

By construction, the regular expressions characterizing the different tapes within a partition are not related. It is a strong restriction, especially when the lexical and surface representation are closely related, when they are basically identical with only small local changes. It would be interesting to define a less restrictive definition of partition, while preserving the uniqueness of canonical representation which is essential for intersection.

Another interesting topic deals with composition of transducers having different partitionings, without loss of information. At the moment, only partitioning composition would work, and one of the two partitioning would be lost in the operation. There are applications where forms are partitioned in a different way using respectively a morphological or a graphemic point of view.

References

1. H. Ganchev, S. Mihov, and K. U. Schulz. One-letter automata: How to reduce k tapes to one. Technical Report IS-Bericht-03-133, Centrum für Informations- und Sprachverarbeitung, Universität München, Munich (Germany), 2003.
2. E. Grimley-Evans, G. Kiraz, and S. Pulman. Compiling a partition-based two-level formalism. In *COLING*, pages 454-459, Copenhagen, Denmark, 1996.
3. R. M. Kaplan and M. Kay. Regular models of phonological rule systems. *Computational Linguistics*, 20:3:331-378, 1994.
4. A. Kempe, F. Guingne, and F. Nicart. Algorithms for weighted multi-tape automata. Technical Report 2004/031, XRCE, Grenoble, France, 2004.
5. E. Roche and Y. Schabes, editors. *Finite-State Language Processing*. Bradford Book. MIT Press, Cambridge, Massachusetts, USA, 1997.

Squeezing the Infinite into the Finite:
Handling the OT Candidate Set with Finite State Technology

Tamás Bíró

Humanities Computing, University of Groningen
t.s.biro@rug.nl

Abstract. Finite State approaches to Optimality Theory have had two goals. The earlier and less ambitious one was to compute the optimal output by compiling a finite state automaton for each underlying representation. Newer approaches aimed at realizing the OT-systems as FS transducers mapping any underlying representation to the corresponding surface form. After reviewing why the second one fails for most linguistically interesting cases, we use its ideas to accomplish the first goal. Finally, we present how this approach could be used in the future as a—hopefully cognitively adequate—model of the mental lexicon.

1 Introduction

Although very popular in linguistics, *Optimality Theory* by Prince and Smolensky (OT, [17], [18]) poses a serious problem for being computationally very complex. This fact could question the relevance of much contemporary linguistic work both for cognitive research, and language technology. Is our brain doing such a hard computation? Could language technology make us of OT models? Fortunately, things are not so bad.

Figure 1 presents the architecture of an Optimality Theoretical grammar, which consists of two modules, *Gen* and *Eval*. The input—the underlying representation (UR)—is mapped by the universal Gen onto a *set of candidates*. The candidate set, or a subset of it, reflects language typology: for each language, the language-specific Eval chooses the element (or elements) that appears as the surface form SR. Eval is a function assigning a harmony value to each candidate, and the most harmonic one will surface. Alternatively, Eval can also be seen as a pipeline in which the constraints filter out the sub-harmonic candidates. This second approach is most often used in practice, and the finite state realizations presented in this paper are also based on this vision of an OT system.

In many models advanced by theoretical linguists, the set of candidates is infinite, leading to serious questions. How could our brain process an infinite set? How could language technology make use of a model involving an infinite set?

Different approaches have been, then, proposed in order to handle an infinite candidate set. Chart parsing (dynamic programming) is probably the best known among them (chapter 8 in [19] for syllabification; [16] for implementing it to OT

A. Yli-Jyrä, L. Karttunen, and J. Karhumäki (Eds.): FSMNLP 2005, LNAI 4002, pp. 21–31, 2006.
© Springer-Verlag Berlin Heidelberg 2006

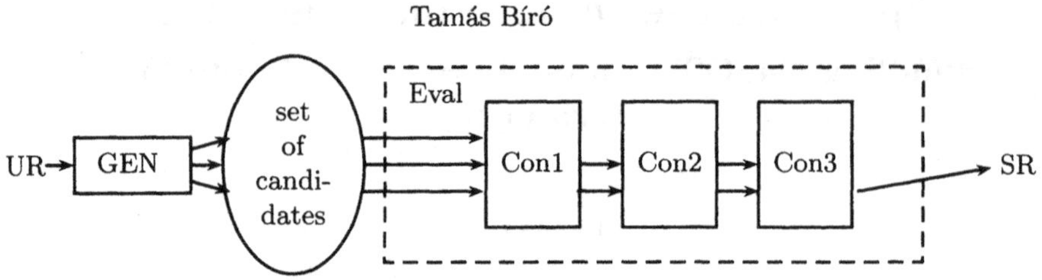

Tamás Bíró

Fig. 1. The architecture of an OT grammar, which maps the underlying representation onto the surface representation. Gen is followed by the Eval module: the latter is a series of constraints, acting as filters.

LFG). It presupposes on the one hand that applying a recursive rule (usually insertion) incurs some constraint violation; and on the other, that "all constraints are structural descriptions denoting bounded structures". The interplay of these two assumptions guarantees that the algorithm may stop applying the recursive rule after a finite number of steps, for no hope is left to find better candidates by more insertions.

Alternatives include using heuristic optimization techniques. Genetic algorithms were proposed by Turkel [20], whereas simulated annealing by Bíró [5]. Such approaches involve only relatively low computational cost; nonetheless, they do not guarantee finding the optimal candidate. Simulated annealing, for instance, returns a "near-optimal" form within constant time, but you cannot know if the algorithm has found the good solution. Even though Bíró [4] argues that this algorithm models language production, one may still wish to have a perfectly working algorithm for language technology.

The present paper proposes an alternative: determining the optimal candidate by using *finite state* technologies. We first present the previous approaches to Finites State Optimality Theory (FS OT) in section 2, with an emphasis on the *matching approach*. This is followed by a new proposal in section 3, further developed into a model of the lexicon in section 4.

2   Finite State Optimality Theory

The idea of computing the optimal candidate of an OT system by building a finite state (FS) automaton goes back to Ellison [10].[1] He requires the set of candidates for a given input be a regular expression, and realizes the constraints as transducers (weighted automata) assigning violation marks. The number of violation marks assigned by a constraint to a candidate is reflected by the sum of the weights along the path representing the given candidate. Ellison subsequently proposes a series of algorithms resulting in an automaton in which "the only paths from the initial state to the final state will be optimal and define optimal candidates." This approach builds a new automaton for each input.

---

[1] Eisner [9] summarizes existing work on FS OT, and proposes a framework very similar to the one to be presented here.

Later work in FS OT aims at realizing the OT-system as a regular relation mapping any correct UR to the corresponding surface form. By compiling such a transducer, one would enjoy all advantages of finite state techniques, such as robustness, speed and relatively low memory requirements in both directions (production and parsing). This approach includes Frank and Satta [11] and Karttunen [15], on the one hand (the *counting approach*), as well as Gerdemann and van Noord [12], generalized by Jäger [13], on the other (the *matching approach*). The hope for a regular mapping from the UR to the SR goes back to Douglas Johnson [14].

In short, finite state approaches to OT require Gen, as well as each of the constraints be realizable—in some sense—as a regular expression or transduction. In many linguistic theories, Gen produces a regular set, as exemplified by syllabification [12] or metrical stress assignment [3]. However, many further examples, such as reduplicative morphology or numerous phenomena in syntax, are not finite state-friendly.[2] Concerning Eval, Eisner [7] [8] and Bíró [3] discuss what constraints can be realized as finite transducers. Eisner's Primitive Optimality Theory (OTP) [7] launches a challenging research program the goal of which is to model as many phonological phenomena as possible by restricting ourselves to finite state-friendly constraints.

Nonetheless, the more ambitious program of FS OT to create a transducer mapping any underlying representation to any surface representation cannot be fully carried out. Even with a FS representation of Gen and of the constraints at hand, filtering is not always possible. Frank and Satta [11] (following Smolensky and Hiller) show a simple counter-example:

Example 1: Let Gen map string $a^n b^m$ to the candidate set $\{a^n b^m, b^n a^m\}$, and let the only constraint penalize each occurrence of a. The resulting language is $\{a^n b^m | n \leq m\} \cup \{b^n a^m | n \geq m\}$, which is clearly not regular. And yet, Gen is regular, similarly to the proposed constraint.[3]

Although *Example 1* might look very artificial, its constraint, actually, is a prototype form many constraints used in linguistics. In Syllable Structure Theory [17], each segment may be parsed or underparsed, and constraint PARSE punishes underparsing. Metrical stress may be assigned to each syllable, and constraint WSP ("Weight-to-Stress Principle") requires each heavy syllable to be stressed (cf. e.g. [19]). In fact, most constraints in phonology penalize each occurrence of some local substructure a (underparsed, unstressed,...), and prefer its alternative, substructure b (parsed, stressed,...). The above example shows that all these constraints could realize a non-regular language with some specific input (output of Gen and the previous constraints) [8].

---

[2] Albro [1] shows how to combine a non-finite state Gen with finite state constraints.

[3] Authors differ in what is meant by a "regular constraint". For Frank and Satta [11], the set of strings incurring exactly k violation marks should form a regular set, for all k. Gerdemann and van Noord [12] use transducers inserting violation mark characters into the candidate strings. The given counter-example satisfies both of these definitions, unlike that of Jäger [13].

The *counting approach* proposed by [11] and [15] requires an upper bound on the number of violations a given candidate can incur. The *matching approach* is closer to the model proposed by linguists: it can, in theory, distinguish between any number of level of violations. Yet, in many cases, only an approximation is possible, as we shall soon see. By supposing that the length of candidates is bounded due to restrictions in the working memory, both approaches can be used in applications. Nevertheless, not only do we lose here the linguistic "point", but the size of the automata also increases quickly.

2.1   The Matching Approach

Both the *counting approach* and the *matching approach* share the agenda composed of the following three steps:

- first, formulate a finite state transducer Gen;
- then, formulate an optimality operator oo, which makes use of
- the finite state realizations Con-i of the constraints CON-i.

Once we have all these at hand, the grammar is realized by the finite state transducer obtained after having compiled the following expression:

$$\Big(\big(\text{Gen oo Con-1}\big)\ \text{oo Con-2}\Big)\ldots\ldots\ \text{oo Con-N} \tag{1}$$

From now on, we suppose that a FS transducer Gen is given. The task is to formulate the optimality operator oo; the latter will then determine what realization Con-i of each constraint CON-i is required.

The key idea of the *matching approach* is to build a set $Worse(Input, \text{CON})$ that includes all sub-harmonic candidates of the input *Input* with respect to the constraint CON, as well as possibly other strings; but excludes all harmonic candidates. This set will then serve as a filtering set in the definition of the optimality operator oo:

$$Input\ \text{oo Con} := Input\ \text{o}\ Id\ \overline{_{Worse(Input,\text{Con})}} \tag{2}$$

Here, the identity transduction filters out the elements of $Worse(Input, \text{CON})$, only the elements of its complement may become outputs. This approach is a straightforward implementation of the idea behind OT—supposing that the set $Worse(Input, \text{CON})$ can be constructed.

Without referring to violation marks, Jäger [13] proposes to realize a constraint CON with a transducer Con_J that directly will create the filtering set, a superset of the sub-harmonic candidates. The candidate w is mapped onto a set containing: (1) all candidates of $Gen(Gen^{-1}(w))$ that are less harmonic than w; and (2) possibly strings not belonging to $Gen(Gen^{-1}(w))$. Now, the range of $Input\ \text{o}\ \text{Con}_J$ contains all sub-harmonic elements of *Input* but no harmonic ones. Hence, it can serve as the filter in (2):

$$Input\ \text{oo Con} := Input\ \text{o}\ Id\ \overline{_{Ran(Input\ \text{o}\ \text{Con}_J)}} \tag{3}$$

The draw-back of Jäger's approach is the difficulty of defining the required transducers corresponding to constraints in linguistics. Even worse, it is not possible very often—otherwise a finite automaton could accept a non-regular language in Example 1. A constraint that is finite-state in Jäger's sense would lead automatically to a finite-state realization of OT.

It is more fruitful to realize constraints with transducers assigning violation marks to the strings, as done by Ellison [10], Gerdemann & v. Noord [12] and Eisner [9]. One can simply construct a finite state transducer that inserts a special violation mark symbol after each disfavored substructure—supposing that the latter are simple enough to be recognized with an FSA, which is usually the case. In this sense, most constraints are finite-state.[4] Can we make any use of these transducers?

Suppose that for constraint CON, a transducer Con exists that introduces the required number of violation marks into any candidate string. Importantly, we only know that the output of Con includes the correct number of violation mark symbols, but we do not know how these symbols are dispersed in the string. Furthermore, let remove_viol denote the transducer removing all violation mark symbols from its input. The only task now is to define the transducer make_worse, and then we can rewrite definition (2) as follows:

$$Input \text{ oo } \text{CON} := Input \circ \text{Con} \circ$$
$$\circ Id \overline{Ran(Input \circ Con \circ make\_worse)} \circ \text{ remove\_viol} \qquad (4)$$

Now, we have to define make_worse. Imagine that the set of candidates *Input* entering the constraint filter CON includes only candidates that are assigned N violation marks, or more. Let us add at least one violation mark to each of them: we thus obtain a set of strings with not less than $N + 1$ violation marks. If we ignored the characters other than the violation marks, this latter set could simply be used for filtering, because only the candidates of the input set with the least (namely, N) violation marks are not element of the filtering set thus constructed. Consequently, the finite state transducer make_worse will have to add any positive number of extra violation marks to the input, using a finite state transducer add_viol.

Nevertheless, we cannot ignore the characters in the candidate strings. The filtering set will not yet include all the sub-harmonic candidates, because the candidate strings vary not only in the number of violation marks. The different elements of the candidate set have to diverge from each other, for instance, in the position of parsing brackets. Most probably, the violation marks should also be permuted around the segments of the strings.

Therefore, we redefine make_worse: besides adding extra violation marks (add_viol), it will delete all characters that are not violation marks using the simple transducer delete_char, and then insert any new characters (transducer insert_char) (cf. (4) and (5) to the formalism in Eisner [9]):

$$make\_worse := delete\_char \circ add\_viol \circ insert\_char \qquad (5)$$

The range of *Input* o Con o make_worse is now the set of *all* strings with more violation marks than the minimal in the range of *Input* o Con: all candidates

---

[4] Quadratic alignment constraints assigning a number of violation marks growing faster than the length of the string, are not regular even in that sense [7] [8] [3].

to be filtered out, further uninteresting strings, but no candidates to be left in. This fact guarantees that the harmonic candidates, and only they will survive the filtering in definition (4). Or almost.

Yes, we still face a problem. Suppose that underlying representation W_1 is mapped by *Inp* o Con to candidates involving at least N_1 violation marks, and w_1 is an optimal one. Further, suppose that UR W_2 is mapped to candidates containing N_2 violation marks or more, with an optimal w_2. Suppose also that $N_1 < N_2$. Because W_1 is in the domain of *Inp* o Con o make_worse, the latter's range will include all strings with more than N_1 violation marks, w_2 among them. Consequently, all candidates corresponding to W_2 will be filtered out, and W_2 is predicted to be ineffable, without any corresponding output.

Gerdemann and van Noord [12], therefore, define make_worse such a way that it will keep the underlying material unchanged. Suppose that what Gen does is nothing but to add some extra material, like parsing brackets. In such a case, deleting and reintroducing only the brackets introduced originally by Gen ensures that different underlying representations cannot interfere:

$$\text{make\_worse} = \text{add\_viol o del\_brackets o ins\_brackets} \qquad (6)$$

Nonetheless, a new problem arises! Let the underlying representation abab yield two candidates, namely a[b]ab and [a]b[a]b. Let the constraint insert a violation mark @ after each closing bracket, so the set entering make_worse is {a[b]@ab, [a]@b[a]@b}. By applying the operation make_worse as defined in (6), we get among others the strings [a]b@a[b]@ or [a]@b@[a]b; but not [a]@b[a]@b, the candidate to be filtered out. An extra operation is, therefore, required that will permute the violation marks: in our case, we need to remove the @ between the first b and the second a, and simultaneously insert a @ following one of the a's; the second violation mark will be inserted by add_viol after the other a.

The real problem arises when one has to compare two candidates, such that the first one may have an unbounded number of violation marks in its first part, while the second one any number of violation marks in its last part. This happens in Example 1, and in the many analogous linguistic applications. Then, the transducer should have to keep track of the unbounded number of violation marks deleted at the beginning of the string, before it reaches the end of the string and re-inserts them. That is clearly a non-finite state task.

If the transducer permuting the marks perm is able to move one violation at the same time, then the following definition of make_worse yields an exact OT-system only for the case where not more than n violation marks should be moved at once:[5]

---

[5] The same transducer can move a second violation mark after having accomplished its task with the first one. Note that such a finite-state friendly case can theoretically result from the interplay of Gen and the previously ranked constraints; and not only from restricting the number of violation marks assigned, due, for instance, to a bound in the length of the candidates. Further research should reveal whether the linguistically relevant cases are indeed finite-state, or languages do produce extreme candidate sets, such as the one in Example 1. See the research line launched by Eisner's OTP [8].

$$\texttt{make\_worse} := \texttt{add\_viol} \circ \texttt{del\_brackets}$$

$$\circ \ \texttt{ins\_brackets} \circ \texttt{perm}_1 \circ \texttt{perm}_2 \circ \dots \circ \texttt{perm}_n \qquad (7)$$

Thus, we have run into the "permute marker problem": only an approximation is offered by Gerdemann and van Noord for the general case. Besides, introducing **perm** n times makes the automaton enormous.

3 Planting the Input into the FST

The matching approach, as proposed by Gerdemann and van Noord [12], has two main advantages over its competitors. First, it does not require the number of levels of violations to be finite, as opposed to the counting approach. Second, it makes use of transducers assigning violation marks to the strings, which is much easier to realize than the transducers in Jäger's generalized matching approach.

Example 1 has shown that there is no hope for solving the "permute marker problem" in general. Can we still bring out the most of the the counting approach? Maybe by stepping back to the lesser goal of Ellison: compiling an automaton to each word, instead of creating a general transducer mapping any underlying representation to the corresponding surface form? This is bad news for people believing in FS OT (despite Example 1), and yet, it opens the way to a new model of the mental lexicon.

We have seen that the radical definition of **make_worse** in (5) creates a problem: the candidates corresponding to some underlying representation may discard *all* candidates of another underlying representation. The solution by [12], that is, to modify **make_worse** as (6) and (7), led to the "permute marker problem". Another solution is to keep the more radical **make_worse** transducer, as defined in (5), for the definition (4) of the optimality operator; but, simultaneously, to introduce a filter at the beginning of the pipeline (or, into Gen, as Ellison did). By restricting the domain of the transduction, this filter—an identity transduction on a singleton—ensures that no other input disturbs the computation. So, for hierarchy CON-1 $\gg$ CON-2 $\gg$ ... $\gg$ CON-N, and for *each* underlying representation W we have to compile the following regular expression:

$$\left(\left(\left(Id_{\{W\}} \circ \textbf{Gen} \right) \circ \circ \textit{Con-1} \right) \circ \circ \textit{Con-2} \right) \ \dots \ \circ \circ \textit{Con-N} \qquad (8)$$

Let us prove the correctness of this approach:

Theorem: *Let all constraints* CON-i *be represented by a transducer* Con-i *inserting violation marks, and let*

$$\texttt{make\_worse} := \texttt{delete\_char} \circ \texttt{add\_viol} \circ \texttt{insert\_char}$$

$$Input \ \circ\circ \ \text{CON} := Input \circ Con \ \circ$$

$$\circ \ Id \ \overline{{}_{Ran(Input \, \circ \, Con \, \circ \, \texttt{make\_worse})}} \ \circ \ \textit{remove\_viol}$$

If for hierarchy $H = \langle$ CON-1 $\gg$ CON-2 $\gg \ldots \gg$ CON-N $\rangle$ *and underlying representation* W,

$$OT_0 := Id_{\{W\}} \text{ o Gen} \qquad\qquad OT_i := OT_{i-1} \text{ oo Con-i}$$

then the range of OT_N *is the set of outputs with respect to underlying representation* W *and ranking* H.

Proof: By induction on the number of constraints N. For $N = 0$: by definition, the range of OT_0 is the candidate set corresponding to W.

For $N = k > 0$: We suppose that the range of OT_{k-1} is the set of candidates returned by the part of the pipe-line before constraint CON-k. We have to show that OT_k is the optimal subset of OT_{k-1} with respect to constraint CON-k.

Let m denote the number of violation marks assigned by constraint CON-k to the most harmonic candidates in the range of OT_{k-1}. By the definition of make_worse, the range of OT_{k-1}o Con-k o make_worse includes all strings (words and non-words) with more than m violation marks, and only them. Thus, the identity transduction in the definition of the optimality operator oo transduces all strings with no more than m marks, and only them. Consequently, the range of OT_k will include exactly those elements of the range of OT_{k-1} that violate CON-k m times. □

We have stepped back to the less ambitious proposal of Ellison [10]: we compile a regular expression for each input. One first formulates a finite transducer realizing Gen, as well as transducer adding each candidate string the same number of violation marks as the constraints of the linguistic model do. Then, the range of the regular expression (8) has to be compiled and read. Compilation—even if it is a computationally complex task, primarily due to the set complement operation—can be done automatically, with any package handling regular expressions.

Is stepping back to a ten-year old result something worth writing a paper on? The good news, however, is that the approach proposed opens new perspectives about a finite-state model of the lexicon.

4   Modeling a Complex Lexicon

Many linguistic phenomena can be described by using "co-phonologies", by referring to exceptions or to "minor rules". The discussion about the interaction between morphology and phonology (here we just refer to the well-known "past tense debate") has also affected OT [6]. On-going and further research shall analyze whether a finite-state Optimality Theoretical approach has something interesting to say about the issue. In the remaining space of the present paper, we shall present the possible first steps of such a research line.

Equation (8) allows for generalization. If SL is a subset of the lexicon, the following expression will define the surface representation of elements of SL:

$$\left(\left(\left(Id_{SL} \; \mathtt{o} \; \mathtt{Gen}\right) \; \mathtt{oo} \; Con\text{-}1\right) \; \mathtt{oo} \; Con\text{-}2\right) \; \ldots \; \mathtt{oo} \; Con\text{-}N \qquad (9)$$

Note that elements of SL may "extinguish" each other: if a candidate w_1 corresponding to some element $W_1 \in SL$ incurs less violation marks than the optimal candidate corresponding to another W_2, then no output is returned for W_2. Therefore, SL should be the set of "analogous" words in the language.

The phonology of the language is then modeled thus:

$$\bigcup_i \left(\left(\left(Id_{SL_i} \; \mathtt{o} \; \mathtt{Gen}\right) \; \mathtt{oo} \; Con_{i_1}\right) \; \mathtt{oo} \; Con_{i_2}\right) \; \ldots \; \mathtt{oo} \; Con_{i_N} \qquad (10)$$

The lexicon is composed of subsets of words. Each subset SL_i is associated with a hierarchy $Con_{i_1} \gg Con_{i_2} \gg \ldots \gg Con_{i_N}$. Different subsets may be associated with the same hierarchy, but cannot be unified, unless some words are erased from the language, as explained. Yet, once we have this structure, nothing prohibits us to associate different subsets with different hierarchies.[6]

Until now, if the sub-lexicons are finite, the complex expression in (10) is compiled into a simple finite set of UR-SR pairs. Yet, we claim that expression (10) together with linguistically motivated constraints have a cognitive explanatory value by restricting the possible lexicons: *what* UR-SR mappings are thinkable?

Additionally, our on-going research tries to introduce some sort of *generalization* into the sub-lexicons. Let the *hash* $a\#$ of an element a of the alphabet be the following concatenation:

$$a\# := \mathtt{pc*} \; | \; \{\mathtt{a}, \; \mathtt{pc}\} \; | \; \mathtt{pc*}, \qquad (11)$$

where pc is a *punished change*: whatever character followed by a special *punishment symbol*. Thus, the *hash* of a character is its generalization: you can replace it, you can add anything before and after it, but whatever change introduced is marked by a *punishment symbol*. In the next step, the generalization $W\#$ of a memorized word W is the concatenation of the hash of its characters in the corresponding order. Last, we propose that if a learned (memorized) word $W \in SL_i$, then also $W\# \in SL_i$.

With this generalization, the input of the grammar model (10) can also be an unseen word—yet, not *any* unseen word. The punishment symbols measure the "distance" of the input from previously memorized, "similar" words, in terms of letter changes. An input may match the hash of several learnt lexical items, possibly in different sublexicons, in which case more outputs are generated

---

[6] One can speculate about how co-phonologies have emerged in languages. Decomposing the lexicon into sub-lexicons is necessary, otherwise some words would be ineffable, *i.e.*, unpronounceable. Thus, an acquisition model should be able to open new sub-lexicons. Then, as the constraint pipe-line is connected to each sub-lexicon independently, nothing prohibits constraint re-ranking for certain sub-lexicons. A prediction is that language varieties differ in the constraint ranking corresponding exactly to these sub-lexicons, which reminds us the similar proposal of [2].

simultaneously in various pipe-lines.[7] These symbols are preserved during the transduction, and the output with the minimal number of punishment symbols is the predicted form. We can use a FS OT-style filter on the punishment symbols, and we obtain a sort of memory-based learning. The consequences of this proposal, learnability issues and its possible cognitive relevance are subject to future research.

5 Conclusion

In the introduction, we have raised the problem of how one can handle the infinite set of OT candidates appearing in contemporary linguistic work within the framework of a plausible psycholinguistic model or a working language technology application. In this paper, we have proposed a new way of using finite state technology in order to solve that problem. We have reviewed why it is not possible to create a FS transducer realizing an OT-system in general, even if Gen is a regular relation, and constraints are also regular (at least in some sense). Subsequently, we have proposed to make the *matching approach* exact by planting a filter before Gen.

This way we have obtained an alternative to Ellison's algorithm [10]. By compiling (8) for each input separately, we can calculate the optimal element of the possibly infinite candidate set. Finally, we have shown how this result can be generalized into a model of the lexicon, yet further research has to prove the cognitive adequateness of such a model. For instance, does it account for observed morpho-phonological minor rules? Preliminary results show that different hierarchies are compiled in significantly different time. If so, do less frequently attested language typologies correspond to rankings more difficult to compile?

The present paper hope to have paved the way for such future research.

Acknowledgments

I wish to acknowledge the support of the University of Groningen's Program for High-Performance Computing. I also would like to thank Gosse Bouma and Gertjan van Noord for valuable discussions.

References

1. D. M. Albro. Taking primitive Optimality Theory beyond the finite state. In *Eisner, J. L. Karttunen and A. Thériault (eds.): Finite-State Phonology: Proc. of the 5th Workshop of SIGPHON*, pages 57–67, Luxembourg, 2000.

---

[7] The input may turn out to be ineffable in some—or all—of the pipe-lines. Importantly, constraints and the definition of the hash operation should be such that $W\#$ may not render W ineffable in its own subset. Many, yet not all constraints assign an equal or higher number of violation marks to the best candidate of a longer input. This is also the reason why a *punished change* does not include an empty string, allowing for shortening—at any rate, it is quite rare that longer forms influence shorter forms by analogy.

2. A. Anttila and Y. Cho. Variation and change in optimality theory. *Lingua*, 104(1-2):31–56, 1998.

3. T. Bíró. Quadratic alignment constraints and finite state Optimality Theory. In *Proc. of the Workshop on FSMNLP, at EACL-03, Budapest*, pages 119–126, also: ROA-600,[8] 2003.

4. T. Bíró. When the hothead speaks: Simulated Annealing Optimality Theory for Dutch fast speech. presented at CLIN 2004, Leiden, 2004.

5. T. Bíró. How to define simulated annealing for optimality theory? In *Proc. of the 10th Conference on Formal Grammar and the 9th Meeting on Mathematics of Language*, Edinburgh, August 2005.

6. L. Burzio. Missing players: Phonology and the past-tense debate. *Lingua*, 112:157–199, 2002.

7. J. Eisner. Efficient generation in primitive Optimality Theory. In *Proc. of ACL 1997 and EACL-8, Madrid*, pages 313–320, 1997.

8. J. Eisner. Directional constraint evaluation in Optimality Theory. In *Proc. of COLING 2000, Saarbrücken*, 2000.

9. J. Eisner. Comprehension and compilation in Optimality Theory. In *Proc. of ACL 2002, Philadelphia*, 2002.

10. T. M. Ellison. Phonological derivation in Optimality Theory. In *COLING-94, Kyoto*, pages 1007–1013, also: ROA-75, 1994.

11. R. Frank and G. Satta. Optimality Theory and the generative complexity of constraint violability. *Computational Ling.*, 24(2):307–315, 1998.

12. D. Gerdemann and G. van Noord. Approximation and exactness in finite state Optimality Theory. In *J. Eisner, L. Karttunen, A. Thriault (eds): SIGPHON 2000, Finite State Phonology*, 2000.

13. G. Jäger. Gradient constraints in finite state OT: The unidirectional and the bidirectional case. *ROA-479*, 2002.

14. D. C. Johnson. *Formal Aspects of Phonological Description*. Mouton, The Hague [etc.], 1972.

15. L. Karttunen. The proper treatment of Optimality Theory in computational phonology. In *Finite-state Methods in NLP*, pages 1–12, Ankara, 1998.

16. J. Kuhn. Processing optimality-theoretic syntax by interleaved chart parsing and generation. In *Proc. of ACL-2000, Hongkong*, pages 360–367, 2000.

17. A. Prince and P. Smolensky. Optimality Theory, constraint interaction in generative grammar. RuCCS-TR-2, ROA Version: 8/2002, 1993.

18. A. Prince and P. Smolensky. *Optimality Theory: Constraint Interaction in Generative Grammar*. Blackwell, Malden, MA, etc., 2004.

19. B. Tesar and P. Smolensky. *Learnability in Optimality Theory*. The MIT Press, Cambridge, MA - London, England, 2000.

20. B. Turkel. The acquisition of optimality theoretic systems. m.s., ROA-11, 1994.

---

[8] ROA stands for *Rutgers Optimality Archive* at `http://roa.rutgers.edu/`.

A Novel Approach to Computer-Assisted Translation Based on Finite-State Transducers*

Jorge Civera[1], Juan M. Vilar[2], Elsa Cubel[1], Antonio L. Lagarda[1],
Sergio Barrachina[2], Francisco Casacuberta[1], and Enrique Vidal[1]

[1] Departamento de Sistemas Informáticos y Computación
Universitat Politècnica de València
Instituto Tecnológico de Informática, E-46071 València, Spain
tt2iti@iti.upv.es
[2] Departamento de Lenguajes y Sistemas Informáticos
Universitat Jaume I, E-12071 Castellón de la Plana, Spain

Abstract. Computer-Assisted Translation (CAT) is an alternative approach to Machine Translation, that integrates human expertise into the automatic translation process. In this framework, a human translator interacts with a translation system that dynamically offers a list of translations that best completes the part of the sentence already translated. Stochastic finite-state transducer technology is proposed to support this CAT system. The system was assessed on two real tasks of different complexity in several languages.

1 Introduction

State-of-the-art Machine Translation (MT) techniques are still far from producing high quality translations. This drawback leads us to introduce an alternative approach to the translation problem that brings human expertise into the MT scenario. This idea was proposed in [13] and can be illustrated as follows. Initially, the human translator is provided with a possible translation for the sentence to be translated. Unfortunately, in most cases, this translation is far from being perfect, so the translator amends it and asks for a translation of the part of the sentence still to be translated (completion). This latter interaction is repeated as many times as needed until the final translation is achieved.

The scenario described in the previous paragraph can be seen as an iterative refinement of the translations offered by the translation system, that while not having the desired quality, can help the translator to increase his/her productivity. Nowadays, this lack of translation excellence is a common characteristic in all Machine Translation systems. Therefore, the human-machine synergy represented by the Computer-Assisted Translation (CAT) paradigm seems to be more promising than fully-automatic translation in the near future.

The CAT approach has two important aspects: the models need to provide adequate completions and they have to do so efficiently under usability constrains.

* This work has been supported by the European Union under the IST Programme (IST-2001-32091) and the Spanish project TIC2003-08681-C02.

A. Yli-Jyrä, L. Karttunen, and J. Karhumäki (Eds.): FSMNLP 2005, LNAI 4002, pp. 32–42, 2006.
© Springer-Verlag Berlin Heidelberg 2006

To fulfill these two requirements, Stochastic Finite-State Transducers (SFST) have been selected since they have proved to be able to provide adequate translations [12, 1, 3]. In addition, efficient parsing algorithms can be easily adapted in order to provide completions.

The rest of the paper is structured as follows. Next section introduces the general setting for MT and finite-state models. In Section 3, the search procedure for interactive translation is explained. Experimental results are presented in Section 4. Finally, some conclusions and future work are exposed in Section 5.

2   Machine Translation with Finite-State Transducers

In a probabilistic framework, given a source sentence $\mathbf{s}$, the goal of MT is to find a target sentence $\hat{\mathbf{t}}$ that:

$$\hat{\mathbf{t}} = \underset{\mathbf{t}}{\operatorname{argmax}} \Pr(\mathbf{t} \mid \mathbf{s}) = \underset{\mathbf{t}}{\operatorname{argmax}} \Pr(\mathbf{t}, \mathbf{s}). \tag{1}$$

It should be noted that the maximisation problem stated above is NP-hard [10]. The joint distribution $\Pr(\mathbf{t}, \mathbf{s})$ can be modelled by a SFST $\mathcal{T}$ [15]:

$$\hat{\mathbf{t}} = \underset{\mathbf{t}}{\operatorname{argmax}} \Pr(\mathbf{t}, \mathbf{s}) \approx \underset{\mathbf{t}}{\operatorname{argmax}} \Pr_{\mathcal{T}}(\mathbf{t}, \mathbf{s}). \tag{2}$$

A SFST $\mathcal{T}$ is defined as a tuple $\langle \Sigma, \Delta, Q, q_0, F, \delta, p, f \rangle$ where Σ and Δ are finite sets of source and target symbols respectively, Q is a finite set of states, q_0 is the initial state, $F \subseteq Q$ is the set of final states, $\delta \subseteq Q \times \Sigma \times \Delta^\star \times Q$ is the set of transitions, $p : Q \times \Sigma \times \Delta^\star \times Q \to [0, 1]$ is a transition probability function and $f : Q \to [0, 1]$ is the state probability function. The functions p and f satisfy:

$$f(q) + \sum_{q' \in Q,\, a \in \Sigma,\, \omega \in \Delta^\star} p(q, a, \omega, q') = 1 \quad \forall q \in Q . \tag{3}$$

SFSTs have been successfully applied into many translation tasks [1, 5]. Furthermore, there exist efficient search algorithms like Viterbi [16] for the best path and the Recursive Enumeration Algorithm (REA) [11] for the n-best paths.

A possible way of inferring SFSTs is the Grammatical Inference and Alignments for Transducer Inference (GIATI) technique [7]. Given a finite sample of string pairs, it works in three steps:

1. Building training strings. Each training pair is transformed into a single string from an extended alphabet to obtain a new sample of strings. The "extended alphabet" contains words or substrings from source and target sentences coming from training pairs.
2. Inferring a (stochastic) regular grammar. Typically, a smoothed n-gram is inferred from the sample of strings obtained in the previous step.
3. Transforming the inferred regular grammar into a transducer. The symbols associated to the grammar rules are adequately transformed into source/target symbols, thereby transforming the grammar inferred in the previous step into a transducer.

The transformation of a parallel corpus into a corpus of single sentences is performed with the help of statistical alignments: each word is joined with its translation in the output sentence, creating an "extended word". This joining is done taking care not to invert the order of the output words. The third step is trivial with this arrangement. In our experiments, the alignments are obtained using the GIZA++ software [14], which implements IBM statistical models [4].

3   Interactive Search

The concept of interactive search is closely related to the CAT paradigm. This paradigm introduces a new factor t_p into the general MT equation (Eq. 1). t_p represents a prefix of the target sentence obtained as a result of the interaction between the human translator and the MT system.

An example of this interaction is shown in Fig. 1. In each iteration, a prefix (t_p) of the target sentence has somehow been fixed by the human translator in the previous iteration and the CAT system computes its best (or n-best) translation suffix hypothesis $(\hat{t}_s)$ to complete this prefix.

ITER-0	(t_p)	( )
ITER-1	$(\hat{t}_s)$	*(Haga clic para cerrar el diálogo de impresión)*
	(a)	*(Haga clic)*
	(k)	(en)
	(t_p)	(Haga clic en)
ITER-2	$(\hat{t}_s)$	*(ACEPTAR para cerrar el diálogo de impresión)*
	(a)	*(ACEPTAR para cerrar el)*
	(k)	(cuadro)
	(t_p)	(Haga clic en ACEPTAR para cerrar el cuadro)
FINAL	$(\hat{t}_s)$	*(de diálogo de impresión)*
	(a)	*(de diálogo de impresión)*
	(k)	(#)
	$(t_p \equiv t)$	(Haga clic <u>en</u> ACEPTAR para cerrar el <u>cuadro</u> de diálogo de impresión)

Fig. 1. Example of a CAT system interaction to translate into Spanish the English sentence *"Click OK to close the print dialog"* extracted from a printer manual. Each step starts with a previously fixed target language prefix t_p, from which the system suggests a suffix $\hat{t}_s$. Then the user accepts part of this suffix (a) and types some keystrokes (k), in order to amend the remaining part of t_s. This produces a new prefix, composed by the prefix from the previous iteration and the accepted and typed text, (a) (k), to be used as t_p in the next step. The process ends when the user enters the special keystroke "#". In the final translation, t, all the text that has been typed by the user is underlined.

Given $t_p\hat{t}_s$, the CAT cycle proceeds by letting the user establish a new, longer acceptable prefix. To this end, he or she has to accept a part (a) of $t_p\hat{t}_s$ (or, more typically, just a prefix of $\hat{t}_s$). After this point, the user may type some keystrokes (k) in order to amend some remaining incorrect parts. Therefore, the new prefix (typically) encompasses t_p followed by the accepted part of the system suggestion, **a**, plus the text, **k**, entered by the user. Now this prefix, $\mathbf{t}_p \mathbf{a} \mathbf{k}$, becomes a new $\mathbf{t}_p$, thereby starting a new CAT prediction cycle.

Ergonomics and user preferences dictate exactly when the system can start its new cycle, but typically, it is started after each user-entered word or even after each new user keystroke.

Perhaps the simplest formalization of the process of hypothesis suggestion of a CAT system is as follows. Given a source text **s** and a user validated *prefix* of the target sentence $\mathbf{t}_p$, search for a *suffix* of the target sentence that maximises the *a posteriori* probability over all possible suffixes:

$$\hat{\mathbf{t}}_s = \operatorname*{argmax}_{\mathbf{t}_s} \Pr(\mathbf{t}_s \mid \mathbf{s}, \mathbf{t}_p) \ . \tag{4}$$

Taking into account that $\Pr(\mathbf{t}_p \mid \mathbf{s})$ does not depend on $\mathbf{t}_s$, we can write:

$$\hat{\mathbf{t}}_s = \operatorname*{argmax}_{\mathbf{t}_s} \Pr(\mathbf{t}_p \mathbf{t}_s \mid \mathbf{s}) \ , \tag{5}$$

where $\mathbf{t}_p \mathbf{t}_s$ is the concatenation of the given prefix $\mathbf{t}_p$ and a suffix $\mathbf{t}_s$. Eq. 5 is similar to Eq. 1, but here the maximisation is carried out over a set of suffixes, rather than full sentences as in Eq. 1. This joint distribution can be adequately modeled by means of SFSTs [9].

The solution to this maximisation problem has been devised in two phases. The first one copes with the extraction of a word graph $\mathcal{W}$ from a SFST $\mathcal{T}$ given a source sentence **s**. In a second phase, the search of the best translation suffix (or suffixes) according to the Viterbi approach [16] is performed over the word graph $\mathcal{W}$ given a prefix $\mathbf{t}_p$ of the target sentence.

3.1   Word Graph Derivation

A word graph is a compact representation of all the possible translations that a SFST $\mathcal{T}$ can produce from a given source sentence **s** [9, 8]. In fact, the word graph could be seen as a kind of weighted finite-state automaton in which the probabilities are not normalized.

Formally, given a SFST $\mathcal{T} = \langle \Sigma, \Delta, Q, q_0, F, \delta, p, f \rangle$ and a source sentence $\mathbf{s} = s_1, \cdots, s_i, \cdots s_{|\mathbf{s}|}$, the constructed word graph is defined as a tuple $\mathcal{W} = \langle \Delta, Q', q_0', F', \delta', p, f \rangle$:

$$Q' = Q \times i : 0 \leq i \leq |\mathbf{s}|$$
$$\delta' = \{((q, i-1), t, (q', i)) \mid (q, s_i, t, q') \in \delta\}$$
$$q_0' = (q_0, 0)$$
$$F' = \{(q', |\mathbf{s}|) \mid ((q, s_{|\mathbf{s}|}, t, q') \in \delta) \wedge (q' \in F)\}$$

There are a couple of minor issues to deal with in this construction. On the one hand, the output symbol for a given transition could contain more than one word. In this case, auxiliary states were created to assign only one word for each transition and simplify the posterior search procedure. On the other hand, it is possible to have words in the input sentence that do not belong to the input vocabulary in the SFST. This problem is solved with the introduction of a special generic "unknown word" in the input vocabulary of the SFST.

Intuitively, the word graph generated retains those transitions in the SFST that were compatible with the source sentence along with their transition probability and output symbol(s). Those states that are reached at the end of the parsing process of the source sentence, over the SFST, are considered final states (as well as those states reachable with λ-transitions from them).

Once the word graph is constructed, it can be used to find the best completions for the part of the translation typed by the human translator. Note that the word graph depends only on the input sentence, so it is used repeatedly for finding the completions of all the different prefixes provided by the user.

3.2   Search for N-best Translations Given a Prefix of the Target Sentence

Ideally, the search problem consists in finding the target suffix $\mathbf{t}_s$ that maximises the *a posteriori* probability given a prefix $\mathbf{t}_p$ of the target sentence and the input sentence $\mathbf{s}$, as described in Eq. 5. To simplify this search, it will be divided into two steps or phases. The first one would deal with the parsing of $\mathbf{t}_p$ over the word graph $\mathcal{W}$. This parsing procedure would end reaching a set of states Q'_p that define paths from the initial state whose associated translations include $\mathbf{t}_p$. To clarify this point, it is important to note that each state q in the word graph defines a set of translation prefixes P_q. This set of translation prefixes is obtained from the concatenation of the output symbols of the different paths that reach this state q from the initial state. Therefore, the set P_q of each state in Q'_p includes $\mathbf{t}_p$. The second phase would be the search of the most probable translation suffix from any of the states in Q'_p. Finally, the complete search procedure extracts a translation from the word graph whose prefix is $\mathbf{t}_p$ and its remaining suffix is the resulting translation suffix $\mathbf{t}_s$.

Error-Correcting Parsing. In practice, however, it may happen that $\mathbf{t}_p$ is not present in the word graph $\mathcal{W}$. The solution is not to use $\mathbf{t}_p$ but a prefix $\mathbf{t}'_p$ that is the *most similar* to $\mathbf{t}_p$ in some string distance metric. The metric that will be employed is the well-known minimum edit distance based on three basic edit operations: insertion, substitution and deletion. Therefore, the first phase introduced in the previous paragraph needs to be redefined in terms of the search of those states in $\mathcal{W}$ whose set P_q contains $\mathbf{t}'_p$, that is, the set of states Q'_p. It should be remarked that $\mathbf{t}'_p$ is not unique, but there exist a set of prefixes in $\mathcal{W}$ whose minimum edit distance to $\mathbf{t}_p$ is the same and the lowest possible.

Given a translation prefix $\mathbf{t}_p$, the computation of Q'_p is efficiently carried out by applying an adapted version of the error-correcting algorithm for regular grammars over the word graph $\mathcal{W}$. This algorithm returns the minimum edit cost $c(q)$ with respect to $\mathbf{t}_p$ for each state q in $\mathcal{W}$. To be more precise, this minimum edit cost is the lowest minimum edit cost between $\mathbf{t}_p$ and the set of prefixes P_q of each state q. Finally, Q'_p is defined as:

$$Q'_p = \operatorname*{argmin}_{q \in Q'} c(q) \qquad (6)$$

The asymptotic cost of this algorithm is $O(|\mathbf{t}_p| \cdot |Q'| \cdot B)$, where B is the (average) branching factor of the word graph $\mathcal{W}$.

The implementation of the error-correcting parsing is further improved by visiting the states in $\mathcal{W}$ in topological order, and incorporating beam-search techniques to discard those states whose minimum edit cost is worse than the best minimum edit cost at the current stage of the parsing by a given constant. Moreover, given the incremental nature of $\mathbf{t}_p$, the error-correcting algorithm takes advantage of this peculiarity to parse only the new suffix of $\mathbf{t}_p$ provided by the user in the last interaction, that is, the concatenation of $\mathbf{a}$ and $\mathbf{k}$.

As mentioned before, once the set Q'_p has been computed, the search of the most probable translation suffix could be calculated from any of the states in Q'_p. In practice, only one state q_p from Q'_p is selected to find the suffix $\mathbf{t}_s$. This selected state q_p maximises the *a posteriori* probability of the word-graph prefix $\mathbf{t}'_p$ defined during the error-correcting parsing process. This maximisation is performed according to the Viterbi approximation [16].

N-best Search. The actual implementation of this CAT system is able to provide a set of different translation suffixes, instead of a single suggestion. To this purpose, an algorithm that searches for the n-best translation suffixes in a word graph is required. Among the n-best algorithms available, the Recursive Enumeration Algorithm (REA) described in [11] was selected. The main two reasons that support this decision are its simplicity to calculate best paths on demand and its smooth integration with the error-correcting parsing algorithm. Basically, the interaction between these two algorithms, error-correcting and n-best, consists in the supplement of the state q_p by the former, so that the n-best translation suffixes can be calculated from this state by the latter.

The version of REA included in the CAT system, which is being described, stores for each state q in $\mathcal{W}$, the sorted list of current best paths (in the form of next state in the best path) from q to any final state. The length of this sorted list depends on the number of transitions leaving q. During the initialisation of REA, the initial sorted list of best paths for each state is calculated starting from the final states and visiting the rest of states in backward topological order. This last condition imposes a total order in Q' that favours the efficient calculation of the sorted list of best paths. This is so because each state is visited only once, and once the best paths of the preceding states have already been computed.

Then, given a state q_p from which the n-best translation suffixes need to be calculated, REA first extracts the 1-best path from the state q_p, since it was precomputed during REA initialisation. If $n > 1$, then the next best path from q_p will be obtained. The next best path at state q_p can be found among the candidate paths still left in the sorted list of this state and the second best path through the transition traversed in the 1-best path just extracted. This fact requires the recursive calculation of the second best path (whenever exists) through the states visited in the 1-best path. This same rationale is applied to the calculation of subsequent best paths until n-best different translation suffixes have been obtained or no more best paths can be found.

4   Experimental Framework and Results

The SFST models introduced in the previous sections were assessed through some series of experiments with two different corpora that were acquired and preprocessed in the framework of the TransType2 (TT2) project [2]. In this section, these corpora, the assessment metrics and the results are presented.

4.1   XRCE and EU Corpora

Two bilingual corpora extracted from different semantic domains were used in the evaluation of the CAT system described. The language pairs involved in the assessment were English/Spanish, English/French and English/German.

The first corpus, namely *XRCE* corpus, was obtained from a miscellaneous set of printer user manuals. Some statistics of this corpus are shown in Table 1.

Table 1. The "XRCE" and "EU" corpora English(En) to/from Spanish(Sp), German(Ge) and French(Fr). Trigrams models were used to compute the test perplexity. (K denotes ×1.000, and M denotes ×1.000.000).

		XRCE			EU		
		En/Sp	En/Ge	En/Fr	En/Sp	En/Ge	En/Fr
Train	Sent. pairs (K)	56	49	53	214	223	215
	Run. words (M)	0.6/0.7	0.6/0.5	0.6/0.7	5.9/6.6	6.5/6.1	6.0/6.6
	Vocabulary (K)	26/30	25/27	25/37	84/97	87/153	85/91
Test	Sentences (K)	1.1	1.0	1.0	0.8	0.8	0.8
	Run. words (K)	8/9	9/10	11/10	20/23	20/19	20/23
	Perplexity	107/60	93/169	193/135	96/72	95/153	97/71

It is important to remark that the English manuals are different in each pair of languages. The size of the vocabulary in the training set is about 25.000 words in most of the language pairs that can be considered to be a broad lexicon. In the test set, even though all test sets have similar size, the perplexity varies abruptly over the different language pairs.

The second dataset was compiled from the Bulletin of the European Union, which exists in the 11 official languages of the European Union. This dataset is known as the *EU* corpus and is publicly available on the Internet. A summary of its features is presented in Table 1.

The size of the vocabulary of this corpus is at least three times larger than that of the *XRCE* corpus. These figures together with the amount of running words and sentences reflect the challenging nature of this task. However, the perplexity of the *EU* test set is similar to that of the *XRCE*. This phenomenon can be intuitively explained through the more uniform grammatical structure of the sentences in the *EU* corpus.

4.2 Translation Quality Evaluation

The assessment of the CAT system has been carried out based on two measures:

1. *Translation Word Error Rate* (TWER). It is defined as the minimum number of word substitution, deletion and insertion operations required to convert the target sentence provided by the translation system into the reference translation, divided by the number of words of the reference translation. It can also be seen as the ratio of the minimum edit distance between the system and the reference translation, and the number of words of the reference translation [1, 6].

   This metric is employed to evaluate the quality of the complete translations offered by the system when no prefix is taken into consideration, that is, no interaction with the user is assumed.

2. *Key-Stroke Ratio* (KSR). Number of interactions, as the sum of mouse actions (to select **a**) and keystrokes (to type **k**), that are necessary to achieve the reference translation plus the final translation-acceptance keystroke divided by the number of characters of the reference translation [9, 8].

   KSR reflects the ratio between the number of interactions of a fictitious user when translating a given text using a CAT system compared to the number of interactions, which this user would need, to translate the same text without using a CAT system. Thus, this measure gives a clear idea of the amount of work that a translator would be saving when translating using a CAT system.

4.3 Experimental Results

These experimental results were obtained with GIATI transducers based on smoothed trigram language models for the *XRCE* corpus and smoothed 5-gram language models for the *EU* corpus (see Table 2).

The translation metrics presented in the previous section were calculated on the test set for all the pairs of languages and both directions, translating from English to a non-English language and from a non-English language to English, as shown on the left-most column of Table 2. Moreover, the results were obtained assuming two possible cases, the CAT system only offers the best translation or the 5-best translations. In the latter case, the calculation of a given assessment metric was conducted considering that translation out of the five suggested translations that most minimises the corresponding error measure. As expected, there is a notable improvement when comparing 1 to 5-best translation error measures.

Analysing the results accomplished in the *XRCE* corpus, it is observed that the TWER and KSR rates for English/Spanish language pairs are substantially lower than those obtained in the rest of language pairs. A possible reason behind the error rate discrepancies between English/Spanish pairs with respect to English/German and English/French pairs could be found in the perplexity differences shown in Table 1. The Spanish test perplexity is significantly lower than that of the rest of languages and this fact is transformed into better translation results. Another reason for the outperforming results of the English/Spanish

Table 2. Results comparing 1-best to 5-best translations based on 3-gram language models for the *XRCE* corpus and on 5-gram language models for the *EU* corpus

XRCE	1-best KSR	1-best TWER	5-best KSR	5-best TWER
En-Sp	24.4	30.8	21.7	25.2
Sp-En	30.1	33.5	26.4	25.1
En-Ge	52.1	70.7	48.1	63.4
Ge-En	50.7	64.0	46.4	57.0
En-Fr	48.7	63.2	45.0	54.8
Fr-En	52.2	57.8	48.5	51.4

EU	1-best KSR	1-best TWER	5-best KSR	5-best TWER
En-Sp	38.9	54.5	35.5	49.8
Sp-En	37.2	51.0	33.6	46.8
En-Ge	45.6	64.2	42.4	59.2
Ge-En	49.1	65.7	45.6	59.2
En-Fr	35.7	51.8	32.3	47.6
Fr-En	34.1	47.5	30.7	43.2

pairs comes from the hand of the random partition in training and test datasets, that could have been resulted in a simpler test set for the English/Spanish pairs.

This rationale is compatible with the results obtained for the *EU* corpus. In these results, English/Spanish pairs exhibit similar error rates to those of the English/French pairs, but significantly better than those of the English/German pairs. This same tendency is followed by perplexity values appearing in Table 1. As observed, the German language seems to be more complex than the other languages and this is reflected in the translation results.

As the reader would notice, TWER results in both corpora are not sufficiently good to support a pure MT system based on SFSTs inferred by the GIATI technique. However, if the system is evaluated as a CAT system (KSR), a productivity gain is clearly manifested. For example in the *XRCE* corpus, using five suggestions and translating from English to Spanish, the user would only need to perform 21.7% of the interactions that would be required without this CAT system. On the other hand, the KSR results are about 50% for the English/French and English/German pairs. Even in these cases, the number of interactions is halved with respect to the effort that would entail translating the same test set without a CAT system.

In the *EU* corpus, the best KSR results were obtained for the English/French language pairs, followed by the results in the English/Spanish language pairs, and finally the worst results were achieved in English/German language pairs. Despite the important difference in size between *XRCE* and *EU*, the results are similar and for some language pairs even lower in the *EU* corpus. The perplexity numbers on both corpora partially explain these results being somewhat correlated with the TWER and KSR results. For instance, the English/French language pair presents lower perplexity and better results in the *EU* corpus than in the *XRCE* corpus.

5   Conclusions and Future Work

In the present work, SFSTs have been revisited and applied to CAT. In this case, SFSTs that are easily learnt from parallel corpora were inferred by the GI-ATI technique, which was briefly reviewed. Moreover, the concept of interactive search has been introduced in this paper along with some well-known techniques, i.e. error-correcting parsing and n-best paths, that allow the calculation of the suffix translation that better completes the prefix written by the user. It is fundamental to remember that usability and response-time are vital features for CAT systems. CAT systems need to provide translation suffixes after each user interaction and this imposes the necessity of efficient algorithms to solve the search problem.

As preempted in the introduction, current MT systems are not able to provide high quality translations and SFST techniques are not an exception. Nevertheless, the capability of SFSTs to suggest translation suffixes that aid a human translator to increase his or her productivity in a CAT framework should not be neglected. The results presented on two different corpora support the idea of the benefits of the incorporation of MT techniques into the translation process to reduce human translator effort without sacrificing high quality translations.

Finally, the introduction of morpho-syntactic information, bilingual categories or more powerful smoothing techniques on the source and target languages, in SFSTs, are topics still to be explored in future research.

References

1. J. C. Amengual et al. The EuTrans-I speech translation system. *Machine Translation*, 15:75–103, 2000.
2. Atos Origin, Instituto Tecnológico de Informática, RWTH Aachen, RALI Laboratory, Celer Soluciones and Société Gamma and Xerox Research Centre Europe. TransType2 - Computer Assisted Translation. Project Technical Annex., 2001.
3. S. Bangalore and G. Ricardi. A finite-state approach to machine translation. In *Proc. of NAACL'01*, 2001.
4. P. F. Brown et al. The mathematics of statistical machine translation: Parameter estimation. *Computational Linguistics*, 19(2):263–312, 1993.
5. F. Casacuberta et al. Some approaches to statistical and finite-state speech-to-speech translation. *Computer Speech and Language*, 18:25–47, 2004.
6. F. Casacuberta et al. Some approaches to statistical and finite-state speech-to-speech translation. *Computer Speech and Language*, 18:25–47, 2004.
7. F. Casacuberta and E. Vidal. Machine translation with inferred stochastic finite-state transducers. *Computational Linguistics*, 30(2):205–225, 2004.
8. J. Civera et al. From machine translation to computer assisted translation using finite-state models. In *Proc. of EMNLP04*, Barcelona, 2004.
9. J. Civera et al. A syntactic pattern recognition approach to computer assisted translation. In A. Fred, T. Caelli, A. Campilho, R. P. Duin, and D. de Ridder, editors, *Advances in Statistical, Structural and Syntactical Pattern Recognition*, Lecture Notes in Computer Science, pages 207–215. Springer-Verlag, 2004.
10. F.Casacuberta and C. de la Higuera. Computational complexity of problems on probabilistic grammars and transducers. In A. Oliveira, editor, *Grammatical Inference: Algorithms and Applications*, volume 1891 of *Lecture Notes in Computer Science*, pages 15–24. Springer-Verlag, 2000.

11. V. M. Jiménez and A. Marzal. Computing the k shortest paths: a new algorithm and an experimental comparison. In J. S. Vitter and C. D. Zaroliagis, editors, *Algorithm Engineering*, volume 1668 of *Lecture Notes in Computer Science*, pages 15–29. Springer-Verlag, July 1999.

12. K. Knight and Y. Al-Onaizan. Translation with finite-state devices. In E. H. D. Farwell, L. Gerber, editor, *Proc. of AMTA'98*, volume 1529, pages 421–437, October 1998.

13. P. Langlais, G. Foster, and G. Lapalme. Unit completion for a computer-aided translation typing system. *Machine Translation*, 15(4):267–294, 2000.

14. F. J. Och and H. Ney. Improved statistical alignment models. In *Proc. of ACL'00*, pages 440–447, Hong Kong, China, October 2000.

15. D. Picó and F. Casacuberta. Some statistical-estimation methods for stochastic finite-state transducers. *Machine Learning*, 44:121–142, July-August 2001.

16. A. Viterbi. Error bounds for convolutional codes and a asymptotically optimal decoding algorithm. *IEEE Transactions on Information Theory*, 13:260–269, 1967.

Finite-State Registered Automata and Their Uses in Natural Languages

Yael Cohen-Sygal and Shuly Wintner

Department of Computer Science
University of Haifa
{yaelc, shuly}@cs.haifa.ac.il

Abstract. We extend *finite-state registered automata* (FSRA) to account for medium-distance dependencies in natural languages. We provide an extended regular expression language whose expressions denote arbitrary FSRAs and use it to describe some morphological and phonological phenomena. We also define several dedicated operators which support an easy and efficient implementation of some non-trivial morphological phenomena. In addition, we extend FSRA to *finite-state registered transducers* and demonstrate their space efficiency.

1 Introduction

Finite-state (FS) technology is considered adequate for describing the morphological processes of natural languages since the pioneering works of [1] and [2]. Several toolboxes provide extended regular expression description languages and compilers of the expressions to finite-state automata (FSAs) and transducers (FSTs) [3,4,5]. While FS approaches for natural languages processing have generally been very successful, it is widely recognized that they are less suitable for non-concatenative phenomena. In particular, FS techniques are assumed not to be able to efficiently account for medium-distance dependencies, whereby some elements that are related to each other in some deep-level representation are separated on the surface. These phenomena do not lie outside the descriptive power of FS systems, but their implementation can result in huge networks that are inefficient to process.

To constrain dependencies between separated morphemes in words, [6] propose *flag diacritics*, which add features to symbols in regular expressions to enforce dependencies between separated parts of a string. The dependencies are forced by different kinds of unification actions. In this way, a small amount of finite memory is added, keeping the total size of the network relatively small. The main disadvantage of this method is that it is not formally defined, and its mathematical and computational properties are not proved. Furthermore, flag diacritics are manipulated at the level of the extended regular expressions, although it is clear that they are compiled into additional memory and operators in the networks themselves. The presentation of [6] and [7] does not explicate the implementation of such operators and does not provide an analysis of

A. Yli-Jyrä, L. Karttunen, and J. Karhumäki (Eds.): FSMNLP 2005, LNAI 4002, pp. 43–54, 2006.
© Springer-Verlag Berlin Heidelberg 2006

their complexity. Moreover, they do not present any dedicated regular expression operations for non-concatenative processes.

A related formalism is *vectorized finite-state automata* (VFSA) [8], where both the states and the transitions are represented by vectors of elements of a partially ordered set. Two kinds of operations over vectors are defined: *unification* and *overwriting*. The vectors need not be fully determined, as some of the elements can be unknown (free). In this way information can be moved through the transitions by the overwriting operation and traversing these transitions can be sanctioned through the unification operation. The free symbols are also the source of the efficiency of this model, where a vector with k free symbols actually represents t^k vectors, t being the number of different values that can be stored in the free places. As one of the examples of the advantages of the model, [8] shows that it can efficiently solve the problem of 32-bit binary incrementor. The goal of this example is to construct a transducer over $\Sigma = \{0, 1\}$ whose input is a number in 32 bit binary representation and whose output is the result of adding 1 to the input. The naïve solution is a transducer with only 5 states and 12 arcs, but this transducer is neither sequential nor sequentiable. A sequential transducer for an n-bit binary incrementor would require 2^n states and a similar number of transitions. Using vectorized finite-state automata, a 32-bit incrementor is constructed where first, using overwriting, the input is scanned and stored by the vectors, and then, using unification, the result is calculated where the carry can be computed from right to left. This allows a significant reduction in the network size. The main disadvantage of VFSA lies in the fact that it significantly deviates from the standard methodology of developing finite-state devices, and integration of vectorized automata with standard ones remains a challenge. Moreover, it is unclear how, for a given problem, the corresponding network should be constructed: programming with vectorized automata seems to be unnatural, and no regular expression language is provided for them.

Finite state registered automata (FSRA) ([9]) augment finite-state automata with finite memory (registers) in a restricted way that saves space but does not add expressivity. The number of registers is finite, usually small, and eliminates the need to duplicate paths as it enables the automaton to 'remember' a finite number of symbols. Each FSRA defines an alphabet, Γ, whose members can be stored in registers. In this model, each arc is associated not only with an alphabet symbol, but also with a series of actions on the registers. There are two kinds of possible actions, *read* and *write*. The read action, denoted R, allows traversing an arc only if a designated register contains a specific symbol. The write action, denoted W, allows traversing an arc while writing a specific symbol into a designated register. Then, the FSRA model is extended to allow up to k register operations on each transition, where k is determined for each automaton separately. The register operations are defined as a sequence (rather than a set), in order to allow more than one operation on the same register over one transition. [9] prove that FSRAs are equivalent to FSAs, and use them to efficiently describe some non-concatenative phenomena of natural languages, including interdigitation (root-and-pattern morphology) and limited reduplication.

In this work we extend the model of *FSRA* to account for medium-distance dependencies in natural languages. We provide an extended regular expression language whose expressions denote FSRAs in section 2. Section 3 defines several dedicated operators which support an easy and efficient implementation of some non-trivial morphological phenomena. We then extend FSRA to finite-state registered *transducers* in section 4. Furthermore, the model is evaluated through an actual implementation in section 5. We conclude with a comparison with similar approaches and suggestions for future research.

2 A Regular Expression Language for FSRAs

The first limitation of [9] is that no regular expression language is provided for constructing FSRAs. We begin by proposing such a language, the denotations of whose expressions are FSRAs. In the following discussion we assume the regular expression syntax of XFST ([7]) for basic expressions[1].

Definition 1. *Let $Actions_n^{\Gamma} = \{R, W\} \times \{0, 1, 2, \ldots, n-1\} \times \Gamma$, where n is the number of registers and Γ is the register alphabet. If R is a regular expression and $\boldsymbol{a} \in \left(Actions_n^{\Gamma}\right)^{+}$ is a series of register operations, then the following are also regular expressions: $\boldsymbol{a} \triangleright R$, $\boldsymbol{a} \triangleright \triangleright R$, $\boldsymbol{a} \triangleleft R$ and $\boldsymbol{a} \triangleleft \triangleleft R$.*

We now define the denotation of each of the above expressions. Let R be a regular expression whose denotation is the FSRA A, and let $\boldsymbol{a} \in \left(Actions_n^{\Gamma}\right)^{+}$. The denotation of $\boldsymbol{a} \triangleleft R$ is an FSRA A' obtained from A by adding a new node, q, which becomes the initial node of A', and an arc from q to the initial node of A; this arc is labeled by ϵ and associated with $\boldsymbol{a}$. Notice that in the regular expression $\boldsymbol{a} \triangleleft R$, R and $\boldsymbol{a}$ can contain operations on joint registers. In some cases, one would like to distinguish between the registers used in $\boldsymbol{a}$ and in R. Usually, it is up to the user to correctly manipulate the usage of registers, but in some cases automatic distinction seems desirable. For example, if R includes a circumfix operator (see below), its corresponding FSRA will contain register operations created automatically by the operator. Instead of remembering that circumfixation always uses register 1, one can simply distinguish between the registers of $\boldsymbol{a}$ and R via the $\boldsymbol{a} \triangleleft \triangleleft R$ operator. This operator has the same general effect as the previous one, but the transition relation in its FSRA uses fresh registers which are added to the machine.

In a similar way, the operators $\boldsymbol{a} \triangleright R$ and $\boldsymbol{a} \triangleright \triangleright R$ are translated into networks. The difference between these operators and the previous ones is that here, the register operations in $\boldsymbol{a}$ are executed *after* traversing all the arcs in the FSRA denoted by R. It is easy to show that every FSRA has a corresponding regular expression denoting it.

Example 1. *Consider the case of vowel harmony in Warlpiri [10], where the vowel of suffixes agrees in certain aspects with the vowel of the stem to which it is attached. A simplified account of the phenomenon is that suffixes come in two*

---

[1] In particular, concatenation is denoted by space and ϵ is denoted by 0.

varieties, one with 'i' vowels and one with 'u' vowels. Stems whose last vowel is
'i' take suffixes of the first variety, whereas stems whose last vowel is 'u' or 'a'
take the other variety. The following examples are from [10] (citing [11]):

1. maliki+kiḷi+ḷi+lki+ji+li
   (dog+PROP+ERG+then+me+they)
2. kuḍu+kuḷu+ḷu+lku+ju+lu
   (child+PROP+ERG+then+me+they)
3. minija+kuḷu+ḷu+lku+ju+lu
   (cat+PROP+ERG+then+me+they)

An FSRA that accepts the above three words is denoted by the following complex
regular expression:

```
define LexI [m a l i k i]; % words ending in 'i'
define LexU [k u d u];     % words ending in 'u'
define LexA [m i n i j a]; % words ending in 'a'
! Join all the lexicons and write to register 1
! 'u' or 'i' according to the stem's last vowel.
define Stem [<(W,1,i)> ◁ LexI] |
            [<(W,1,u)> ◁ [LexU | LexA]];
! Traverse the arc only if the scanned symbol is
! the content of register 1.
define V [<(R,1,i)> ▷ i] | [<(R,1,u)> ▷ u];
define PROP [+ k V l V]; % PROP suffix
define ERG  [+ l V];     % ERG suffix
define Then [+ l k V];   % suffix indicating 'then'
define Me   [+ j V];     % suffix indicating 'me'
define They [+ l V];     % suffix indicating 'they'
! define the whole network
define WarlpiriExample Stem PROP ERG Then Me They;
```

Register 1 stores the last vowel of the stem, eliminating the need to duplicate
paths for each of the different cases. The lexicon is divided into three separate
lexicons (LexI, LexU, LexA), one for each word ending ('i', 'u' or 'a' respec-
tively). The separate lexicons are joined into one (the variable Stem) and when
reading the last letter of the base word, its type is written into register 1. Then,
when suffixing the lexicon base words, the variable V uses the the content of reg-
ister 1 to determine which of the symbols 'i', 'u' should be scanned and allows
traversing the arc only if the correct symbol is scanned. Note that this solution is
applicable independently of the size of the lexicon, and can handle other suffixes
in the same way.

Example 2. *Consider the following Arabic nouns: qamar (moon), kitaab*
(book), $ams (sun) and daftar (notebook). The definite article in Arabic is the prefix
''al', which is realized as ''al' when preceding most consonants; however, the 'l' of
the prefix assimilates to the first consonant of the noun when the latter is 'd', '$',

etc. Furthermore, Arabic distinguishes between definite and indefinite case mark-
ers. For example, nominative case is realized as the suffix 'u' on definite nouns, 'un'
on indefinite nouns. Examples of the different forms of Arabic nouns are:

word	nominative definite	nominative indefinite
qamar	'alqamaru	qamarun
kitaab	'alkitaabu	kitaabun
$ams	'a$$amsu	$amsun
daftar	'addaftaru	daftarun

The FSRA of Figure 1 accepts all the nominative definite and indefinite forms
of these nouns. In order to account for the assimilation, register 2 stores infor-
mation about the actual form of the definite article. Furthermore, to ensure that
definite nouns occur with the correct case ending, register 1 stores information
of whether or not a definite article was seen. This FSRA can be denoted by the
following regular expression:

```
! Read the definite article (if present).
! Store in register 1 whether the noun is definite
! or indefinite.
! Store in register 2 the actual form of the
! definite article.
define Prefix [<(W,1,indef)> ◁ 0] |
               [<(W,1,def),(W,2,1)> ◁ 'al] |
               [<(W,1,def),(W,2,$)> ◁ 'a$] |
               [<(W,1,def),(W,2,d)> ◁ 'ad];
! Normal base - definite and indefinite
define Base [ [<(R,2,1)> ◁ 0]|[<(R,1,indef)> ◁ 0] ]
           [ [k i t a a b]|[q a m a r] ];
! Bases beginning with $ - definite and indefinite
define $Base [ [<(R,2,$)> ◁ 0]|[<(R,1,indef)> ◁ 0] ]
              [$ a m s];
! Bases beginning with d - definite and indefinite
define dBase [ [<(R,2,d)> ◁ 0]|[<(R,1,indef)> ◁ 0] ]
              [d a f t a r];
! Read definite and indefinite suffixes.
define Suffix [<(R,1,def)> ▷ u]|[<(R,1,indef)> ▷ un];
! The complete network.
define ArabicExample Prefix [Base | $Base | dBase]
                Suffix;
```

The variable Prefix denotes the arcs connecting the first two states of the FSRA,
in which the definite article (if present) is scanned and information indicating
whether the word is definite or not is saved into register 1. In addition, if the
word is definite then register 2 stores the actual form of the definite article. The
lexicon is divided into several parts: the Base variable denotes nouns that do not
trigger assimilation. Other variables ($Base, dBase) denote nouns that trigger

assimilation, where for each assimilitaion case, a different lexicon is constructed. Each part of the lexicon deals with both its definite and indefinite nouns by allowing traversing the arcs only if the register content is appropriate. The variable Suffix denotes the correct suffix, depending on whether the noun is definite or indefinite. This is possible using the information that was stored in register 1 by the variable Prefix.

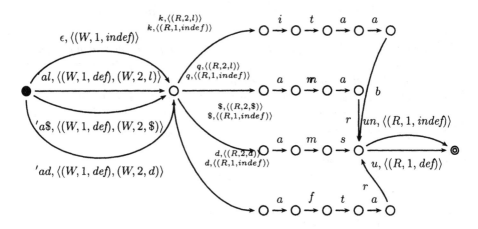

Fig. 1. FSRA-2 for Arabic nominative definite and indefinite nouns

3   Dedicated Regular Expressions for Linguistic Applications

3.1   Circumfixes

The usefulness of FSRAs for non-concatenative morphology is demonstrated by [9], who show a specific FSRA accounting for circumfixation in Hebrew. We introduce a dedicated regular expression operator for circumfixation and show how expressions using this operator are compiled into the appropriate FSRA. The operator accepts a regular expression, denoting a set of bases, and a set of circumfixes, each of which containing a prefix and a suffix regular expressions. It yields as a result an FSRA obtained by prefixing and suffixing the base with each of the circumfixes. The main purpose of this operator is to deal with cases in which the circumfixes are pairs of strings, but it is defined such that the circumfixes can be arbitrary regular expressions.

Definition 2. *Let Σ be a finite set such that $\Box, \{, \}, \langle, \rangle, \otimes \notin \Sigma$. We define the $\otimes$ operation to be of the form*

$$R \otimes \{\langle\beta_1\Box\gamma_1\rangle\langle\beta_2\Box\gamma_2\rangle \ldots \langle\beta_m\Box\gamma_m\rangle\}$$

where: $m \in \mathbb{N}$ is the number of circumfixes; R is a regular expression over Σ denoting the set of bases and β_i, γ_i for $1 \leq i \leq m$ are regular expressions over Σ denoting the prefix and suffix of the i-th circumfix, respectively.

Notice that R, β_i, γ_i may denote infinite sets. To define the denotation of this operator, let β_i, γ_i be regular expressions denoting the FSRAs A_i^β, A_i^γ, respectively. The operator yields an FSRA constructed by concatenating three FSRAs. The first is the FSRA constructed from the union of the FSRAs $A'^\beta_1, \ldots, A'^\beta_m$, where each A'^β_i is an FSRA obtained from A_i^β by adding a new node, q, which becomes the initial node of A'^β_i, and an arc from q to the initial node of A_i^β; this arc is labeled by ϵ and associated with $\langle (W, 1, \beta_i \square \gamma_i) \rangle$. In addition, the register operations of the FSRA A_i^β are shifted by one register in order not to cause undesired effects by the use of register 1. The second FSRA is the FSRA denoted by the regular expression R (again, with one register shift) and the third is constructed in the same way as the first one, with the difference that the FSRAs are those denoted by $\gamma_1, \ldots, \gamma_m$ and the associated register operation is $\langle (R, 1, \beta_i \square \gamma_i) \rangle$. Notice that the concatenation operation, defined by [9], adjusts the register operations in the FSRAs to be concatenated, to avoid undesired effects caused by using joint registers. We use this operation to concatenate the three FSRAs, leaving register 1 unaffected (to handle the circumfix).

Example 3. *Consider the participle-forming combinations in German, e.g., the circumfix ge-t. A simplified account of the phenomenon is that German verbs in their present form take an 'n' suffix but in participle form they take the circumfix ge-t. The following examples are from [10]:*

säuseln 'rustle' gesäuselt 'rustled'
brüsten 'brag' gebrüstet 'bragged'

The FSRA of Figure2, which accepts the four forms, is yielded by the regular expression

$$[s\ \ddot{a}\ u\ s\ e\ l\ |\ b\ r\ \ddot{u}\ s\ t\ e] \otimes \{\langle \epsilon \square n \rangle \langle g\ e \square t \rangle\}$$

This regular expression can be easily extended to accept more German verbs in other forms. More circumfixation phenomena in other languages such as Indonesian, Arabic etc. can be modeled in the same way using this operator.

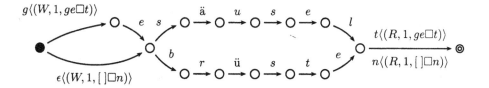

Fig. 2. Participle-forming combinations in German

3.2   Interdigitation

For interdigitation, [9] introduce a dedicated regular expression operator, *splice*, which accepts a set of strings of length n over Σ^*, representing a set of roots, and a list of patterns, each containing exactly n 'slots', and yields a set containing all the strings created by splicing the roots into the slots in the patterns. Formally, if Σ is such that $\square, \{, \}, \langle, \rangle, \oplus \notin \Sigma$, then the *splice* operation is of the form

$$\{\langle \alpha_{1\ 1}, \alpha_{1\ 2}, ..., \alpha_{1\ n} \rangle, ..., \langle \alpha_{m\ 1}, \alpha_{m\ 2}, ..., \alpha_{m\ n} \rangle\}$$

$$\oplus$$

$$\{\langle \beta_{1\ 1} \square \beta_{1\ 2} \square ... \beta_{1\ n} \square \beta_{1\ n+1} \rangle, ..., \langle \beta_{k\ 1} \square \beta_{k\ 2} \square ... \beta_{k\ n} \square \beta_{k\ n+1} \rangle\}$$

where $n \in \mathbb{N}$ is the number of slots (represented by '$\square$'); $m \in \mathbb{N}$ is the number of roots; $k \in \mathbb{N}$ is the number of patterns and $\alpha_{ij}, \beta_{ij} \in \Sigma^*$. This operator suffers from lack of generality as the set of roots and patterns must be strings; we generalize the operator in a way that supports *any* regular expression denoting a language for both the roots and the patterns. This extension is done by simply allowing α_{ij}, β{ij} to be arbitrary regular expressions (including regular expressions denoting FSRAs). The construction of the FSRA denoted by this generalized operation is done in the same way as in the case of circumfixes with two main adjustments. The first is that in this case the final FSRA is constructed by concatenating $2n + 1$ intermediate FSRAs (n FSRAs for the n parts of the roots and $n + 1$ FSRAs for the $n + 1$ parts of the patterns). The second is that here, 2 registers are used to remember both the root and the pattern. We suppress the detailed description of the construction. The circumfixation operator may seem redundant, being a special case of interdigitation. However, it results in a more compact network without any unnecessary register operations.

4   Finite-State Registered Transducers

We extend the FSRA model to *finite-state registered transducers* (FSRT), denoting relations over two finite alphabets. The extension is done by adding to each transition an output symbol. This facilitates an elegant solution to the problem of binary incrementors which was introduced in section 1.

Example 4. *Consider again the 32-bit incrementor example mentioned in section 1. Recall that a sequential transducer for an n-bit binary incrementor would require 2^n states and a similar number of transitions. Using the FSRT model, a more efficient n-bit transducer can be constructed. A 4-bit FSRT incrementor is shown in Figure 3. The first four transitions copy the input string into the registers, then the input is scanned (using the registers) from right to left (as the carry moves), calculating the result, and the last four transitions output the result (in case the input is 1^n, an extra 1 is added in the beginning). Notice that this transducer guarantees linear recognition time, since from each state only one arc can be traversed in each step, even when there are ϵ-arcs. In the same way, an n-bit transducer can be constructed for all $n \in \mathbb{N}$. Such a transducer will have n registers, $3n + 1$ states and $6n$ arcs. The FSRT model solves the incrementor problem in much the same way it is solved by vectorized finite-state automata, but the FSRT solution is more intuitive and is based on existing finite-state techniques.*

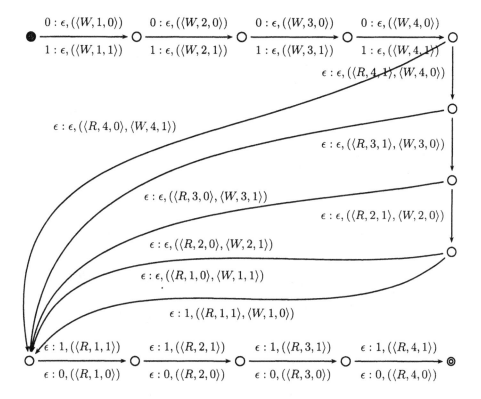

Fig. 3. 4-bit incrementor using FSRT

It is easy to show that FSRTs, just like FSRAs, are equivalent to their non-registered counterparts. It immediately implies that FSRTs maintain the closure properties of regular relations. Thus, performing the regular operations on FSRTs can be easily done by converting them first into finite-state transducers. However, such a conversion may result in an exponential increase in the size of the network, invalidating the advantages of FSRTs. Therefore, as in FSRAs, implementing the closure properties directly on FSRTs is essential for benefiting from their space efficiency. Implementing the common operators such as union, concatenation etc. is done in the same ways as in FSRAs ([9]). Direct implementation on FSRTs of composition is a naïve extension of ordinary transducers composition, based on the intersection construction of FSRAs ([9]). We explicitly define these operations in [12].

5   Implementation and Evaluation

In order to practically compare the space and time performance of FSRAs and FSAs, we have implemented the special operators introduced in section sec: regular expression for nl for circumfixation and interdigitation, as well as direct

Table 1. Space comparison between FSAs and FSRAs

Operation	Network type	States	Arcs	Registers	File size
Circumfixation	FSA	811	3824	–	47kb
(4 circumfixes, 1043 roots)	FSRA	356	360	1	16kb
Interdigitation	FSA	12,527	31,077	–	451kb
(20 patterns, 1043 roots)	FSRA	58	3259	2	67kb
10-bit incrementor	Sequential FST	268	322	–	7kb
	FSRT	31	60	10	2kb
50-bit incrementor	Sequential FST	23,328	24,602	–	600kb
	FSRT	151	300	50	8kb
100-bit incrementor	Sequential FST	176,653	181,702	–	4.73Mb
	FSRT	301	600	100	17kb

Table 2. Time comparison between FSAs and FSRAs

		200 words	1000 words	5000 words
Circumfixation	FSA	0.01s	0.02s	0.08s
(4 circumfixes, 1043 roots)	FSRA	0.01s	0.02s	0.09s
Interdigitation	FSA	0.01s	0.02s	1s
(20 patterns, 1043 roots)	FSRA	0.35s	1.42s	10.11s
10-bit incrementor	Sequential FST	0.01s	0.05s	0.17s
	FSRT	0.01s	0.06s	0.23s
50-bit incrementor	Sequential FST	0.13s	0.2s	0.59s
	FSRT	0.08s	0.4s	1.6s

construction of FSRAs. We have compared FSRAs with ordinary FSAs by building corresponding networks for circumfixation, interdigitation and n-bit incrementation. For circumfixation, we constructed networks for the circumfixation of 1043 Hebrew roots and 4 circumfixes. For interdigitation we constructed a network accepting the splicing of 1043 roots into 20 patterns. For n-bit incrementation we constructed networks for 10-bit, 50-bit and 100-bit incrementors. Table 1 displays the size of each of the networks in terms of states, arcs and actual file size.

Clearly, FSRAs provide a significant reduction in the network size. In particular, we could not construct an n-bit incrementor FSA for any n greater than 100 as a result of memory problems, whereas using FSRAs we had no problem constructing networks even for $n = 50,000$.

In addition, we compared the recognition times of the two models. For that purpose, we used the circumfixation, interdigitation, 10-bit incrementation and 50-bit incrementation networks to analyze 200, 1000 and 5,000 words. As can be seen in Table 2, time performance is comparable for the two models, except for interdigitation, where FSAs outperform FSRAs by a constant factor. The reason is that in this network the usage of registers is massive and thereby, there is a higher cost to the reduction of the network size, in terms of analysis time. This is an instance of the common tradeoff of time versus space: FSRAs improve the network size at the cost of slower analysis time in some cases. When using finite-state devices for natural language processing, often the generated networks become too large to be practical. In such cases, using FSRAs can make network size manageable. Using the closure constructions one can build desired networks of reasonable size, and at the end decide whether to convert them to ordinary FSAs, if time performance is an issue.

6   Conclusions

We have shown how FSRAs can be used to model non-trivial morphological processes in natural languages, including vowel-harmony, circumfixation and interdigitation. We also provided a regular expression language to denote arbitrary FSRAs. In addition, we extended FSRAs to transducers and demonstrated their efficiency. Moreover, we evaluated FSRAs through an actual implementation.

While our approach is similar in spirit to Flag Diacritics ([6]), we provide a complete and accurate description of the FSRAs constructed from our extended regular expressions. The transparency of the construction details allows further insight into the computational efficiency of the model and provides an evidence to its regularity. Moreover, the presentation of dedicated regular expression operations for non-concatenative processes allows easier construction of complex registered networks, especially for more complicated processes such as interdigitation and circumfixes.

In section 5 we discuss an implementation of FSRAs. Although we have used this system to construct networks for several phenomena, we are interested in constructing a network for describing the complete morphology of a natural language containing many non-concatenative phenomena, e.g., Hebrew. A morphological analyzer for Hebrew, based on finite-state calculi, already exists [13], but is very space-inefficient and, therefore, hard to maintain. It would be beneficial to compact such a network using FSRTs, and to inspect the time versus space tradeoff on such a comprehensive network.

Acknowledgments

This research was supported by The Israel Science Foundation (grant number 136/01). We are grateful to Dale Gerdemann for his help.

References

1. Koskenniemi, K.: Two-Level Morphology: a General Computational Model for Word-Form Recognition and Production. The Department of General Linguistics, University of Helsinki (1983)
2. Kaplan, R.M., Kay, M.: Regular models of phonological rule systems. Computational Linguistics **20** (1994) 331–378
3. Karttunen, L., Chanod, J.P., Grefenstette, G., Schiller, A.: Regular expressions for language engineering. Natural Language Engineering **2** (1996) 305–328

4. Mohri, M.: On some applications of finite-state automata theory to natural language processing. Natural Language Engineering **2** (1996) 61–80

5. van Noord, G., Gerdemann, D.: An extendible regular expression compiler for finite-state approaches in natural language processing. In Boldt, O., Jürgensen, H., eds.: Automata Implementation. Number 2214 in Lecture Notes in Computer Science. Springer (2001)

6. Beesley, K.R.: Constraining separated morphotactic dependencies in finite-state grammars. In: FSMNLP-98., Bilkent, Turkey (1998) 118–127

7. Beesley, K.R., Karttunen, L.: Finite-State Morphology: Xerox Tools and Techniques. Cambridge University Press (Forthcoming)

8. Kornai, A.: Vectorized finite state automata. In: Proceedings of the workshop on extended finite state models of languages in the 12th European Conference on Artificial Intelligence, Budapest (1996) 36–41

9. Cohen-Sygal, Y., Gerdemann, D., Wintner, S.: Computational implementation of non-concatenative morphology. In: Proceedings of the Workshop on Finite-State Methods in Natural Language Processing, an EACL'03 Workshop. (2003) 59–66

10. Sproat, R.W.: Morphology and Computation. MIT Press, Cambridge, MA (1992)

11. Nash, D.: Topics in Warlpiri Grammar. PhD thesis, Massachusetts Institue of Technlogy (1980)

12. Cohen-Sygal, Y.: Computational implementation of non-concatenative morphology. Master's thesis, University of Haifa (2004)

13. Yona, S., Wintner, S.: A finite-state morphological grammar of hebrew. In: Proceedings of the ACL-2005 Workshop on Computational Approaches to Semitic Languages. (2005)

TAGH: A Complete Morphology for German Based on Weighted Finite State Automata

Alexander Geyken[1] and Thomas Hanneforth[2]

[1] Berlin-Brandenburg Academy of Sciences
[2] University of Potsdam

Abstract. TAGH is a system for automatic recognition of German word forms. It is based on a stem lexicon with allomorphs and a concatenative mechanism for inflection and word formation. Weighted FSA and a cost function are used in order to determine the correct segmentation of complex forms: the correct segmentation for a given compound is supposed to be the one with the least cost. TAGH is based on a large stem lexicon of almost 80.000 stems that was compiled within 5 years on the basis of large newspaper corpora and literary texts. The number of analyzable word forms is increased considerably by more than 1000 different rules for derivational and compositional word formation. The recognition rate of TAGH is more than 99% for modern newspaper text and approximately 98.5% for literary texts.

1 Introduction

Compounding in German is productive, therefore full-form lexicons cannot cover German morphology completely. Hence morphology programs such as Gertwol (Haapalainen and Majorin[6]) or canoo [http://www.canoo.net] generally use stem lexicons together with decomposition and derivation rules. The present approach differs from the aforementioned morphology systems in that it is not based on a two-level-morphology but on a concatenative mechanism. The formal prerequisites for that are presented in section 2, 'Morphology and Weighted Finite State Automata'. In section 3 we will describe the linguistic aspects of the TAGH-morphology, the lexicon and the word formation rules. In addition, the semantic types of LexikoNet, a shallow semantic hierarchy for German nouns will be described. All noun entries of the stem-lexicon are annotated with these semantic types. Thus, it is possible to use semantic types both for expressing word formation rules as well as for the semantic typing of semantically transparent compounds. In section 4, the problem of disambiguation of ambiguous morphological analysis is addressed. Section 5 and 6 summarize the current state of development of the presented system and sketch out some ideas for future work.

A. Yli-Jyrä, L. Karttunen, and J. Karhumäki (Eds.): FSMNLP 2005, LNAI 4002, pp. 55–66, 2006.
© Springer-Verlag Berlin Heidelberg 2006

2   Morphology and Weighted Finite State Automata

2.1   The Morphology Problem

Basically the morphology problem can be stated as follows: given an input alphabet Σ_I, an output alphabet Σ_0 and a morphological alphabet[1] Σ_M, a morphology realizes a partial function $\Sigma_I^* \to \wp(\Sigma_0^*.\Sigma_M^*)$. The morphological alphabet consists of letters, morpheme boundary symbols ($\#,\sim$), categories (like NN, NSTEM, NSUFF), and features like 3, sg, nom.

Since a string in Σ_I^* can be mapped to several output strings we need the power set operator $\wp$. Usually this function is considered a rational one, that is, both Σ_I^* and $\Sigma_0^*.\Sigma_M^*$ are supposed to be regular languages. This decision rules out constructing word-syntactic trees and also the treatment of unrestricted reduplication phenomena in certain languages. How do we construct such morphology functions? There are at least two ways based on closure properties: one is based on the fact that regular languages are closed under substitution, the other exploits the closure of regular languages/relations under intersection/composition (e.g. Hopcroft [7]). In the next section we will sketch the algebraic specification of a weighted finite state transducer representing a morphology function for German.

2.2   Algebraic Specification of a Morphology for German

The first building blocks of the system are two lexicons, one for stems and one for affixes. Fig. 1 shows a very small fraction of the stem lexicon containing two verbs and a noun.[2] We have decided to handle irregular, nonpredictable allomorphy like *Umlaut* and *Ablaut* in the lexicon, that is, the stem lexicon is represented by a finite state transducer (Fig. 3 in appendix), which maps lemmas to allomorphic stems (cf. also Karttunen [9]).

For example, the irregular verb **werfen** (to throw) is mapped to its five allomorphic stems. A number of mostly boolean features like *StPret* encodes important morphological properties like co-occurrence restrictions, in particular the fact, that a certain stem can be used only in an inflected form of a certain type. *StPret = yes* for example means that a stem marked in that way must be used in preterite verb forms. In effect the seven boolean stem features define the stem equivalence classes for every irregular German verb. The affix lexicon which similarly contains categorized prefixes, derivational and inflectional suffixes, infixes etc. is compiled into a finite state acceptor. The next step consists in taking the union of the lexicons and afterwards the closure of this union:

---

[1] We assume the morphology alphabet to be disjoint from the input and output alphabet.

[2] We use the AT&T LexTools notation, cf. Sproat [14]. Symbols in [ ] denote possibly underspecified categories. Features are defined with respect to an inheritance hierarchy and are represented as transition labels. Underspecification is realized as the disjunction of all maximal subtypes of a super type.

```
(rett:rett)   [VREG VType=main PrefVerb=no Latinate=no PartIIIrreg=no]
(werf:warf)   [VIRREG VType=main PrefVerb=no\
              Latinate=no StDef=no St23SgInd=no StPret=yes StSubjI=no\
              StSubjII=no StPartII=no StImpSg=no St23SgIndVowelChange=yes]\
(werf:werf)   [VIRREG VType=main PrefVerb=no
              Latinate=no StDef=yes St23SgInd=no StPret=no StSubjI=yes \
              StSubjII=no StPartII=no StImpSg=no St23SgIndVowelChange=yes]\
(werf:wirf)   [VIRREG VType=main PrefVerb=no Latinate=no StDef=no\
              St23SgInd=yes StPret=no StSubjI=no StSubjII=no StPartII=no\
              StImpSg=yes St23SgIndVowelChange=yes]\
(werf:worf)   [VIRREG VType=main PrefVerb=no Latinate=no StDef=no\
              St23SgInd=no StPret=no StSubjI=no StSubjII=no StPartII=yes\
              StImpSg=no St23SgIndVowelChange=yes]\
(werf:w\"urf) [VIRREG VType=main PrefVerb=no Latinate=no StDef=no \
              St23SgInd=no StPret=no StSubjI=no StSubjII=yes StPartII=no\
              StImpSg=no St23SgIndVowelChange=yes]\
(Haus:Haus)   [NSTEM Gender=neut NICSg=ic_sg1 NICPl=ic_pl3\
              StemType=deko Bound=no DecoActive=yes]\
(Haus:H\"aus) [NSTEM Gender=neut NICSg=ic_sg1 NICPl=ic_pl3\
              StemType=deko Bound=no DecoActive=yes]
```

Fig. 1. Extract of the stem lexicon

$$Morph^* =_{def} (Stems \cup ID(Affixes) \cup ID(MorphBoundaries))^* \ [3]$$

The regular relation $Morph^*$ denotes the infinite language of all sequences of stems and affixes and their features without taking into account word-grammatical restrictions or phenomena of regular allomorphic variation when certain morphemes are concatenated. To solve the first problem, $Morph^*$ is composed with a word grammar:

$$Morph_{WG} =_{def} Morph^* \circ ID(WordGrammar).$$

This filters out all sequences which are ill-formed according to the word grammar. $WordGrammar$ must be defined as a regular set. Fig. 2 shows some example rules given as regular expressions which are disjunctively combined (of course, the actual grammar is defined in a much more modular fashion):

```
(([Letter]*) [NSTEM] #)* ([Letter]*)   [VREG] ~ ung [NSUFF Gen=fem][NINFL Num=sg Case=*]
(([Letter]*) [NSTEM] #)* ([Letter]*)   [VREG] ~ ung [NSUFF Gen=fem] en [NINFL Num=pl Case=*]
(([Letter]*) [ASTEM] #)* ([Letter]*)   [VREG] ~ bar [ASUFF]
(([Letter]*) [NSTEM] #)* ([Letter]*)   [VREG] ~ bar [ASUFF] ~ keit [NSUFF Gen=fem]\
              [NINFL Num=sg Case=*]
```

Fig. 2. Sample regular word grammar

Rules 1 and 2 for example describe the nominalization of regular verbs by means of the suffix -ung: retten (to rescue) $\rightarrow$ rett $\sim$ ung. Rule 3 defines the suffixation of verb stems with the suffix -bar: retten $\vdash$ rettbar (rescuable), while rule 4 allows a further suffixation of -bar-suffixed verbs with the suffix -keit, resulting in forms like rett$\sim$bar$\sim$keit (rescuability). All four rules permit an unlimited

---

[3] ID(A) represents the identity relation of a regular set A; $MorphBoundaries$ is the set of morpheme boundary symbols: $\sim$ for suffixation, $\#$ for compounding etc.

number of noun stems which precede the derived verb stems, resulting in (rather senseless) compounds like Haus#rett∼bar∼keit (house-rescuability). Fig. 4 (appendix) shows the FSA associated with the word grammar.

The next step consists of applying morphographematic rules, so-called spelling rules, to the outcome of $Morph^* \circ WordGrammar$ to handle regular allomorphy like *schwa*-insertion etc. These types of rules are defined by context-sensitive replacement rules, which can be modelled as finite-state transducers with the restriction that they are not applied to its own output, (see Kaplan [8]). The following rule describes the insertion of *schwa* after verb stems ending with *tt* before a set of the verbal inflectional elements:

$$\epsilon \rightarrow e \; / \; tt[VREG] \_ (\; n(d?) \; |t|st|t(e|est|en|et)) \; [VINFL]$$

This accounts for word forms like rettest *(2. sg pres)* or rettetest *(2. sg pret)*. All k spelling rules SRi are composed into a single spelling transducer (of course the ordering of these rules is of importance):

$$Spelling =_{def} SR1 \circ SR2 \circ \cdots \circ SRk$$

After composing $Morph_{WG}$ with *Spelling* we obtain a transducer representing a relation between lexical forms and surface strings, both interleaved with categorical information. To define the input tape of the morphological analyzer we have to delete the symbols of the morphology alphabet and to invert the resulting transducer:

$$MorphAnalyser' =_{def} Invert(Morph^* \circ ID(WordGrammar) \circ Spelling \circ Cap \circ InputBand).$$

InputBand is the composition of a sequence of rules like the following:

$$([NSTEM]|[VREG]|[VIRREG]|[NSUFF]| \sim) \rightarrow \epsilon.$$

Cap ensures the correct capitalization of the surface word: sequences which define nouns start with an uppercase letter, noun stems inside of words start with a lowercase letter etc. The remaining task is to format the output band of the analyzer accordingly:

$$OutputBand =_{def} RHHR \circ MorphFeatToSynFeat.$$

RHHR represents the right-hand-head-rule which says that in German the stem or suffix morpheme standing at the right periphery determines the morphosyntactic properties of the whole word. *RHHR* is represented by a sequence of contextual replacement rules like the following:

$$[NSTEM] \rightarrow \epsilon \; / \; \_ (\#| \sim).$$

This rule deletes noun stem markers preceding morpheme boundaries. Finally *MorphFeatToSynFeat* rewrites sequences of morphological features/categories to morphosyntactic categories (like NN), followed by morphosyntactic features (case, gender, number, etc.) If, for example, the word Rettungen is analyzed, both categories $NSUFF$ and $NINFL$ contribute to the features of the complete word: $NSUFF$ defines its gender and $NINFL$ its number and case. The final morphological transducer is defined by:

$$MorphAnalyser =_{def} MorphAnalyser' \circ OutputBand.$$

As usual, applying the morphology to a word consists in composing the input word given as an identity transducer with $MorphAnalyzer$ and taking the output band:

$$Proj2(ID(input) \circ MorphAnalyzer).$$

2.3 Morphological Complexity and Weighted Automata Morphology

Analyzers like the one sketched in the last section segment longer word forms in a sometimes absurd manner into sets of senseless alternatives amongst which to choose is not an easy task.[4] Therefore, it would be useful to have a notion of morphological complexity which can be integrated into the analyzer and which prefers for example compounds with fewer segments to compounds with more segments or favors lexicalized but morphologically complex compounds over non-lexicalized readings. A simple way to achieve this is to reconstruct the grammar as a weighted regular language where the weights reflecting the morphological complexity of the different word formation rules can be either chosen by hand or acquired through machine learning techniques. To put it a bit more generally: we define a weighted language L where each element in L is a pair consisting of a string $x \in \Sigma^*$ and a weight c chosen from a weight set W. A suitable algebraic structure for this task in the context of finite-state automata is a *semiring*. A structure $< W, \oplus, \otimes, \bar{0}, \bar{1} >$ is a semiring (e.g. Golan [5]), if it fulfils the following conditions:

1. $< W, \oplus, \bar{0} >$ is a commutative monoid with $\bar{0}$ as the identity element for $\oplus$.
2. $< W, \otimes, \bar{1} >$ is a monoid with $\bar{1}$ as the identity element for $\otimes$.
3. $\otimes$ distributes over $\oplus$.
4. $\bar{0}$ is an annihilator for $\otimes$: $\forall w \in W, w \otimes \bar{0} = \bar{0} \otimes w = \bar{0}$.

A weighted finite-state transducer $A = < \Sigma, \Delta, Q, q_0, F, E, \lambda, \rho >$ over a semiring W is an 8-tuple with Σ being the finite input alphabet, Δ the output alphabet, Q the finite set of states, $q_0 \in Q$ the start state, $F \subseteq Q$ the set of final states, $E \subseteq Q \times (\Sigma \cup \epsilon) \times (\Delta \cup \epsilon) \times W \times Q$ the set of edges, $\lambda \in W$ the initial weight and $\rho : F \mapsto W$ the final weight function mapping final states to elements in W. In section 4 we give some examples for an instantiation of the semiring template with $< \Re, min, +, \infty, \bar{0} >$, a so-called tropical semiring (e.g. Mohri [11]). This means that weights along an accepting path of an automaton are additively combined and among different paths accepting the same input string the path with the minimal weight is chosen.

---

[4] We give some examples in section 4.

3 Lexicon and Word Formation Rules

3.1 TAGH-Lexicon

Lexicons for NLP purposes can be represented as full-form lexicons (e.g. Courtois [3]) or as stem-lexicons (e.g. two-level morphology lexicons such as the above mentioned Gertwol or canoo). In the first case each lexicon entry corresponds to an inflected form together with its morphological features. Full-form lexicons are convenient for languages such as English or French where compounding is not productive. The lexicon look-up is then reduced to a pattern matching of a token with a lexicon entry. In the second case, a comparatively small lexicon is related to word formation rules in order to analyze word-forms which are not in the stem-lexicon. It is convenient to encode German as a stem-based lexicon because of its productive derivation and compounding.

Stem-based lexicons can be used in a concatenative or a non-concatenative way. In the latter case one attempts to describe non-concatenative processes such as the formation of irregular stems by an enrichment of the lexical entries with special symbols on which special rules apply (e.g. two-level-morphology). The TAGH-morphology relies on a concatenative stem-based lexicon as described in section 2. Hence, irregular lemmas generally correspond to several allomorphic stems. In the above-mentioned example in Fig. 1, the irregular verb **werfen** (to throw) has five different allomorphic stems: **warf, wirf, werf, worf, würf**. Likewise an irregular noun such as **Haus** (house) has two different allomorphic stems: **Haus** and **Häus**.

In the TAGH-lexicon a difference between simple stems and complex stems is made. A word form in the TAGH-lexicon is a **simple stem** if

(**A**) it cannot be analyzed by a morphophonetic-, derivation- or a composition-rule or a combination of them into two or more non empty segments in a way that at least one segment can be used autonomously;

(**B**) each true decomposition consists of at least one opaque segment. Here, transparency is understood synchronically; e.g. Augst [1];

(**C**) it is unmarked with respect to inflection.

According to that definition the lexicon of simple stems consists of word-forms that cannot be further decomposed (in the above-mentioned sense) in a transparent way into smaller lexemes. Of course, this definition depends on a large extent on the word formation rules as well as on the set of stems. Some examples shall illustrate this definition.

(1) Wand (wall), steh (to stand), grün (green)
(2) vorhersehbar (predictable), Drehtür (revolving door)
(3) Waldmeister (woodruff)
(4) unflätig (bawdy), drollig (funny),
(5) lexikalisch, (lexicalized), marokkanisch (moroccan)

The examples in (1) are all simple forms, those in (2) are transparent compounds since they can be analyzed by word formation rules vorhersehbar ↦

vorherseh + *bar*, Drehtür ↦ Dreh + Tür. Semantically intransparent compounds such as Waldmeister in (3) are stored in the lexicon of complex stems. Even though Waldmeister is morphologically analyzable by a simple N+N compound rule, the complex stem is the preferred lemma (cf. section 2.3 how the preference is computed, and section 4 for some examples).

The examples in (4) are encoded as simple stems since they are consistent with condition **B** of the definition above: here *un-* and *-ig* are active prefixes resp. suffixes, but the remaining word forms Flat (Old High German sauber, clean) and Droll (lower German Knirps (manikin) have no synchronous interpretation.

The examples in (5) are also considered simple stems since the current TAGH-morphology does not consider the following morphophonemic word formation rules: *-al-* in lexik-al-isch or *-an-* in marokk-an-isch.

A word form is a **complex stem** if

(**A**) it consists of at least two simple stems plus additional affixes or linking elements;

(**B**) if the meaning of the word form is either morphologically or semantically opaque, meaning that fully transparent compounds are not stored in the stem-lexicon;

(**C**) it is unmarked with respect to inflection.

Organization of the TAGH-Lexicon. The TAGH-lexicon itself is divided up into several sub-lexicons according to their lexical categories. There are lexicons for nouns, verbs, adjectives, adverbs, closed classes (prepositions, determiners, conjunctions), confixes, abbreviations and acronyms, each stored in a relational database (cf. table 1). Additionally, large lists of proper nouns (first names and family names as well as geographical names) were compiled.

3.2   Shallow Semantic Typing

All noun entries are categorized on the basis of a shallow semantic typing which has been derived from LexikoNet, a lexical ontology of German nouns (Geyken

Table 1. Number of stems in the TAGH-lexicon

stem type	number
nouns	41,000
verbs	21,000
adjectives	11,000
adverbs	2,300
closed forms	1,500
abbrev, acronyms	15,000
confixes	105
family names	150,000
first names	20,000
geogr. names	60,000

and Schrader [4]). LexikoNet is based on a concept hierarchy of more than 1,200 concept nodes that is ordered in a top-down hierarchy beginning with the concepts of CONCRETE NOUNS and ABSTRACT NOUNS.

For its use in the TAGH-morphology the LexikoNet is simplified in order to be tractable for fast analysis. The 1,200 categories are mapped to a shallow hierarchy of types selected for their prevalence in context patterns: the Brandeis Shallow Ontology, (BSO), Pustejovsky ([12]). BSO consists of the following (provisional) types: EVENT, ACTION, SPEECHACT, ACTIVITY, PROCESS, STATE, ENTITY, PHYSICALOBJECT, ARTIFACT, MACHINE, VEHICLE, HARDWARE, MEDIUM, GARMENT, DRUG, SUBSTANCE, VAPOR, ANIMATE, BIRD, HORSE, PERSON, HUMAN GROUP, PLANT, PLANTPART, BODY, BODYPART, INSTITUTION, LOCATION, DWELLING, ACCOMMODATION, ENERGY, ABSTRACT, ATTITUDE, EMOTION, RESPONSIBILITY, PRIVILEGE, RULE, INFORMATION, DOCUMENT, FILM, PROGRAM, SOFTWARE, WORD, LANGUAGE, CONCEPT, PROPERTY, VISIBLEFEATURE, COLOR, SHAPE, TIMEPERIOD, HOLIDAY, COURSE OF STUDY, COST, ASSET, ROUTE.

Shallow semantic typing is used for two purposes: for specifying word formation rules (see section 4) as well as for determining the semantic type of a transparent compound. For example, the compound noun Sprachexperte (language expert) is not part of the stem-lexicon but can be morphologically and semantically analyzed on the basis of its components (note also, that the allomorphic stem Sprach (language) is correctly lemmatized to Sprache):

Sprache/N#Experte[NN SemClass=Human Gender=masc Number=sgCase=nom]

3.3   Word Formation Rules

Approximately 1000 word formation rules are used in the TAGH-morphology in order to recognize new words on the basis of the stem-lexicon. Within the framework of the formalism it is possible to express derivation, conversion and composition rules. These rules generally operate on lexical categories, but it is also possible to restrict the applicability of a rule to subsets of lexical categories that are determined by additional features such as accented suffixes, latinate, compounding activity or semantic type. Additionally, for nouns and adjectives more than 120 non autonomous prefixes and suffixes were collected, each of them being active in word formation. It is beyond the scope of this paper to present all rules. The following examples illustrate how the encoding in the lexicon and the word formation rules interact.

(1) VSTEM + -*bar* ↦ ASTEM
(2) confix + NSTEM ↦ NSTEM
(3) ASTEM [latinate=true] + -*ist* ↦ NSTEM [semClass =Human] if ASTEM ends with --*tär*, -*iv*, -*ell*, -*al*.
(4) -*chen*-derivation (only suffix) for nouns of the semantic classes ARTIFACT, PHYSICAL OBJECT or SUBSTANCE.

(1) describes the simple derivation rule: a verb stem combines with the suffix -*bar* to an adjective. Rule (2) describes a rule that combines confixes and nouns.

Confixes are morphemes such as *Ergo-, Poly-, Giga-*. They are listed in the noun resp. adjective lexicon as stems with two distinctive properties: they are non-autonomous and do not belong to a lexical category. (3) is a non concatenative rule that is used to derive abstract nouns ending with *-ist* from their corresponding adjective, for example monetär (monetary) $\mapsto$ Monetarist with the following morphological analysis: Monetarist $\mapsto$ monetär$/A \sim ist[NNSemClass = Human]$.

Rule (4) demonstrates the use of semantic typing for word formation rules. Here, the diminutive rule induced by the suffix *-chen* only applies to nouns with the semantic type ARTIFACT. This rule does not raise the recognition rate but has an impact on the precision of word formation. An example for this rule is the diminutive noun Kärtchen (engl. small card) which is derived from Karte/N $\sim chen$[NN SemClass=artifact].

4 Compound Segmentation

Since morphology programs display all possible segmentations for compounds, disambiguation rules are required for compounds with ambiguous segmentations. The lexicon of complex stems is used to avoid blunders such as the segmentation of Gendarm (gendarme) into Gen and Darm or of Ration (ration) into rat$\sim$*en* and lon by listing them as lexicalized compounds. However, it is not possible to disambiguate all compounds in that way because of the above mentioned productivity of German. Hence other methods are required to choose the correct lemma in the case of ambiguous compounds. Following the approach of Volk ([15]) we set weights for each segmentation boundary: segmentation costs for a linking element (/) in compounds are 2, for a derivation boundary ($\sim$) 2.5, for weak composition boundaries such as confix boundaries 5, for strong composition boundaries (#) 10. Furthermore, a change of lexical categories corresponds to 5 for a change from adjective to verb, 10 for a change from verb to noun, and 20 for a change proper noun to noun, since we consider compounds with proper nouns much less likely. The weights are additively combined along an accepting path of an automaton (cf. section 2.3) thus defining a cost function. The preferred analysis is the analysis with the least costs.

The following examples using some well known ambiguous German compounds illustrate the efficiency of this simple cost function. In example 1, the correct lemma Abteilung (department) is the one with the least value of the cost function since Abteilung is part of the lexicon of complex stems. On the other hand, the other two possibilities require decomposition and therefore get higher weights. In the second example, the compound Arbeitstag (work day) is correctly decomposed. Note here, that, similarly to other approaches, the wrong segmentation Arbeit/N\#stag is blocked by the TAGH-morphology since the rare noun Stag (stay) is encoded in the lexicon as not being active in compounding. In example 3 the compound Schadstoffanreicherung (accumulation of toxic substance) the correct analysis is preferred because of unlikely category changes (from verb to noun resp. from proper noun to noun) in the other two segmentations.

Example (1)

```
Abteilung[NN SemClass=Human_Group Gender=fem Number=pl Case=*] <0>
ab|teil/V~ung[NN SemClass=Abstract Gender=fem Number=pl Case=*]<5>
Abtei/N#Lunge[NN SemClass=PhysObject Gender=fem Number=pl Case=*]<10>
```

Example (2)

```
Arbeit/N\s#Tag[NN SemClass=abstr Gender=masc Number=sg Case=nom_acc_dat] <12>
```

Example (3)

```
Schadstoff/N#an|reicher/V~ung[NN Sem=Abstract Gen=fem Num=sg Case=*]<15>
schad/V#Stoff/N#an|reicher/V~ung[NN SemClass=Abstract Gender=fem Number=sg Case=*] <25>
Schad/NE#Stoff/N#an|reicher/V~ung[NN SemClass=Abstract Gender=fem Number=sg Case=*] <45>
```

5   Technicalities

The morphology described here has been developed for 5 years. The development is based on the Potsdam FST library which is modelled after the seminal AT&T FST library (Mohri [11]) and implemented in C++. The library implements all operations of the algebra of weighted finite state transducers based on abstract semirings. The library also contains compilers for lexicons, regular expressions, replacement rules etc. The morphology transducer currently has 3.96 million states and 6.75 million transitions. It analyzes, depending on the text genre, up to 50,000 words per second. TAGH-morphology is currently used as an annotation tool for the search engine of the newspaper *Die ZEIT* (http://www.zeit.de) as well as for the morphological analysis of the DWDS-Kerncorpus of the project DWDS at the Berlin-Brandenburg Academy of Sciences (http://www.dwds.de). The DWDS-Kerncorpus is a 100 million word corpus of the 20th century, balanced with respect to text genre. The recognition rate for the archive of *Die ZEIT* (40 m tokens) is 99.1%, the recognition rate for the DWDS-Kerncorpus is 98.2%. An evaluation of the correctness has not been carried out yet due to a lack of training corpora containing manually corrected word segmentation information.

6   Conclusion and Further Work

In this work we have presented TAGH-Morphology, a system, which unlike the two-level approach does not assume to be closed under intersection, i.e. it does not require the input and output tape to be of the same length. We have shown that the system scales up to a full coverage morphology of German and that the implemented mechanism, which is based on weighted transducers, rules out most of the undesired segmentations with a best match strategy. We have also presented a way to integrate a shallow semantic types to the morphological analysis thus allowing to compute a semantic type for compounds that are not in the stem-lexicon.

Future work will concentrate evaluation of the correctness of the system, which amounts to the creation of a manually disambiguated training corpora, as well as to use machine learning methods in order to learn the weights of the cost function.

References

1. Augst, Gerhard: Lexikon zur Wortbildung. Morpheminventar Bd. 1-3. Tübingen, 1975.
2. Cormen, T.H., Leiserson, C.L., Rivest, R.L., Stein, C.: Introduction to Algorithms. MIT Press, 2001.
3. Courtois, B. "Dictionnaires électroniques DELAF anglais et français", in: Leclère C., Laporte E., Piot M., Silberztein M. (eds.). Syntax, Lexis and Lexicon-Grammar. Papers in honour of Maurice Gross, Lingvisticae Investigationes Supplementa 24, Amsterdam-Philadelphia : Benjamins, 2004, p. 113 – 125.
4. Geyken, A. and N. Schrader: LexikoNet - a lexical database based on type and role hierarchies. Technical Report BBAW/DWDS, Berlin, 2005.
5. Golan, Jonathan S.: Semirings and Their Applications. Kluwer, Dordrecht, 1999.
6. Haapalainen, M. and A. Majorin: Gertwol: Ein System zur automatischen Wortformerkennung deutscher Wörter. Lingsoft, Inc., 1994.
7. Hopcroft, J.E. & Ullman, J.D.: Introduction to Automata Theory, Languages, and Computation. Addison-Wesley, Reading, Mass., 1979.
8. Kaplan, R.M., Kay, M.: "Regular Models of Phonological Rule Systems". Computational Linguistics, 20(3), 1994, p. 331–378.
9. Karttunen, L.: "Constructing Lexical Transducers". In: Proceedings of the Fifteenth International Conference on Computational Linguistics. Coling I-94, Kyoto, Japan, 1994, p. 406–411.
10. Klappenbach, Ruth and Wolfgang Steinitz (ed.) (1977). Wörterbuch der deutschen Gegenwartssprache (WDG). Akademie Verlag.
11. Mohri, M.: "Semiring Frameworks and Algorithms for Shortest-Distance Problems". Journal of Automata, Language, and Combinatorics 7 (2002) 3, p. 321–350.
12. Pustejovsky, J., P. Hanks, and A. Rumshisky. "Automated Induction of Sense in Context". 5th International Workshop on Linguistically Interpreted Corpora (LINC-04), Coling, 2004.
13. Riley, M.: "The Design Principles of a Weighted Finite-State Transducer Library". Theoretical Computer Science, 231 (2000), p. 17–32.
14. Sproat, R.: Finite-State Methods in Morphology, Text Analysis and the Analysis of Writing Systems. ROCLING X, 1997.
15. Volk, M.: "Choosing the right lemma when analysing German nouns". In: Multilinguale Corpora: Codierung, Strukturierung, Analyse. Jahrestagung der GLDV 11, Frankfurt, 1999, p. 304–310.

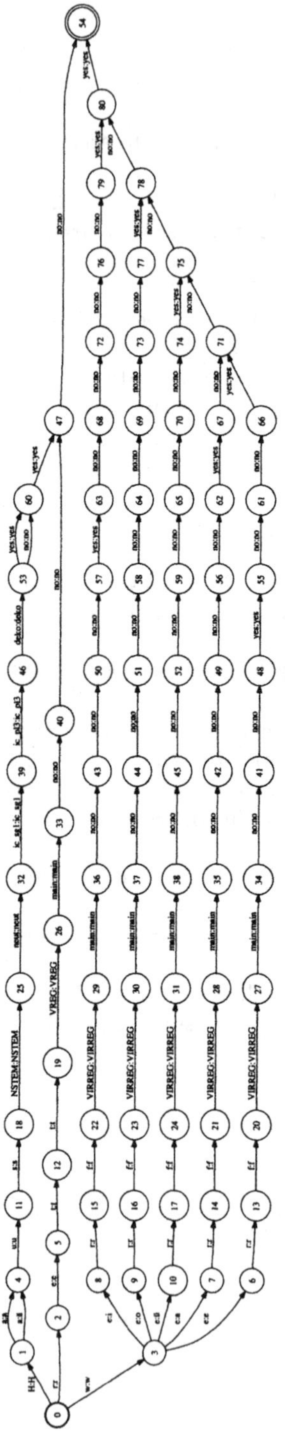

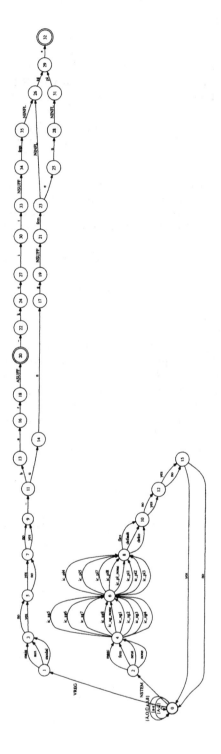

Fig. 3. Stem lexicon as a transducer

Fig. 4. FSA for the grammar fragment of Fig. 2

Klex: A Finite-State Transducer Lexicon of Korean

Na-Rae Han

Department of Linguistics, University of Pennsylvania, Philadelphia, PA 19104, USA
nrh@ling.upenn.edu
http://www.cis.upenn.edu/~nrh/klex.html

Abstract. This paper describes the implementation and system details of Klex, a finite-state transducer lexicon for the Korean language, developed using XRCE's Xerox Finite State Tool (XFST). Klex is essentially a transducer network representing the lexicon of the Korean language with the lexical string on the upper side and the inflected surface string on the lower side. Two major applications for Klex are morphological analysis and generation: given a well-formed inflected lower string, a language-independent algorithm derives the upper lexical string from the network and vice versa. Klex was written to conform to the part-of-speech tagging standards of the Korean Treebank Project, and is currently operating as the morphological analysis engine for the project.

1 Introduction

Korean is a highly agglutinative language, with productive use of post-position markers following nouns, verbal ending suffixes for verbs and adjectives, as well as frequent use of derivational morphology. Breaking up Korean words into smaller morphological components is the necessary first step in any natural language processing system of Korean, as well as an essential task for computerized language-learning tools. Klex is a fully operational Korean lexicon system whose underlying mathematical representation is a form of data structure known as the finite-state transducer or FST[1]. The transducer's upper level consists of strings representing a sequence of lexical forms of morphemes, each followed by their part-of-speech tag; the lower level consists of the fully inflected surface forms produced by concatenation of the morphemes, with relevant phonological and morphotactic processes applied:

---

[1] The name Klex is used somewhat ambiguously: it refers to the binary FST network that constitutes the lexicon; it also loosely refers to the entire morphological analysis and generation system of Korean lexicon built around the binary FST, with a few auxiliary networks, XML database and other helper scripts and utilities.

A. Yli-Jyrä, L. Karttunen, and J. Karhumäki (Eds.): FSMNLP 2005, LNAI 4002, pp. 67–77, 2006.
© Springer-Verlag Berlin Heidelberg 2006

(1) Mapping for 돕+었+다 /top+ess+ta/ 'help+Past+Declarative':

$$돕 /VV+ 었 /EPF+ 다 /EFN$$
$$top \quad\quad ess \quad\quad ta$$
$$\updownarrow$$
$$도 왔 다$$
$$towassta$$

A transducer network as a whole consists of all such possible morpheme-sequence/ word pairs in the language. Given the lower inflected form, a language-independent algorithm can produce the analyzed morpheme sequence (the process of "looking-up"). Conversely, the transducer can be used in producing the fully inflected surface form of grammatical sequence of morphemes (the opposite of "looking-up", hence Xerox's terminology of "looking-down"). These two operations, namely morphological analysis and generation, are the most typical applications of lexical transducers.

In the remainder of the paper, we will present implementation details of the system, and then discuss the main characteristics of Korean morphology and some of the design aspects of Klex which are aimed at providing optimal solutions for Korean.

2   Implementation

The system is implemented using XRCE(Xerox Research Centre Europe)'s XFST software platform. It consists of the main binary FST network, some auxiliary networks, and scripts which perform the morphological analysis and generation operations. The source codes for the networks are built from an XML dictionary and some helper scripts[2].

2.1   Overall Design

The main FST binary of Klex is built with three modules which are FSTs themselves: the lexicon FST, the rule FST, and the encoding-converter FST. These transducers are combined together in an operation known as composition to form the single lexical transducer which erases intermediate levels of representation to directly encode the relation between analysis strings and surface orthographical strings (Figure 1).

The lexicon FST is the backbone of the architecture: it is a network of legitimate Korean words, which maps lexical forms with POS in the upper level to their abstract representation at the bottom. The rule FST is composed at the bottom of the lexicon FST to apply morpho-phonological and orthographical processes to abstract symbols to produce the romanized surface strings.

---

[2] The main binary FST network of Klex, along with its source code, was released by Linguistic Data Consortium (LDC) catalog number LDC2004L01 and ISBN 1-58563-283-x.

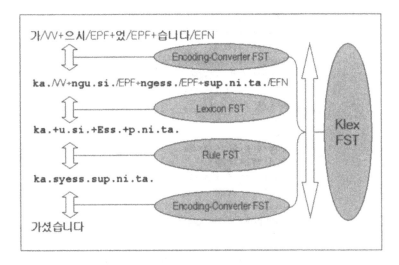

Fig. 1. Klex and component FSTs

Composing the lexicon FST and the rule FST results in a FST lexicon of Korean with roman transliteration of Korean strings on both levels; composing an encoding-converter FST on top and bottom produces the final product which handles Korean-encoded input and output. Currently Klex is configured for KSC-5601 (EUC-KR) encoding; however, it can be recompiled to use other encoding schemes such as UTF-8.

While *hangul*, the Korean script, is an alphabetic system with symbols for consonants and vowels in the language, modern computerized encoding schemes of Korean take the syllabic unit as the encoding block, thereby rendering the internal structure of syllables, e.g. individual alphabetic characters, opaque. This makes the task of writing rules, which must address vowels and consonants in the phonological inventory of the language, impossible with Korean encodings. For this reason, roman transliteration was used for the core part of the system. The romanization scheme adopted in Klex is a variant of the "Yale romanization system", a popular choice among linguists. A few modifications were made: (1) end-of-syllable is marked with "." to ensure a one-to-one mapping between the romanized and Korean alphabets; (2) the Korean consonant alphabet character "ㅇ" is always mapped to "ng" even in the onset position where it actually lacks phonological value, a measure taken in order to facilitate the process of writing rules.

2.2   The Dictionary

Klex relies on a dictionary in XML format, which serves as a database of lexical entries and their lexical properties, including morphotactic information and their underlying forms. Figure (2) shows examples of typical entries.

```
<entry>
  <rom>ngu.lo.</rom>
  <POS>PAD</POS>
  <form>u.lo.</form>
  <lemma>으 로</lemma>
  <morpho>MiddleCosa:MiddleCosa;</morpho>
</entry>

<entry>
  <rom>top.ta.</rom>
  <POS>VVt</POS>
  <form>toP.</form>
  <irr>ㅂ</irr>
  <lemma>돕 다</lemma>
  <morpho>vv</morpho>
</entry>
```

Fig. 2. Dictionary entries for 으로 /ulo/ 'with' and 돕 /top/ 'to help'

Each entry contains the following fields: the romanized form, the part-of-speech, the underlying form and the verbal conjugation class where relevant, the lemma form, and the morpho-syntactic information. There is a set of scripts written in perl which scan this dictionary and then create a source code for the lexicon FST based on the information in the fields.

The vocabulary included in the lexicon was obtained from many sources, including *Minjung Eutteum Korean Dictionary for Elementary School Students* (민중 초등학교 으뜸 국어사전: Minjungseorim, 1998), the Korean English Treebank Annotation (Palmer et al., 2002) and other various texts. The lexicon was expanded and fine-tuned by testing against these various corpora, the process of which included fixing undesirable outputs and adding missing lexical entries. The XML dictionary contains about 148,000 entries: the vast majority of them are nouns (about 133,000), and a small fraction of them belongs to the affix category (total of 622).

2.3 Morphotactics

The morphotactic grammar is formulated as a set of continuation classes in LEXC grammar which are then compiled into the lexicon FST. Much attention was paid to the morphotactics of postposition markers, verbal ending suffixes, derivational morphology and finally, noun compounding.

Some non-local dependencies are observed in the morphotactic grammar of Korean, most of which involve semantic constraints between suffixes encoding aspectual senses and verbal and adjectival stems. For example, final verbal ending 는다 /nunta/ is incompatible with adjective stems, since it encodes the "habitual" aspect, therefore: 먹는다 /meknunta/ "eats (habitual)" vs. *작는다 /*caknunta/ "*is small (habitual)". Other suffixes such as the honorific marker 으시

/usi/ can intervene, which makes the dependency a non-local one. Verb and adjective stems in Korean share the same morphotactics for the most part, which makes the option of writing separate continuation classes for the two categories redundant and impractical. The standard method of Flag Diacritics, available in the XFST platform, provides an economical solution: a bit of Flag Diacritic indicating its POS is set for adjective roots, which is then checked against a matching bit of Flag Diacritic associated with the habitual suffix ending at runtime, ruling out any path that traverses the two incompatible morphemes.

2.4 Rewrite Rules for Morpho-Phonological Alternations

Korean is known to display a wide variety of morpho-phonological processes, which the rule FST was designed to handle. The rule FST itself is a single transducer which maps the abstract morphophonemic strings to the surface orthographical strings, built by applying a composition operation on an ordered sequence of 100 individual replace rules.

The initial input to the set of rules, e.g. the lower strings of the lexicon FST, contains rich abstract information which allows the rules to set their targets precisely. Morpheme boundaries, where all alternations occur, are marked with "+". Morphemes that go through morpho-phonological processes are given abstract representations which deviate from the romanization scheme, such as inclusion of upper-case letters and missing onset consonant. The rules are formulated to target these symbols and environments.

The replace rules, comparable to the rewrite rules used traditionally in phonological derivations (Chomsky and Halle, 1968), handle three major groups of alternations: transformations at the right edge of irregular verbal roots; phonological processes occurring on morpheme boundaries, mostly involving verbal ending suffixes; and allomorphy in post-position markers. The first group of alternations involve six classes of irregular verbs of Korean, whose roots are subject to different sets of phonological processes when followed by transformation-triggering suffixes. The second group of phonological processes mostly involves verbal ending suffixes, such as vowel harmony, epenthesis, glide formation and u deletion[3].

Figure 3 illustrates derivations of three irregular verbal roots 듣 /tut/ "to hear", 자르 /calu/ "to cut", and 젓 /ces/ "to stir"[4] and a regular verbal root 가 /ka/ "to go", followed by any verbal ending with an initial abstract vowel E. The key morpho-phonological processes invloved here are: "T" irregular stem operation, "L" irregular stem operation, "S" irregular stem operation, vowel harmony, vowel merge and u (which is the epenthetic vowel in Korean) deletion. The rule [..] -> ng || . + _ VOW; addresses an orthographic issue: Korean orthography inserts a phonologically empty consonant "ㅇ" into an empty onset position. At the very end, the cleanup rule removes remaining traces of the morpheme boundary.

---

[3] /u/ functions as the epenthetic vowel in Korean phonology.
[4] Called "ㄷ", "ㄹ", and "ㅅ" irregular verbs respectively in the school grammar of Korean.

들+어 ⇒ 들어 "to hear"	자르+어 ⇒ 잘라 "to cut"	젓+어 ⇒ 저어 "to stir"	가+어 ⇒ 가 "to go"	rewrite rule
tuT.+E.	ca.Lu.+E.	ceS.+E.	ka.+E.	

vowel harmony
E -> a ||
[o|a] (CON|. CON u) . + _;
E -> e;

| tuT.+e. | ca.Lu.+a. | ceS.+e. | ka.+a. | |

u deletion
u . + -> [..] || CON _ [e|a];

| n/a | ca.La. | n/a | n/a | |

vowel merge
a . + -> [..],
e . + -> [..] || \w _ VOW

| n/a | n/a | n/a | ka. | |

"T" irregular
T -> l || _ . + E;

| tul.+e. | n/a | n/a | n/a | |

"L" irregular
. L -> 1 . 1 || _ VOW;

| n/a | cal.la. | n/a | n/a | |

"S" irregular
S -> [..] || _ . + VOW;

| n/a | n/a | ce.+e. | n/a | |

insert empty onset consonant
[..] -> ng || . + _ VOW;

| tul.+nge. | n/a | ce.+nge. | n/a | |

remove morpheme boundary
+ -> [..];

| tul.nge. | n/a | ce.nge. | n/a | |

Fig. 3. Cascade of rules applied to verb forms (CON: consonant; VOW: vowel)

The top strings are the abstract representations that are given as the input to the rule FST; the sequence of rules are applied and the bottom strings are resulting surface strings. Note that the precise ordering among the rules is crucial: the vowel merge rule must apply before the "S" irregular rule, otherwise an illegitimate surface string *ce. would be derived instead of the correct string ce.nge.. This dissected view of the rule module easily gives the illusion of a procedural model of rule application; ultimately, the cascade of rules are compiled into a single rule FST which maps the abstract strings on the top directly to the surface strings at the bottom. This "composition of sequential rules" architecture achieves the elegance of the mathematically equivalent model of KIMMO-style two-level morphology (Koskenniemi, 1983, 1984; Karttunen, 1983) while granting the linguist a higher level of flexibility and ease in formulating rules.

3   Language-Specific Issues

3.1   Lexical Representation of Affixes

The analyzed upper strings of Klex take the following form:

$\text{morph}_1/\text{POS}_1+\text{morph}_2/\text{POS}_2+\ldots+\text{morph}_n/\text{POS}_n,$

where morphemes are separated by "+" and each morpheme is followed by "/" and its part-of-speech tag. Korean affixes, therefore, are represented as a lexical item, rather than combinations of grammatical features such as +plural, +honorific and +past-tense, the popular approach taken mostly by finite-state lexicons of European languages. This is a rather inevitable design decision given the sheer number of Korean affixes; currently there are 622 of them listed in the system. Translating each one of them into a combination of binary features is not only an infeasible task but also an undesirable one; many affixes in Korean convey their own semantic and pragmatic senses that are not easily decomposed into matrices of binary features.

The feature representation of affixes can be more useful depending on the nature of applications, especially those that involve generation. The current setup requires the user to supply all component morphemes in their correct representative forms along with their correct part-of-speeches in order to obtain the inflected surface forms, which mandates a sophisticated level of knowledge on user's part. For a system that generates Korean words, however, a single verbal root marked with some grammatical features such as +polite, +past-tense, +interrogative might be considered a more reasonable input, which suits the feature representation scheme well. Although the system is not presently set up to handle such an alternative representation, its flexibility allows it to be modified as such with relative ease. First a subset of affixes would have to be selected excluding those that are inessential from the generation perspective. Their entries in the XML dictionary must then be augmented with appropriate feature representations. Finally a set of modified scripts can then produce a LEXC source script with the feature representations of suffixes instead of their lexical form and the POS in the upper level.

The set of part-of-Speech tags used is fully compliant with the specification of the Korean Treebank Project Phase 2. The set, which includes a total of 33 tags, is based on the one employed by the Korean Treebank Project Phase 1 (Han & Han, 2001) with some newly introduced modifications[5].

---

[5] The POS tagging guideline for the Korean Treebank Phase 1 can be found at: ftp://ftp.cis.upenn.edu/pub/ircs/tr/01-09/.

3.2 Allomorphy in Klex

A large number of inflectional suffixes and post-position markers in Korean have allomorphs, whose ditributions are conditioned by the phonological environment in which they appear. For example, the "topic" proposition marker takes three different forms 은 /un/, 는 /nun/, and ㄴ /n/; the past-tense pre-verbal-ending suffix 었 /ess/, 았 /ass/, and ㅆ /ss/.

The predominant position taken by past and present systems of Korean morphological analysis has been not to posit a single lexical representation for such sets of allomorphs, opting instead to output appropriate allomorphic forms within context.

Klex diverges from other systems by treating allomorphs as having a single representative form. All allomorphs of a given lexical item therefore show up as a single form in the upper (analyzed) string. For example, the topic markers in 학교-는 /hakkyo-nun/ 'school-Top', 학생-은 /haksayng-un/ 'student-Top' and 너-ㄴ /ne-n/ 'you-Top' are equally assigned 은/PAU in the analyzed strings:

(2) 은 /un/ as the representative form for the Korean topic postposition:

학교/NNC+은/PAU	학생/NNC+은/PAU	너/NPN+은/PAU
hakkyo un	haksayng un	ne un
↕	↕	↕
학교는	학생은	넌
hakkyonun	haksayngun	nen

The criteria used in determining the representative form among allomorphs are as follows:

(3) Criteria for determining the representative form

    a. The representative form should be fully syllabic, i.e. 은 /un/ is chosen over ㄴ /n/.

    b. The form for the post-consonantal environment is chosen, i.e. 이 /i/ instead of 가 /ka/.

    c. Epenthetic vowels are included, i.e. 으로 /ulo/ and not 로 /lo/[6].

    d. For vowel harmony, 어 /e/ is chosen over 아 /a/, i.e. 어서 /ese/ and not 아서 /ase/.

Note that these representative forms are to be distinguished from the "abstract underlying representation": the representative forms are those that function as the dictionary entry; the abstract underlying representations are their romanized counterparts with abstract symbols that are used system-internally, and which eventually undergo morpho-phonological transformations through applications of rewrite rules. For example, 었 /ess/ is the representative form for the the past-tense verbal ending suffix with its underlying abstract representation **Ess**..

---

[6] This clause is in fact redundant, as epenthetic vowels are used in post-consonantal environments only which is covered by criterion (b).

3.3 The Guesser Modules

A successful morphological analysis requires that the root of the encountered word be listed in the lexicon database. Even with Klex's extensive dictionary, it certainly cannot provide full coverage for the continuously evolving vocabulary of the language. To handle cases of novel words, two "guesser" modules are implemented: one dealing with novel roots belonging to open classes of part-of-speech and the other dealing with Korean person names.

Some part-of-speech categories, such as affixes, verbs and adjectives of Korean are considered a closed class: they consist of a closed set of vocabulary items, and addition of new vocabulary items is rare. On the other hand, common nouns (NNC), proper nouns (NPR), adverbs (ADV) and interjections (IJ) are open classes which allow novel vocabulary items, including newly formed words or borrowed words, to be added more freely. Phonologically possible roots are defined for each of the four part-of-speeches, and a guesser lexicon is compiled with the guessed roots in place of real roots. The guessed roots are subject to the same morphotactic grammar and morpho-phonological alternations as real roots. Figure 4 shows how 핸섬하다 /haynsemhata/ "is handsome" is handled by the module. 핸섬^Guess/NNC+하/XSJ+다/EFN (haynsem^Guess/ NNC+ha/XSJ+ta/EFN) is the correct guess, with the borrowed word 핸섬 (/haynsem/) is a guessed common noun root (^Guess/NNC) followed by an adjectivization suffix ha/XSV[7].

```
xfst[1]: apply up 핸섬하다
핸섬하^Guess/NPR+이/CO+다/EFN
핸섬하^Guess/NNC+이/CO+다/EFN
핸섬^Guess/NNC+하/XSV+다/EFN
핸섬^Guess/NNC+하/XSJ+다/EFN ⇐ CORRECT GUESS!
핸섬하다^Guess/ADV
핸섬하다^Guess/NPR
핸섬하다^Guess/IJ
핸섬하다^Guess/NNC
```

Fig. 4. Guesser module analyzes novel 핸섬하다 /haynsemhata/ "is handsome"

Korean person names pose another challenge. Klex implements an auxiliary FST module tailored to recognize them. Korean person names in most common cases consist of three-syllables, one for the surname and the the other two for given names[8]. The list of 137 known Korean surnames is obtained from census data. Given names are usually built by combining two syllables from a pool of chinese characters – while the Korean syllabic structure permits 11,172 possible

---

[7] Foreign vocabularies lose their original part-of-speech and are uniformly treated like nouns in Korean.

[8] Only 9 Korean surnames with two syllables are documented. Monosyllabic Korean given names are not rare; given names longer than 2 syllables are a rarity.

syllabic combinations of which 2,350 are in wide use, the range of syllables commonly used in names is relatively small: we hand-picked 262 of them. A model of Korean person names is then described as a regular expression: a syllable from the surname set, followed by two from the pool of syllables for given names. With the regular expression in place for a proper-noun root, the FST for Korean names can recognize legitimate Korean person names followed in some cases by titles or postposition markers. This is by no means a robust model of Korean names, but provides a good enough measure for the task of guessing.

4　Conclusions

Klex is a full-scale FST-based lexicon model for morphological analysis and generation of Korean words. The finite-state technology, which XRCE's XFST suite implements, provides an elegant yet powerful mathematical framework for designing such a system for morphologically complex languages such as Korean. The XFST suite by XRCE provides particularly powerful and flexible tools for a linguist seeking to develop such a system, since their composition-based modular architecture lets the developer model distinct aspects of morphology such as morphotactics and morpho-phonemic alternations into separate modules of transducers, which are then combined into a single transducer network that is both structurally simple and efficient. Klex was developed to fit the specification of the Korean Treebank Project, and is currently employed as the morphological analyzer for the project. It is also available by licensing through the Linguistic Data Consortium (LDC).

Acknowledgements

This research has been partially supported by various sources, including the Korean Treebank Project at the University of Pennsylvania, ARO grant DAAD 19-03-2-0028, a 5-year grant (BCS-998009, KDI, SBE) from the National Science Foundation via TalkBank, and the Linguistic Data Consortium. We would like to thank Xerox (XRCE) for making their tools available to the public. Also special thanks go to: Ken Beesley and Lauri Karttunen who provided valuable insights and guidance through the initial stages of the project; Mike Maxwell for his help in putting together the final product; and finally Martha Palmer for her continuous support throughout the course of the project.

References

1. Back, D.H., Lee, H., Rim, H.C.: A structure of korean electronic dictionary using the finite state transducer. In: Proceedings of the 7th Symposium for Information Processing of Hangul and Korean (한글 및 한국어 정보처리 학술대회). (1995) in Korean.
2. Beesley, K.R., Karttunen, L.: Finite-State Morphology: Xerox Tools and Techniques. CSLI Publications, Stanford, California (2003).

3. Han, C.H., Han, N.R.: Part of speech tagging guidelines for penn korean treebank. Technical report, IRCS, University of Pennsylvania (2001).

4. Han, N.R.: Klex: Finite-state lexical transducer for korean. Linguistic Data Consortium (LDC) catalog number LDC2004L01 and ISBN 1-58563-283-x (2004).

5. Han, N.R.: Morphologically annotated korean text. Linguistic Data Consortium (LDC) catalog number LDC2004T03 and ISBN 1-58563-284-8 (2004).

6. Kim, S.: Korean Morphology (우리말 형태론). Tap Publishing, Seoul, Korea (1992) in Korean.

7. Ko, Y.: A Study of Korean Morphology (국어형태론연구). Seoul National University Press, Seoul, Korea (1989) in Korean.

8. Koskenniemi, K.: Two-level morphology: A general computational model for word form recognition and production. Publication No: 11, Department of General Linguistics, University of Helsinki (1983).

9. Minjungseorim, ed.: Minjung Eutteum Korean Dictionary for Elementary School Students (민중 초등학교 으뜸 국어사전). Minjungseorim, Seoul, Korea (1998) in Korean.

10. Palmer, M., Han, C.H., Han, N.R., Ko, E.S., Yi, H.J., Lee, A., Walker, C., Duda, J., Xue, N.: Korean english treebank annotations. Linguistic Data Consortium (LDC) catalog number LDC2002T26 and ISBN 1-58563-236-8 (2002).

Longest-Match Pattern Matching with Weighted Finite State Automata

Thomas Hanneforth

Universität Potsdam, Institut für Linguistik, PF 601553, 14415 Potsdam, Germany
tom@ling.uni-potsdam.de

Abstract. I present a new method of longest match pattern matching based on weighted finite state automata. Contrary to the approach of Karttunen [9] we do not need expensive complementation operations to construct the pattern matching transducer.

1 Introduction

Longest-match pattern matching has a long tradition as a disambiguation technique in regular expression searching and natural language processing. The problem is addressed by a range of methods which are mostly based on finite-state automata (FSA), sometimes with a little more machinery to find the longest match (cf. the techniques described in Aho/Sethi/Ullman [3, 130ff] or in Abney [1]. In the next subsection I describe an approach by Karttunen [9], called Directed Replacement, which stays completely in the realm of finite state automata. In section 2 I present an improved method with better complexity properties. Section 3 evaluates the new method against Karttunen's approach.

1.1 The Method of Karttunen (1996)

The basic problem of longest-match pattern matching based on FSAs is that we have to compare different accepting paths in a finite state automaton with respect to each other. This is not a standard task for finite state automata and on first sight it's not entirely clear how a FSA can accomplish this. Karttunen's idea is to introduce auxiliary brackets around the found patterns and to then filter out illegal paths in the intermediate FSA representing matches which are shorter than others starting at the same position. I can't go into all the details of Karttunen's method (but some of them are described in section 2.3) but his longest match criterion is defined by a regular set which looks like this[1]:

$$(1) \quad \neg(\Sigma^* \cdot (\{[\} \cdot (\alpha'' \cap (\Sigma^* \cdot \{]\} \cdot \Sigma^*))) \cdot \Sigma^*)$$

The regular language α is the (perhaps infinite) set of our search patterns; α'' is a variant of α where the auxiliary bracket symbols enclosing a pattern in α are

---

[1] I've translated Karttunen's regular expression into the format I will use in this paper. See the appendix for notational details.

A. Yli-Jyrä, L. Karttunen, and J. Karhumäki (Eds.): FSMNLP 2005, LNAI 4002, pp. 78–85, 2006.
© Springer-Verlag Berlin Heidelberg 2006

ignored in non-final pattern positions[2]. The symbols [and] serve as bracketing symbols around the different possible matches of the patterns in α with respect to a given input text. For longest match processing to become effective it is assumed that α contains patterns x and y where x is a prefix of y.

The subexpression $(\{[\} \cdot (\alpha'' \cap (\Sigma^* \cdot \{]\} \cdot \Sigma^*)))$ denotes a regular language where the pattern instances of α following an opening bracket must contain occurrences of the closing bracket (this is achieved through the intersection of α'' with a regular set of all strings which contain a closing bracket]). A construction of the form $\neg(\Sigma^* \cdot A \cdot \Sigma^*)$ defines the *does-not-contain operator* for regular set A. The whole expression in (1) therefore disallows all closing brackets except the "last" one thereby filtering out all shorter matches and leaving the longest one. I will show in the next section that the does-not-contain operator is an expensive tool that can limit the practicability of an approach using it.

2   Longest-Match Pattern Matching with Weighted Finite State Automata

2.1   Weighted Automata

The basic idea of the approach presented here consists in the simplest case in counting the symbols inside the brackets enclosing the found pattern occurrences and afterwards taking the one with the maximum of symbols.

To put it a bit more generally: we define a weighted language L where each element in L is a pair consisting of a string $x \in \Sigma^*$ and a weight c chosen from a weight set W. A suitable algebraic structure for this task in the context of finite-state automata is a *semiring*. A structure $< W, \oplus, \otimes, \bar{0}, \bar{1} >$ is a semiring ([2], [11]) if it fulfils the following conditions:

1. $< W, \oplus, \bar{0} >$ is a commutative monoid with $\bar{0}$ as the identity element for $\oplus$.
2. $< W, \otimes, \bar{1} >$ is a monoid with $\bar{1}$ as the identity element for $\otimes$.
3. $\otimes$ distributes over $\oplus$.
4. $\bar{0}$ is an annilator for $\otimes$: $\forall w \in W, w \otimes \bar{0} = \bar{0} \otimes w = \bar{0}$.

A weighted finite-state transducer (cf. [11]) $A = < \Sigma, \Delta, Q, q_0, F, E, \lambda, \rho >$ over a semiring W is a 8-tuple with Σ being the finite input alphabet, Δ the output alphabet, Q the finite set of states, $q_0 \in Q$ the start state, $F \subseteq Q$ the set of final states, $E \subseteq Q \times (\Sigma \cup \epsilon) \times (\Delta \cup \epsilon) \times W \times Q$ the set of edges, $\lambda \in W$ the initial weight and $\rho : F \mapsto W$ the final weight function mapping final states to elements in W[3]. In section 2.2 I give some examples for an instantiation of the semiring template with $< \mathbb{R}, min, +, \infty, 0 >$, a so-called *tropical semiring*. This means that weights along an accepting path of an automaton are additively combined and among different paths accepting the same input string the path with the minimal weight is chosen.

---

[2] $\alpha'' \equiv Ignore(\alpha, \{[,]\}) - \Sigma^* \cdot \{[,]\}$.
[3] These are the so-called *letter transducers*.

2.2   The New Method

Let α be a search pattern and β a replacement pattern. Let Σ be the pattern matching alphabet. We add three auxiliary symbols @, [, and] to Σ. Following Karttunen [9] α' is a variant of α such that the auxiliary symbol @ may occur freely in all non-final positions of α:

$$\alpha' \equiv Ignore(\alpha, \{@\}) - \Sigma^* \cdot @$$

The new finite state cascade consists of four steps[4]:

1. Initial-match

$$\epsilon \rightarrow @ \ / \ \_ \ \alpha$$

2. Left-to-Right

$$\circ$$

$$(ID(\Sigma - \{@\})^* \cdot (@ \times [\ ) \cdot \alpha \cdot (\epsilon \times]\ ))^* \cdot ID(\Sigma - \{@\})^*$$

$$\circ$$

$$@ \rightarrow \epsilon$$

3. Longest-match

$$\circ$$

$$ID(Arith(\times, -1, (\Sigma - ([\,|\,]))^* \cdot [\cdot (\Sigma - ([\,|\,]))^* < 1 > \cdot])^* \cdot (\Sigma - ([\,|\,]))^*))$$

4. Replacement

$$\circ$$

$$[\cdot (\Sigma - \{]\}^*) \cdot] \rightarrow \beta$$

Steps 1,2, and 4 correspond to the same-named steps in Karttunen (1996). Step 1, *Initial-match*, prefixes all occurrences of the search pattern α with a newly introduced auxiliary symbol @. Step 2, *Left-to-Right*, represents a finite state transducer which repeatedly looks for the first occurrence of the start marker @, replaces it by an opening bracket and inserts a closing bracket after each occurrence of a pattern $x \in \alpha$, while ignoring additional @ markers. After that all remaining occurrences of @ are deleted. The transducer constructed after step 2 inserts curly brackets around all occurrences of pattern instances of α found in a given input automaton. The new step is step 3. For each alphabet symbol inside a pair of brackets [and] we add the arbitrarily chosen weight 1. After the definition of a FSM with a tropical semiring as the underlying algebraic weight structure the weights along a path are abstractly multiplied and therefore actually added. For example, a string $x[abc]y$ receives the weight 3. After weighting all strings inside the brackets all weights are multiplied with -1. Step 4 follows Karttunen again. All strings inside and including the curly brackets are replaced by the patterns in β. If the replacement step consists simply in bracketing the found occurrences of α with open bracket *lb* and closing bracket *rb* (*lb* and *rb* can denote arbitrary regular sets) step 4 can be replaced by 4':

4'. Replacement $([\rightarrow lb) \ \circ \ (] \rightarrow rb)$

---

[4] For reasons of readability I sometimes omit set parentheses around single symbols. That is, @ means {@} etc.

Let **LMPM** be the composition of the four finite state transducers. Basically the application of **LMPM** to an input text given as a finite state acceptor **input** consists of composing **input** with **LMPM** and taking the best path, that is, the path with the minimal weight:

$$Arith(\times, 0, BestPath(Proj_2(ID(\mathbf{input}) \circ \mathbf{LMPM})))$$

After that all weights are multiplied by zero effectively removing them.

2.3 Hierarchical Evaluation

Although this simple method of counting symbols inside of brackets works for many cases there are patterns where we need a more sophisticated evaluation technique. Consider for example the search pattern $a|aa$ applied to the search text aa. We get two bracketings $[aa]$ and $[a][a]$ with the same weight of -2. To achieve a disambiguated result we have to impose a further constraint:

a. In case of several bracketings having the same weight prefer the one with the least number of brackets.

But even then there are cases where we do not get a unique result, as can be seen by applying the above pattern to the string aaa where we get two minimal bracketings again with the same weight: $[a][aa]$ and $[aa][a]$. So we have to add another constraint:

b. In case of several bracketings having the same weight and the same number of brackets prefer the one where the sum of the index positions of the closing bracket is maximal.

Formally this is achieved by the Cartesian product of three semirings (cf. [5] and [7] how to implement criterium b. as a semiring). The ranking is guaranteed by imposing a total order on the resulting semiring based on the hierarchical ordering of the constraints.

2.4 An Example

I will exemplify the method with the help of the example in [9]. The search pattern is $d? \cdot a^* \cdot n^+$ and the "search text" is given as $dannvaan$; let lb be $[_{np}$ and rb $_{np}]$.

Step	Patterns	Description
Start	dannvaan	Input pattern
Initial-Match	@d@a@n@nv@a@a@n	Every start of a pattern was marked with @
Left-to-Right	[dan][n]v[aan] [dann]v[aan]	Patterns starting further to the right were removed; simultaneously [and] were introduced.

Longest-Match	[dan][n]v[aan]<-7> [dann]v[aan]<-7>	Both analysises receive the same weight.
Replacement	$[_{np}$dan$_{np}][_{np}$n$_{np}]$v$[_{np}$aan$_{np}]$<-7> $[_{np}$dann$_{np}]$v$[_{np}$aan$_{np}]$<-7>	The auxiliary brackets were replaced by the final ones.
BestPath	$[_{np}$dann$_{np}]$v$[_{np}$aan$_{np}]$<-7>	Filter out non-minimal analysises according to the criteria given in sec. 2.3

2.5 Complexity

The most expensive FSM operation is the complementation of a finite state acceptor A because A must be deterministic and determinisation in the worst case can show exponential behaviour due to the implicit power set construction. Step 1 prefixes all patterns in alpha with a marker symbol with the help of a conditional replacement rule. Following the method of Kaplan & Kay ([8]) the right context α is processed by the *prefix-iff-suffix(P,S)* operator which needs four complementations and one intersection. However we (and also Karttunen) can do better if we make use of the method of Mohri & Sproat (1996) ([12]) which is based on the determinisation of $\Sigma^* \cdot reverse(\alpha)$ and an additional reversal of the result. Step 2, *Left-to-Right*, consists only of the inexpensive operations concatenation and closure which are linear in the size of the operands. Constructing an acceptor α' which ignores certain symbols is also linear in the size of α. Step 3, *Longest-Match*, also uses only the operations concatenation and closure. The complexity of *Arith* is linear to the size of the operand FSM. The replacement transducer in step 4 does not depend on the search pattern α and is also very easy to compute. To summarize we don't use any complementation during the construction of **LMPM**; only a single determinisation of $\Sigma^* \cdot reverse(\alpha)$ and the composition of four FSTs are necessary. The application of the pattern matching FST to an acceptor **input**[5] representing the input text involves a composition, a linear arithmetic operation, a linear projection and the determination of the best path. Since **input** is a linear, acyclic acceptor the size of the FST after composing input with **LMPM** is proportional to the size of **input**. Since **input** is acyclic and so is **input** ∘ **LMPM** we can use Lawler's algorithm ([10]) of relaxation in topological order to find the best path[6] which is in $O(|Q| + |\delta|)$ ([6]). Putting it all together the application of **LMPM** to an input text of length n is in $O(n)$.

3   Evaluation

Our method has been implemented in a longest-match pattern matching compiler based on the Potsdam FST library. Karttunen's pattern matcher was

---

[5] In practice, **input** would never be constructed and instead an incremental composition algorithm would be used.

[6] The algorithm of relaxation in topological order has no problems with negative weights.

implemented in the same framework. For both approaches we used two regular grammars from a named entity recognition task, a small one and a slightly bigger one. Both grammars were compiled to minimal finite state acceptors. The grammars are complicated by the fact that it must be possible to reconstruct the positions of recognised named entities in the original text. Therefore the grammars allows for triples of the form $< line, column, length >$ which are added to the input automaton during the preprocessing and morphological analysis of the input text. The automaton alphabet we need is quite big because the preprocessing steps add very detailed morphosyntactic and semantic information encoded in distinct symbols for each word to the input FSA. Basically the input automaton can be described by a regular expression

$$(position\_information \;\; lemma \;\; syntactic\_features \;\; semantic\_features)^+$$

To achieve a fair comparison, the resulting transducers in both methods were optimised as much as possible (by so-called encoded minimisation[7]). The same is true for all intermediate transducers emerging from the construction steps.

Table 1. Properties of the FSAs describing the search patterns

Size of FSA for grammar 1 ($\|\Sigma\| = 970$)	112 states, 4612 transitions
Size of FSA for grammar 2 ($\|\Sigma\| = 970$)	177 states, 7449 transitions

Table 2. FSA Sizes and Compilation Times

		Karttunen's method	The method described here
Grammar 1	*Size of LMPM*	2,228 states	271 states
		1,604,617 transitions	88,036 transitions
	Compilation time	66.7s	2.5s
	Memory peak during compilation	485 MB	10 MB
Grammar 2	*Size of LMPM*	4,115 states	441 states
		2,992,666 transitions	108,888 transitions
	Compilation time	241.8s	3.7s
	Memory peak during compilation	600 MB	12 MB

As can be seen from table 2[8] Karttunen's method is very sensitive to small changes in the size of the FSM representing the search patterns and results in

---

[7] This means encoding the transition labels (and if present the weights) into a single symbol, after which the resulting acceptor is determinised and minimised and then decoded back to a transducer.

[8] All measurements were made on a 3 GHz Pentium 4 PC with 1 GB memory running Windows XP.

very large automata which quickly become impracticable for realistic grammar sizes. The method described here does not lead to such a blow-up of automata size; compilation times and FSM sizes seem to grow linearly. This was also verified by the complete grammar for the named entity recognizer which has 1060 states and nearly 34,000 transitions and was compiled into a corresponding longest match automaton with 1600 states and approximately 550,000 transitions in 20 s. Of course the problem of Karttunen's approach is the fact that it depends on the does-not-contain operator which leads to almost complete automata where every state has $|\Sigma|$ outgoing transitions. To solve this problem one can introduce a special "otherwise"-symbol, in which most of the outgoing transitions of a state (those which do not contribute to the recognition of a pattern) are collapsed into a single transition. This technique was for example implemented in the Xerox Finite State Tools, the framework in which Karttunen's method originally emerged ([4]). But the approach of using "otherwise" symbols leads to special processing mechanisms (nearly all algebraic operations of the underlying FSA library must be adapted) which can be a complicated task especially in the context of automata based on abstract semirings. The approach described here on the other hand shows that standard algorithms will do. The price one has to pay for having quite compact longest match automata is a linear best path operation at run time which can nevertheless be implemented in a very efficient way.

4   Conclusion and Further Work

Since the approach described in section 2 does not depend on complementation even the input language describing the patterns can be a weighted language represented by a weighted FSA (weighted languages are not closed under complementation). This leads to interesting possibilities of assigning weights to patterns either by hand or by machine learning techniques. The last approach is currently under investigation. In addition, the longest-match-constraint employed in section 2.3 might not simply count the symbols inside the brackets but instead realise an arbitrary weight function. For example after preprocessing and morphological annotation of the input text, the longest-match-constraint can refer to all morphological categories and features added during the preprocessing phase and weight them appropriately.

Acknowledgements. I would like to thank Jörg Didakowski for helping implementing the compiler based on the described method and Sigrid Beck for correcting my English. Many thanks also to Alexander Geyken for help with respect to the morphology.

References

1. S. Abney. Partial parsing via finite-state cascades. In *Proceedings of ESSLLI 96, Robust Parsing Workshop*, 1996.
2. A. Aho, J. Hopcroft, and J. Ullman. *The Design and Analysis of Computer Algorithms*. Addison-Wesley, Reading, MA, 1974.

3. A. Aho, R. Sethi, and J. Ullman. *Compilers. Principles, Techniques, and Tools.* Addison-Wesley, Reading, MA, 1986.
4. K. R. Beesley and L. Karttunen. *Finite State Morphology.* CSLI Studies in Computational Linguistics. CSLI Publications, Stanford, CA, 2003.
5. S. Bistarelli. *Semirings for Soft Constraint Solving and Programming*, volume 2962 of *Lecture Notes in Computer Science.* Springer, Berlin, 2004.
6. T. H. Cormen, C. L. Leiserson, R. L. Rivest, and C. Stein. *Introduction to Algorithms.* The MIT Electrical Engineering and Computer Science Series. The MIT Press, second edition, 2001.
7. J. Didakowski. Robustes parsing und disambiguierung mit gewichteten transduktoren. Diploma thesis, University of Potsdam, 2005.
8. R. Kaplan and M. Kay. Regular models of phonological rule systems. *Computational Linguistics*, 20(3):331–378, 1994.
9. L. Karttunen. Directed replacement. In *Proceedings of the 34rd Annual Meeting of the ACL*, Santa Cruz, CA, 1996.
10. E. Lawler. *Combinatorial Optimization: Networks and Matroids.* Holt, Rinehart & Winston, New York, NY, 1976.
11. M. Mohri. Semiring frameworks and algorithms for shortest-distance problems. *Journal of Automata, Language, and Combinatorics*, 7(3):321–350, 2002.
12. M. Mohri and R. Sproat. An efficient compiler for weighted rewrite rules. In *Proceedings of the 34rd Annual Meeting of the ACL*, Santa Cruz, CA, 1996.

Appendix: Notation

α^*	Kleene-Star
$\alpha \mid \beta$	Union
$\alpha \cdot \beta$	Concatenation
$\alpha \circ \beta$	Composition
$\alpha - \beta$	Difference
$\neg \alpha$	Complementation
$\alpha \times \beta$	Product (sometimes also multiplication)
$\alpha \rightarrow \beta$	Denotes an FST which replaces α by β without regarding the context
$\alpha \rightarrow \beta/\gamma \_ \delta$	Denotes an FST which replaces α by β if γ precedes and δ follows α
$BestPath(M)$	Returns an FSM which represents the path in M with the minimal weight.
$ID(M)$	Identity relation consisting of all pairs $< x, x >$ where $x \in M$
$Arith(op, k, M)$	Application of an arithmetic operation op with factor k to all transition weights in M
$Proj_i(M)$	ith projection of transducer M ($i = 1$ means projecting the input band, $i = 2$ the output band)
$Reverse(\alpha)$	The mirror image of α
Σ	Alphabet
ϵ	Epsilon
$< w >$	Weights

Finite-State Syllabification

Mans Hulden

The University of Arizona
Department of Linguistics
PO BOX 210028
Tucson AZ, 85721-0028
USA
mhulden@email.arizona.edu

Abstract. We explore general strategies for finite-state syllabification and describe a specific implementation of a wide-coverage syllabifier for English, as well as outline methods to implement differing ideas encountered in the phonological literature about the English syllable. The syllable is a central phonological unit to which many allophonic variations are sensitive. How a word is syllabified is a non-trivial problem and reliable methods are useful in computational systems that deal with non-orthographic representations of language, for instance phonological research, text-to-speech systems, and speech recognition. The construction strategies for producing syllabifying transducers outlined here are not theory-specific and should be applicable to generalizations made within most phonological frameworks.

1   The Syllable[1]

Phonological alternations are often expressed efficiently by reference to syllables. Most phonological descriptions presume a regular grouping of C or V elements into syllables which other phonological rules can subsequently refer to.

An example of syllables being used as a domain of phonological alternations is given by Kahn [1], who noted that an underlying [t] phoneme in English may behave in various different ways, conditioned mainly by its position in the syllable. A [t] can surface:

- as aspirated [tʰ], as in **creativity**
- as glottalized [tˀ], as in **create**
- as [t], as in **stem**
- as a flap [ɾ], as in **creating**
- as [čʰ], as in **train**
- as [č], as in **strong**

Many other phenomena are sensitive to syllable boundaries. A further example would be, for instance, syncope (schwa-deletion) where words like **licorice** may surface either as [lɪ.kə.rɪš] or as syncopated [lɪk.rɪš], as noted by Hooper [2].

---

[1] Thanks to Mike Hammond, Lauri Karttunen, and two anonymous reviewers for guidance, comment, and discussion. Any errors are my own.

A. Yli-Jyrä, L. Karttunen, and J. Karhumäki (Eds.): FSMNLP 2005, LNAI 4002, pp. 86–96, 2006.
© Springer-Verlag Berlin Heidelberg 2006

More abstract levels of representation in phonological theory—such as metrical systems in which the structure involves the laying down of feet—also assume the existence of syllables at some lower level.

To make accurate predictions about syllabification, both in phonological behavior and in empirically attested preferences, requires—as in the case of [t] mentioned above—subtle differentiation of syllabification patterns with respect to consonant cluster affiliation. We present an approach based on a fairly traditional view of the syllable that largely follows the sonority hierarchy and the maximum onset principle. Knowledge of word stress is not assumed in the syllabifier—cases where word stress appears to affect syllabification have been modelled by sensitivity to the quality of syllabic nuclei and of the surrounding consonant clusters.

Table 1. Regular expression operators

A*	Kleene star
A+	Kleene plus
A | B	Union
(A)	Optionality, equivalent to A|0
˜A	The complement of A
A B	Concatenation
A.l	Extraction of the lower language in relation A (the range of A)
A.u	Extraction of the upper language in relation A (the domain of A)
A .o. B	Composition
A .P. B	Upper-side priority union, equal to A | [˜[A.u] .o. B]
A -> B || L _ R	Directed replacement with context restriction
A @-> B || L _ R	Left-to-right longest replace with context restriction
A @> B || L _ R	Left-to-right shortest replace with context restriction
A -> B . . . C	Left-to-right marking operator with context restriction

2   Finite-State Syllabification Methods

The finite-state formalism owes much of its conceptual background to phonological rewrite systems originating in the Sound Pattern of English [3]. Kaplan and Kay [4] subsequently provided a strong connection between classical generative phonology and finite-state systems. The syllable, however, had no official recognition in much of the early generative work, and when it later entered into the scope of research, a rich internal structure of the syllable was assumed to the extent that syllabification processes were no longer commonly described with rewrite rules— although verbal descriptions of syllabification "algorithms" were often given.

The finite-state calculus rewrite operators (see table 1) provide most of the functionality required for a convenient description of most details in syllabification processes.[2] Depending on the complexity of a language's syllables, syllabifiers may need to have refined knowledge of the types or quality of

---

[2] The description here assumes the Xerox xfst formalism [5].

phonemes—consonants in particular. Finnish, as an example of a language with a relatively simple syllabification process, can be treated with little regard to consonant clusters:[3]

$$\text{C* V+ C* @-> ... "." } \| \_ \text{C V}$$

However, languages such as English that feature a variety of syllable types will need to be treated with detailed attention to the quality and order of segments.

For designing the syllabifier described here, the syllabifications of 1,920 words that all contained consonant clusters were extracted from Merriam-Webster's Collegiate Dictionary and used as a set of empirical data to compare against.[4] Barring internal inconsistencies, the final predictions made by the syllabifier agreed with the source.[5]

3   Sonority

Languages that contain complex clusters of consonants are usually guided in their syllable structure by the concept of a sonority hierarchy. The principle states that more "sonorous" elements appear closer to the syllable nucleus, which in turn is the most sonorous element. The onset of a syllable thus mirrors the coda in sonority.[6]

Table 2. The sonority hierarchy

Increasing → sonority					
Voiceless Obstruents	Voiced Obstruents	Nasals	Liquids	Glides	Vowels
p,t,k,s,..	b,d,g,z...	m,n,ŋ	l,r,..	y,w,...	a,e,o,u...

---

[3] It is assumed that the legal vowels and consonants are defined in the sublanguages C, V. This treatment requires some further elaboration about legal dipthongs. The syllabification here is the traditional treatment [6]. It may be argued that the Finnish syllable is subject to additional sonority constraints—the rewrite rule here would yield /abstrakti/ → /abst .rak.ti/, whereas most native speakers prefer /abs.trak.ti/ or /ab.strak.ti/. Insofar as the syllable is permitted independent status as an entity outside language-internal phonological processes, accurate modelling of even Finnish, which has a relatively poor syllable inventory, is probably best treated in the manner outlined in this paper.

[4] http://www.britannica.com/dictionary

[5] In some cases the dictionary showed conflicting syllabifications for highly similar words. For instance, the words **poster**, **toaster**, and **coaster** were syllabified [pos.tər], [to.stər], and [kos.tər], respectively. The majority account was followed whenever the data were inconsistent. In this case, it was concluded that [(p|t|k)os.tər] would be the preferred syllabification.

[6] This observation is often attributed to O. Jespersen, *Phonetische Grundfragen* (1904).

In English, the word **comptroller**, for example, has a four-consonant medial cluster. This will be divided by the sonority sequence requirement into **mp.tr**.

English, by and large, adheres to the sonority requirements, with the exception of [s] which (in this treatment) must occur syllable-initially or syllable-finally (in word-medial position) and [h], which only occurs syllable-initially, never syllable-finally.

From a finite-state point of view, the sonority hierarchy is a statement dictating a particular order in which elements must occur in a legal syllable. The requirements of sonority are, however, not sufficient to syllabify correctly—an approach that only followed sonority requirements will massively overgenerate (see table 3):

```
define Onset [(VLObs) (VObs) (Nas) (Liq) (Gli)];
define Coda [(Gli) (Liq) (Nas) (VObs) (VLObs)];
define Syllable [Onset Vow Coda];
define Syllabify [Syllable -> ... "." || _ Syllable];
```

Here, we define the syllable to consist of onsets and codas, which are mirror images of each other according to the sonority hierarchy. We then introduce syllable boundaries between all legal syllables.

Table 3. Syllabifying by only sonority

/æbrəkədæbrə/	/kæləforniə/
æb.rək.əd.æb.rə	kæ.ləf.or.ni.ə
æb.rək.əd.æ.brə	kæ.ləf.orn.i.ə
æb.rək.ə.dæb.rə	**kæ.lə.for.ni.ə**
æb.rək.ə.dæ.brə	kæ.lə.forn.i.ə
æb.rə.kəd.æb.rə	kæl.əf.or.ni.ə
æb.rə.kəd.æ.brə	kæl.əf.orn.i.ə
æb.rə.kə.dæb.rə	kæl.ə.for.ni.ə
æb.rə.kə.dæ.brə	kæl.ə.forn.i.ə
æ.brək.əd.æb.rə	
æ.brək.əd.æ.brə	
æ.brək.ə.dæb.rə	
æ.brək.ə.dæ.brə	
æ.brə.kəd.æb.rə	
æ.brə.kəd.æ.brə	
æ.brə.kə.dæb.rə	
æ.brə.kə.dæ.brə	

3.1 Sonority Distance

Phonological theory also makes use of the concept of sonority distance, which states that consecutive sounds within a syllable must be sufficiently distant from each other in terms of sonority [7]. The exact requirements vary from language to language: in English, [p] (a stop) may not be followed by an [n] (a nasal), although this is possible in e.g. French.

4 Maximum Onset

Another generalization about syllabification processes is that, given a choice between affiliating a consonant to a coda or to an onset, affiliating with the onset is preferable, cf. [1,8].

Application of this principle can be used to eliminate overgeneration, and immediately narrows down the eligible syllabifications to a single one, i.e. [æbrəkədæbrə] → [æ.brə.kə.dæ.brə].

The combination of sonority requirements and onset maximization can be economically expressed through the shortest replace operator [5], assuming we have a definition of allowed onsets and coda clusters.

```
define Syllable Onset Vow Coda;
define MainRule Syllable @> ... "." || _ Syllable;
```

Table 4. Legal two consonant onsets in English. The obstruents are not quite symmetrical with respect to the consonants that are allowed to follow them. The phonemes {y,r} behave more alike than for instance the natural grouping of glides, {w,y}. This is also true for three-consonant onsets. Circles mark clusters that are legal only word-initially, and thus not included in the grammar.

	Gli		Liq		Nas		Sto		
	w	y	r	l	m	n	p	t	k
p		•	•	•					
t	•		•	•					
k	•	•	•	•					
b		•	•	•					
d	•	•	•						
g	•	•	•	•					
f		•	•	•					
θ	•	•	•						
š			○						
s	•	•		•	•	○	•	•	•

Table 5. Three consonant onsets in English

	w	y	r	l	m	n
sp		•	•	•		
st		•	•			
sk	•	•	•	○		

The shortest replace operator @> works like the standard replace operator, but will construct a transducer that follows a strategy such that the application site of the left hand side of the rule will be kept to a mimimum if there are alternative ways of applying the rule (i.e. if there are several legal ways to distribute the syllable boundary at the coda-onset juncture). Technically, this minimizes the coda instead of maximizing the onset, but the end result is equivalent. See tables 4 and 5 for the particulars of allowed onsets and codas in the English implementation here.

5   Stress

Many treatments of the English syllable found in the literature also depend on knowledge of stress. The generalization is that at least some consonants, [s] and the nasals in particular, tend to affiliate with a stressed syllable, going against the Onset Maximization principle. In the M-W data used for this implementation, some pairs where this is seen include [æm.yʊ.lɛt] vs. [ə.myuz] and [æs.pɛkt] vs. [ə.spɛ.rə.ɾi].

In this treatment, the goal has been to give an account of English syllabification without knowledge about the particular stress of a word, but based on the quality of vowels and surrounding consonant clusters. Still, most speakers of English do have a strong intuition about consonants affiliating to a coda in some syllables based on what appear to be stress factors. So, for instance, there is a tendency to syllabify **astir** as [ə.str̩], but the proper name **Astor**, as [æs.tr̩].

To solve this without relying on knowledge of word stress, we have modeled consonant affiliation by adding two rules where nasals and [s] affiliate to the left when preceded by an open syllable where the nucleus is not {ə,i} to give the desired predictions.[7] These rules apply before the main syllabification rule:

```
define sRule[s -> ...".." || ([[Cons]|[(Stop) r]]) [Vow - ə - i] _ Cons+ Vow]];
define NasRule [Nas -> ...".." || [Vow - ə - i] _ y ];
```

6   Medial vs. Marginal Clusters

Often the types of onset that are found word-initially can be used as clues to deduce further restrictions on top of the sonority considerations [9]. As English allows, for instance, initial [spr] in many words (spring, spray, etc.), the conclusion can be drawn that [spr] should be legal in word-medial onsets as well. However, in modeling the syllabifications of a particular source (M-W), it has become clear that there is a tendency to avoid generalizing from some attested

---

[7] The syllabifier described was designed to be used as part of research concerning generalizations about English stress where an underlying representation was assumed that was close to the phonetic form of the word. Part of this research involved the separation of syllabification and stress rules, where syllabification would apply first, and stress later, and where the two would function as independent processes.

word-initial onsets to legal medial onsets. Although [sn] is a cluster very commonly encountered word-initially, as in e.g. **snow**, allowing the same cluster in word-medial position will not yield correct syllabifications in words such as **pilsner**, which, if [sn] were permitted, would be incorrectly syllabified as [pɪl.snɹ].[8]

Thus, certain initial clusters can probably not be used as a basis for legitimizing medial clusters of the same type. The initial-cluster [skl], for instance (which only occurs in a handful of words: sclerosis, sclaff, etc.), is one that has not been permitted syllable-initially in the syllabifier. Similarly with final clusters, e.g. [sɪksθs] is a unique and highly marked four-consonant cluster and does not seem to warrant the inference that [ksθs] would be a legal coda. For such coda clusters, this is in most cases not significant because of the tendency to maximize onsets—long codas will rarely be allowed except word-finally. In fact, the set of permitted codas have been modelled simply as any maximally two-consonant combination.[9] This makes exactly the same predictions as a model where codas are constrained to actually attested ones.

Onsets, on the other hand, must be attended to in more detail than the guiding sonority principles. In this implementation we have only marked syllable *boundaries*. In such a process, the main syllabification rule (above) applied to a word with an initial [skl]-cluster will never match [skl] since it is not a legal onset. But as the input language to the transducer is the universal language ?*, [s] will be transduced to [s], and [kl] will be matched as a legal onset as the syllabification proceeds. In effect, the initial [s] will be treated as "extrametrical."

Incidentally, the exclusion of onset clusters such as [skl] yields different syllabifications for word pairs such as **exclaim** and **explain** ([ɪks.klem], [ɪk.splen]).[10]

This strategy will not affect the final syllabification as long as we are content with marking syllable boundaries, not beginnings and endings. Such an approach should be sufficient for most applications since any phonological rule that later needs to refer to a syllable boundary in its conditioning environment will not need to know whether the boundary marks the beginning or the end of syllable.

If we wanted to "wrap" every syllable with both a beginning and end marker, [$_\sigma$ and]$_\sigma$, this issue would have to be addressed. However, we know of no simple phonological process in English that would require a differentiation between [$_\sigma$ and]$_\sigma$.

It should be noted that this implementation assumes an underlying form that is very close to the phonetic form. Applications that make use of more abstract underlying forms can derive further predictions through wrapping

---

[8] The discrepancy between acceptable word-medial and word-marginal syllable types has been the subject of much recent research. For a stochastic perspective, see Coleman and Pierrehumbert [10], and for an OT-related analysis, see Hammond [9].

[9] That this approach works has an interesting parallel in the OT literature, where a constraint with a similar function, such as ALIGN-3μ, is sometimes seen [11]. This constraint prohibits syllables heavier than 3 moras, except word-finally. For English, the prediction is quite similar to disallowing more than two coda consonants.

[10] M-W has this syllabification. This example pair 1) [ɪks.klem] and 2) [ɪk.splen] would indirectly make the subtle prediction that the [k] is aspirated [k^h] in 1), whereas the [p] would remain unaspirated in 2).

syllables with beginning and end markers instead of simply marking boundaries. For instance, the phonological phenomenon of Stray Erasure [12], where
coda segments that cannot be legally parsed into syllables remain unpronounced,
could be described by wrapping syllables. Supposing the underlying form of a
word such as **damn** were [dæmn], instead of [dæm], as here, and supposing syllables would be grouped instead of boundary-marked, the output of the transducer
would be [dæm]n. However, in [dæm][ne][šən], the first [n] would be parsed into
a new onset, allowing it to be pronounced.

7   Polymorphemic Words

Some polymorphemic words will not be treated properly given the description above. For instance, **transplant** will receive the unorthodox syllabification
[træn.splænt]. Assuming the system knows of morpheme boundaries, a preference
for syllabifications where syllable breaks coincide with morpheme boundaries can
be stated. This is accomplished by the upper-side priority union operator [13].

```
define Syllabify [
[sRule .o. NasRule .o. MainRule .o. SyllableWellFormedness]
                           .P.
[IgnoreMorphBoundaries .o. sRule .o. NasRule .o. MainRule]
];
```

We also define a SyllableWellFormedness filter that disallows parses where a
syllable violates the the well-formedness of onsets or codas in English:

```
define SyllableWellFormedness [[SSP "."]* SSP];
define IgnoreMorphBoundaries "|" -> 0;
```

The motivation for the .P. construction is to allow words that would syllabify
correctly when morpheme boundaries are treated as syllable boundaries. The
syllabification [træns.plænt] contains no illegal onsets or codas, and is accepted.
But there are words where morpheme boundaries cannot be respected without
incurring an illegal onset, e.g. **deca|$_\mu$(a)thlon** should not yield [dɛ.kæ.θlɑn] since
the sequence [θl] is not a well-formed onset in English. The first part of the rule
in this case will have no output (it is blocked by SyllableWellFormedness) since
[θl] is not among the legal onsets, and is prevented by well-formedness filter. The
priority union operator ensures that only the lower rule cascade applies if the
output language of the upper rule is 0, giving in this case the correct final output
[dɛ.kæθ.lɑn]. The lower rule simply removes the morpheme boundary markers,
and syllabification proceeds normally.

8   Implementing Alternative Approaches

The phonological literature is rife with differing proposals for the syllabification
of English, and agreement seems to be rare. This is why we chose a standard

source whose syllabifications seemed natural (M-W), and the principles of the syllabifier were then developed according to this specific set of empirical data.

This results in a fairly conservative and traditional view of English syllabification—one that does not allow more complex phonological representations such as ambisyllabicity (where a single consonant is seen to belong to two adjacent syllables, as in Kahn's treatment [1]), or gemination (where a single consonant is represented as two segments, following e.g. Hammond [9]).

Most approaches to English syllabification are implementable with the basic methods outlined here. Four other approaches were encoded as FSTs to compare their respective predictions. These were the generative views of Kahn [1] and Selkirk [14], as well as the more recent Optimality Theory based views in Hammond [9], and Hall [11]. This simplicity of implementation crucially hinges on the existence of a shortest-replace operator (@>) and the upper-side priority union operator. Defining these through more primitive operators would severely complicate the task of constructing correct transducers.

When implemented as FST rewrite rules, the generative approaches were shown to be quite similar, differing only in the minutiae of the rewrite rules, despite the fact that the original descriptions often follow an involved formalism. However, these small differences often lead to wide variety of predictions, as seen in table 6.

Table 6. A sampling of the differing views on the English syllable. The second column represents the predictions made by the implementation described here. It should be noted that many of the examples here are not provided by the original authors—rather, a finite-state syllabifier has been reconstructed based on information given by the original sources. In the phonological literature, many details are often abstracted away from, and some essentials are presumed to be known, such as the set of allowed onsets. Often such details must be inferred from the specific examples given by the authors.

		Kahn (1976)	Hammond (1999)	Hall (2004)
feisty	fɑys.ti	[fɑy[s]ti]	fɑyst.i	fɑy.sti
cascade	kæs.ked	[kæ][sked]	kæs.sked	kæ.sked
pity	pɪ.ti	[pɪ[t]i]	pɪt.i	pɪ.ti
vanity	væ.nə.ti	[væ[n]ə][ti]	væn.ət.i	væ.nə.ti
texture	tɛks.čr̩	[tɛks][čr̩]	tɛks.čr̩	tɛk.sčr̩

9 Concluding Notes

We have presented general strategies to handle syllabification by finite-state means, as well as the details of an English syllabifier (see table 7 for examples of the output). The particular implementation is compact and the end result is a transducer with 52 states if the special handling that respects morpheme boundaries is ignored, and 188 states with this addition. This compares favorably with optimality theoretical implementations we have also evaluated as a comparison—the smallest of which (following Hall [11]), using the construction method given by Gerdemann and Van Noord [15] is minimally represented by 1768 states.

Table 7. Example outputs of the syllabifier. No morpheme boundaries were present in the input.

acquiesce	æ.kwɪ.ɛs	aspen	æs.pɛn
atrocious	ə.tro.šəs	atrophy	æ.trə.fi
comptroller	kamp.tro.lər	computer	kəm.pyu.tər
deluge	dɛl.yuj̆	esquire	ɛs.kwayr
establishment	ɪs.tæ.blɪš.mɛnt	exclaim	ɛks.klem
explain	ɛk.splen	exquisite	ɛk.skwɪ.zət
extra	ɛk.strə	formula	for.myu.lə
gestation	j̆ɛs.te.šn̩	inkling	ɪŋ.klɪŋ
manipulate	mə.nɪ.pyʊ.let	manual	mæn.yu.l̩
mattress	mæ.trəs	metro	mɛ.tro
Mississippi	mɪ.sə.sɪ.pi	mistrust	mɪs.trʌst
tenuous	tɛn.yu.əs	transcribe	træn.skrayb
venue	vɛn.yu	Venusian	vɛ.nu.šn̩

References

1. Kahn, D.: Syllable-based Generalizations in English Phonology. PhD thesis, MIT (1976)
2. Hooper, J.: Constraints on schwa-deletion in American English. In Fisiak, K., ed.: Recent Developments in Historical Phonology. Mouton, The Hague (1978) 183–207
3. Chomsky, N., Halle, M.: The Sound Pattern of English. Harper and Row (1968)
4. Kaplan, R.M., Kay, M.: Regular models of phonological rule systems. Computational Linguistics **20** (1994) 331–378
5. Beesley, K., Karttunen, L.: Finite-State Morphology. CSLI, Stanford (2003)
6. Laaksonen, K., Lieko, A.: Suomen kielen äänne- ja muoto-oppi [Finnish Phonology and Morphology]. Finn Lectura (1998)
7. Kenstowicz, M.: Phonology in Generative Grammar. Blackwell (1994)
8. Clements, G.N., Keyser, S.J.: CV Phonology: A Generative Theory of the Syllable. MIT Press (1983)
9. Hammond, M.: The Phonology of English. Oxford (1999)
10. Coleman, J., Pierrehumbert, J.: Stochastic phonological grammars and acceptability. Proceedings of the 3rd Meeting of the ACL Special Interest Group in Computational Phonology (1997) 49–56
11. Hall, T.A.: English syllabification as the interaction of markedness constraints. ZAS Papers in Linguistics **37** (2004) 1–36
12. Blevins, J.: The syllable in phonological theory. In Goldsmith, J.A., ed.: The Handbook of Phonological Theory. Blackwell (1995)
13. Karttunen, L.: The proper treatment of optimality theory in computational phonology. In: Finite-state Methods in Natural Language Processing, Ankara (1998) 1–12

14. Selkirk, E.O.: The syllable. In: Phonological Theory: The Essential Readings. Blackwell (1999)
15. Gerdemann, D., van Noord, G.: Approximation and exactness in finite state optimality theory. In Jason Eisner, Lauri Karttunen, A.T., ed.: Proceedings of the Fifth Workshop of the ACL Special Interest Group in Computational Phonology. (2000)

Algorithms for Minimum Risk Chunking

Martin Jansche

Center for Computational Learning Systems
Columbia University, New York

Abstract. Stochastic finite automata are useful for identifying substrings (chunks) within larger units of text. Relevant applications include tokenization, base-NP chunking, named entity recognition, and other information extraction tasks. For a given input string, a stochastic automaton represents a probability distribution over strings of labels encoding the location of chunks. For chunking and extraction tasks, the quality of predictions is evaluated in terms of precision and recall of the chunked/ extracted phrases when compared against some gold standard. However, traditional methods for estimating the parameters of a stochastic finite automaton and for decoding the best hypothesis do not pay attention to the evaluation criterion, which we take to be the well-known F-measure. We are interested in methods that remedy this situation, both in training and decoding. Our main result is a novel algorithm for efficiently evaluating expected F-measure. We present the algorithm and discuss its applications for utility/risk-based parameter estimation and decoding.

1 Introduction

Finding regions of interest in texts is a fundamental task in Natural Language Processing. Typical regions of interest include noun phrases [1, 2, 3, 4], subject-verb phrases [5], named entities [6, 7], and word tokens [8], among others. We consider this task abstractly and speak of *chunks* or *phrases* (substrings) to be located inside larger strings. Phrase chunking – the process of finding chunks/ phrases – is evaluated like an information retrieval task, in terms of precision and recall: we compare the set of chunks found by a system against a given gold standard dataset annotated with chunk information. Precision refers to the number of true positive chunks divided by the number of hypothesized chunks (fraction correct). Recall refers to the number of true positive chunks divided by the number of true chunks according to the gold standard (fraction found). Precision and recall values are combined into a single quantity, which can be either the risk-like E-measure [9], or the utility-like F-measure.

Our larger goal is to formulate a stochastic approach to phrase chunking that is informed by these evaluation criteria: we want to minimize E-measure (risk) or maximize F-measure (utility) during training [10] and decoding. In this paper we focus on the foundational aspects of this approach and on algorithmic issues surrounding minimum-risk/maximum-utility estimation in particular. The main result is a novel algorithm for evaluating the expected utility of a hypothesis. The

A. Yli-Jyrä, L. Karttunen, and J. Karhumäki (Eds.): FSMNLP 2005, LNAI 4002, pp. 97–109, 2006.
© Springer-Verlag Berlin Heidelberg 2006

key insight is that the number of true positives (matched chunks) of a hypothesis string compared to a gold standard label string can be computed by a weighted infinite transducer. This infinity poses no problems, since transducers can be implemented in a lazy fashion [11] and only finite prefixes have to be considered. The algorithm also makes use of weighted transducer composition and algebraic path computations (not discussed here).

Building automatic chunkers is simplified by the use of supervised machine learning. In this scenario, a learner is presented with examples of strings together with a set of chunks[1] occurring in those strings and asked to infer regularities that will allow similar chunks to be found inside previously unseen strings. Since this is not a standard learning task, it is transformed into a more conventional sequence learning task. Learning with sequential data is ubiquitous in Natural Language Processing and well understood [12, 13, 14].

Several reductions from the real learning task to sequence learning tasks are possible. The most common schemes annotate each string of words with an equally long string of labels, which indicate, directly or indirectly, whether a symbol is part of a chunk, and whether it occurs at the start, in the middle, or at the end of a chunk. Tjong Kim Sang et al. [4] compare several labeling schemes. The examples and techniques in this paper are based on what they refer to as the IOB2 scheme. This choice is convenient, but not essential; our techniques could be adapted to work with other schemes as well. The IOB2 scheme goes back to Ratnaparkhi ([15], pp. 57ff.), who used the labels 'Start', 'Join', and 'Other', which are known here as as B, I, and O, respectively. Their function is perhaps best illustrated by an example.

Example 1. The following sentence appears in the Dutch language training data provided for the Shared Task of the 2002 Workshop on Computational Natural Language Learning [16], in which named entity chunks are indicated by square brackets (we do not care about entity sorts here):

De liberale minister van [Justitie] [Marc Verwilghen] is geen kandidaat op de lokale [VLD-lijst] bij de komende gemeenteraadsverkiezingen in [Dendermonde].[2]

The same sentence is represented in the IOB2 scheme as follows:

⟨De, O⟩ ⟨liberale, O⟩ ⟨minister, O⟩ ⟨van, O⟩ ⟨Justitie, B⟩ ⟨Marc, B⟩
⟨Verwilghen, I⟩ ⟨is, O⟩ ⟨geen, O⟩ ⟨kandidaat, O⟩ ⟨op, O⟩ ⟨de, O⟩ ⟨lokale, O⟩
⟨VLD-lijst, B⟩ ⟨bij, O⟩ ⟨de, O⟩ ⟨komende, O⟩
⟨gemeenteraadsverkiezingen, O⟩ ⟨in, O⟩ ⟨Dendermonde, B⟩ ⟨., O⟩

---

[1] In the simplest case, a chunk is a substring of the string of words. This is the definition we will assume throughout this paper. More complex scenarios where chunks come in different varieties (e.g. different types of named entities) are easily accommodated.

[2] [Marc Verwilghen], the liberal minister of [Justice], is not on the local [VLD (the Flemish liberal democrats) list] as a candidate in the upcoming city council elections in [Dendermonde].

In the IOB2 scheme, the label B signals the beginning of a chunk, I marks the inside (continuation) of a chunk, and O denotes that a word is outside of any chunk. Note that an I label cannot occur immediately after an O label. A total of three types of labels is needed in order to encode adjacent chunks, as in 'minister van [Justitie] [Marc Verwilghen]'.

Formally, an unsupervised instance is a nonempty string $w \in \Sigma^+$ over some finite alphabet Σ (Dutch words, in the above example). Let $\Gamma = \{I, O, B\}$ be the set of IOB2 labels. A supervised instance is then a pair $\langle w, x \rangle$ consisting of a word string $w \in \Sigma^+$ of length $|w| = \ell > 0$ together with a label sequence x of the same length $|x| = \ell$. The language of valid label sequences, of which x is a member, is the local language $L_{lbl} = \{O, B\}\Gamma^* - \Gamma^*\{OI\}\Gamma^*$. Excluded from L_{lbl} are label strings that either start with the label I or contain OI as a substring. A pair $\langle w, x \rangle$ of same-length strings is isomorphic to a string of pairs, which was the representation used in the example.

2 Two Related Processing Tasks

2.1 Minimum Risk Decoding

Thanks to the IOB2 encoding of chunks, we are now dealing with a familiar sequence labeling problem: instead of finding chunks in an instance w, we have to find a label string x corresponding to w in the transformed problem. However, we also need to recover a solution to the original information extraction problem from a solution to the sequence labeling problem. This is known as *decoding*.

Say a sequence labeling module is presented with a word string $w \in \Sigma^n$ and produces a probability distribution over label string hypotheses $y \in \Gamma^n \cap L_{lbl}$. A naive decoding approach might consider only the most likely label string and read chunks off that string. This does not use information from runners-up, which might contradict the most likely string and collectively outweigh it.

The Bayes Decision Rule [17] tells us that the best hypothesis $\hat{x}_w$ is one with minimum average cost under the distribution of label strings (this is also known as *minimum risk decoding*):

$$\hat{x}(w) = \operatorname*{argmin}_x \mathcal{R}(x \mid w) = \operatorname*{argmin}_x \sum_y \lambda(x \mid y) \Pr(y \mid w), \qquad (1)$$

where $x, y \in \Gamma^{|w|} \cap L_{lbl}$ range over valid label strings such that $|w| = |x| = |y|$. The *loss function* λ is a task-dependent function into the nonnegative rational numbers; $\lambda(x \mid y)$ is the loss incurred for choosing hypothesis x when the true state of affairs is y. Finally, $\mathcal{R}(x \mid w)$ is the *conditional risk*, or expected loss, of hypothesis x under a probability distribution conditional on w.

Instead of minimizing the expectation of a loss function, we can also maximize the expectation of the negative loss function, which we call the expected *utility*.[3] In general, the choice of loss or utility function depends on the application. In Natural Language Processing, various loss/utility functions have been

---

[3] Maximizing expected utility and minimizing expected loss amount to the same if optimization is exact. In the rest of this paper we will treat them as equivalent.

proposed for decoding and evaluation of chunking [5, 18, 19, 20] and other tasks (for example [21, 22] among many others). For the phrase chunking applications we are concerned with, the evaluation criteria are based on the concepts of precision and recall from Information Retrieval. Both of these criteria compare a hypothesis h against a gold standard g. Precision is defined as the number of correctly identified chunks (true positives, or $tp(g, h)$) divided by the number of hypothesized chunks (positive margin, or $m(h)$). We write this as

$$P(h \mid g) = \begin{cases} \dfrac{tp(g,h)}{m(h)} & \text{if } m(h) > 0 \\ 1 & \text{if } m(h) = 0 \end{cases} \tag{2}$$

Recall is conversely defined as the number of correctly identified chunks $tp(g, h)$ divided by the true number of chunks $m(g)$ (true margin): $R(h \mid g) = P(g \mid h)$. Note that a special case arises when the denominator is zero, in which case the numerator $tp(g, h)$ is also necessarily zero.

Precision and recall are combined into a single loss function, namely van Rijsbergen's ([9], p. 372) effectiveness measure E with parameter $\alpha \in (0; 1)$:

$$E_\alpha(h \mid g) = 1 - \left[\alpha \frac{1}{P(h \mid g)} + (1 - \alpha) \frac{1}{R(h \mid g)} \right]^{-1}$$

An analogous, and much more familiar, utility function can be defined in terms of $1 - E_\alpha(h \mid g)$. This is the α-weighted harmonic mean of precision and recall, also known as the F-measure and often mistakenly attributed to [23]. Letting $\alpha = 1/(\beta + 1)$ with $\beta > 0$, the F_β-measure is defined as follows:

$$F_\beta(h \mid g) = 1 - E_\alpha(h \mid g) = \frac{(\beta + 1) \, P(h \mid g) \, R(h \mid g)}{\beta \, P(h \mid g) + R(h \mid g)}$$

It is more convenient to express the F_β-measure in terms of the number of matched chunks $tp(g, h)$, hypothesized chunks $m(h)$, and actual chunks $m(g)$:

$$F_\beta(h \mid g) = \begin{cases} \dfrac{(\beta + 1) \, tp(g,h)}{m(h) + \beta \, m(g)} & \text{if } m(h) + m(g) > 0 \\ 1 & \text{otherwise} \end{cases} \tag{3}$$

This equation gives us the parametric family of utility functions F_β that will be used throughout the rest of this paper for the phrase chunking task. The optimization tasks underlying decoding and parameter estimation involve maximizing the expectation of the utility $F_\beta(h \mid g)$, or, equivalently, minimizing the expectation of the loss $1 - F_\beta(h \mid g)$. The following symmetry will be useful later: Because $\alpha = 1/(1 + \beta)$, therefore $1 - \alpha = 1/(1 + 1/\beta)$ and so

$$F_\beta(h \mid g) = F_{1/\beta}(g \mid h). \tag{4}$$

With these definitions in place, we are in a position to formally state the decoding problem for the phrase chunking task. The hypothesis with minimum expected loss (minimum risk) or maximum expected utility (MEU) is now

$$\hat{x}_{\text{MEU}}(w) = \operatorname*{argmax}_{x} \sum_{y} F_\beta(x \mid y) \Pr(y \mid w) = \operatorname*{argmax}_{x} \mathcal{U}_\beta(x \mid w). \qquad (5)$$

The conditional expectation of F_β will also be written as $\mathcal{U}_\beta(x \mid w)$. In order to carry out the discrete optimization of the decoding task (5), we need an efficient algorithm for evaluating the expected utility $\mathcal{U}$. We will show that $\mathcal{U}$ can be represented as a weighted transducer whenever the probability model is provided by a stochastic finite automaton.

2.2 Parameter Estimation by Empirical Risk Minimization

A second task in which the expected utility $\mathcal{U}$ plays a role is the estimation of parameters of the underlying probability model of a chunker given a sequence of supervised instances $\langle w_1, x_1 \rangle, \ldots, \langle w_n, x_n \rangle$. We assume that the probability model is parameterized by a vector θ. In Empirical Risk Minimization, our estimate of θ is one which minimizes the average risk on the training data. We reformulate this again as maximizing the average utility (using F_β as the utility function) instead of minimizing expected loss:

$$\hat{\theta} = \operatorname*{argmax}_{\theta} \frac{1}{n} \sum_{i=1}^{n} F_\beta(\hat{x}(w_i; \theta) \mid x_i).$$

For simplicity, we use as the decoded hypothesis $\hat{x}$ the maximum a posteriori (MAP) hypothesis (6) instead of the MEU hypothesis (5).

$$\hat{x}(w; \theta) = \operatorname*{argmax}_{x} \Pr(x \mid w; \theta). \qquad (6)$$

The factor $1/n$ does not depend on θ and can be ignored in the maximization. The parameter estimation task is then the following optimization problem:

$$\hat{\theta} = \operatorname*{argmax}_{\theta} \sum_{i=1}^{n} F_\beta(\operatorname*{argmax}_{z} \Pr(z \mid w_i; \theta) \mid x_i). \qquad (7)$$

Because of the nested discrete maximization step involving z, the outer maximization problem involving θ is not well-behaved: the outer optimization objective is a piecewise constant function of θ whose gradient is zero almost everywhere. We reformulate this problem and approximate the inner maximization in a way that will regularize the outer optimization problem. Let δ be the Kronecker delta, whose value is one if its two arguments are equal, and zero otherwise. Then:

$$\hat{\theta} = \operatorname*{argmax}_{\theta} \sum_{i=1}^{n} \sum_{y} F_\beta(y \mid x_i) \, \delta(y, \operatorname*{argmax}_{z} \Pr(z \mid w_i; \theta))$$

$$\approx \operatorname*{argmax}_{\theta} \sum_{i=1}^{n} \sum_{y} F_\beta(y \mid x_i) \, \frac{\Pr(y \mid w_i; \theta)}{\max_z \Pr(z \mid w_i; \theta)}$$

$$= \operatorname*{argmax}_{\theta} \sum_{i=1}^{n} \frac{1}{\max_z \Pr(z \mid w_i; \theta)} \, \mathcal{U}_{1/\beta}(x_i \mid w_i; \theta)$$

The approximate equality between the first and second line holds because

$$\delta(y, \operatorname{argmax}_z \Pr(z)) = \lim_{\gamma \to \infty} \left(\frac{\Pr(y)}{\max_z \Pr(z)} \right)^\gamma$$

We chose a fixed sharpening parameter $\gamma = 1$ to approximate this limit in the above derivation; larger values of γ can be used with minor changes. We again encounter the expected utility $\mathcal{U}$, whose parameter $1/\beta$ is due to the symmetry (4) observed earlier. The net result is that the outer optimization objective depends continuously on θ so that an iterative numerical optimization can be carried out[4] provided that $\mathcal{U}$ can be evaluated efficiently.

2.3   A Common Subexpression: Expected Utility

The conditional expected utility $\mathcal{U}$ occurs both in the Maximum Expected Utility (or Minimum Risk) decoding task and in the Empirical Risk Minimization parameter estimation task. It can be expressed as follows:

$$\mathcal{U}_\beta(x \mid w; \theta) = \begin{cases} (\beta + 1) \sum_y \dfrac{tp(x, y)}{m(x) + \beta\, m(y)} \Pr(y \mid w; \theta) & \text{if } m(x) > 0 \\[2mm] \Pr(x \mid w; \theta) & \text{if } m(x) = 0 \end{cases} \tag{8}$$

The special case is due to the fact that $m(x) + m(y) = 0$ iff both x and y are comprised exclusively of O labels, in which case $x = y$.

Expected utility cannot be evaluated efficiently by direct summation, since there are exponentially many label strings y one has to sum over. Let the number of label strings of length ℓ (recall that $\ell = |w| = |x| = |y|$) be known as $N(\ell) = |\Gamma^\ell \cap L_{\mathrm{lbl}}|$. It is easy to show that the asymptotic growth of N is exponential in ℓ: observe that $\{O, B\}^\ell \subsetneq (\Gamma^\ell \cap L_{\mathrm{lbl}}) \subsetneq \Gamma^\ell$ for $\ell \geq 2$, and therefore $N(\ell) \in \omega(2^\ell)$ and $N(\ell) \in o(3^\ell)$. The tight bound is $\Theta((1 + \phi)^\ell)$ where $\phi = (1 + \sqrt{5})/2$; hence $1 + \phi \approx 2.618$. The hidden constant of proportionality in the tight bound is $1/2 + \sqrt{1/20}$, and so for a moderately long sentence with 21 words (including punctuation) like in Example 1, one would have to sum over $433\,494\,437$ distinct label strings. The longest "sentence" in the dataset which Example 1 was taken from [16] comprises 859 tokens – it is a linearized table – and corresponds to about 79 centumoctodecillion (79×10^{357}) potential label strings.

3   Algorithms

3.1   Computing Expected Precision

Consider the problem of evaluating the expectation of precision (2) for fixed w, x and θ:

$$\sum_y P(x \mid y) \Pr(y \mid w; \theta) = \begin{cases} \dfrac{1}{m(x)} \sum_y tp(x, y) \Pr(y \mid w; \theta) & \text{if } m(x) > 0 \\[2mm] 1 & \text{if } m(x) = 0 \end{cases}$$

---

[4] This involves ignoring the term $\max_z \Pr(z \mid w_i; \theta)$ or holding it fixed in each iteration.

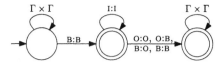

Fig. 1. Nondeterministic finite transducer that counts true positive chunks

Computing expected precision boils down to evaluating the expected number of true positives,

$$\sum_y tp(x, y)\; \Pr(y \mid w; \theta). \tag{9}$$

The significance of (9) is that it also occurs in the derivation of the expected utility (8). The technique developed in this section for evaluating expected true positives will be generalized in Sec. 3.2 to apply to expected utility.

In general, sums of products of the form $\sum_y f(x, y)\, g(y, z)$ can be calculated efficiently for certain forms of f and g even when naive summation would be inefficient. This holds in particular when f and g can be computed by finite state transducers (FSTs), in which case the summation corresponds to weighted transducer composition [24].

The expected number of true positives as expressed in (9) is of the requisite form. In order for transducer composition to be applicable, we need to show that we can compute tp by a finite state transducer.[5] Since we require the evaluation algorithm to be efficient, we also need to demonstrate that the size of all finite state machines involved in the computation is small enough to enable the evaluation to be carried out in polynomial time. We begin by formulating a finite state machine for computing tp.

A transducer that computes tp is a two-tape automaton that maps a pair of strings $x, y \in \Gamma^n$ to a count of the number of chunks that x and y agree on (true positives). An individual true positive chunk is described by the regular expression B:B (I:I)* ($:$ | O:O | O:B | B:O | B:B). This expression describes all pairs of string that both start with B followed by an equal amount of I's, and then both signal the end of the chunk. A chunk ends on either tape if the end of the string is reached ($), or if I is followed by a label other than I.

From this regular expression one can then construct a nondeterministic transducer that counts the number of occurrences of true positive chunks, using the generalized counting technique of Allauzen et al. [25]. The resulting weighted transducer over the real semiring, call it T_{nd}, is shown in Fig. 1 (all edge weights and final weights are unity). The crucial observation is that $tp(x, y) = t$ if and only if there are precisely t paths through T_{nd} labeled with $\langle x, y \rangle$. For further background on weighted transducers see [25] and references cited therein.

---

[5] We also need to formulate a suitable probability model $\Pr(y \mid w; \theta)$ that can likewise be expressed as a weighted finite state transducer. It is clear that HMMs, CMMs, MEMMs and related models have this property.

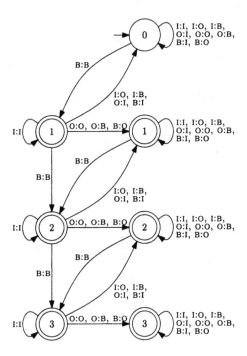

Fig. 2. Initial portion of T_{ua}

Assume that there is a transducer M_θ over alphabets Γ and Σ with behavior $[M_\theta](y, w) = \Pr(y \mid w; \theta)$. The composition of T_{nd} with M_θ then has the following behavior, as desired: $[T_{\mathrm{nd}} \circ M_\theta](x, w) = \sum_y tp(x, y) \Pr(y \mid w; \theta)$.

The next issue is to show how this calculation can be done for fixed $\langle x, w \rangle$. We write $\mathrm{Str}(x)$ to denote a transducer[6] that maps the string pair $\langle x, x \rangle$ to 1 and all other pairs to 0. In order to evaluate (9) for fixed $\langle x, w \rangle$, construct the transducer

$$\mathrm{Str}(x) \circ T_{\mathrm{nd}} \circ M_\theta \circ \mathrm{Str}(w), \qquad (10)$$

which has the property that all paths leaving its start state are labeled with $\langle x, w \rangle$. Its behavior can be computed efficiently by a single-source algebraic path algorithm on the acyclic transition graph of the transducer (10) (see [26], §25.4).

We can simplify the construction of (10). When we build $\mathrm{Str}(x) \circ T_{\mathrm{nd}}$, we do not actually care about the first tape of the composed transducer and can eliminate it by projection/marginalization. Notice that the second projection $\pi_2(\mathrm{Str}(x) \circ T_{\mathrm{nd}})$ does not generally result in a deterministic automaton; however, we can directly construct an equivalent deterministic automaton. The reason for doing so is to obtain a simple upper bound on the state and arc complexity of a transducer that carries out the same computation as $\mathrm{Str}(x) \circ T_{\mathrm{nd}}$.

---

[6] The construction of $\mathrm{Str}(x)$ is a special case of the prefix tree (a. k. a. "trie") representation of a finite dictionary.

Tdet(x):

1: $\langle x_0, \ldots, x_{\ell-1} \rangle \leftarrow x$
2: $S \leftarrow \{\}$ // set of states
3: $F \leftarrow \{\}$ // set of final states
4: $E \leftarrow \{\}$ // set of transitions
5: $Q \leftarrow$ **new** Queue() // an empty queue
6: Q.enqueue($\langle 0, \top, 0, 0 \rangle$) // push start state
7: **while** $\neg Q$.isEmpty() **do**
8:     $q \leftarrow Q$.dequeue()
9:     **if** $q \in S$ **then**
10:        **continue** // already visited q
11:     $S \leftarrow S \cup \{q\}$
12:     $k \leftarrow q[0]$ // index
13:     **if** $k = \ell$ **then**
14:        $F \leftarrow F \cup \{q\}$
15:        **continue** // final state
16:     $outside \leftarrow q[1]$ // outside a match?
17:     $tp \leftarrow q[2]$ // matching chunks so far
18:     **if** $x_k = $ B $\vee$ $x_k = $ O $\vee$ ($outside \wedge x_k = $ I) **then**
19:        addEdge($E, Q, q, $ O $, \top, 0$)
20:        **if** $x_k = $ B **then**
21:           addEdge($E, Q, q, $ B $, \bot, +1$)
22:        **else**
23:           addEdge($E, Q, q, $ B $, \top, 0$)
24:        **if** $outside = \top$ **then**
25:           addEdge($E, Q, q, $ I $, \top, 0$)
26:     **else if** $x_k = $ I **then**
27:        **assert** $tp > 0$
28:        addEdge($E, Q, q, $ I $, \bot, 0$)
29:        addEdge($E, Q, q, $ O $, \top, -1$)
30:        addEdge($E, Q, q, $ B $, \top, -1$)
31:     **else**
32:        **assert** $tp > 0$
33:        addEdge($E, Q, q, $ I $, \top, -1$)
34: **return** $\langle S, \langle 0, \top, 0, 0 \rangle, F, E \rangle$

(a) Construction of T_{det}.

addEdge($E, Q, q, osym, outside, \Delta tp$):

1: $k \leftarrow q[0] + 1$
2: $tp \leftarrow q[2] + \Delta tp$
3: $r \leftarrow \langle k, outside, tp, 0 \rangle$ // target
4: $E \leftarrow E \cup \{\langle q, osym, r \rangle\}$
5: $Q \leftarrow Q \cup \{r\}$

(b) Computing exp. true positives.

addEdge($E, Q, q, osym, outside, \Delta tp$):

1: $k \leftarrow q[0] + 1$
2: $tp \leftarrow q[2] + \Delta tp$
3: **if** $osym = $ B **then**
4:    $pm \leftarrow q[3] + 1$
5: **else**
6:    $pm \leftarrow q[3]$
7: $r \leftarrow \langle k, outside, tp, pm \rangle$ // target
8: $E \leftarrow E \cup \{\langle q, osym, r \rangle\}$
9: $Q \leftarrow Q \cup \{r\}$

(c) Computing expected utility.

U(x, w, θ, β):

1: $mx \leftarrow$ num. occurrences of B in x
2: **if** $mx = 0$ **then**
3:    **return** $\Pr(x \mid w; \theta)$
4: $T \leftarrow$ Tdet(x)
5: $\langle D, F \rangle \leftarrow$ algPathCompose(T, θ)
6: $u \leftarrow 0$
7: **for each** $q \in F$ **do**
8:    $tp \leftarrow q[2]$
9:    $my \leftarrow q[3]$
10:    $u \leftarrow u + D[q] \, tp/(mx + \beta \, my)$
11: **return** $(\beta + 1) \, u$

(d) Overall computation.

Fig. 3. Algorithm for constructing T_{det}

We construct a complete and unambiguous transducer T_{ua} that is equivalent to T_{nd}, meaning for each pair of same-length strings $\langle x, y \rangle$ there is precisely one accepting path through T_{ua}. Furthermore, the composition $\text{Str}(x) \circ T_{\text{ua}}$ is an output-deterministic transducer: its second projection is a deterministic automaton. Note that it is possible to have an unambiguous transducer for counting matching chunks in string pairs of a known length, but disambiguation of T_{nd} is impossible because T_{nd} can be used to count matching chunks in strings of unbounded length. In fact, the path multiplicity of T_{nd} is at the core of its design as a counter. However, an unambiguous version of T_{nd} can be constructed if we allow the set of states to be countably infinite. The initial portion of T_{ua} is shown in Fig. 2 (all edge weights are one; final weights are as indicated). In order to understand the correctness of T_{ua} (Fig. 2), observe its similarity to T_{nd} (Fig. 1). In both cases there are B:B transitions from the start state to a state with an I:I loop, as well as O:O, O:B and B:O transitions out of that state. However, whereas the B:B transition out of the second state of Fig. 1 signals the end of a chunk, it simultaneously signals the beginning of a new chunk (this is precisely the rationale for the B label – to encode adjacent junks), hence the vertical B:B transitions in Fig. 2. The final weight of each state corresponds to the number of matching chunks encountered. The states there are organized in two columns, with those on the left indicating that the inside of a matching chunk is being processed. The only way to get to the left column is to take a diagonal B:B transition that signals the beginning of a potential matching chunk. There are two ways to proceed from the left column to the right column: take an upward diagonal transition, which indicates a failed potential match; or take a horizontal transition, which successfully completes a true positive match.

In an implementation of finite state machines based on lazy data structures (e.g. [11]), infinite transducers like T_{ua} can be represented directly. For simplicity we will present a more traditional algorithm, shown in Fig. 3 (a+b), which constructs a deterministic finite automaton $T_{det}(x) = \pi_2(\text{Str}(x) \circ T_{ua})$. The states of $T_{det}(x)$ can be thought of as triples $\langle k, o, t \rangle$ where k is an index into x; o is a boolean variable that indicates if the state is part of a matching chunk; and t is the number of matching chunks encountered so far (equal to the final weights). Conceptually, k is a state of $\text{Str}(x)$ and $\langle o, t \rangle$ is a state of T_{ua}, where o selects the left ($o = \perp$) or right ($o = \top$) column of states in Fig. 2. There are at most $(|x| + 1) \times (2|x| + 1)$ states and a constant number of outgoing edges per state.

This is sufficient to guarantee that (10) can be evaluated efficiently. $M_\theta \circ \text{Str}(w)$ has $\Theta(3^j |w|)$ states when M_θ is a jth-order Markov model. Since j is fixed and x and w are of the same length and thus do not require separate indices, the composed automaton (10) has $O(|x|^2)$ states. Because the algebraic path computation runs in linear time, the overall computation of the expected number of true positives (9) runs in quadratic time. Moreover the hidden constant of proportionality is small when j is small and when there are few B labels in a label sequence, as is typically the case.

3.2   Computing Expected Utility

Evaluating expected F_β also involves computing the expected number of hypothesized chunks $\sum_y m(y) \Pr(y \mid w; \theta)$. This is straightforward: whenever one encounters the label B, one increments a counter. An FST which counts (up to a fixed threshold of n) the chunks it sees on its second tape is shown in Fig. 4.

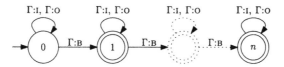

Fig. 4. Output-deterministic transducer that counts hypothesized chunks

An FST that computes $\langle tp(x,y), m(y) \rangle$ in parallel can be obtained[7] by a composition-like combination of the transducers in Fig. 2 and Fig. 4. This is quite simple: the algorithm in Fig. 3 (a+b) can be extended by making states quadruples instead of triples, changing only the function "addEdge", so that the number of hypothesized chunks can be tracked directly. The extended algorithm in Fig. 3 (a+c) constructs a transducer with at most $(|x|+1)^2 \times (2\,m(x)+1)$ states, whose behavior can therefore be computed in cubic time. The corresponding algorithm is shown in Fig. 3 (a+c+d) and requires a subroutine (not shown for reasons of space) that computes (i) the composition of T_{det} with the automaton $M_\theta \circ \text{Str}(y)$ representing the probability model and (ii) the algebraic path weights for the final states of the composed transducer. The key insight here is that these final states partition the probability mass of the probability model in such a way that all label strings with the same number of true positive matches and the same number of predicted chunks contribute to just one final state. While there are exponentially many label sequences, there are only quadratically many final states. This allows us to evelute the expected utility $\mathcal{U}$ in polynomial time.

4   Conclusion

An efficient algorithm for computing the expected utility of chunking hypotheses was presented within the framework of weighted automata. This has direct applications for the loss-sensitive training and minimum risk decoding of stochastic chunkers. The key insight is that the number of matching chunks in two label sequences can be counted efficiently using an unambiguous infinite transducer. This does not transcend the boundaries of finite state computations – only finite prefixes and finitely many hypotheses are considered – and it enabled us to state simple bounds on the size of derived machines. The chunk counting transducer was extended trivially to also keep track of predicted chunks, thus computing both matching and predicted chunks in parallel, as required for the computation of expected utility.

Acknowledgments

This research was supported by the Office of the Dean, Fu Foundation School of Engineering and Applied Science, Columbia University. I would like to thank

---

[7] More precisely, since this computation involves pairs of real numbers, the weights of the component transducers must be thought of as having been mapped into a direct product of the real semiring with itself. Composition takes place in that product semiring. The final weights are tuples $\langle tp, pm \rangle$.

Julia Hirschberg, Phil Long, Owen Rambow, and the Columbia NLP group for helpful feedback. The usual disclaimers apply.

References

1. Church, K.W.: A stochastic parts program and noun phrase parser for unrestricted text. In: ANLP. (1988) 136–143
2. Voutilainen, A.: NPtool, a detector of English noun phrases. In: WVLC. (1993) 48–57
3. Ramshaw, L.A., Marcus, M.P.: Text chunking using transformation-based learning. In: WVLC. (1995) 82–94
4. Tjong Kim Sang, E.F., Veenstra, J.: Representing text chunks. In: EACL. (1999) 173–179
5. Punyakanok, V., Roth, D.: The use of classifiers in sequential inference. In: NIPS. (2000) 995–1001
6. Bikel, D.M., Miller, S., Schwartz, R., Weischedel, R.: Nymble: A high-performance learning name-finder. In: ANLP. (1997) 194–201
7. Freitag, D.: Toward general-purpose learning for information extraction. In: COLING-ACL. (1998) 404–408
8. Zhou, G.: Chunking-based Chinese word tokenization. In: SIGHAN. (2003)
9. van Rijsbergen, C.J.: Foundation of evaluation. Journal of Documentation **30** (1974) 365–373
10. Jansche, M.: Maximum expected F-measure training of logistic regression models. In: HLT-EMNLP. (2005) 692–699
11. Mohri, M., Pereira, F., Riley, M.: The design principles of a weighted finite-state transducer library. Theoretical Computer Science **231** (2000) 17–32
12. Bengio, Y.: Markovian models for sequential data. Neural Computing Surveys **2** (1999) 129–162
13. Dietterich, T.G.: Machine learning for sequential data: A review. Lecture Notes in Computer Science **2396** (2002)
14. Collins, M.: Machine learning methods in natural language processing. Tutorial presented at COLT (2003)
15. Ratnaparkhi, A.: Maximum Entropy Models for Natural Language Ambiguity Resolution. PhD thesis, University of Pennsylvania (1998)
16. Tjong Kim Sang, E.F.: Introduction to the CoNLL-2002 shared task. In: CoNLL. (2002) 155–158
17. Duda, R.O., Hart, P.E., Stork, D.G.: Pattern Classification. 2nd edn. Wiley (2000)
18. Zhang, T., Damerau, F., Johnson, D.: Text chunking using regularized winnow. In: ACL. (2001) 539–546
19. Zhang, T., Damerau, F., Johnson, D.: Text chunking based on a generalization of winnow. Journal of Machine Learning Research **2** (2002) 615–637
20. Zhang, T., Johnson, D.: A robust risk minimization based named entity recognition system. In: CoNLL. (2003) 204–207
21. Stolcke, A., König, Y., Weintraub, M.: Explicit word error minimization in n-best list rescoring. In: EuroSpeech. (1997)
22. Kumar, S., Byrne, W.: Minimum Bayes-risk decoding for machine translation. In: HLT-NAACL. (2004) 169–176
23. van Rijsbergen, C.J.: Information Retrieval. 1st edn. Butterworths (1975)

24. Mohri, M., Pereira, F., Riley, M.: Weighted automata in text and speech processing. In: ECAI'96 Workshop on Extended Finite State Models of Language. (1996) 46–50
25. Allauzen, C., Mohri, M., Roark, B.: Generalized algorithms for constructing language models. In: ACL. (2003) 40–47
26. Cormen, T.H., Leiserson, C.E., Rivest, R.L.: Introduction to Algorithms. 1st edn. MIT Press (1990)

Collapsing ϵ-Loops in Weighted Finite-State Machines

J. Howard Johnson

Institute for Information Technology,
National Research Council Canada,
Ottawa Canada
Howard.Johnson@nrc-cnrc.gc.ca

Abstract. Weighted finite-state automata pose a number of challenges for software developers. One particular difficulty is that ϵ-transitions must be treated more carefully than is necessary for unweighted automata. The usual weighted ϵ-closure algorithm always produces $O(n^2)$ transitions for a ϵ-loop with n states. An approach that removes ϵ-loops without performing a full ϵ-closure is proposed and it is shown how this can be efficiently implemented using sparse matrix operations.

1 Introduction

Weighted finite state automata and transducers have become quite popular as an underlying model for natural language processing. After much success in simplifying and generalizing the foundations of Automatic Speech Recognition [8, 12], they are now being successfully used as a framework for Statistical Machine Translation [7].

Non-weighted finite state automata and transducers have also achieved a lot of success in modelling various aspects of morphology and syntax of natural language [2] but suffer from a lack in trainability that the weighted form of machine can handle naturally. Thus there is interest in extending toolkits that handle non-weighted models so that they handle weights in a meaningful way [6].

INR [5] was developed as a demonstration that large automata could be constructed efficiently in the early 1980s but never was extended to handle semirings other than the Boolean semiring. This extension (with working name wINR) is currently being undertaken at NRC to support a number of research projects.

There are many issues that adding weights brings up for an implementation of finite automata and transducers but one of the first ones that is encountered is the handling of ϵ-transitions [9, 11, 10]. One problem that has been observed is that automata with large ϵ-loops experience the addition of $O(n^2)$ transitions when the standard ϵ-closure algorithm is used. This has led to the development of approximate methods to handle the large transducers that occur in some applications [9].

INR [5] had an ϵ-closure algorithm that reduced the network of ϵ transitions using a local rewrite rule mechanism. Then ϵ-loops can be collapsed to a single

A. Yli-Jyrä, L. Karttunen, and J. Karhumäki (Eds.): FSMNLP 2005, LNAI 4002, pp. 110–119, 2006.
© Springer-Verlag Berlin Heidelberg 2006

state by means of merging through state renaming. A more general ε-closure algorithm is still needed (and implemented) but it can assume that there are no ε-loops remaining.

This approach had the advantage of keeping the number of states and transitions small as long as possible to optimize space and time of implementation. In the weighted case, this becomes even more important because the more compact representations of a machine will often have ε-transitions [15, 16].

The idea of collapsing strongly connected components in the ε-network does not generalize easily for other semirings. A more general approach is needed. Fortunately this can be handled using an approach based on Gaussian elimination and that is the topic of this paper.

Note that this approach to handling ε-transitions differs from most others in that the only goal is the removal of loops. The remaining ε-transitions can be kept or removed as suits the convenience of downstream operations using simpler algorithms that do not have to handle loops.

Section 2 discusses one simple special case, that of a one tape finite automaton with weights taken from the real numbers ($\Re$). To help clarify ideas, section 3 provides an example of the approach. Section 4 shows how the technology developed for the efficient processing of sparse matrices can be applied, reducing the problem of storage cost to that of the amount of fill-in for a LU decomposition. Section 5 shows that the restrictions imposed for section 2 can be removed so that any *-semiring can be used for weights and any number of tapes can be handled. Section 6 provides some concluding remarks.

2   The Technique (for a One-Tape Automaton over $\Re$)

In order to simplify the presentation, we will fix on the weights being drawn from the real numbers $\Re$ with addition and multiplication being the usual operations on numeric quantities. A second simplification will be to assume that there is only one input stream so that we consider only a weighted finite state recognizer. This is an important case of interest and will provide important insight into the more general cases discussed in section 5.

This section will present the idea in terms of matrix operations since it is easier to see in this guise. Gaussian elimination is used and this is the standard technique introduced in numerical analysis courses and more easily discussed in terms of matrices. A discussion in terms of weighted directed graphs is also possible but is less direct.

Suppose, then, that we have a weighted finite state automaton M:

$$M = \langle Q, \Sigma, S, F, E, \{T_x | x \in \Sigma\} \rangle$$

Here S is a row vector of $|Q|$ elements from $\Re$, F is a column vector of $|Q|$ elements from $\Re$, and E and $\{T_x | x \in \Sigma\}$ are all square matrices of order $|Q|$ with elements from $\Re$. This presentation, though slightly different from the usual, is easily interconvertible with other definitions. The only wrinkle is that only one transition with given label or ϵ is possible between any pair of states but this does not result in any loss in expressiveness.

By considering Q as the set of row (and column) indices $\{1, 2, 3, \ldots, |Q|\}$, T_x transitions with a label of x together in a matrix T_x. For the transition from state i to j with label x and weight w, we will set $[T_x]_{ij} = w$.

Next, we will collect together all of the ϵ-transitions into a matrix E by setting E_{ij} to the weight of the ϵ-transition from state i to j (if it exists).

Any unassigned cells in E or T_x will be set to 0.

We will begin with a row vector S with the appropriate weight for each state indicated. If only one state is possible, then that element will have weight 1 and the others will have weight 0. We will terminate with a column vector F having the appropriate weights for each state.

Now if the automaton is ϵ-free, $E = 0$, and the total weight $f(w)$ associated with an input $w = x_1 x_2 \cdots x_l$:

$$f(w) = S \cdot T_{x_1} \cdot T_{x_2} \cdot \cdots \cdot T_{x_l} \cdot F$$

where the $\cdot$ indicates the normal matrix multiplication.

If, on the other hand $E \neq 0$, we will note that E represents all ϵ-paths of exactly length 1, $E^2 = E \cdot E$ all ϵ-paths of exactly length 2, and, in general, E^i (the product of i copies of E), represents all ϵ-paths of exactly length i.

Then we can define E^* as the reflexive and transitive closure of E:

$$E^* = I + E + E^2 + E^3 + \ldots = \lim_{n \to \infty} \sum_{i=0}^{n} E^i$$

If this limit is defined, E^* is a matrix that brings together in one package the total effect of all of the possible finite paths using only ϵ-transitions. E^* will be defined if all of the weights are probabilities and the largest eigenvalue has magnitude less than 1, as is usually the case. If E^* is not defined then the problem will probably need to be reformulated to explicitly handle the infinities or to avoid them. This might mean removing states that are not co-accessible (i.e., from which a final state can be reached) with non-zero probability and renormalizing the weights so that the total probability is 1.

Then we interpose the matrix E^* between every matrix multiplication in the formula for $f(w)$ to get:

$$f(w) = SE^* T_{x_1} E^* T_{x_2} E^* \cdots E^* T_{x_l} E^* F$$

Here we have reverted to the more common convention of not explicitly marking the matrix multiplication operations.

Since we are assuming that E is over field $\Re$, and that E^* is defined, $E^* = (I - E)^{-1}$ is also defined. This is easily seen by verifying that $(I - E) \cdot E^* = I$.

If $I - E$ is invertible, we can use Gaussian elimination to factor it into a product of a lower triangular matrix L, a diagonal matrix D, and an upper triangular matrix U:

$$I - E = LDU = (I - L')D(I - U')$$

Here L is a lower triangular matrix that has 1s on the diagonal, and U is an upper triangular matrix also with 1s on the diagonal. Then L' is a strictly lower triangular matrix and U' is a strictly upper triangular matrix.

Up to this point, we are following the usual approach for inverting $I - E$. The next step would be to use back solving with U and L to calculate the individual elements of the inverse. Instead, we will go in another direction and recode U' and L' back into regular ε-transitions.

Now

$$(I - E)^{-1} = (I - U')^{-1} D^{-1} (I - L')^{-1}$$

using standard properties of the matrix inverse. It is easy to see that all three inverses are defined.

But

$$U'^* = \sum_{i=0}^{n-1} U'^i$$

since every path involving arcs of U' are strictly monotonically increasing. Similarly

$$L'^* = \sum_{i=0}^{n-1} L'^i$$

since every path involving arcs of U' are strictly monotonically decreasing. Thus $L'^* = (I - L')^{-1}$ and $U'^* = (I - U')^{-1}$ are both defined and

$$(I - E)^{-1} = U'^* D^{-1} L'^*$$

Thus the value for $w = x_1 x_2 \cdots x_l$ is

$$f(w) = S U'^* D^{-1} L'^* T_{x_1} U'^* D^{-1} L'^* T_{x_2} U'^* D^{-1} L'^*$$
$$\cdots U'^* D^{-1} L'^* T_{x_l} U'^* D^{-1} L'^* F$$

This is not in a form that can be easily converted back to an automaton but with a small trick, this can be achieved. Let

$$\overline{M} = \langle Q \times \{0, 1\}, \Sigma, \overline{S}, \overline{F}, \overline{E}, \{\overline{T_x} | x \in \Sigma\} \rangle$$

where

$$\overline{S} = \begin{bmatrix} S & 0 \end{bmatrix} \quad \overline{F} = \begin{bmatrix} 0 \\ F \end{bmatrix} \quad \overline{E} = \begin{bmatrix} U' & D^{-1} \\ 0 & L' \end{bmatrix} \quad \overline{T_x} = \begin{bmatrix} 0 & 0 \\ T_x & 0 \end{bmatrix}$$

It is then easy to demonstrate that:

$$\overline{E}^* = \begin{bmatrix} U'^* & U'^* D^{-1} L'^* \\ 0 & L'^* \end{bmatrix}$$

Definition: $\mathcal{B}(M) = \{(w, p) | f(w) = p\}$.

Theorem 1. $\mathcal{B}(M) = \mathcal{B}(\overline{M})$

Proof: Easily shown by induction on the length of $w \in \Sigma^*$.   ∎

3 An Example

Let

$$M = \left\langle Q = \{1,2,3,4\}, \quad \Sigma = \{a,b\}, \quad S = \begin{bmatrix} 1\,0\,0\,0 \end{bmatrix}, \quad F = \begin{bmatrix} 0 \\ 0 \\ \frac{1}{2} \\ 0 \end{bmatrix},\right.$$

$$E = \begin{bmatrix} \frac{1}{7} & 0 & 0 & 0 \\ 0 & 0 & \frac{1}{5} & 0 \\ 0 & 0 & 0 & \frac{1}{2} \\ 0 & \frac{1}{3} & 0 & 0 \end{bmatrix}, \quad T_a = \begin{bmatrix} 0 & \frac{6}{7} & 0 & 0 \\ 0 & 0 & \frac{3}{5} & 0 \\ 0 & 0 & 0 & 0 \\ 0 & 0 & \frac{2}{3} & 0 \end{bmatrix}, \quad T_b = \begin{bmatrix} 0 & 0 & 0 & 0 \\ 0 & 0 & 0 & \frac{1}{5} \\ 0 & 0 & 0 & 0 \\ 0 & 0 & 0 & 0 \end{bmatrix} \right\rangle$$

be a weighted automaton over $\Re$. Figure 1 shows M in the more familiar directed graph form.

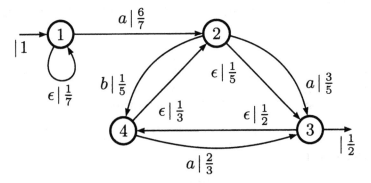

Fig. 1. An example

Then the *LDU* factorization of $I - E$ is:

$$I - E = \begin{bmatrix} \frac{6}{7} & 0 & 0 & 0 \\ 0 & 1 & -\frac{1}{5} & 0 \\ 0 & 0 & 1 & -\frac{1}{2} \\ 0 & -\frac{1}{3} & 0 & 1 \end{bmatrix} = \begin{bmatrix} 1 & 0 & 0 & 0 \\ 0 & 1 & 0 & 0 \\ 0 & 0 & 1 & 0 \\ 0 & -\frac{1}{3} & -\frac{1}{15} & 1 \end{bmatrix} \cdot \begin{bmatrix} \frac{6}{7} & 0 & 0 & 0 \\ 0 & 1 & 0 & 0 \\ 0 & 0 & 1 & 0 \\ 0 & 0 & 0 & \frac{29}{30} \end{bmatrix} \begin{bmatrix} 1 & 0 & 0 & 0 \\ 0 & 1 & -\frac{1}{5} & 0 \\ 0 & 0 & 1 & -\frac{1}{2} \\ 0 & 0 & 0 & 1 \end{bmatrix}$$

and $\overline{E}$ is:

$$\overline{E} = \begin{bmatrix} 0 & 0 & 0 & 0 & \frac{7}{6} & 0 & 0 & 0 \\ 0 & 0 & \frac{1}{5} & 0 & 0 & 1 & 0 & 0 \\ 0 & 0 & 0 & \frac{1}{2} & 0 & 0 & 1 & 0 \\ 0 & 0 & 0 & 0 & 0 & 0 & 0 & \frac{30}{29} \\ 0 & 0 & 0 & 0 & 0 & 0 & 0 & 0 \\ 0 & 0 & 0 & 0 & 0 & 0 & 0 & 0 \\ 0 & 0 & 0 & 0 & 0 & 0 & 0 & 0 \\ 0 & 0 & 0 & 0 & 0 & \frac{1}{3} & \frac{1}{15} & 0 \end{bmatrix}$$

Then
$$\overline{M} = \langle\{1,2,3,4,5,6,7,8\}, \Sigma, \overline{S}, \overline{F}, \overline{E}, \{\overline{T_a}, \overline{T_b}\}\rangle$$
where $\overline{S}$, $\overline{F}$, $\overline{T_a}$, and $\overline{T_b}$ are defined in terms of S, F, T_a, and T_b as above. The resulting automaton is displayed in Figure 2.

The result $\overline{M}$ has no ε-loops but yields the same weight for any word w without the need for any infinite summations of ε-loops. This automaton is not Markovian since the exit probabilities from each state do not sum to 1 but it can be converted to one if needed.

Although this automaton has twice the number of states and 4 more transitions, it is easily converted to an equivalent 4-state, 10-transition machine by observing that states 1 and 4 can only be exited by a single ε-transition and so they can be removed by merging them into the single following state with an appropriate push-back of the weights.

Furthermore, state 7 is a mandatory-exit state and can only be entered with ε-transitions. A similar merging and push-back can be done by making the preceding states optionally-exit states.

Finally, state 2 can be merged into state 5 by a dual process of pushing forward the label a and weight $\frac{6}{7}$. The result of all of this is shown in Figure 3.

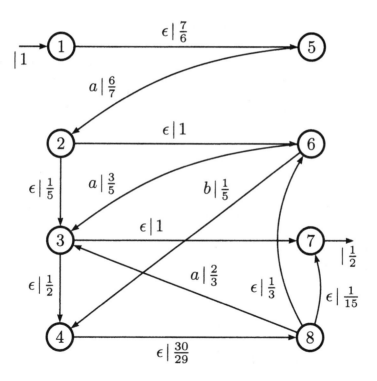

Fig. 2. Example converted: $\overline{M}$

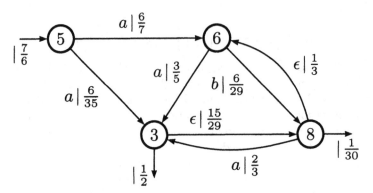

Fig. 3. Example $\overline{M}$ after state rewriting

4   The Sparse Matrix Connection

If the result of the preceding work had been just to introduce an algorithm that spent $O(n^2)$ space to store zeros and $O(n^2)$ time to perform all of the necessary arithmetic operations with them, we would not have improved the situation at all.

Fortunately, there is a well-studied branch of numerical analysis concerned with the handling of matrices with a lot of 0-elements called sparse matrix computations. This study is concerned with the identification of algorithms that retain the sparsity, that is, keep as many cells provably zero and therefore not represented in the data structure except implicitly [4].

What this means in the present case is that partial pivoting will be used during the Gaussian elimination to minimize the fill-in or introduction of non-zero elements that need to be explicitly represented. This problem has been shown to be NP-complete [13] but there have been a number of heuristic approaches that do reasonably well in practice.

To sum up, since the fill-in corresponds exactly to the number of introduced transitions in the process of Section 2 and minimizing fill-in is NP-complete, we have reduced this problem to the problem of minimizing the number of added ϵ-transitions, we have shown that the latter problem is also NP-complete.

Furthermore, because of the direct correspondence, we have a number of practical and tested heuristic approaches that usually do well.

An encouraging example occurs when there is a loop of n states:

$$E_{i,i+1} = p_i, 0 \leq i < n, E_{n,1} = p_n$$

In this case, we end up by removing the transition $E_{n,1}$, adding n states $n + 1, n+2, \ldots, 2n$, adding $n-1$ transitions $E_{i,i+n} = 1$, adding a transition $E_{n,2n} = \frac{1}{1-p_1 p_2 \cdots p_n}$, and adding $n-1$ transitions $E_{2n,i+n} = p_1 p_2 \cdots p_{i-1} \cdot p_n$.

This is an $O(n)$ growth in states and transitions for this simple case.

5 Generalizing to More Tapes and Other Semirings

5.1 Weights from a Field Other than $\Re$

By looking carefully at the presentation of Section 2, it should be clear that, in fact, the only properties of $\Re$ that were used were those that are available for any field. In fact, the example of Section 3 used weights that were explicitly represented as rational numbers.

The generalization is obvious and achieved simply by changing any reference to $\Re$ and elements of $\Re$ by appropriate elements of the desired field. In particular 0 and 1 will be replaced by the additive and multiplicative identities.

5.2 Weights from a $*$-Semiring That Is not a Field

This generalization is a little more difficult but has also been studied extensively.

Tarjan [14] describes a notion of *path sequence* that can be expressed in matrices as described in Section 2.

To show a simple example, suppose our example of Section 3 was modified to M_2 by replacing the weights from an unspecified $*$-semiring that is not necessarily commutative. Let

$$M_2 = \left\langle Q = \{1, 2, 3, 4\}, \quad \Sigma = \{a, b\}, \quad S = \begin{bmatrix} 1\,0\,0\,0 \end{bmatrix}, \quad F = \begin{bmatrix} 0 \\ 0 \\ r_2 \\ 0 \end{bmatrix}, \right.$$

$$E = \begin{bmatrix} p_7 & 0 & 0 & 0 \\ 0 & 0 & p_5 & 0 \\ 0 & 0 & 0 & p_2 \\ 0 & p_3 & 0 & 0 \end{bmatrix}, \quad T_a = \begin{bmatrix} 0 & q_7 & 0 & 0 \\ 0 & 0 & q_5 & 0 \\ 0 & 0 & 0 & 0 \\ 0 & 0 & q_3 & 0 \end{bmatrix}, \quad T_b = \begin{bmatrix} 0 & 0 & 0 & 0 \\ 0 & 0 & 0 & r_5 \\ 0 & 0 & 0 & 0 \\ 0 & 0 & 0 & 0 \end{bmatrix} \right\rangle$$

be a weighted automaton over a $*$-semiring.

Figure 4 shows the result of the transformation and state rewriting that was done in Section 3 now applied to this more general $*$-semiring.

Many details are being glossed over here, specifically the details of Gaussian elimination involving matrices over $*$-semirings but this is well-known in the literature [1].

5.3 More Tapes

This generalization is even more direct and has been described elsewhere [3]. Suppose there are k tapes and that the alphabet for the jth tape is Σ_j. We then form the disjoint union of the $\{\Sigma_j | 1 \leq j \leq k\}$ (This mathematical construction is like a discriminated union in Ada or a tagged union in Pascal and retains a tag that identifies the origin of any symbol). We then perform the construction on the 1-tape automaton where the tape number and the symbol have been encoded in the element of the disjoint union.

If the labels are unpacked after applying the algorithm, the required transducer is produced.

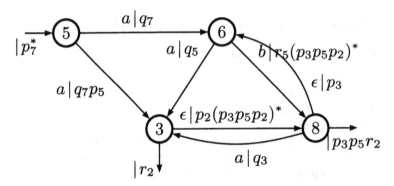

Fig. 4. Example $\overline{M_2}$ for a general ∗-semiring

6   Conclusion

The main observation that follows from the above discussion is that it is possible to collapse the ϵ-loops in a weighted transducer by introducing some new states and transitions. In general, this will result in $O(n^2)$ new transitions being added but in many practical situations, an off-the-shelf sparse matrix technology can be used to produce results that are closer to linear growth.

This algorithm hase been implemented in a simple form in wINR and some experimentation has been done. There is a need to further study the particular heuristics that work best with typical automata encountered in applications.

References

1. R. C. Backhouse and B. A. Carré. Regular Algebra applied to path-finding problems. *Journal of the Institute of Mathematics and its Applications*, 15:161–186, 1975.
2. K. R. Beesley and L. Karttunen. *Finite State Morphology*. CSLI Studies in Computational Linguistics. CSLI Publications, Stanford, CA, 2003. http://www.fsmbook.com.
3. J. Berstel. *Transductions and context-free languages*. BG Teubner, Stuttgart, 1979.
4. A. George and J. W. Liu. *Computer solution of large sparse positive definite systems*. Prentice-Hall, Englewood Cliff, NJ, 1981.
5. J. H. Johnson. INR - a program for computing finite state automata. Unpublished manuscript, 1986.
6. A. Kempe, C. Baeijs, T. Gaál, F. Guingne, and F. Nicart. WFSC - a new weighted finite state compiler. In *Proceedings of CIAA 2003*, pages 108–120, Santa Barbara, CA, 2003.
7. S. Kumar and W. Byrne. A weighted finite state transducer implementation of the alignment template model for statistical machine translation. In *Proceedings of HLT-NAACL 2003*, pages 142–149, Edmonton, Canada, 2003.
8. M. Mohri. Finite-state transducers in language and speech processing. *Computational Linguistics*, 23(2):269–312, 1997.
9. M. Mohri. Generic ϵ-removal algorithm for weighted automata. In *Proceedings of CIAA 2000*, pages 230–242, London, Canada, 2000.

10. M. Mohri. Generic ε-removal and input ε-normalization algorithms for weighted transducers. 2002.

11. M. Mohri, F. Pereira, and M. Riley. The design principles of a weighted finite-state transducer library. *Theoretical Computer Science*, 231(1):17–32, 2000.

12. F. Pereira and M. Riley. Speech recognition by composition of weighted finite automata. In E. Roche and Y. Schabes, editors, *Finite-state Language Processing*, pages 431–453, Cambridge, MA, 1997. The MIT Press.

13. D. J. Rose and R. E. Tarjan. Algorithmic aspects of vertex elimination. In *Proceedings of the 7th ACM Symposium on the Theory of Computing (STOC 1975)*, pages 245–254, 1975.

14. R. E. Tarjan. Fast algorithms for solving path problems. *Journal of the ACM*, 28(3):594–614, 1981.

15. G. van Noord. Treatment of epsilon moves in subset construction. *Computational Linguistics*, 26(1):61–76, 2000.

16. G. van Noord and D. Gerdemann. An extendible regular expression compiler for finite-state approaches in natural language processing. In *Proceedings of WIA '99*, Potsdam, Germany, 2001.

WFSM Auto-intersection and Join Algorithms

A. Kempe[1], J.-M. Champarnaud[2], F. Guingne[1,3], and F. Nicart[1,3]

[1] Xerox Research Centre Europe – Grenoble Laboratory
6 chemin de Maupertuis – 38240 Meylan – France
Andre.Kempe@xrce.xerox.com
http://www.xrce.xerox.com
[2] PSI Laboratory (Université de Rouen, CNRS)
76821 Mont-Saint-Aignan – France
Jean-Marc.Champarnaud@univ-rouen.fr
http://www.univ-rouen.fr/psi/
[3] LIFAR Laboratory (Université de Rouen)
76821 Mont-Saint-Aignan – France
{Franck.Guingne, Florent.Nicart}@univ-rouen.fr
http://www.univ-rouen.fr/LIFAR/

Abstract. The join of two n-ary string relations is a main operation regarding to applications. n-Ary rational string relations are realized by weighted finite-state machines with n tapes. We provide an algorithm that computes the join of two machines via a more simple operation, the auto-intersection. The two operations generally do not preserve rationality. A delay-based algorithm is described for the case of a single tape pair, as well as the class of auto-intersections that it handles. It is generalized to multiple tape pairs and some enhancements are discussed.

1 Introduction

Multi-tape finite-state machines (FSMs) [1,2,3,4,5] are a natural generalization of the familiar finite-state acceptors (one tape) and transducers (two tapes). The n-ary relation defined by a (weighted) FSM is a (weighted) *rational* relation. Finite relations are of particular interest since they can be viewed as relational databases.[1] Multi-tape machines have been used in the morphological analysis of Semitic languages, to synchronize the vowels, consonants, and templatic pattern into a surface form [3,7]. The operation of *join on multiple pairs of tapes*, that is similar to *natural join* of databases, is a crucial operation in many practical applications. In this paper, we focus on its computation through more basic operations such as the auto-intersection. The rationality of a join relation is generally undecidable, and so is the rationality of an auto-intersection relation [6]. In the case of a single pair of tapes, a class Θ of triples $\langle A, i, j \rangle$ can be defined so that the auto-intersection of the machine A w.r.t. tapes i and j can be computed by a delay-based algorithm. This algorithm is generalized to the case of

---

[1] The connection to databases and associated notation was pointed out by J. Eisner in the joint work [6]. We thank him for allowing us to re-use this material.

A. Yli-Jyrä, L. Karttunen, and J. Karhumäki (Eds.): FSMNLP 2005, LNAI 4002, pp. 120–131, 2006.
© Springer-Verlag Berlin Heidelberg 2006

multiple pairs of tapes, leading to a basic algorithm for computing the join of two machines and to an improved version based on the notion of filtering and on the operation of equi-join on a single pair of tapes.

Weighted n-ary relations and their machines are introduced in Section 2. Join and auto-intersection operations are presented in Section 3. A basic algorithm for computing the join of two machines and the embedded auto-intersection algorithm are described in Section 4. We conclude by some enhancements.

2 Definitions

We recall some definitions about n-ary weighted relations and their machines, following the usual definitions for multi-tape automata [2,8], with semiring weights added just as for acceptors and transducers [9,10]. For more details see [6].

Weighted n-Ary Relations: A weighted n-ary relation is a function from $(\Sigma^*)^n$ to $\mathbb{K}$, for a given finite alphabet Σ and a given weight semiring $\mathcal{K} = \langle \mathbb{K}, \oplus, \otimes, \bar{0}, \bar{1} \rangle$. Such a relation assigns a weight to any n-tuple of strings. A weight of $\bar{0}$ means that the tuple is not in the relation.[2] We are especially interested in *rational* (or *regular*) n-ary relations, i.e. relations that can be encoded by n-tape weighted finite-state machines, that we now define. By convention, the names of objects containing n-tuples of strings include a superscript $^{(n)}$.

Multi-tape Weighted Finite-State Machines: An *n-tape weighted finite-state machine* (WFSM or n-WFSM) $A^{(n)}$ is defined by a six-tuple $A^{(n)} = \langle \Sigma, Q, \mathcal{K}, E^{(n)}, \lambda, \varrho \rangle$, with Σ being a finite alphabet, Q a finite set of states, $\mathcal{K} = \langle \mathbb{K}, \oplus, \otimes, \bar{0}, \bar{1} \rangle$ the semiring of weights, $E^{(n)} \subseteq (Q \times (\Sigma^*)^n \times \mathbb{K} \times Q)$ a finite set of weighted n-tape transitions, $\lambda : Q \to \mathbb{K}$ a function that assigns initial weights to states, and $\varrho : Q \to \mathbb{K}$ a function that assigns final weights to states. Any transition $e^{(n)} \in E^{(n)}$ has the form $e^{(n)} = \langle p, \ell^{(n)}, w, n \rangle$. We refer to these four components as the transition's source state $p(e^{(n)}) \in Q$, its label $\ell(e^{(n)}) \in (\Sigma^*)^n$, its weight $w(e^{(n)}) \in \mathbb{K}$, and its target state $n(e^{(n)}) \in Q$. We refer by $E(q)$ to the set of out-going transitions of a state $q \in Q$ (with $E(q) \subseteq E^{(n)}$).

A *path* $\gamma^{(n)}$ of length $k \geq 0$ is a sequence of transitions $e_1^{(n)} e_2^{(n)} \cdots e_k^{(n)}$ such that $n(e_i^{(n)}) = p(e_{i+1}^{(n)})$ for all $i \in [\![1, k{-}1]\!]$. The label of a path is the element-wise concatenation of the labels of its transitions. The weight of a path $\gamma^{(n)}$ from q to q' is the product of the initial weight of q, the weights of the successive transitions and the final weight of q'. The path is said to be *successful*, and to *accept* its label, if $w(\gamma^{(n)}) \neq \bar{0}$. We denote by $\Gamma_{A^{(n)}}$ the set of all successful paths of $A^{(n)}$, and by $\Gamma_{A^{(n)}}(s^{(n)})$ the set of successful paths that accept the n-tuple of strings $s^{(n)}$. The machine $A^{(n)}$ defines a weighted n-ary relation

---

[2] It is convenient to define the *support* of an arbitrary weighted relation $\mathcal{R}^{(n)}$, as being the set of tuples to which the relation gives non-$\bar{0}$ weight.

$\mathcal{R}(A^{(n)}) : (\Sigma^*)^n \to \mathbb{K}$ that assigns to each n-tuple $s^{(n)}$ the total weight of all paths accepting it.

3 Operations

We now describe some central operations on n-ary weighted relations and their n-WFSMs [11]. The auto-intersection operation is introduced, with the aim of simplifying the computation of the join operation. Our notation is inspired by relational databases. Mathematical details can be found in [6].

Simple Operations: Any n-ary weighted rational relation can be constructed by combining the basic rational operations of *union*, *concatenation* and *closure*. Rational operations can be implemented by simple constructions on the corresponding nondeterministic n-tape WFSMs [12]. These n-tape constructions and their semiring-weighted versions are exactly the same as for acceptors and transducers, since they are indifferent to the n-tuple transition labels.

The *projection* operator $\pi_{\langle j_1, \ldots j_m \rangle}$, with $j_1, \ldots j_m \in [\![1, n]\!]$, maps an n-ary relation to an m-ary one by retaining in each tuple components specified by the indices $j_1, \ldots j_m$ and placing them in the specified order. Indices may occur in any order, possibly with repeats. Thus the tapes can be permuted or duplicated: $\pi_{\langle 2,1 \rangle}$ inverts a 2-ary relation. The *complementary projection* operator $\overline{\pi}_{\{j_1, \ldots j_m\}}$ removes the tapes $j_1, \ldots j_m$ and preserves the order of other tapes.

Join Operation: Our *join* operator differs from database join in that database columns are named, whereas our tapes are numbered. Tapes being explicitly selected by number, join is neither associative nor commutative.

For any distinct $i_1, \ldots i_r \in [\![1, n]\!]$ and any distinct $j_1, \ldots j_r \in [\![1, m]\!]$, the *join* operator $\bowtie_{\{i_1 = j_1, \ldots i_r = j_r\}}$ combines an n-ary and an m-ary relation into an $(n + m - r)$-ary relation defined as follows:[3]

$$\left(\mathcal{R}_1^{(n)} \bowtie_{\{i_1 = j_1, \ldots i_r = j_r\}} \mathcal{R}_2^{(m)} \right) (\langle u_1, \ldots u_n, s_1, \ldots s_{m-r} \rangle) =_{\text{def}} \mathcal{R}_1^{(n)}(u^{(n)}) \otimes \mathcal{R}_2^{(m)}(v^{(m)}) \tag{1}$$

$v^{(m)}$ being the unique tuple s. t. $\overline{\pi}_{\{j_1, \ldots j_r\}}(v^{(m)}) = s^{(m-r)}$ and $(\forall k \in [\![1, r]\!])\ v_{j_k} = u_{i_k}$.

The *intersection* of two n-ary relations is the n-ary relation defined by the join operator $\bowtie_{\{1=1, 2=2, \ldots n=n\}}$. A join on a single pair (resp. multiple pairs) of tapes is said to be a *single-pair* (resp. *multi-pair*) one. Examples of single-pair join are the join $\bowtie_{\{1=1\}}$ (the intersection of two acceptors) and the join $\bowtie_{\{2=1\}}$ that can be used to express transducer composition.

A lot of practical applications could not be performed without the multi-tape join operation, for example: multi-tape transduction (mapping n-tuples to m-tuples of strings), probabilistic normalization of n-WFSMs conditioned on multiple tapes,[4] or searching for cognates [14].

---

[3] For example the tuples $\langle abc, def, \epsilon \rangle$ and $\langle def, ghi, \epsilon, jkl \rangle$ combine in the join $\bowtie_{\{2=1, 3=3\}}$ and yield the tuple $\langle abc, def, \epsilon, ghi, jkl \rangle$, with a weight equal to the product of their weights.

[4] This can be obtained by a straightforward generalization of J. Eisner's algorithm for probabilistic normalization of transducers conditioned on one tape [13].

Unfortunately, rational relations are *not* closed under arbitrary joins [6]. For example, transducers are not closed under intersection [1]. The join operation is, however, so useful that it is helpful to have a partial algorithm: hence our motivation for studying auto-intersection.

Auto-intersection: For any distinct $i_1, j_1, \ldots i_r, j_r \in [\![1, n]\!]$, we define an *auto-intersection* operator $\sigma_{\{i_1=j_1, i_2=j_2, \ldots i_r=j_r\}}$. It maps a relation $\mathcal{R}^{(n)}$ to a subset of that relation, preserving tuples $s^{(n)}$ whose elements are equal in pairs as specified, but removing other tuples from the support of the relation:[5]

$$\left(\sigma_{\{i_1=j_1, \ldots i_r=j_r\}}(\mathcal{R}^{(n)})\right)(\langle s_1, \ldots s_n \rangle) =_{\text{def}} \begin{cases} \mathcal{R}^{(n)}(\langle s_1, \ldots s_n \rangle) & \text{if } (\forall k \in [\![1, r]\!]) s_{i_k} = s_{j_k} \\ \bar{0} & \text{otherwise} \end{cases} \quad (2)$$

Auto-intersecting a relation is different from joining it with its own projections. For example, $\sigma_{\{1=2\}}(\mathcal{R}^{(2)})$ is supported by tuples of the form $\langle w, w \rangle \in \mathcal{R}^{(2)}$. By contrast, $\mathcal{R}^{(2)} \bowtie_{\{1=1\}} \left(\pi_{\langle 2 \rangle}(\mathcal{R}^{(2)})\right)$ is supported by tuples $\langle w, x \rangle \in \mathcal{R}^{(2)}$ such that w can also appear on tape 2 of $\mathcal{R}^{(2)}$ (but not necessarily paired with a copy of w on tape 1).[6]

Actually, join and auto-intersection are related by the following equalities:

$$\mathcal{R}_1^{(n)} \bowtie_{\{i_1=j_1, \ldots i_r=j_r\}} \mathcal{R}_2^{(m)} = \overline{\pi}_{\{n+j_1, \ldots n+j_r\}} \left(\sigma_{\{i_1=n+j_1, \ldots i_r=n+j_r\}}(\mathcal{R}_1^{(n)} \times \mathcal{R}_2^{(m)}) \right) \quad (3)$$

$$\sigma_{\{i_1=j_1, \ldots i_r=j_r\}}(\mathcal{R}^{(n)}) = \mathcal{R}^{(n)} \bowtie_{\{i_1=1, j_1=2, \ldots i_r=2r-1, j_r=2r\}} \left(\pi_{\langle 1,1 \rangle}(\Sigma^*)\right)^r \quad (4)$$

Thus, for any class of difficult join instances whose results are non-rational or have undecidable properties [6], there is a corresponding class of difficult auto-intersection instances, and vice-versa. Conversely, a partial solution to one problem would yield a partial solution to the other.

An auto-intersection on a single pair (resp. multiple pairs) of tapes is said to be a *single-pair* (resp. *multi-pair*) one. It may be wise to compute $\sigma_{\{i_1=j_1, \ldots i_r=j_r\}}$ all at once rather than one tape pair at a time, since a sequence of single-pair auto-intersections such as $\sigma_{\{i_r=j_r\}}(\cdots(\sigma_{\{i_1=j_1\}})\cdots)$ could fail due to non-rational intermediate results, even if the final result is rational.[7]

4   Join Via Auto-intersection: A First Construction

Following (3), a multi-pair join can be computed via a multi-pair auto-intersection. A first version of such a join algorithm is presented in this

---

[5] The requirement that the $2r$ indices be distinct mirrors the similar requirement on join and is needed in (4). But it can be evaded by duplicating tapes.

[6] Applying $\sigma_{\{1=2\}}$ to $\{\langle a, b \rangle, \langle b, a \rangle\}$ yields the empty relation, whereas joining it with its own projection (either $\bowtie_{\{1=1\}} \pi_{\langle 2 \rangle}$ or $\bowtie_{\{2=1\}} \pi_{\langle 1 \rangle}$) does not change the relation.

[7] Applying $\sigma_{\{2=3,4=5\}}$ to $\{\langle a^i b^j, c^i, c^j, x, y \rangle \mid i, j \in \mathbb{N}\}$ yields the empty relation, while applying $\sigma_{\{2=3\}}$ yields the non-rational relation $\{\langle a^i b^i, c^i, c^i, x, y \rangle \mid i \in \mathbb{N}\}$.

section. The embedded multi-pair auto-intersection algorithm is a generalization of the single-pair one, that has been proved to work for a specific class
of auto-intersections [15].

4.1   Multi-pair Join: A Basic Algorithm

The Algorithm JOIN1 attempts to construct the join of two WFSMs, $A_1^{(n)}$ and
$A_2^{(m)}$, on multiple pairs of tapes specified by a set of constraints $T = \{t_1 = (i_1 = j_1), \ldots t_r = (i_r = j_r)\}$. We write $\bowtie_T$ instead of $\bowtie_{\{i_1 = j_1, \ldots i_r = j_r\}}$.

$\text{JOIN1}(A_1^{(n)}, A_2^{(m)}, T) \rightarrow A^{(n+m-r)} :$ $[\, T = \{t = (i=j)\};\ |T| = r;\ A^{(n+m-r)} = A_1^{(n)} \bowtie_T A_2^{(m)} \,]$

1     $A^{(n+m)} \leftarrow A_1^{(n)} \times A_2^{(m)}$
2   if $|T| \neq 0$
3   then
4             $A^{(n+m)} \leftarrow \text{AUTOINTERSECTION}(A^{(n+m)}, T)$
5   if $A^{(n+m)} = \bot$ [error code]
6   then return $\bot$
7             $A^{(n+m-r)} \leftarrow \overline{\pi}_{\{n+j_h \mid t_h = (i_h = j_h) \in T\}}(A^{(n+m)})$
8   return $A^{(n+m-r)}$

We compile first the cross-product $A^{(n+m)}$ of $A_1^{(n)}$ and $A_2^{(m)}$. If T is empty,
we simply return the crossproduct $A^{(n+m)}$ (Line 2). Otherwise we compile the
auto-intersection of $A^{(n+m)}$ for all specified pairs of tapes (Line 4). The auto-
intersection may fail and return an error code, in which case the join algorithm
must return an error code as well (Lines 5, 6).

4.2   A Class of Rational Single-Pair Auto-intersections

We now introduce a single-pair auto-intersection algorithm and the class of
bounded delay auto-intersections that this algorithm can handle. For a detailed
exposure see [15].

Although due to Post's Correspondence Problem there exists no fully general
algorithm of auto-intersection [6], $A^{(n)} = \sigma_{\{i=j\}}(A_1^{(n)})$ can be compiled for a class
of triples $\langle A_1^{(n)}, i, j \rangle$ whose definition is based on the notion of *delay* [16,17], i.e.,
the difference of length of two strings of an n-tuple: $\delta_{\langle i,j \rangle}(s^{(n)}) = |s_i| - |s_j|$
(with $i, j \in [\![1, n]\!]$). The delay of a path $\gamma = \gamma_1 \gamma_2 \cdots \gamma_r$, or of any of its factors γ_h,
results from its respective labels on tapes i and j: $\delta_{\langle i,j \rangle}(\gamma) = |\ell_i(\gamma)| - |\ell_j(\gamma)|$. We
call the delay *bounded* if its absolute value does not exceed some limit. A path
has bounded delay if all its prefixes have bounded delay,[8] and an n-WFSM has
bounded delay if all its successful paths have bounded delay.

---

[8] Any finite path has bounded delay (since its label is of finite length). An infinite
path (traversing cycles) may have bounded or unbounded delay. For example, the
delay of a path labeled with $(\langle ab, \varepsilon \rangle \langle \varepsilon, xz \rangle)^h$ is bounded by 2 for any h, whereas that
of a path labeled with $\langle ab, \varepsilon \rangle^h \langle \varepsilon, xz \rangle^h$ is unbounded for $h \longrightarrow \infty$.

We construct $A^{(n)}$ without creating invalid paths with $\ell_i(\gamma) \neq \ell_j(\gamma)$, which is equivalent to creating them with $w(\gamma) = \bar{0}$. Thus, all paths of $A^{(n)}$ have a delay equal to 0 : Let Γ^0 be the set of accepting paths of $A_1^{(n)}$ with a 0-delay. Then it holds: $\Gamma_{A^{(n)}} \subseteq \Gamma^0 \subseteq \Gamma_{A_1^{(n)}}$. The sum of the delays of the factors of a path is equal to its delay, and it holds: $\forall \gamma = \gamma_1 \gamma_2 \cdots \gamma_r \in \Gamma^0$, $\delta_{\langle i,j \rangle}(\gamma) = \sum_{h=1}^{r} \delta_{\langle i,j \rangle}(\gamma_h) = 0$.

Let us traverse $A_1^{(n)}$ in-depth,[9] both left-to-right and right-to-left, and memorize the global maxima $\hat{\delta}_{\langle i,j \rangle}^{LR}(A_1^{(n)})$ and $\hat{\delta}_{\langle i,j \rangle}^{RL}(A_1^{(n)})$, and global minima $\check{\delta}_{\langle i,j \rangle}^{LR}(A_1^{(n)})$ and $\check{\delta}_{\langle i,j \rangle}^{RL}(A_1^{(n)})$ of the delay on any path. Let us then observe the delay along a path $\gamma \in \Gamma^0$: It would begin and end with $\delta_{\langle i,j \rangle} = 0$, and have a global maximum $\hat{\delta}_{\langle i,j \rangle}(\gamma)$ and a global minimum $\check{\delta}_{\langle i,j \rangle}(\gamma)$.

Proposition 1. *Let Θ be the class of all the triples $\langle A_1^{(n)}, i, j \rangle$ such that $A_1^{(n)}$ does not contain a path traversing both a cycle with positive delay and a cycle with negative delay (w.r.t. tapes i and j). Then for all paths $\gamma \in \Gamma_{A^{(n)}}$ of $A^{(n)} = \sigma_{\{i=j\}}(A_1^{(n)})$, the delay is bounded by*

$$\delta_{\langle i,j \rangle}^{\max} = \max(\ |\hat{\delta}_{\langle i,j \rangle}^{LR}(A_1^{(n)})|,\ |\hat{\delta}_{\langle i,j \rangle}^{RL}(A_1^{(n)})|,\ |\check{\delta}_{\langle i,j \rangle}^{LR}(A_1^{(n)})|,\ |\check{\delta}_{\langle i,j \rangle}^{RL}(A_1^{(n)})|\ ) \quad (5)$$

Proof. If a path $\gamma \in \Gamma^0$ has only cycles with positive delay, traversing a cycle raises the delays in γ's suffix. These cycles have, however, no impact on the delays in the in-depth traversals, where cycles are not traversed. Therefore $(\ \check{\delta}_{\langle i,j \rangle}^{LR}(A_1^{(n)}) \leq \check{\delta}_{\langle i,j \rangle}(\gamma) \leq 0\ )$ and $(\ \hat{\delta}_{\langle i,j \rangle}^{RL}(A_1^{(n)}) \geq \hat{\delta}_{\langle i,j \rangle}(\gamma) \geq 0\ )$ which means

$$\forall \gamma \in \Gamma^0,\ \max(\ |\hat{\delta}_{\langle i,j \rangle}(\gamma)|, |\check{\delta}_{\langle i,j \rangle}(\gamma)|\ ) \ \leq\ \max(\ |\check{\delta}_{\langle i,j \rangle}^{LR}(A_1^{(n)})|, |\hat{\delta}_{\langle i,j \rangle}^{RL}(A_1^{(n)})|\ ) \quad (6)$$

This still holds if we also admit cycles with 0-delay on γ, since traversing them has no impact on the delays of γ's suffix. If all cycles of γ had negative or 0-delay instead, we would obtain

$$\forall \gamma \in \Gamma^0,\ \max(\ |\hat{\delta}_{\langle i,j \rangle}(\gamma)|, |\check{\delta}_{\langle i,j \rangle}(\gamma)|\ ) \ \leq\ \max(\ |\hat{\delta}_{\langle i,j \rangle}^{RL}(A_1^{(n)})|, |\check{\delta}_{\langle i,j \rangle}^{LR}(A_1^{(n)})|\ ) \quad (7)$$

Since $\Gamma_{A^{(n)}} \subseteq \Gamma^0$, (6) (7) and Proposition 1 hold for all paths $\gamma \in \Gamma_{A^{(n)}}$. ∎

Joining $A_1^{(n)}$ beforehand with its own (neutrally weighted) projections yields a superset of $A^{(n)}$: $\text{support}((A_1^{(n)} \bowtie_{\{i=1\}} \pi_{\langle j \rangle}(A_1^{(n)})) \bowtie_{\{j=1\}} \pi_{\langle i \rangle}(A_1^{(n)})) \supseteq \text{support}(A^{(n)})$. The triple $\langle A_1^{(n)}, i, j \rangle$ is placed into Θ, as soon as this operation removes from $A_1^{(n)}$ all cycles in conflict with Θ. This method is referred to as *filtering* and performed prior to any auto-intersection (it is the function FILTERTAPEPAIRS of the Algorithm AUTOINTERSECTION in Section 4.4). Based on Proposition 1, an algorithm can be designed to compute $\sigma_{\{i=j\}}(A_1^{(n)})$ as far as $\langle A_1^{(n)}, i, j \rangle \in \Theta$. This algorithm is now described in a more general case.

---

[9] We optionally trim the automaton to restrict it to accepting paths. Then, to find (for example) $\hat{\delta}_{\langle i,j \rangle}^{LR}$, we exhaustively explore all acyclic paths from the start state, and record the maximum delay on any path prefix. This takes exponential time in general, which is unavoidable since the longest-acyclic-path problem is NP-complete.

4.3   Multi-pair Auto-intersection: A Basic Construction

Our construction bears resemblance to known transducer synchronization pro-
cedures [16,17]. However the algorithm of Frougny and Sakarovitch [16] is based
on a $\mathbb{K}$-covering of the transducer and it works only for non-empty input labels
whereas our single-pair auto-intersection algorithm supports unrestricted labeling. Our algorithm is based on a general reachability-driven construction, as it is
the case for the synchronization algorithm of Mohri [17]. But the labeling of the
transitions is quite different since our algorithm performs a copy of the original
labeling, and we also construct only such paths whose delay does not exceed
some limit that we are able to determine.

We now address the case of a multi-pair auto-intersection $\sigma_{\{i_1=j_1,\ldots i_r=j_r\}}$ such
that for all $h \in [\![1,r]\!]$, $\langle A_1^{(n)}, i_h, j_h \rangle \in \Theta$. As an example, we consider the WFSM
$A_1^{(4)}$ in Figure 1a and the auto-intersection $\sigma_{\{1=2,3=4\}}(A_1^{(4)})$, with $\langle A_1^{(4)}, 1, 2 \rangle \in \Theta$
and $\langle A_1^{(4)}, 3, 4 \rangle \in \Theta$; the associated delay limits are $\delta_{\langle 1,2 \rangle}^{max} = 1$ and $\delta_{\langle 3,4 \rangle}^{max} = 2$.
The support $(a{:}a{:}dc{:}cd \cup a{:}\varepsilon{:}c{:}\varepsilon)^* (ba{:}ab{:}c{:}\varepsilon)^* \varepsilon{:}a{:}\varepsilon{:}cc$ of $A_1^{(4)}$ is equal to the set
$\{ \langle a^{i+j}(ba)^h, a^i(ab)^h a, ([dc]^i \sqcup c^j)c^h, (cd)^i c^2 \rangle \mid i,j,h \in \mathbb{N} \}$.[10]

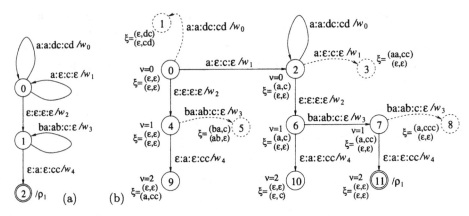

Fig. 1. (a) A WFSM $A_1^{(4)}$ and (b) its auto-intersection $A^{(4)} = \sigma_{\{1=2,3=4\}}(A_1^{(4)})$ (dashed
parts are not constructed)

We construct simultaneously the two auto-intersections $\sigma_{\{1=2\}}$ and $\sigma_{\{3=4\}}$. We
copy states and transitions one by one from $A_1^{(4)}$ (Figure 1a) to $A^{(4)}$ (Figure 1b),
starting with the initial state $q_1 = 0$. We assign to each state q of $A^{(4)}$ two
variables: $\nu[q] = q_1$ is the corresponding state q_1 of $A_1^{(4)}$, and $\xi[q] = (s^{(r)}, u^{(r)})$
expresses the leftover string tuple $s^{(r)}$ (resp. $u^{(r)}$) from the tapes $\langle i_1, \ldots i_r \rangle$
(resp. $\langle j_1, \ldots j_r \rangle$), yet unmatched on the tapes $\langle j_1, \ldots j_r \rangle$ (resp. $\langle i_1, \ldots i_r \rangle$). In
particular, we have: $\nu[0] = 0$ and $\xi[0] = (\langle \varepsilon, \varepsilon \rangle, \langle \varepsilon, \varepsilon \rangle)$.

---

[10] A square-bracketted string cannot be split by shuffle: in $([ab]^i \sqcup [cd]^j)$, any number
of cd can occur between two occurrences of ab, but not inside one ab.

$\text{AUTOINTERSECTMULTIPAIR}(A_1^{(n)}, i^{(r)}, j^{(r)}, (\delta_{(i,j)}^{max})^{(r)}) \rightarrow A^{(n)}$:

1    $A^{(n)} \leftarrow \langle \Sigma \leftarrow \Sigma_1, Q \leftarrow \emptyset, \mathcal{K} \leftarrow \mathcal{K}_1, E^{(n)} \leftarrow \emptyset, \lambda, \rho \rangle$

2    $Stack \leftarrow \emptyset$

3   for $\forall q_1 \in Q_1 : \lambda(q_1) \neq \bar{0}$ do

4        $\text{GETPUSHSTATE}(q_1, (\varepsilon^{(r)}, \varepsilon^{(r)}))$

5   while $Stack \neq \emptyset$ do

6        $q \leftarrow pop(Stack)$

7        $q_1 \leftarrow \nu[q]$

8        $(s^{(r)}, u^{(r)}) \leftarrow \xi[q]$

9   for $\forall e_1 \in E(q_1)$ do

10            $(s'^{(r)}, u'^{(r)}) \leftarrow \text{GETLEFTOVERSTRINGS}(s^{(r)} \cdot \pi_{i^{(r)}}(\ell(e_1)), u^{(r)} \cdot \pi_{j^{(r)}}(\ell(e_1)))$

11   if $\forall h \in [1, r] : (s'_h = \varepsilon \vee u'_h = \varepsilon) \wedge (||s'_h| - |u'_h|| \leq (\delta_{(i_h, j_h)}^{max})_h)$

12   then $q' \leftarrow \text{GETPUSHSTATE}(n(e_1), (s'^{(r)}, u'^{(r)}))$

13                    $E \leftarrow E \cup \{ \langle q, \ell(e_1), w(e_1), q' \rangle \}$

14   return $A^{(n)}$

$\text{GETLEFTOVERSTRINGS}(\acute{s}^{(r)}, \acute{u}^{(r)}) \rightarrow (s'^{(r)}, u'^{(r)})$:

15    $x^{(r)} \leftarrow longestCommonPrefix(\acute{s}^{(r)}, \acute{u}^{(r)})$

16   return $((x^{(r)})^{-1} \cdot \acute{s}^{(r)}, (x^{(r)})^{-1} \cdot \acute{u}^{(r)})$

$\text{GETPUSHSTATE}(q_1, (s'^{(r)}, u'^{(r)})) \rightarrow q'$:

17   if $\exists q \in Q : \nu[q] = q_1 \wedge \xi[q] = (s'^{(r)}, u'^{(r)})$

18   then $q' \leftarrow q$

19   else $q' \leftarrow createNewState()$

20            $\nu[q'] \leftarrow q_1$

21            $\xi[q'] \leftarrow (s'^{(r)}, u'^{(r)})$

22   if $s'^{(r)} = \varepsilon^{(r)} \wedge u'^{(r)} = \varepsilon^{(r)}$

23   then $\lambda(q') \leftarrow \lambda(q_1)$

24                    $\rho(q') \leftarrow \rho(q_1)$

25   else $\lambda(q') \leftarrow \bar{0}$

26                    $\rho(q') \leftarrow \bar{0}$

27            $Q \leftarrow Q \cup \{q'\}$

28            $push(Stack, q')$

29   return q'

Then, we attempt to copy the three outgoing transitions of $q_1 = 0$ with their original labels and weights, as well as their respective target states. The $\xi[n(e)]$ of the target state of a transition e results from the $\xi[p(e)]$ of its source state, concatenated with the relevant components of its label $\ell(e)$. The longest common prefix[11] of the two string tuples in $\xi[n(e)]$ is removed. A target q that has the same $\nu[q]$ and $\xi[q]$ as an existing state q', it is not created and q' is used instead. For example, for the cyclic transition e on $q = 2$ (Figure 1b), the leftover tuples of the source, $\xi[p(e)] = (\langle a, c \rangle, \langle \varepsilon, \varepsilon \rangle)$, are concatenated with the relevant

---

[11]   The longest common prefix of two string tuples is compiled element-wise.

projections of the label, $\pi_{\langle 1,3 \rangle}(\ell(e)) = \langle a, dc \rangle$ and $\pi_{\langle 2,4 \rangle}(\ell(e)) = \langle a, cd \rangle$, yielding $\xi' = (\langle aa, cdc \rangle, \langle a, cd \rangle)$; since $lcp(\xi') = \langle a, cd \rangle$, the leftover tuples of the target are finally $\xi[n(e)] = (\langle a, c \rangle, \langle \varepsilon, \varepsilon \rangle)$, which implies that $p(e) = n(e)$.

State $q = 3$ (resp. $q = 1$) and its incoming transition are not created because $\delta^{max}_{\langle 1,2 \rangle}$ is exceeded (resp. dc and cd are incompatible leftover strings). State $q = 9$ is non-final, although $\nu[9] = 2$ is final, because its leftover tuples are not $(\langle \varepsilon, \varepsilon \rangle, \langle \varepsilon, \varepsilon \rangle)$. As expected, the support $a{:}\varepsilon{:}c{:}\varepsilon$ $(a{:}a{:}dc{:}cd)^*$ $ba{:}ab{:}c{:}\varepsilon$ $\varepsilon{:}a{:}\varepsilon{:}cc$ of the auto-intersection is equal to the set $\{\langle a^{i+1}ba, a^{i+1}ba, (cd)^i c^2, (cd)^i c^2 \rangle \mid i \in \mathbb{N}\}$.

Algorithm: The Algorithm AUTOINTERSECTMULTIPAIR computes the auto-intersection $\sigma_{\{i_1 = j_1, \ldots i_r = j_r\}}$ in the case where $\forall h \in [1, r]$, $\langle A_1^{(n)}, i_h, j_h \rangle \in \Theta$. The tape indices are specified in two tuples, $i^{(r)} = \langle i_1, \ldots i_r \rangle$ and $j^{(r)} = \langle j_1, \ldots j_r \rangle$, that are also used for projection, $\pi_{i^{(r)}} = \pi_{\langle i_1, \ldots i_r \rangle}$. The delay limits, related to the two index tuples, are specified in one tuple, $(\delta^{max}_{\langle i,j \rangle})^{(r)} = \langle (\delta^{max}_{\langle i_1,j_1 \rangle})_1, \ldots (\delta^{max}_{\langle i_r,j_r \rangle})_r \rangle$. The function GETPUSHSTATE checks whether a target state already exists or not; a new state is created if necessary and pushed onto the stack.

The construction of $A^{(n)} = \sigma_{\{i_1 = j_1, \ldots i_r = j_r\}}(A_1^{(n)})$ is guaranteed to terminate because each auto-intersection $\sigma_{\{i_h = j_h\}}$ terminates. Only such states are created for $\sigma_{\{i_1 = j_1, \ldots i_r = j_r\}}$, that would also have been created for each $\sigma_{\{i_h = j_h\}}$ separately. Therefore, the number $|Q|$ of states in $A^{(n)}$ cannot exceed that of each separate auto-intersection. Finally we get $|Q| < 2 |Q_1| \frac{|\Sigma_1|^{\min(\delta^{max}_{\langle i_h,j_h \rangle})} - 1}{|\Sigma_1| - 1}$.

4.4   Multi-pair Auto-intersection: Iterative Construction

We now address the case of a multi-pair auto-intersection $\sigma_{\{i_1 = j_1, \ldots i_r = j_r\}}$ such that there may exist $h \in [1, r]$ with $\langle A_1^{(n)}, i_h, j_h \rangle \notin \Theta$. As an example we consider the WFSM $A_1^{(4)}$ of Figure 2a and the auto-intersection $\sigma_{\{1=2,3=4\}}(A_1^{(4)})$. The support $(a{:}a{:}dc{:}cd \;\cup\; a{:}\varepsilon{:}c{:}\varepsilon)^*$ $(ba{:}ab{:}c{:}\varepsilon)^*$ $\varepsilon{:}a{:}\varepsilon{:}c$ of $A_1^{(4)}$ is equal to the set $\{ \langle a^{i+j}(ba)^h, a^i(ab)^h a, ([dc]^i \sqcup c^j), (cd)^i c^h c \rangle \mid i, j, h \in \mathbb{N} \}$. Since $\langle A_1^{(4)}, 1, 2 \rangle \in \Theta$ with $\delta^{max}_{\langle 1,2 \rangle} = 1$ and $\langle A_1^{(4)}, 3, 4 \rangle \notin \Theta$, $\sigma_{\{1=2\}}(A_1^{(4)})$ is first compiled (Figure 2b); its support $(a{:}a{:}dc{:}cd)^* a{:}\varepsilon{:}c{:}\varepsilon$ $(a{:}a{:}dc{:}cd)^*(ba{:}ab{:}c{:}\varepsilon)^* a{:}\varepsilon{:}\varepsilon{:}c$ is the set $\{ \langle a^{i+j+1}(ba)^h, a^{i+j+1}(ba)^h, (dc)^i(cd)^j c, (cd)^i(cd)^j c^{h+1} \rangle \mid i, j, h \in \mathbb{N} \}$.   Since $\langle \sigma_{\{1=2\}}(A_1^{(4)}), 3, 4 \rangle \in \Theta$ with $\delta^{max}_{\langle 3,4 \rangle} = 2$, we now can compile the second auto-intersection (Figure 2c), whose support $a{:}\varepsilon{:}c{:}\varepsilon$ $(a{:}a{:}dc{:}cd)^*$ $\varepsilon{:}a{:}\varepsilon{:}c$ is equal to the set $\{ \langle a^{i+1}, a^{i+1}, (cd)^i c, (cd)^i c \rangle \mid i \in \mathbb{N} \}$.

Algorithm: The Algorithm AUTOINTERSECTION attempts to construct iteratively the auto-intersection $\sigma_T(A_1^{(n)})$ on tape pairs specified by the set T. The function FILTERTAPEPAIRS implements the filtering of $\sigma_T(A_1^{(n)})$ and the function SELECTTAPEPAIRS selects tapes satisfying $\langle A_1^{(n)}, i, j \rangle \in \Theta$. The function COMPILEDELAYLIMIT computes the limit $\delta^{max}_{\langle i,j \rangle}$.

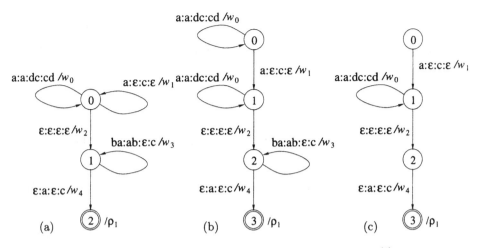

Fig. 2. Iterative compilation of auto-intersection: (a) a WFSM $A_1^{(4)}$, (b) its auto-intersection $\sigma_{\{1=2\}}(A_1^{(4)})$, and (c) a second auto-intersection $\sigma_{\{3=4\}}(\sigma_{\{1=2\}}(A_1^{(4)}))$

AUTOINTERSECTION$(A_1^{(n)}, T) \rightarrow A^{(n)}$: $[\ T = \{t=(i=j)\}\,;\ A^{(n)} = \sigma_T(A_1^{(n)})\ ]$

1    $A^{(n)} \leftarrow A_1^{(n)}$
2   while $T \neq \emptyset$ do
3        $A^{(n)} \leftarrow$ FILTERTAPEPAIRS$(A^{(n)}, T)$
4        $T' \leftarrow$ SELECTTAPEPAIRS$(A^{(n)}, T)$
5   if $T' = \emptyset$
6   then return $\perp$ [error code]
7   else $i^{(r=0)} \leftarrow j^{(r=0)} \leftarrow (\delta_{\langle i,j\rangle}^{\max})^{(r=0)} \leftarrow \langle\ \rangle$
8   for $\forall t = (i=j) \in T'$ do
9                    $\delta_{\langle i,j\rangle}^{\max} \leftarrow$ COMPILEDELAYLIMIT$(A^{(n)}, i, j)$
10                   $i^{(r+1)} \leftarrow$ append$(\ i^{(r)}, i\ )$
11                   $j^{(r+1)} \leftarrow$ append$(\ j^{(r)}, j\ )$
12                   $(\delta_{\langle i,j\rangle}^{\max})^{(r+1)} \leftarrow$ append$(\ (\delta_{\langle i,j\rangle}^{\max})^{(r)}, \delta_{\langle i,j\rangle}^{\max}\ )$
13               $A^{(n)} \leftarrow$ AUTOINTERSECTMULTIPAIR$(A^{(n)}, i^{(r)}, j^{(r)}, (\delta_{\langle i,j\rangle}^{\max})^{(r)})$
14               $T \leftarrow T \setminus T'$
15   return $A^{(n)}$

As long as T is not empty (Line 2), the algorithm filters all tape pairs (see Section 4.2) then selects all constraints $t = (i = j)$ on which the auto-intersection is constructible (Line 4), and compiles a limit of the delay $\delta_{\langle i,j\rangle}^{\max}$ for each of those pairs (Line 8–9). Finally, it constructs an auto-intersection simultaneously on all selected pairs (Line 10–13). In the next iteration, it tries the same for the set of remaining pairs (Line 14, 2). The test of constructibility may now succeed on a pair of tapes on which it previously failed, because the cycles that made it fail may have disappeared in between. The algorithm terminates either successfully if all tape pairs can been processed ($T = \emptyset$) or not if some pairs remain ($T \neq \emptyset \wedge T' = \emptyset$). In the latter case, an error code is returned (Line 5–6).

5   Conclusion

We conclude by briefly describing an improved version of the Algorithm JOIN1. It is based on the operation of single-pair equi-join.[12] A single-pair join $A_1^{(n)} \bowtie_{\{i=j\}} A_2^{(m)}$ can be compiled in one step, rather than first building the cross-product, $A_1^{(n)} \times A_2^{(m)}$, and then deleting most of its paths by the auto-intersection $\sigma_{\{i=n+j\}}$. Our single-pair join algorithm is very similar to the classical transducer composition; it simulates the behaviour of an ε-filter (cf [10]) for aligning ε-transitions in the two transducers.

The improved join algorithm selects arbitrarily one pair of tapes and performs on it a single-pair equi-join (that always yields a rational result, at least for weights over a commutative semiring) followed by an auto-intersection for the remaining pairs (that may fail). So far we found no evidence that would allow us to decide whether the choice of the first pair of tapes, that is used in the equi-join, matters for the success of the whole algorithm.

Acknowledgments

We wish to thank Jason Eisner for allowing us to use a bulk of relevant notation that he elaborated (cf. Footnote 1), Mark-Jan Nederhof for pointing out the relationship between auto-intersection and Post's Correspondence Problem (personal communication), and the anonymous reviewers of our paper for their valuable advice.

References

1. Rabin, M.O., Scott, D.: Finite automata and their decision problems. IBM Journal of Research and Development **3** (1959) 114–125
2. Elgot, C.C., Mezei, J.E.: On relations defined by generalized finite automata. IBM Journal of Research and Development **9** (1965) 47–68
3. Kay, M.: Nonconcatenative finite-state morphology. In: Proc. 3rd Int. Conf. EACL, Copenhagen, Denmark (1987) 2–10
4. Harju, T., Karhumäki, J.: The equivalence problem of multitape finite automata. Theoretical Computer Science **78** (1991) 347–355
5. Kaplan, R.M., Kay, M.: Regular models of phonological rule systems. Computational Linguistics **20** (1994) 331–378
6. Kempe, A., Champarnaud, J.M., Eisner, J.: A note on join and auto-intersection of n-ary rational relations. In Watson, B., Cleophas, L., eds.: Proc. Eindhoven FASTAR Days. Number 04–40 in TU/e CS TR, Eindhoven, Netherlands (2004) 64–78
7. Kiraz, G.A.: Multitiered nonlinear morphology using multitape finite automata: a case study on Syriac and Arabic. Computational Lingistics **26** (2000) 77–105
8. Eilenberg, S.: Automata, Languages, and Machines. Volume A. Academic Press, San Diego (1974)

---

[12] According to database notation an equi-join does not discard any tape.

9. Kuich, W., Salomaa, A.: Semirings, Automata, Languages. Number 5 in EATCS Monographs on Theoretical Computer Science. Springer Verlag, Berlin, Germany (1986)

10. Mohri, M., Pereira, F.C.N., Riley, M.: A rational design for a weighted finite-state transducer library. Lecture Notes in Computer Science **1436** (1998) 144–158

11. Kempe, A., Guingne, F., Nicart, F.: Algorithms for weighted multi-tape automata. Research report 2004/031, Xerox Research Centre Europe, Meylan, France (2004)

12. Rosenberg, A.L.: On n-tape finite state acceptors. In: IEEE Symposium on Foundations of Computer Science (FOCS). (1964) 76–81

13. Eisner, J.: Parameter estimation for probabilistic finite-state transducers. In: Proc. of the 40th Annual Meeting of the Association for Computational Linguistics, Philadelphia (2002)

14. Kempe, A.: NLP applications based on weighted multi-tape automata. In: Proc. 11th Conf. TALN, Fes, Morocco (2004) 253–258

15. Kempe, A., Champarnaud, J.M., Eisner, J., Guingne, F., Nicart, F.: A class of rational n-WFSM auto-intersections. In Ibarra, O.H., Dang, Z., eds.: Proc. 10th Int. Conf. CIAA, Sophia Antipolis, France (2005) *(to appear)*.

16. Frougny, C., Sakarovitch, J.: Synchronized rational relations of finite and infinite words. Theoretical Computer Science **108** (1993) 45–82

17. Mohri, M.: Edit-distance of weighted automata. In: Proc. 7th Int. Conf. CIAA (2002). Volume 2608 of Lecture Notes in Computer Science., Tours, France, Springer Verlag, Berlin, Germany (2003) 1–23

Further Results on Syntactic Ambiguity of Internal Contextual Grammars

Lakshmanan Kuppusamy

School of Technology and Computer Science
Tata Institute of Fundamental Research
Homi Bhabha Road, Colaba
Mumbai - 400 005, India
laksh@tifr.res.in

Abstract. Ambiguity plays an important role in checking the relevances of formalism for natural language processing. As contextual grammars were shown to be an appropriate description for natural languages, analyzing syntactic ambiguity of contextual grammars deserves a special attention. The levels of ambiguity of internal contextual grammars are defined depending on the information used for describing a derivation. In this paper, we continue the study on ambiguity of internal contextual grammars which was investigated in [3] and [13]. We achieve solutions to the following open problems addressed in the above papers. For each $(i,j) \in \{(2,1),(1,0),(0,1)\}$, are there languages which are inherently i-ambiguous with respect to grammars with arbitrary selector, but j-ambiguous with respect to grammars with finite selector?

1 Introduction

The syntactic and semantic analysis of natural language processing has a wide range of application to many areas including artificial intelligence, where the knowledge representation is very crucial for simulating the human understanding. In syntactic analysis of natural languages, if one wants to check the relevance of formal description (i.e. parsing), then ambiguity is the most important question since ambiguity of any programming or natural language is the most difficult barrier to the development of robust, efficient and powerful language technology. We consider contextual grammars, an appropriate model for syntax of natural languages [11], to investigate the syntactic ambiguity of the grammar.

Contextual grammars were introduced by Marcus in 1969 [9] as 'intrinsic grammars', without auxiliary symbols, based on the fundamental linguistic operation of inserting words in given phrases, according to certain contextual dependencies [8]. More precisely, contextual grammars produce languages starting from a finite set of *axioms* and adjoining *contexts*, iteratively, according to the *selector* present in the current sentential form. As introduced in [9], adjoining the contexts are done at the ends of the strings. Internal contextual grammars were introduced by Păun and Nguyen in 1980 [17], where the contexts are adjoined to the selector strings appeared as substrings of the derived string. Later on,

A. Yli-Jyrä, L. Karttunen, and J. Karhumäki (Eds.): FSMNLP 2005, LNAI 4002, pp. 132–143, 2006.
© Springer-Verlag Berlin Heidelberg 2006

many variants of contextual grammars were introduced consequently by imposing restriction to the selectors, viz., *maximal use of selector* [10], *depth-first* [12].
For more technical details and comprehensive study on contextual grammars,
we refer to [15] and the monograph on contextual grammars by Gh. Păun [16].

We now recall some results from previous papers on contextual grammars
where the aim was given to analyze the relevances with natural languages. In
[11], it was shown that contextual grammars can be considered as a good model
for natural languages and when some restriction is imposed on the selector of
the grammar, the grammars were able to straightforwardly describe all the usual
restrictions appearing in natural and artificial languages, which lead to the *non-
context-freeness* of these languages, which are *reduplication, crossed dependencies, and multiple agreements*. Some other classes of contextual grammars were
also shown to generate the non-context-free constructions, refer [4], [6], [7]. In
fact, these classes of languages were shown to satisfy the properties of *mildly
context sensitive* (*MCS*) languages [5], which are (i) they contain non-context-
free constructions, (ii) they are *parsable* in polynomial time, (iii) they contain
semilinear languages only. Showing such a result is very significant in natural
languages since the formalism of *MCS* resembles natural languages to a greater
extent. Besides, in [2] some variants of contextual grammars were translated into
equivalent *range concatenation grammars* [1] and thus the classes of contextual
grammars can be parsed in polynomial time. With the information provided
above we can conclude that contextual grammars provide an appropriate model
for the description of natural languages. So, analyzing ambiguity of contextual
grammars would substantially contribute to natural languages also.

For any class of grammars, the natural and important question that can be
raised is (syntactic) ambiguity of the grammar. Generally, the ambiguity for
a grammar is defined as given a grammar, are there words in the generated
language have two distinct derivations? For Chomsky grammars, the notion of
ambiguity is clear, but defining ambiguity for contextual grammars is not so
obvious since the derivation of contextual grammars consists many components
such as axioms, contexts, selectors. Based on the information used for describing a derivation, five levels of ambiguity for internal contextual grammars were
defined in [13]. The information are based on the components of contextual grammars and they are: (1) the axiom and the contexts used in the derivation but not
their order; (2) the axiom, the contexts and the selectors used in the derivation
(but not their order); (3) considering order in (1); (4) considering order in (3);
and (5) the axiom, the contexts and also the places where they are used in the
derivation. Consequently, a new type of ambiguity called *0-ambiguity* was introduced in [3] by taking into the account of axioms only. There are many open
problems addressed in [3], [13] on different aspects of ambiguity including the
one on 'inherent ambiguity' of internal contextual grammars. We also refer to
section 7.5 of [16] for an extensive study of the ambiguity of internal contextual
grammars.

In this paper, we make an attempt to solve the open problems which are
based on 'inherently 1-ambiguous' and 'inherently 2-ambiguous'. For internal

contextual grammar, we cannot find any inherently 2-ambiguous language which is 1-unambiguous, but for depth-first contextual grammars (a variant of internal contextual grammars), we are able to show that there are inherently 2-ambiguous languages which are 1-unambiguous. The result on 'inherently 1-ambiguous' is also interesting because, earlier the result on inherently 1-ambiguous was proved for internal contextual grammars without choice only and here we (im)prove it for grammars with choice. We prove the similar existence result of 'inherently 1-ambiguous' for deterministic contextual grammars.

This paper is organized as follows: Section 2 encompasses the preliminaries in formal language theory, contextual grammars and the types of ambiguity in internal contextual grammars; Section 3 reminiscences the related results on ambiguity of internal contextual grammars and their open problems; Section 4 presents the main results of this paper which are solutions to the open problems addressed in [3], [13] and Section 5 concludes the paper with the final remarks.

2   Preliminaries

In this section, we start with introducing some formal language theory notions which are used in this paper. A finite non-empty set V is called an *alphabet*. We denote by V^* the free monoid generated by V, by λ its identity or the *empty string*, and by V^+ the set $V^* - \{\lambda\}$. The elements of V^* are called *words* or *strings*. For more details on formal language theory, we refer to [18].

Now we shall see some basic definitions of contextual grammars. An *internal contextual grammar with choice* is a construct $G = (V, A, (S_1, C_1), ...(S_n, C_n))$, $n \geq 1$, where

- V is a finite set of *alphabets*,
- $A \subseteq V^*$ is a finite set called the set of *axioms*,
- $S_i \subseteq V^*$, $1 \leq i \leq n$, are the sets of *selectors* or *choice*,
- $C_i \subseteq V^* \times V^*$, C_i finite, $1 \leq i \leq n$, are the sets of *contexts*.

The usual derivation in the *internal mode* is defined as

$$x \Longrightarrow_{in} y \text{ iff } x = x_1 x_2 x_3, y = x_1 u x_2 v x_3, \text{ for } x_1, x_2, x_3 \in V^*, x_2 \in S_i, (u, v) \in C_i,$$

for some $1 \leq i \leq n$. The language generated by the above grammar G is given as

$$L_{in}(G) = \{x \in V^* \mid w \Longrightarrow_{in}^* x, \ w \in A\},$$

where $\Longrightarrow_{in}^*$ is the reflexive transitive closure of the relation $\Longrightarrow_{in}$.

When all the selectors S_i's are empty, G is said to be internal contextual grammar *without choice*. In such a case, we can apply any context $(u, v) \in C_i$, $1 \leq i \leq n$, to any substrings of the derivation as there is no specified selector.

A contextual grammar G is said to be *deterministic* if and only if for every selector in G there exists at most only one corresponding context (u, v) in G. That is, $Card(C_i) \leq 1$ for $1 \leq i \leq n$.

Depth-first contextual grammars were introduced by Martin-Vide *et. al.* in [12]. In depth-first contextual grammars, at each derivation step (except the first derivation), at least one of the contexts u or v which was introduced in the previous derivation must be a subword of the currently used selector. More formally, given a contextual grammar $G = (V, A, (S_1, C_1), \ldots, (S_n, C_n))$, $n \geq 1$, the *depth-first derivation* in G as a derivation $w_1 \Longrightarrow_{df} w_2 \Longrightarrow_{df} \cdots \Longrightarrow_{df} w_m$, $m \geq 1$, where

(i) $w_1 \in A$, $w_1 \Longrightarrow w_2$ in the usual sense,
(ii) for each $i = 2, 3, \ldots, m$, if $w_{i-1} = x_1 x_2 x_3$, $w_i = x_1 u x_2 v x_3$ ((u, v) is the context adjoined to w_{i-1} in order to get w_i), then $w_i = y_1 y_2 y_3$, $w_{i+1} = y_1 u' y_2 v' y_3$, such that $y_2 \in S_j$, $(u', v') \in C_j$, for some j, $1 \leq j \leq n$, and y_2 contains one of the contexts u or v (which were adjoined in the previous derivation) as a substring.

The set of all words generated by a grammar G in this way is denoted by $L_{df}(G)$.

Now, we formally define the ambiguity for internal contextual grammars and the types of ambiguity of them. Given a contextual grammar $G = (V, A, (S_1, C_1), \ldots, (S_n, C_n)$ and a derivation δ of a word z is given by

$$\delta = w_1 \Longrightarrow_{in} w_2 \Longrightarrow_{in} \cdots \Longrightarrow_{in} w_m = z, \ m \geq 1, \text{ such that } w_1 \in A \text{ and}$$
$$w_j = x_{1,j} x_{2,j} x_{3,j}, \ x_{1,j}, x_{2,j}, x_{3,j} \in V^*,$$
$$w_{j+1} = x_{1,j} u_j x_{2,j} v_j x_{3,j}, \text{ for } x_{2,j} \in S_j, \ (S_j, (u_j, v_j)) \in P, \ 1 \leq j \leq m-1.$$

The sequence of used axiom and the used context can be given as

$$w_1, (u_1, v_1), (u_2, v_2), \ldots, (u_{m-1}, v_{m-1})$$

and is called the *control sequence* associated to the derivation δ. The control sequence does not identify the derivation, because the contexts might be adjoined in different positions. Thus, we define the *description* of δ as follows:

$$w_1, \ x_{1,1}(u_1)x_{2,1}(v_1)x_{3,1}, \ldots, x_{1,m-1}(u_{m-1})x_{2,m-1}(v_{m-1})x_{3,m-1},$$

the parentheses identify exactly the contexts used and the places at which they are adjoined.

An intermediate case is to specify only the used contexts and their corresponding selectors. Such a sequence will be of form

$$w_1, ((u_1, v_1), x_{2,1}), \ ((u_2, v_2), x_{2,2}), \ldots, ((u_{m-1}, v_{m-1}), x_{2,m-1}).$$

We call this as *complete control sequence* of δ. If we take into consideration the contexts (and selectors) used and not the order in which they are applied, then we obtain the *unordered control sequence* (and the *unordered complete control sequence*).

A contextual grammar G is said to be *1-ambiguous* if there are two derivations in G having different unordered control sequences and which generate the same string. Replacing the above definition with the words, "unordered control sequences" by "unordered complete control sequences", "control sequences", "complete control sequences", and "descriptions", respectively, we say that the grammar is 2-, 3-, 4-, 5- ambiguous, respectively. A contextual grammar G is said to be 0-*ambiguous* if there exists at least two different axioms $w_1, w_2 \in A$, $w_1 \neq w_2$ such that they both derive the same word z. i.e., $w_1 \Longrightarrow^+ z$, $w_2 \Longrightarrow^+ z$. More formally, the types of ambiguity are given as follows:

$$0 - ambiguity = \text{two axioms,}$$

$$1 - ambiguity = \text{two unordered control sequences,}$$

$$2 - ambiguity = \text{two unordered complete control sequences,}$$

$$3 - ambiguity = \text{two (ordered) control sequences,}$$

$$4 - ambiguity = \text{two (ordered) complete control sequences,}$$

$$5 - ambiguity = \text{two descriptions.}$$

A grammar which is not i-ambiguous, for some $i = 0, 1, 2, 3, 4, 5$, is said to be i-*unambiguous*. A language L is *inherently i-ambiguous* if every grammar G with F selection generating L is i-ambiguous. A language for which a i-unambiguous grammar exists is called i-*unambiguous*. From definition, it is clear that if a grammar is i-ambiguous, it is j-ambiguous too, for $(i, j) \in \{(0, 1), (1, 2), (1, 3), (2, 4), (3, 4), (4, 5)\}$.

Here, we give some of the conventional notions which are prevalently used in this paper. We call selector as choice some times. When the selectors S_i's are of a particular family of languages, the grammar G is said to be contextual grammars with F selector (or F choice or F selection) where F is the family of languages. Arbitrary selectors does not mean that the selectors have no restriction (which are called grammars without choice), rather it means the selectors can be of any type like $finite$, $regular$, etc.. As we are not discussing external contextual grammars or any other grammars, we simply refer internal contextual grammars as grammars in many occurrences.

3   Related Results and Open Problems

In this section we recall some of the results obtained so far in ambiguity of internal contextual grammars. These results are presented in order to facilitate insight into inherent ambiguity of internal contextual grammars. We also mention some open problems which were formulated in [3], [13].

In [14], the notion of ambiguity was considered first time in this field, where the ambiguity was defined for external contextual grammars. The rigorous study on ambiguity of internal contextual grammars were analyzed by L. Ilie in [3] and by Martin-Vide *et al.* in [13]. Ilie investigated the ambiguity in connection with contextual grammars without choice, deterministic grammars and grammars over one-letter alphabet whereas Martin-Vide *et. al.* analyzed the inherent ambiguity of internal contextual grammars with arbitrary selection. Here, we list some of the results and open problems which are relevant to this paper.

We first consider some results and open problems on ambiguity of contextual grammars without choice. The proof of these results can be found in [3]. When we consider contextual grammars without choice, from the definition of types of ambiguity, it is not hard to conclude that there is no need to consider the cases of 2-, 3-, 4-, 5- ambiguity as the selectors are empty. Therefore, only 0-ambiguity and 1-ambiguity are worth to be considered.

Result 1. *There are inherently 0-ambiguous languages with respect to internal contextual grammars without choice which are 0-unambiguous with respect to internal contextual grammars with finite choice.*

Result 2. *There are inherently 1-ambiguous languages with respect to internal contextual grammars without choice which are 0-unambiguous with respect to internal contextual grammars with finite choice as well as without choice.*

Open problem 1. *Are there inherently 0-ambiguous languages with respect to internal contextual grammars without choice which are 1-unambiguous (or j-unambiguous, $j = 2,3,4,5$) with respect to internal contextual grammars with finite choice?*

We now consider some results and open problems on ambiguity of contextual grammars with arbitrary selector. More detailed results can be seen in [13].

Result 3. *There are inherently 5-ambiguous languages with respect to internal contextual grammars with arbitrary selection which are 4-unambiguous with respect to internal contextual grammars with finite choice.*

Result 4. *There are inherently 4-ambiguous languages with respect to internal contextual grammars with arbitrary selection which are 2- and 3- unambiguous with respect to internal contextual grammars with finite choice.*

Result 5. *There are inherently 3-ambiguous languages with respect to internal contextual grammars with arbitrary selection which are 1- and 2- unambiguous with respect to internal contextual grammars with finite choice.*

The remaining cases of existence of inherently ambiguity were unsolved in that paper and left as open. They are:

Open problem 2. *Whether or not there are inherently 2-ambiguous languages with respect to internal contextual grammars with arbitrary choice and 1- or 3-unambiguous with respect to internal contextual grammars with finite choice?*

Open problem 3. *Whether or not there are languages which are inherently 1-ambiguous with arbitrary choice which are 0-unambiguous with respect to internal contextual grammars with finite selection?*

Unlike, contextual grammars without choice, the notion of six types of ambiguity are meaningful to deterministic grammars. The above results 3,4,5 hold well for deterministic case too, because the grammars considered in the proof are deterministic (each selector in the grammar has only one context at most). Regarding the open problems for deterministic grammars, the above two open problems 2 and 3 can also be raised to deterministic case too.

4   Main Results

In this section, we present our results which are solutions to the open problems 1,2,3 discussed in the previous section.

Theorem 1. *There are inherently 0-ambiguous languages with respect to internal contextual grammars without choice (selector) which are 1-unambiguous with respect to internal contextual grammars with finite selector.*

Proof. In [3] it is proved that the language $L = \{a, b\}^+$ is inherently 0-ambiguous with respect to internal contextual grammars without selector. Nevertheless, we restate the proof here for the sake of completeness.

Consider the above language L and an arbitrary contextual grammar $G = (\{a, b\}, A, \{(S_1, C_1), \ldots, (S_n, C_n)\})$ where each $S_i = \lambda$, $1 \le i \le n$ (without choice) which generates L. As the string a^+ is in L, there must be a context of the form (a^{r_1}, a^{r_2}), $r_1, r_2 \ge 0$, $r_1 + r_2 \ge 1$ in C_i, $1 \le i \le n$. Similarly, as the string b^+ is in L, there must be a context of the form (b^{s_1}, b^{s_2}), $s_1, s_2 \ge 0$, $s_1 + s_2 \ge 1$ in C_i, $1 \le i \le n$. Because the strings $a^{r_1} a^{r_2}$ and $b^{s_1} b^{s_2}$ are in L, there are two axioms w_1, w_2 in A derives them. That is, $w_1 \Longrightarrow^* a^{r_1} a^{r_2}$, $w_2 \Longrightarrow^* b^{s_1} b^{s_2}$. As L does not contain any empty string, $w_1 \ne w_2$. As G is without choice, we can have the derivation $a^{r_1} a^{r_2} \Longrightarrow b^{s_1} a^{r_1} b^{s_2} a^{r_2}$, and $b^{s_1} b^{s_2} \Longrightarrow b^{s_1} a^{r_1} b^{s_2} a^{r_2}$. Therefore, L is inherently 0-ambiguous.

On the other hand, consider the following grammar G' with finite selector

$$G' = (\{a, b\}\{a, b\}, \{(\{a, b\}, \{(\lambda, a), (\lambda, b)\})\}).$$

It is obvious that $L(G') = L$. As a and b are present only on the right side of the context, all words can be generated from left to right in an unique way. Therefore, the grammar G' is 1-unambiguous. $\qquad\square$

Theorem 2. *There are inherently 1-ambiguous languages with respect to internal contextual grammars with arbitrary selector which are 0-unambiguous with respect to internal contextual grammars with finite choice.*

Proof. Consider the following language

$$L = \{a^n b a^m \mid n \ge m \ge 0\} \cup \{a^r d a^s \mid s \ge r \ge 0\} \cup \{a^i d a^j b a^k \mid j \ge i+k, \ i, j, k \ge 0\}.$$

Let us begin with considering first part of the language L. The number of occurrences of a appeared to the left of b must be at least as much as the number of occurrences of a appeared to the right of b. Therefore, P will have the selector-context of the form $(S_1, C_1) = (a^* b a^*, (a^{m_1}, a^{m_1}))$, $m_1 \ge 1$. To increment more a's to the left of b and since $a^+ b$ is in L, P will have the selector-context of the form $(S_2, C_2) = (a^* b a^*, (a^{n_1}, \lambda))$, $n_1 \ge 1$. Applying the similar argument to the second part, we can see that P will have the selector-context of the form $(S_3, C_3) = (a^* d a^*, (a^{r_1}, a^{r_1}))$, $r_1 \ge 1$, and $(S_4, C_4) = (a^* d a^*, (\lambda, a^{s_1}))$, $s_1 \ge 1$. To generate the third part, the selector-contexts which were discussed above are sufficient.

Now we claim that the grammar G is inherently 1-ambiguous. Consider the third part, set $i = m_1$, $j = m_1 + r_1 + s_1 n_1$, $k = r_1$. Then, the word will be of the form $a^{m_1} da^{m_1+s_1 n_1+r_1} ba^{r_1}$. This can be generated by applying $(S_1, C_1), (S_2, C_2)$, (S_3, C_3) or $(S_1, C_1), (S_4, C_4), (S_3, C_3)$. Therefore, there exists two different unordered control sequences which derive the same word present in the language L.

In order to prove that the language is 0-unambiguous with respect to internal contextual grammar with finite selector, consider the following grammar

$$G' = (\{a, b, d\}, \{b, d, db\}, \{(b, \{(a, a), (a, \lambda)\}), (d, \{(a, a), (\lambda, a)\})\}).$$

It is easy to see that $L(G') = L$ and G' is 0-ambiguous since there exists only one axiom for each part of the language.   □

The above grammar is not deterministic since the selector b and d has more than one context. Therefore, the immediate question can be raised is whether the statement holds for deterministic case too? We prove it in the affirmative way in the following theorem.

Theorem 3. *There are inherently 1-ambiguous languages with respect to deterministic internal contextual grammars with arbitrary choice which are 0-unambiguous with respect to internal contextual grammars with finite selection.*

Proof. Consider the language

$$\{a^n ca^n \mid n \geq 0\} \cup \{ba^i ca^j d \mid i, j \geq 0\}.$$

We start with considering the first part. Obviously, the selector $a^* ca^*$ must have the context (a^r, a^r), $r \geq 1$. Considering the second part, the selectors of the form $a^* ca^*$ and a^+ will have no context of the form (a^{s_1}, a^{s_2}), $s_1 \neq s_2$, $s_1, s_2 \geq 0$, $s_1 + s_2 \geq 1$. Otherwise, unequal number of a's can be derived in the first part of L. Therefore, the selector ba^* (or the selector $ba^* ca^*$) must have the context of the form (λ, a^{s_3}), $s_3 \geq 1$ and the selector $a^* d$ (or the selector $a^* ca^* d$) must have the context of the form (a^{s_4}, λ), $s_4 \geq 1$.

Now, we claim that this grammar G is inherently 1-ambiguous. Whenever, we set $i = j$ in the second part, the word can be derived by two ways: either using the context (a^r, a^r) or by using the contexts (λ, a^{s_3}) and (a^{s_4}, λ). Therefore, there exists two different unordered control sequences such that one will have the context (a^r, a^r) and the other will have the contexts $(\lambda, a^{s_3}), (a^{s_4}, \lambda)$, both control sequences derive the same word in L. We can see that all the selectors are having only one context and therefore G is deterministic.

To prove the second part of the statement, consider the following grammar

$$G' = (\{a, b, c, d\}, \{c, bcd\}, \{(c, (a, a)), (b, (\lambda, a)), (d, (a, \lambda))\}).$$

Its is easy to see that $L(G') = L$ and G' is 0-unambiguous since to produce each part of the language G' has only one axiom.   □

From the results 3,4,5 and theorem 2, we can see that there exists languages which are inherently ambiguous for every level of ambiguity in contextual grammars, otherthan the level 2. Regarding 2-ambiguity, we can neither come up with a language which is inherently 2-ambiguous with respect to internal contextual grammar with arbitrary choice nor we can claim that there exists no language which is inherenly 2-ambiguous with respect to internal contextual grammar with arbitary choice. So, the open problem 2 mentioned in the previous section remains unsolved. But, surprizing, we can solve this open problem for the variant depth-first contextual grammars in the following theorem.

Theorem 4. *There are inherently 2-ambiguous languages with respect to depth-first internal contextual grammars with arbitrary selector which are 1-unambiguous with respect to internal contextual grammars (with arbitrary selector).*

Proof. Consider the following language

$$L = \{a^n ba^m \mid n \geq m \geq 1\} \cup \{ba^k d \mid k \geq 1\}.$$

Let G be an arbitrary contextual grammar which generates the language L under the depth-first derivation mode. Consider the first part of L. Obviously, the contexts are of the form (a^p, a^p), $p \geq 1$, and (a^q, λ), $q \geq 1$ present in the grammar G (as $a^r b$, $r \geq 1$ is in L).

For the case of selectors (with respect to first part only), all the selectors must have a subword b. Otherwise, if a's were the only selector, then, more a's can be incremented on the right of b than the number of a's on the left of b which is not in the language. At the same time, b alone can not be a selector, because whenever (a^p, a^p) is introduced, the derivation of the next step should contain either the left a^p or the right a^p which was introduced in the previous step. So, the possible selectors are of the form $a^+ b$, ba^+ and $a^+ ba^+$. But ba^+ can not be a selector. Because, if $(ba^+, \{(a^p, a^p), (a^{q_3}, \lambda)\})$ is in P, then this can be applied to the axiom of the second part of L which generates the word of the form $a^r ba^k d$, $r, k \geq 1$, not in L. Note that when we start from the axiom, we need not check whether the selector contains any context since no contexts are introduced yet to the axiom. Therefore, the possible selector-context for the first part will be of the form $(a^+ b, a^+ ba^+, \{(a^p, a^p), (a^{q_1}, a^{q_2}), (a^{q_3}, \lambda)\})$, $p, q_1, q_3 \geq 1$, $q_2 \geq 0$, $q_1 \geq q_2$.

Now, consider the second part. ba^* can not have the context (λ, a^{s_1}), $s_1 \geq 1$. Otherwise, applying this to the axiom of first part generates more a's on the right of b than the a's on the left of b, which is not allowed in the first part. Therefore, $a^* d$ could be the only possible selector and the context should have λ on the right. Therefore, the possible selector-context for the second part is $(a^* d, (a^s, \lambda))$, $s \geq 1$.

Now we claim that this grammar G with arbitrary selector is inherently 2-ambiguous with respect to depth-first mode. Let P be having the first selector $a^+ b$, then whenever we apply the context (a^p, a^p), the left context a's which are adjoined in the previous step of the derivation can be covered by the selector $a^+ b$. Whenever, we apply the context (a^{q_1}, λ) in a derivation, we will have two choices to cover the last introduced context: either the left a's of the context can be included in the selector $a^+ b$ or without including the left context, we can include the right context λ to the selector $a^+ b$ as λ was inserted on the right of b in the last step of the derivation. So, whenever we apply the context (a^{q_1}, λ), we can have two different selectors: the first selector covers the inserted left context a's and the second selector covers the inserted right context λ. Obviously, both the selectors derive the same word. The similar argument can be raised to the other selector a^+ba^+. In fact, whenever we apply the context (a^p, a^p) itself, we can have two different selectors: the first one consists the left of last inserted a's and the second one consists the right of last inserted a's. Therefore, the complete control sequences will have two different selectors (but the contexts are same) which derive the same word in L. It follows that G is inherently 2- ambiguous with respect to depth-first internal contextual grammars.

To prove L is 1-unambiguous, consider the following grammar G' with finite selector

$$G' = (\{a, b, d\}, \{aba, aaba, bad\}, \{(\{aab, aba\}, \{(a, a), (a, \lambda)\}), (d, (a, \lambda))\})$$

It is easy to see that $L_{df}(G') = L$. First we shall make sure that G' is 2-ambiguous with respect to depth-first derivation. Assume that the word $a^j \underline{a}aba\underline{a}a^j$, $j \geq 0 \in L$ is derived from axiom under depth-first mode and the last selector used was aba (the underlined letters are the contexts which were introduced in the previous step). Now consider the next derivation step and we want to apply the context (a, λ). The only possible selector which contain one of the previous introduced context is aab. Once the context (a, λ) is applied using the selector aab, we will have the word $a^j \underline{a}aab\underline{\lambda}aaa^j$. Now the next selector should contain one of the context $\underline{a}$ or $\underline{\lambda}$. Then we can have two choices: either we can choose $aab\lambda$ or $ab\lambda a$. Hence G' is 2-ambiguous. As G' has no other alternative contexts for (a, a) and (a, λ), G' is 1- unambiguous.   □

When the ordered control sequence of the derivation is considered, G' is 3-ambiguous since the order of applying (a, a) and (a, λ) can be interchanged. It is worth to note that L can not be inherently 2-ambiguous with respect to internal contextual grammars with arbitrary selector because b and d itself are sufficient selectors for the above contexts. That is, $(b, \{(a, a), (a, \lambda)\})$ and $(d, (a, \lambda))$ would be sufficient to generate L in internal contextual grammar. Obviously, we can not choose some other substitutes for the selectors b and d, the grammar is 2-unambiguous and thus L is not inherently 2-ambiguous with respect to internal contextual grammars. Also, note the above grammar G' is not deterministic. So, proving a similar result with deterministic grammar is left *open*. That is, whether there are inherently 2-ambiguous languages with respect to a variant of deterministic internal contextual grammar with arbitrary choice are 1-ambiguous is *open*.

5 Final Remarks

In this paper, we have given solutions to the following open problems on ambiguity of internal contextual grammars which were addressed in [3], [13]. For each $(i, j) \in \{(2, 1), (2, 3), (1, 0), (0, 1)\}$, are there languages which are inherently i-ambiguous with respect to grammars with arbitrary choice which are

j-ambiguous with respect to grammars with finite choice (except for $(0,1)$ case - where contextual grammars without choice was considered)? Though, we did not prove any result for $(2,3)$ of the above problem, we presume that when there exists a language (like in the case of depth-first grammars) which is inherently 2-ambiguous, there is no need to analyze whether it is 3-unambiguous or not. The reason to our argument is 2-ambiguity does not mean that 3-ambiguity and so there is no direct relation exists between 2- and 3- ambiguity. But, we can not discard the similar question to 1-ambiguity. Because, whenever a grammar is 1-ambiguous it is 2-ambiguous too. So, whenever we claim a language is of inherently 2-ambiguous (with respect to internal or depth-first contextual grammars), we need to verify that it does not follow from 1-ambiguous and so proving 1-unambiguity for that language is valid and unavoidable.

The results shown in this paper are important since now a more clear picture of the existence of inherently ambiguous languages (of all types) for internal contextual grammars is obtained. Regarding the further work on this topic, it would be interesting to find a language which is inherently 2-ambiguous with respect to internal contextual grammar with arbitrary choice, but 1-unambiguous with respect to finite selector. The result will be of more interesting if the grammar is deterministic.

References

1. P. Boullier. Range Concatenation Grammars. In proceedings of the sixth International Workshop on Parsing Technologies (IWPT'00), Trento, Italy, 2000, pp. 53–64.
2. P. Boullier. From Contextual Grammars to Range Concatenation Grammars. Electronic Notes in Theoretical Computer Science, 53, 2001.
3. L. Ilie. On Ambiguity in Internal Contextual Languages. *II Intern. Conf. Math. Linguistics '96*, Tarragona, (C. Martin-Vide ed.), John Benjamins, 1997, 29–45.
4. L. Ilie. On Computational Complexity of Contextual Languages. *Theoretical Computer Science*, 183(1), 1997, 33–44.
5. A.K. Joshi, How much Context-Sensitivity is Required to Provide Structural Descriptions: Tree Adjoining Grammars, In David Dowty, Lauri Kartunen and Arnold Zwicky (eds.), Natural Language Processing: Psycholinguistic, Computational, and Theoretical Perspectives, Cambridge University Press, 1986, 206–250.
6. M. Kudlek, C. Martin-Vide and A. Mateescu. An Infinite Hierarchy of Mildly Context-Sensitive Families of Languages. TUCS Technical Report No. 163, 1998.
7. K. Lakshmanan, S.N. Krishna, R. Rama and C. Martin-Vide, Internal Contextual Grammars for Mildly Context Sensitive Languages, to appear in *Research on Language and Computation*, 2006.
8. S. Marcus, *Algebraic Linguistics, Analytical Models*, Academic Press, New York, 1967.
9. S. Marcus. Contextual Grammars. *Rev. Roum. Pures. Appl.*, 14, 1969, 1525–1534.
10. S. Marcus, C. Martin-Vide and Gh. Păun, On Internal contextual grammars with maximal use of selectors, *Proc.8th Conf. Automata and Formal Languages*, Salgotarjan, 1996.
11. S. Marcus, C. Martin-Vide and Gh. Păun. Contextual Grammars as Generative Models of Natural Languages. *Computational Linguistics*, 1998, 245–274.

12. C. Martin-Vide, J. Miquel-Verges and Gh. Păun. Contextual Grammars with Depth-first Derivation. *Tenth Twente Workshop on Language Technology; Algebraic Methods in Language Processing, Twente*, 1995, 225–233.
13. C. Martin-Vide, J. Miguel-Verges, Gh. Păun and A. Salomaa. Attempting to Define the Ambiguity in Internal Contextual Languages. *II Intern. Conf. Math. Linguistics '96*, Tarragona, (C. Martin-Vide ed.), John Benjamins, Amsterdam, 1997, 59–81.
14. Gh. Păun, *Contextual Grammars*, The Publ. House of the Romanian Academy of Sciences, Bucuresti, 1982.
15. Gh. Păun, Marcus Contextual Grammars: After 25 years, *Bulletin of EATCS*, **52**, 1995, 183–194.
16. Gh. Păun. *Marcus Contextual Grammars*. Kluwer Academic Publishers, 1997.
17. Gh. Păun and X.M. Nguyen. On the Inner Contextual Grammars. *Rev. Roum. Pures. Appl.*, 25, 1980, 641–651.
18. A. Salomaa. *Formal Languages*. Academic Press, 1973.

Error-Driven Learning with Bracketing Constraints

Takashi Miyata[1] and Kôiti Hasida[2,1]

[1] Core Research for Evolutional Science and Technology,
Japan Science and Technology Agency
[2] Information Technology Research Institute,
National Institute of Advanced Industrial Science and Technology

Abstract. A chunking algorithm with a Markov model is extended to accept bracketing constraints. The extended algorithm is implemented by modifying a state-of-the-art Japanese dependency parser. Then the effect of bracketing constraints in preventing parsing errors is evaluated. A method for improving the parser's accuracy is proposed. That method adds brackets according to a set of optimal brackets obtained from a training corpus. Although the method's coverage is limited, the F-measure for the sentences to which the method adds brackets is improved by about 7%.

1 Introduction

One important topic in recent studies of statistical parsers is how to weaken the independence assumptions of probabilistic context-free grammar (PCFG). Two issues are included in the problem: lexicalization and structural context [1].

Charniak [2] reduced the probability of the parse to the product of the probabilities of the pre-terminal of each constituent, the lexical head of the constituent, and expansion of the constituent. These three kinds of probabilities are conditioned by information outside the constituent. Consequently, the parser described in that study can address both lexicalization and structural context.

CaboCha [3], which is a state-of-the-art Japanese parser that adopts cascaded chunking; its language model is n-gram. Cascaded chunking [4] is a parsing method that iteratively produces chunks of words or constituents in a sentence. Chunks that are built in the $(n-1)$-th stage are regarded as words in the n-th stage. The chunking process is repeated until the entire sentence becomes one chunk. A word in the n-th stage inherits some information about the chunk in the $(n-1)$-th stage, such as the head word and the subcategorization. Therefore, cascaded chunking shares similar properties with lexicalized PCFG.

This study specifically examines cascaded chunking and is intended to improves its accuracy through error-driven learning. We first detect the parser's deficiency by correcting errors through the use of *bracketing*. Then, we generalize the obtained bracketing patterns and apply them to raw sentences.

A. Yli-Jyrä, L. Karttunen, and J. Karhumäki (Eds.): FSMNLP 2005, LNAI 4002, pp. 144–155, 2006.
© Springer-Verlag Berlin Heidelberg 2006

2 Chunking Under Bracketing Constraints

2.1 Chunking with IOB Model

Chunking can be reduced to labeling B or I on each word [5,6], where label B means the beginning of a chunk and label I denotes the middle or the end of a chunk[1]. The formal specification of the language model is as follows:

- Two states, B and I, exist at respective positions of words in a sentence. Each state produces a word according to a fixed distribution $\Pr(w_i \mid L)$, where w_i is the i-th word in a sentence and L is B or I[2].
- The probability of the transition through a sequence of states L_{i-h}, L_{i-h+1}, ..., and L_{i-1} to state L_i is specified by conditional probabilities $\Pr(L_i \mid L_{i-1}, \ldots, L_{i-h})$, in which L_i is the i-th state and h is a fixed size of history[3].

Given a sentence $(w_1, w_2, \ldots, w_n)$ as a sequence of words, we can calculate the most likely transition of states, or labels, using the Viterbi algorithm[4]. Note that every combination of two types of states (B→B, B→I, I→B, and I→I) can be a valid transition in this language model.

The following examples show encoding of some possible parses for the phrase "bank books and account" in this model[5]:

1. $(\text{Bank}_n$ books_n and_{cnj} $\text{account}_n)_{NP}$
     B   I   I   I

2. $[\, (\text{Bank}_v)$ $(\text{books}_n)_{NP}\,]_{VP}$ (and_{cnj}) $(\text{account}_v)_{VP}$
     B   B   B   B

3. (Bank_v) $(\text{books}_n$ and_{cnj} $\text{account}_n)_{NP}$
     B   B   I   I

Each suffix of a word indicates the part-of-speech (POS), and each suffix of a bracket indicates the phrasal category. The pair of square brackets in the second parse ($[\,]_{VP}$) is not encoded by the labels, but we annotate it for clarity.

---

[1] The original algorithm uses another label O to indicate the outsides of chunks. We omit label O by ignoring the bar levels of single-branching phrases. Labels may have subsorts such as B_{NP}, which indicates the beginning of a noun phrase.

[2] This explanation neglects other information like POSs and phrasal categories for clarity.

[3] These conditional probabilities are inferred as already obtained by some means such as a forward-backward algorithm [7]. The parser described in the remainder of this paper uses support vector machines [5]. We first prepare a classifier for labels B and I. Subsequently, the probabilities are calculated as $\Pr(L_i \mid L_{i-1}, L_{i-2}, \ldots, L_{i-h}) = \{1 + \tanh(d(\boldsymbol{h}))\}/2$, where $d(\boldsymbol{h})$ is the distance between the point corresponding to the features $\boldsymbol{h}$ representing the history $(L_{i-1}, L_{i-2}, \ldots, L_{i-h})$ and the separating hyperplane.

[4] In the remaining explanation, we consider only the calculation of the most likely parse for clarity, but that algorithm would be readily extensible to output multiple candidates.

[5] We assume that "bank" has two meanings as a noun and a transitive verb and "account" as a noun and an intransitive verb.

The following pair of brackets which partially specifies syntactic structure, restricts the possibility of chunking:

4. (Bank   books)   and   account

Note that this pair of brackets only excludes the third parse and chunks are producible both inside and outside specified brackets. That is, we use bracketing for specification of both intra-chunk and inter-chunk structures. It is also noteworthy that parsing the bracketed part separately fails to draw the best performance out of a language model because of the lexicalization and structural context.

2.2 Extension of the Chunking Algorithm

To process the bracketing constraints described above, we introduce another type of state that does not correspond to a word but rather to a sequence of bracketed words. Figure 1 shows the states for the bracketed word sequence "w_1 ((w_2 w_3 w_4) w_5 (w_6) w_7) w_8," where unreachable states are omitted for clarity. In Fig. 1,

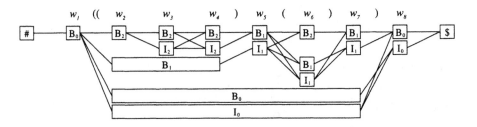

Fig. 1. Lattice Structure for Chunking with Bracketing Constraints

a sharp sign (#) and a dollar sign ($) respectively denote the beginning and the end of the paths. The suffix of each state symbol is *depth* of the brackets. For example, the depth of state B that spans bracketed words w_2, w_3, and w_4 is 1, which means that the state is surrounded by another pair of brackets (spanning from w_2 to w_7). This state is depicted as the middle-sized rectangle labeled by B_1 in the figure. We call states that spans several words surrounded by a pair of brackets *bracket states* and ordinary states corresponding to words *word states*, respectively. There are 5 bracket states and 13 word states shown in Fig. 1.

To reflect bracketing constraints to paths, transitions are restricted as follows:

- The immediate after the beginning of paths must be a state labeled by B.
- If a left bracket is shown between state L_i and its next state L_{i+1}, the following transitions are allowed:

(	$L_{i+1} = I$	$L_{i+1} = B$
$L_i = I$	OK	OK
$L_i = B$	same depth	OK

The transition from L_i labeled by B to L_{i+1} labeled by I is allowed only if L_i and L_{i+1} have the same depth.

– If a right bracket is shown between state L_i and its next state L_{i+1}, the following transitions are allowed:

)	$L_{i+1} = \text{I}$	$L_{i+1} = \text{B}$
$L_i = \text{I}$	same depth	OK
$L_i = \text{B}$	same depth	L_i is word state

The transition from L_i (with any label) to L_{i+1} labeled by I allowed only if L_i and L_{i+1} have the same depth. The transition from L_i labeled by B to L_{i+1} labeled by B is allowed only if L_i is a word state (i.e. the deepest state among the states whose end points are the same as L_i)[6].

Bracket states are considered to generate a sequence of words in their brackets according to the product of each generation probability and transition probability. Bracket state S spanning from w_i to w_{i+j} generates word sequence $(w_i, w_{i+1}, \ldots, w_{i+j})$ according to (1):

$$\prod_{k=0}^{j} \left\{ \Pr(w_{i+k} \mid L_{i+k}) \sum_{\text{path}} \Pr(L_{i+k} \mid L_{i+k-1}, \ldots, L_{i+k-h}) \right\}. \qquad (1)$$

Note that each bracket state is read as a sequence of word states in the above calculation. That is, bracket state B is read as a sequence of word states (B I ...I) and bracket state I as (I I ...I). As a result, word states $L_i, \ldots, L_{i+j}$ are fixed to $L_i = \text{B}$ (I) and $L_{i+1} = \cdots = L_{i+j} = \text{I}$ if bracket state S is labeled as B (I), whereas $L_{i-1}, \ldots, L_{i-h}$ runs over the possible paths within the summation.

Note that the above extended algorithm makes the best use of the original language model's performance. For example, the score of the label for w_3 in Fig. 1 is estimated correctly according to the preceding path (# B_0 B_2). If the bracketed part (w_2, w_3, w_4) were parsed separately, the score of the label for w_3 would be estimated incorrectly.

We use the Viterbi algorithm for label estimation. Let d be the maximum depth of the brackets. As displayed in Fig. 1, each pair of brackets adds, at most, two extra states within it. For that reason, the number of states at each position is $2(d+1)$ at most. In each transition from L_i to L_{i+1}, histories at L_i should be also distinguished. The number of possible histories that each state must hold is 2^{h-1} at most. The computational complexity is therefore $O(\{2(d+1)\}^2 2^{h-1}n) = O(n(d+1)^2 2^{h+1})$, where n is the sentence length and h is the size of history[7].

2.3   Examples of Extended Chunking

Figure 2 depicts examples of our extended algorithm. The left column is the output to sentence "逐次調査を依頼する (He asks someone(s) for investigation sequentially / He asks someone for sequential investigation)," which is the same as

---

[6] The last restriction is to remove redundant paths. The correctness of this algorithm is proved by induction on the depth of brackets.

[7] Since brackets that span the same range need not be distinguished, d is less than n.

```
* 0                        * 0
逐次 (sequentially)        # <x>
* 1                        逐次 (sequential)
調査 (investigation)       調査 (investigation)
を    (OBJ)               # </x>
* 2                        を    (OBJ)
依頼 (ask)                * 1
する (do)                 依頼 (ask)
                           する (do)
```

Fig. 2. Parses for Non-bracketed (Left) and Bracketed (Right) Sentences

the output of original chunker (YamCha). The right column is the output to the bracketed sentence "<x>逐次調査</x>を依頼する (He asks someone for sequential investigation)." In both columns, each morpheme is represented as a row. The beginning of a chunk is indicated by a row marked by *; the chunk's ID number.

Ambiguities of the non-bracketed sentence result from the morpheme "逐次" which has two meanings: sequentially and sequential. Our chunker disambiguates the morpheme in the non-bracketed sentence as 'sequentially' and chunks it as an adverbial phrase. On the other hand, the morpheme in the bracketed sentence is differently disambiguated and the sentence is parsed as two chunks. Note that the added brackets themselves do not prohibit the possibility of parsing "逐次" as a single chunk. Chunking this morpheme as one chunk, however, causes particle "を" to be located at the beginning of a chunk as "<x>(逐次)(調査)</x>(を...)" because of the added brackets. The score of such a parse is low because particles rarely appear at the beginning of a chunk in Japanese. Consequently, the right column in the figure is output as the most probable parse.

2.4 Notes on Morphological and Dependency Analyses

As shown above, the algorithm parses both inside and outside pairs of brackets. Nevertheless, a case exists in which a user seeks to parse a certain part of a sentence as one morpheme in morphological analysis. This is easily achievable merely by restricting looking-up morphemes so as to select those that span the same range of the part. We have extended the morphological analyzer *ChaSen* by introducing a special sort of bracket that similarly surrounds just one morpheme.

We have also extended the dependency analyzer *CaboCha*, which can be seen as a variant of the cascaded chunker. CaboCha verifies each pair of adjacent chunks to determine whether they are dependent or not. If they do, they are combined to form a larger chunk. This process is repeated until all chunks are combined to one. Introducing bracketing constraints in this parser merely restricts the case in which a pair of adjacent chunks depends; it must not depend when brackets exist between them. Aside from combining chunks, a pair of brackets surrounding just one chunk is removed in each step.

We have pipelined these three parsers: the extended ChaSen; the chunker described in the above sections, which is implemented based on *YamCha* [5];

and the extended CaboCha. This integrated parser can handle arbitrary levels
of bracketing constraints and output dependency structures from raw sentences.

3   Upper Bound of Bracketing Effect

This section evaluates the upper bound of the effect of bracketing to correct
the parser's errors. We modify YamCha and CaboCha to accept bracketing constraints, as described above, and use the smaller sets of parameters distributed
with the parsers. These sets of parameters are estimated from part of the Kyoto
University Corpus [8] (7,615 sentences), in which the POSs are converted by
ChaSen[8]. The rest of the corpus (30,768 sentences) is used for evaluation.

Evaluation measurements are *bracket precision*, *bracket recall*, and *F-measure*. The bracket precision is the ratio of the number of correct brackets against
the number of brackets the parser outputs. Bracket recall is the ratio of the number of correct brackets against the number of brackets the sentence in the corpus
has. The F-measure is calculated as $(2 \times \text{precision} \times \text{recall})/(\text{precision} + \text{recall})$.
The bracket precisions, recalls, and F-measures of original chunker (YamCha),
dependency analyzer (CaboCha), and their combination are as follows:

	chunk	dependency	chunk+dependency
precision	0.9749	0.8723	0.9268
recall	0.9743	0.8720	0.9263
F-measure	0.9746	0.8721	0.9265

3.1   Evaluation Procedure

We evaluate how many errors are corrected in the best case if we give a few pairs
of brackets to a sentence before parsing it. The procedure is as follows:

1. Exclude sentences (a) which are already parsed correctly, and (b) whose
   parses have more brackets than all brackets in their correct parses. We call
   the latter kind of sentence *over-split* ones.
2. For each remaining sentence, add brackets to it and obtain the parse as
   follows:
   i. Select a pair of brackets in the correct parse in the corpus that did
      not appear in the parser output. Add the pair of brackets to the raw
      sentence. This procedure produces *m* sentences if the output parse lacks
      for *m* pairs of brackets in the correct one.
   ii. Parse these *m* bracketed sentences and choose the most correctly parsed
      result as the parse for that sentence. We call the pair of brackets in the
      most correctly parsed sentence *optimal brackets* for the sentence.

---

[8] Kyoto University Corpus collects Japanese articles printed in the Mainichi Newspaper from 1/1 to 1/17 and monthly columns of January–December in 1995. They are
annotated in morphemes, chunks (*bunsetsu*), and dependency among chunks.

3. Calculate the bracket precision, recall, and F-measure for the sentences.

The above procedure is repeated by adding 2, 3, 4, and 5 pairs of brackets while excluding correctly parsed and over-split sentences in the previous stage. In the second step in each stage, $\binom{m}{2}$, $\binom{m}{3}$, $\binom{m}{4}$, and $\binom{m}{5}$ sentences are produced from one sentence if the parse output by the parser lacks for m pairs of brackets in the correct one[9].

3.2 Result

Figure 3 portrays the bracket precision and recall against the number of pairs of brackets added to the sentence. The figure shows that only two pairs of optimal

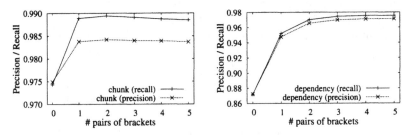

Fig. 3. Precisions and Recalls of Chunk and Dependency against # Pairs of Brackets

brackets drastically improve the accuracy of the outputs. For example, the recall of chunks increases from 0.9743 to 0.9894 and the precision of dependency from 0.8723 to 0.9655. The F-measure for the combination increases from 0.9143 to 0.9746. The figure also indicates that the upper bound of the effects of bracketing constraints saturates with two or three pairs of brackets. The precision and recall of chunks decrease slightly when more than two optimal brackets are added.

The following table lists the numbers of sentences that were (a) parsed, (b) correctly parsed, and (c) over-split at each stage, where the stage corresponds to the number of pairs of optimal brackets added in a sentence:

stage	0	1	2	3	4	5
parsed	30768	16845	7429	3465	1836	1057
corrected	13894	8598	3377	1163	382	107
over-split	29	818	587	466	**397**	**276**

The table indicates that the number of over-split sentences becomes larger than the number of correctly parsed ones when four pairs of optimal brackets are added. This coincides with the saturation of the improvement shown in Fig. 3.

Figure 4 illustrates distributions of the widths and positions of the center of the brackets that correct all errors in a sentence at each stage. The width and the position are normalized by the sentence length and quantized by 5%. For

---

[9] The sentences s.t. $m < b$ are also regarded as over-split ones and are thus excluded in each stage, where b is the number of pairs of brackets to be added in the stage.

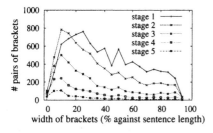
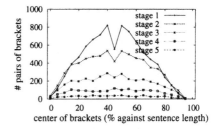

Fig. 4. Distribution of Brackets' Widths and Positions

example, Fig. 4 shows that the brackets with width of 25–30% of the sentence appear the most frequently (763 times) in stage 1. The figure indicates that most optimal brackets are narrow in each stage; relatively wider brackets appear in stages 1 and 2.

Figure 4 also displays that the optimal brackets are apt to be located around the center of the sentences in each stage. The average of the positions, however, is 47%, which is slightly left of the sentence center. The reason why the centers of distributions in early stages sink is currently under investigation. We suspect that the head-final property of Japanese is related to this phenomenon.

4   Improved Accuracy with Bracketing Constraints

The procedure described in the previous section provides optimal brackets for each sentence in a corpus, which can be seen as a compensation for the parser's deficiency. If we can generalize these optimal brackets in a certain manner, they will improve the parser's accuracy for unseen sentences.

4.1   Algorithm and Evaluation Procedure

As mentioned previously, we use the smaller part of the corpus (7,615 sentences) for parameter estimation and training. The remainder of the corpus (30,768 sentences) is used for evaluation. The procedure is as follows:

1. Apply the procedure described in the previous section to the training corpus.
2. Obtain the optimal brackets with four morphemes before and after the brackets that form the bracketing context. For example, the optimal brackets surrounding morphemes $(w_i, w_{i+1}, \ldots, w_j)$ produce a morpheme sequence: $w_{i-2}, w_{i-1}, (w_i, \ldots, w_j), w_{j+1}, w_{j+2}$. A sharp sign (#) and a dollar sign ($) are used as w_k if $k < 1$ and $n < k$ (n is the length of the sentence), respectively. We call these sequences *base patterns*.
3. Count the frequency of each POS in the obtained base patterns and determine the level of generalization for each POS[10] manually considering their frequencies.

---

[10] ChaSen adopts a hierarchical POS system.

4. Generalize each base pattern by abstracting their POSs according to the levels determined in the above step. We call these generalized base patterns *bracketing rules*.
5. Apply these bracketing rules to raw sentences in the test corpus. If bracketing rules that are mutually inconsistent are applicable, the narrowest one is preferred. If their widths are the equal, the leftmost one is preferred.

As indicated in the previous section, adding many brackets does not effectively improve the parser's accuracy. For that reason, we only use the base patterns obtained in stages 1 and 2: 837 base patterns in all and 825 different ones. The number of POSs in the base patterns was 61. We chose 21 POSs that appear most frequently and determined their levels of generalization. The remaining POSs were generalized to the coarsest level. Thereafter, we obtained 805 bracketing rules following POS abstraction.

The bracketing rules were applied 309 times to 302 sentences in the test corpus. This is only a small part of the test corpus (1%) and hardly affects the overall parser accuracy, but the parses for the sentences to which the bracketing rules were applied were greatly improved as follows:

		chunk	dependency	chunk+dependency
without brackets	precision	0.9295	0.7277	0.8389
	recall	0.8833	0.6839	0.7932
	F-measure	0.9057	0.7050	0.8153
with brackets	precision	0.9468	0.7855	0.8737
	recall	0.9612	0.7999	0.8882
	F-measure	0.9539	0.7926	0.8809

4.2 Examples of Optimal Brackets, Base Patterns, and Bracketing Rules

Figure 5 displays two examples of incorrectly parsed sentences and the obtained optimal brackets in the training corpus. Each morpheme is separated by slash sign (/) while each chunk and dependency is enclosed by round brackets. The first line in each block is an incorrect parser output, whereas the second line is the correct parse in the training corpus. Optimal brackets are represented as square brackets ([ ]).

1. *((((ブザー / が) (鳴っ / た)) (瞬間 / 、)) ((その / 場 / に) (座り込ん / だ)))
   ((((ブザー / が) (鳴っ / た)) (瞬間 / 、)) (((その) [場 / に]) (座り込ん / だ)))
   buzzer / NOM strike / past moment   that / field / at   fall / past
   (At the moment the buzzer struck, he fell down there.)

2. *(((((３０ / カ国 / を)   (対象 / に))(し / て))   (行っ / た)) (分析))
   ((((３０ / カ国 / を) [(対象 / に) (し / て)]) (行っ / た)) (分析))
              30 / nations / OBJ subject / to do / and perform / past analysis
   (An analysis that is carried out subject to 30 nations)

Fig. 5. Incorrect Parses and Optimal Brackets in the Training Corpus

1.

		base pattern	bracketing rule
base form		POS	abstracted POS
、	，	symbol–punctuation	symbol–punctuation
その	(that)	adnominal	adnominal
# <x>			
場	(field)	noun–general	noun–general
に	(at)	particle–case_marker–general	particle–case_marker
# </x>			
座り込む	(fall)	verb–content	verb–content
だ	(past)	auxiliary	auxiliary

2.

		base pattern	bracketing rule
base form		POS	abstracted POS
カ国	(nations)	noun–suffix–ordinal	noun–suffix
を	(OBJ)	particle–case_marker–general	particle–case_marker–general
# <x>			
対象	(subject)	noun–general	noun–general
に	(to)	particle–case_marker–general	particle–case_marker–general
する	(do)	verb–content	verb–content
て	(and)	particle–conjunctive	particle–conjunctive
# </x>			
行く	(go)	verb–functional[11]	verb
た	(past)	auxiliary	auxiliary

Fig. 6. Base Patterns and Bracketing Rules Obtained from Examples in Fig. 5

Figure 6 shows the base patterns and the bracketing rules that are obtained from the examples in Fig. 5. Each table consists of three columns: morphemes in base form, POSs, and abstracted POSs. The left two columns form a base pattern while the rightmost column is a bracketing rule. The POSs hierarchy is demarcated by dashes (–).

The first examples in Fig. 5 and Fig. 6 are optimal brackets and a bracketing rule which corrects a chunking error around morphemes "その (that)" and "場 (field)." This type of bracketing rule is applicable to simple cases where the errors mainly arise from insufficient training data and are corrected locally. In fact, this bracketing rule was the most frequently applied (34 sentences).

The second examples in Fig. 5 and Fig. 6 are optimal brackets and a bracketing rule that correct a dependency error. The five chunks that comprise this sentence are identified correctly without bracketing constraints, but dependencies among them are not parsed correctly. In the correct parse, the chunk that represents quantity "３０カ国を (30 nations, OBJ)" depends on the light verb "して (do, and)", not the adjacent chunk "対象に (subject to)." Such an idiosyncrasy is difficult to manage, but the optimal brackets and the derived bracketing rule partially capture its property. This bracketing rule was applied to 18 sentences.

---

[11] This is an error in the corpus, which should be "行なう (perform) verb–content."

5   Discussion

As described in Sect. 3, even the effect of optimal brackets saturates in relatively early stages because of the increase of over-split sentences. Moreover, Fig. 4 shows that most optimal brackets are narrow. Consequently, the effect of bracketing constraints that compensates the locality of Markov model is limited. If we were able to devise some bias that reduces over-splitting within a pair of brackets, bracketing constraints could be used more effectively. Brackets that surround just one constituent explained in Sect. 2.4 would be one solution for this problem.

In Sect. 4, we hand-crafted an abstraction scheme for POSs because very few base patterns were obtained. A more systematic method, however, should be adopted when a larger training corpus is available. Moreover, we applied each bracketing rule independently, which was not problematic because the coverage of the bracketing rules was quite low and most bracketing rules were applicable at most once in a sentence. However, we have obtained optimal combinations of brackets by the procedure described in Sect. 4. Use of a larger training corpus could yield more sophisticated bracketing rules by a pattern mining method such as that proposed by Asai and others [9].

Note that brackets that are not optimal are also useful. Notwithstanding, we have addressed only optimal bracketing in this study. Adding brackets that are already output by the parser does not affect the parser's output.

6   Related Work

To manage numerous ambiguities efficiently, several studies have examined structure sharing, mainly in the context of syntactic parsing [10, 11]. A lattice structure with a Markov model incorporated into a Cost Minimization Method in morphological analysis [12] and Cascaded Chunking [4] are special cases of those studies. The difference between those methods and ours is that our method has no fixed dictionary or grammar. A pair of brackets introduces a new 'constituent,' but it also allows the 'constituent' to be parsed in more detail.

Brill and Resnik [13] approach prepositional phrase attachment disambiguation by error-driven learning. They first parse a raw sentence in a training corpus and obtain transformation rules that correct errors in the parser's output. Note that their transformation rules are applied repeatedly and that the order of the application is important. For example, one effect of a rule is sometimes canceled by another rule that is applied later. For that reason, it is difficult to interpret transformation rules even if each of them were quite simple. On the other hand, our bracketing constraints can be interpreted independently.

7   Conclusion

This paper has presented an algorithm that introduces bracketing constraints into chunking based on a Markov model. This paper has also reported the effect of adding optimal brackets into a raw sentence before parsing it and has shown that the use of only two pairs of brackets can increase the F-measure from 0.9143 to 0.9746 at best.

A method for improving the parser's accuracy with bracketing constraints has also been proposed. Optimal brackets obtained from a training corpus are generalized by abstracting hierarchical POSs around them; bracketing rules are derived. Coverage of bracketing rules is quite limited, but they improve the F-measure from 0.8153 to 0.8809 for sentences to which the rules are applicable.

Our algorithm has numerous potential applications; information from various analysis modules such as named entity identification can be integrated easily into our parser through bracketing constraints.

References

1. Manning, C.D., Schütze, H.: Chap. 12 Probabilistic Parsing. In: Foundations of Statistical Natural Language Processing. MIT Press (1999) 407–460.
2. Charniak, E.: A maximum-entropy-inspired parser. In: Proceedings of the 6th Applied Natural Language Processing Conference (ANLP) and the 1st Meeting of the North American Chapter of the Association for Computational Linguistics (NAACL), USA (2000) NAACL 132–139.
3. Kudo, T., Matsumoto, Y.: Japanese dependency analysis using cascaded chunking. In: CoNLL 2002: Proceedings of the 6th Conference on Natural Language Learning 2002 (COLING 2002 Post-Conference Workshops). (2002) 63–69.
4. Brants, T.: Cascaded Markov models. In: Proceedings of the 6th Conference of the European Chapter of the ACL, Bergen, Norway (1999) 118–125.
5. Kudo, T., Matsumoto, Y.: Chunking with support vector machines. In: Proceedings of the 2nd Meeting of the North American Chapter of the Association for Computational Linguistics (NAACL), Pittsburgh, PA, USA (2001) 192–199.
6. Sang, E.F.T.K., Veenstra, J.: Representing text chunks. In: Proceedings of the 6th Conference of the European Chapter of the ACL, Bergen, Norway (1999) 173–179.
7. Rabiner, L.R., Juang, B.H.: An introduction to hidden Markov models. IEEE ASSP Magazine (1986) 4–16.
8. Kurohashi, S., Nagao, M.: Kyoto University text corpus project. In: Proceedings of the Third Annual Meeting of the Association for Natural Language Processing, The Association for Natural Language Processing (1997) 115–118 (in Japanese).
9. Asai, T., Abe, K., Kawasoe, S., Arimura, H., Sakamoto, H., Arikawa, S.: Efficient substructure discovery from large semi-structured data. In: Proceedings of the 2nd Annual SIAM Symposium on Data Mining. (2002) 158–174.
10. Boyer, R.S., Moore, J.S.: The sharing of structure in theorem-proving programs. Machine Intelligence **7** (1972) 101–116.
11. Miyao, Y.: Packing of feature structures for efficient unification of disjunctive feature structure. In: Proceedings of the 37th Annual Meeting of the Association for Computational Linguistics (ACL), Maryland, USA (1999) 579–584.
12. Matsumoto, Y., Kitauchi, A., Yamashita, T., Hirano, Y., Matsuda, H., Takaoka, K., Asahara, M.: Japanese Morphological Analysis System ChaSen version 2.2.1. Computational Linguistics Laboratory, Graduate School of Information Science, Nara Institute of Science and Technology. (2000).
13. Brill, E., Resnik, P.: A rule-based approach to prepositional phrase attachment disambiguation. In: Proceedings of the 15th International Conference on Computational Linguistics (COLING '94), Kyoto, Japan (1994) 1198–1204.

Parsing with Lexicalized Probabilistic Recursive Transition Networks

Alexis Nasr[1] and Owen Rambow[2]

[1] Lattice-CNRS (UMR 8094),
Université Paris 7, Paris, France
alexis.nasr@linguist.jussieu.fr
[2] Center for Computational Learning Systems,
Columbia University, New York, NY, USA
rambow@cs.columbia.edu

Abstract. We present a formalization of lexicalized Recursive Transition Networks which we call Automaton-Based Generative Dependency Grammar (GDG). We show how to extract a GDG from a syntactically annotated corpus, present a chart parser for GDG, and discuss different probabilistic models which are directly implemented in the finite automata and do not affect the parser.

1 Introduction

While finite-state methods are becoming ever more popular in natural language processing (NLP), parsing (as opposed to chunking) has resisted the use of finite-state methods, presumably because of the difficulty of properly modeling structure using only finite state methods (but see [1]). An early proposal to extend finite state methods for syntax were the Recursive Transition Networks (RTNs) of Woods [2], which add a stack mechanism to a collection of finite-state automata (FSMs). RTNs have been used to implement context-free grammars.

In the field of syntax, there has been much interest since the 1990's in lexicalized formalisms, in which each elementary structure of a grammar formalism represents the syntactic behavior of a single lexical item. The question arises what happens if we add lexicalization to RTNs. In this paper, we present probabilistic lexicalized RTN, which we call *Probabilistic Automaton-Based Generative Dependency Grammar* or PGDG. A PGDG is a collection of weighted FSMs, such that in each of these FSMs, every path includes at least one lexical transition. As with all lexicalized generative formalisms, the derivation tree is a dependency tree. GDG as a formalization allows us to relate RTNs to Tree Adjoining Grammars (TAG), and thus to profit from work on extracting TAGs from treebanks. We show how to convert a TAG extracted from a treebank into a GDG. We also show we can vary the conversion algorithm to obtain different automata which represent different ways of probabilistically modeling multiple attachments of the same type (such as adjectives attaching to a noun). Thus, in our approach, the automata represent both the algebraic part of the grammar and the probabilistic model. As a result the same algorithms (for parsing and searching for the best parses) are used for different probabilistic models.

A. Yli-Jyrä, L. Karttunen, and J. Karhumäki (Eds.): FSMNLP 2005, LNAI 4002, pp. 156–166, 2006.
© Springer-Verlag Berlin Heidelberg 2006

The outline of the paper is as follows. We start out by presenting related work in section 2, and then present our definitions in section 3. We very briefly present a simple parsing algorithm for GDG in section 4. We then turn to the key contributions of this paper: we present probabilistic models of adjunction in section 5, and then show how to extract a PGDG from a treebank (section 6).

2   Related Work

This work is based on previous work in string rewriting systems for dependency grammars, as well as on the notion of Recursive Transition Networks [2]. In this section, we quickly review the literature on such string-rewriting systems. The formalism presented here can be seen as having some similarities with the work of Hays and Gaifman [3, 4], who proposed generative formalisms for string rewriting. These formalisms were basically context-free grammars in which there is, on the right-hand side of rules, at least one terminal symbol. To overcome the inadequacy of such formalisms, Abney [5] suggests extending the notation of [4] with regular expressions in the right-hand side, similar to the approach used in extended context-free grammars (for example, [6]). This approach was worked out in some detail by Lombardo [7], and in a similar manner in previous work by us [8], in which we present a string-rewriting version of GDG.

There has been some work on modeling syntactic dependency between words using automata. Alshawi *at al.* [9] use cascaded head automata to derive dependency trees, but leave the nature of the cascading under-formalized. Eisner [10] provides a formalization of a system that uses two different automata to generate left and right children of a head. His formalism bears some similarity to the one we present.

3   Generative Dependency Grammars

3.1   Informal Definition

A GDG is a set of finite-state automata (FSMs) of a particular type, namely *lexicalized automata*. In a lexicalized automaton, every path from a start state to a final state includes at least one lexical transition. A lexicalized automaton with the anchor (word) m describes all possible dependents of m. Each automaton has a name, which defines not only the part-of-speech of m, but also the active valency of m (i.e., all word classes that can depend on it), as well as their linear order. Thus this name can be thought of as a *supertag* in the sense of Bangalore and Joshi [11], and we will adopt the name "supertag" here to avoid confusion with simple part-of-speech tags. A sample lexicalized automaton is shown in Figure 1[1]. For expository purposes, in these examples, the supertags are simply standard part-of-speech tags. The transitions of the automaton are labeled with

---

[1] The initial state of an automaton is labeled 0 while its accepting states are indicated in boldface. The empty transitions are represented in dotted lines.

pairs $\langle f, c \rangle$, where f is a grammatical function (subject, object, different types of adjuncts, etc.), and c is a supertag, or by pairs $\langle \text{LEX}, m \rangle$, where m is an anchor of the automaton. This automaton indicates that the verb *eat* has a dependent which is its subject, obligatory and non-repeatable, and whose category is noun or pronoun; a dependent which is its object that is optional and non-repeatable; and an adjunct prepositional phrase which is repeatable.

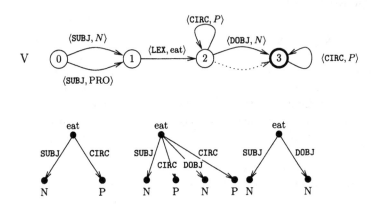

Fig. 1. A lexicalized automaton and three elementary trees that can be derived from it

Each word (in the formal language theory sense), i.e., each sentence (in the linguistic sense) accepted by an automaton is a sequence of pairs $\langle f, c \rangle$. Each such sequence corresponds to a dependency tree of depth one, which we will call an *elementary tree* of the grammar. Three sample elementary trees can be seen in the lower part of figure 1. The word corresponding to the leftmost tree is: $\langle \text{SUBJ}, N \rangle \; \langle \text{LEX}, \text{mange} \rangle \; \langle \text{CIRC}, P \rangle$.

A GDG derivation is defined like a derivation in an RTN [2]. It uses a stack, which contains pairs $\langle c, e \rangle$ where c is the name of an automaton from the grammar, and e is a state of c. When $\langle c, e \rangle$ is on the top of the stack, and a transition of type $\langle f, c' \rangle$ goes from state e to state e' in automaton c, $\langle c, e \rangle$ is popped and $\langle c, e' \rangle$ is pushed as well as the machine c' in its initial state ($\langle c', q \rangle$). When we reach an accepting state q' in c', the pair $\langle c', q' \rangle$ is popped, uncovering $\langle c, e' \rangle$, and the traversal of automaton c resumes. We need to use a stack because, as we saw, during a derivation, several automata can be traversed in parallel, with one invoking the next recursively.

Since our automata are lexicalized, each traversal of a non-lexical arc (i.e., an arc of the form $\langle f, c \rangle$ of automaton c) corresponds to the establishment of a dependency between the lexical anchor of c (as governor), and the lexical anchor of automaton c' (as dependent). Thus, the result of a derivation can be seen as a sequence of transitions, which can be bijectively mapped to a dependency tree.

A probabilistic GDG (PGDG), is a GDG in which the automata of the grammar are weighted finite state automata. For each state in an automaton of the grammar, the weights of the outgoing arcs represent a probability distribution over possible transitions out of that state.

3.2   The Sites of an Automaton

The transitions of a lexicalized automaton do not all play the same role. We have already seen the lexical transitions which provide the words that anchor the automaton. In addition, we will distinguish the *argument transitions* which attach an argument as a dependent to the lexical anchor. All argument transitions which share the same grammatical function label constitute an *argument site* of the automaton. An example can be seen in Figure 2, where site 1 is the subject site, while site 4 is the object site. Note that since we consider in this example the grammatical object of *eat* to be optional, site 4 can be skipped using an ε -transition.

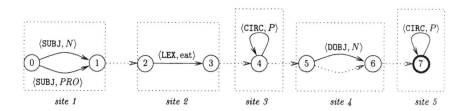

Fig. 2. Sites of the automaton in figure 1

The transitions associated with adjuncts are called *adjunct transitions*. They are grouped into *adjunct sites*, such as sites 3 and 5 in figure 2. Some adjunct sites are repeatable, while others (such as determiners in some languages) are not. When several dependencies are generated by the same repeatable adjunct site, we distinguish them by their *position*, which we mark with integers. The argument and adjunct sites are distinguished from the lexical transitions, which are called *lexical sites*.

4   Parsing with FSMs

The parsing algorithm is a simple extension of the chart parsing algorithm for context-free grammar (CFG). The difference is in the use of finite state machines in the items in the chart. In the following, we will call an FSM a t-FSM if its supertag is t. If T is the parse table for input sentence $W = w_1 \cdots w_n$ and GDG G, then $T_{i,j}$ contains (M, q) where M is a t-FSM and q is one of the accepting states of M, iff we have a complete derivation of substring $w_i \cdots w_j$ such that the root of the corresponding dependency tree is the lexical anchor of M with supertag t. If $T_{i,j}$ contains (M, q_1), if there is a transition in M from q_1 to q_2 labeled t, and if $T_{j+1,k}$ contains (M', q') where M' is a t-FSM and q' is an accepting state, then we add (M, q_2) to $T_{i,k}$. Note that because our grammars are lexicalized, each such step corresponds to one attachment of a lexical head to another as a dependent.

Before starting the parse, we create a tailored grammar by selecting those automata associated with the words in the input sentence. An important question is how to associate automata with words in a sentence; we do not discuss this issue in this paper, and refer to the literature on supertagging (for example, [11]). The parsing algorithm is extended to lattice input in the usual manner. The lattice represents several supertag sequences that can be associated to the sentence to parse. At the end of the parsing process, a packed parse forest has been built. The nonterminal nodes are labeled with pairs (M, q) where M is an FSM and q a state of this FSM. Obtaining the dependency trees from the packed parse forest is performed in two stages. In a first stage, a forest of binary phrase-structure trees is obtained from the packed forest and in a second stage, each phrase-structure tree is transformed into a dependency tree.

In order to deal with PGDG, we extend our parser by augmenting entries in the parse table with probabilities. The algorithm for extracting parses is augmented to choose the best parse (or n-best parses) in the usual manner.

5   Probabilistic Models

The parser introduced in Section 4 associates to a supertag sequence $S = S_1 \ldots S_n$ one or several analyses. Each analysis $\mathcal{A}$ can be seen as a set of $n-1$ attachment operations (either adjunction or substitution) and the selection of one supertag token as the root of the analysis (the single supertag that is not attached in another supertag). For the sake of uniformity, we will consider the selection of the root as a special kind of attachment, $\mathcal{A}$ is therefore of cardinality n.

From a probabilistic point of view, each attachment operation is considered as an event and an analysis $\mathcal{A}$ as the joint event $A_1, \ldots, A_n$. A large range of different models can be used to compute such a joint probability, from the simplest which considers that all events are independent to the model that considers that they are all dependent. The two models that we describe in this section vary in the way they model multiple adjuncts attaching at the same adjunct site. Put differently, the internal structure of repeatable adjunct sites is the only difference between the models. The reason to focus on this phenomenon comes from the fact that it is precisely at this level that much of the structural ambiguity occurs. The two models described below consider that attachments at argument sites are independent of all the other attachments that make up an analysis.

What is important is that the models we present in this section change the automata, but the changes are fully within sites; if we abstract to the level of sites, the automata are identical. Note that this hypothesis is not entailed by the PGDG formalism, one can produce a PGDG which changes the topology of the automata.

The two models for adjunction will be illustrated on a simple example where two automata c_1 and c_2 are candidates for attachment at a given repeatable adjunct site (which we will simply refer to as a "site"). Both sites can generate $(c_1|c_2)*$ but associate different probabilities to the generated strings. Recall that when several adjunctions occur at the same site, the first one is said to be of order 1, the second of order 2 and so on. The two models described below differ mainly in the fact the the first one (the positional model) focuses on the nature of the attachment at order i (how probable is it to have an attachment at order i) as well as on the number of attachments (how probable is it to have n attachments on this site). The second model (the bigram model) focuses on the dependency between an attachement and the preceding one (how probable is it to have a prepositional attachment following another prepositional attachment or an adjectival one). Both models have been used extensively in probabilistic models for parsing, but our use is slightly different as we only use these models for ordering within the same adjunct site. In the context of standard probabilistic context-free grammars, these models are ususally used to model the entire right-hand side of context-free rules.

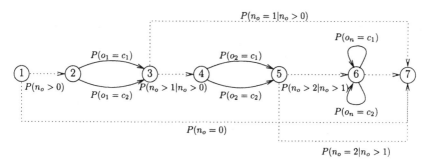

Fig. 3. Repeatable site with two distinguished positions

5.1   Model 1: Positional Model

The automaton for a repeatable site with two positions is shown in Figure 3. It consists of a series of transitions between consecutive pairs of states. The first "bundle" of transitions models the first attachment at the site, the second bundle, the second attachment, and so on, until the maximum number of explicitly modeled attachments is reached. The number of explicitly modeled attachments is a parameter of the model. This limit on the number of attachments concerns only the probabilistic part of the automaton, more attachments can occur on this node, but their probabilities will not be distinguished. These additional attachments correspond to the loops on state 6 of the automaton. ϵ-transitions allow the attachments to stop at any moment by transitioning to state 7. Under Model 1, the probability of the sequences c_1c_2 and $c_1c_2c_1c_2$ being adjoined are:

$$P(c_1c_2) = P(o_1 = c_1) \times P(o_2 = c_2) \times P(n_o = 2)$$

$$P(c_1c_2c_1c_2) = P(o_1 = c_1) \times P(o_2 = c_2) \times P(o_n = c_1) \times P(o_n = c_2) \times P(n_o > 2)$$

Where variables o_1 and o_2 represent the first and second order adjunctions. Variable o_n represents adjunctions of order higher than 2. Variable n_o represents the total number of adjunctions performed.

5.2 Model 2: N-Gram Model

The previous model takes into account the nature of an attachment at a given order as well as the total number of attachements but disregards the nature of the attachments that happened before (or after) a given attachment. The model described here is, in a sense, complementary to the previous one since it takes into account, in the probability of an attachment, the nature of the $n-1$ attachments that occurred before and ignores the order of the current attachment. The probability of a series of attachments on the same side of the same node will be computed by an order-n Markov chain. The order of the Markov chain is a parameter of the model. The first order Markov chain for our sample repeatable site is represented as a finite state automaton in Figure 4. The transitions with probabilities $P(x|\text{START})$ ($P(\text{END}|x)$, respectively) correspond to the occurrence of automaton x as the first (the last, respectively) attachment at this node and the transition with probability $P(\text{END}|\text{START})$ corresponds to the null adjunction (the probability that no adjunction occurs at a node). The probability of the sequence $c_1 c_2 c_1 c_2$ being adjoined is now:

$$P(c_1 c_2 c_1 c_2) = P(c_1|\text{START}) \times P(c_2|c_1) \times P(c_1|c_2) \times P(c_2|c_1) \times P(\text{END}|c_2)$$

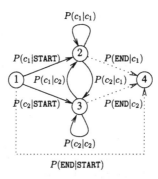

Fig. 4. Repeatable site with bigram modeling

6   Extracting a PGDG From a Corpus

We first describe the algebraic part of the extraction process, then briefly describe the estimation of the parameters of the probabilistic models.

6.1   Basic Approach

To extract a GDG (i.e., a lexicalized RTN) from the Penn Treebank (PTB), we first extract a TAG, and then convert it to a GDG. We make the detour via TAG for the following reason: we must extract an intermediate representation first in any case, as the automata in the GDG may refer in their transitions to any other automaton in the grammar. Thus, we cannot construct the automata until we have done a first pass through the treebank. We use TAG as the result of the first pass because this work has already been done, and we can reuse previous work, specifically the approach of Chen [12] (which is similar to that of Xia *et al.* [13] and that of Chiang [14]). Note that the different models discussed in Section 5 only affect the manner in which the TAG grammar extracted from the corpus is converted to an FSM; the parsing algorithm (and code) is always the same.

We first briefly describe the work on TAG extraction, but refer the reader to the just cited literature for details. For our purposes, we optimize the head percolation in the grammar extraction module to create meaningful dependency structures, rather than (for example) maximally simple elementary tree structures. For example, we include long-distance dependencies (*wh*-movement, relativization) in elementary trees, we distinguish passive transitives without *by*-phrase from active intransitives, and we include strongly governed prepositions (as determined in the PTB annotation, including passive *by*-phrases) in elementary verbal trees as secondary lexical heads. Generally, function words such as auxiliaries or determiners are dependents of the lexical head,[2] conjunctions (including punctuation functioning as conjunction) are dependent on the first conjunct and take the second conjunct as their argument, and conjunction chains are represented as right-branching rather than flat.

In the second step, we directly compile this TAG into a set of FSMs which constitute the GDG and which are used in the parser. An FSM is built for each elementary tree of the TAG, during its depth-first traversal. In most cases, the tree traversal proceeds from the root to the root in a depth-first manner (but excluding the root and foot nodes of adjunct auxiliary trees). Non-leaf nodes are visited twice: first during the downward traversal, and then again during upward traversal. Special attention must be paid to predicative auxiliary trees, i.e., trees which are headed by a predicate that has a clausal argument. For predicative auxiliary trees which are left auxiliary trees (in the sense of [15], i.e., all nonempty frontier nodes are to the left of the footnode), the traversal ends at the footnode. For right auxilary predicative trees (which do not occur for English), the traversal would start at the footnode.

Each time a node is visited in the depth-first traversal, a site is built in the corresponding automaton. Each transition in the site corresponds to an attachment that can be performed at the node, or to a lexical transition. If the node visited is a substitution node of category X, a substitution site will be created in the FSM. The transitions in the substitution site are labeled with all the initial trees of the TAG whose root has category X. If the leaf node is the lexical root of the elementary tree, a lexical site is created with one transition, labelled with the lexical anchor, if the elementary tree is lexicalized, or with the special

---

[2] This is a linguistic choice and not forced by the formalism or the PTB. We prefer this representation as the resulting dependency tree is closer to predicate-argument structure.

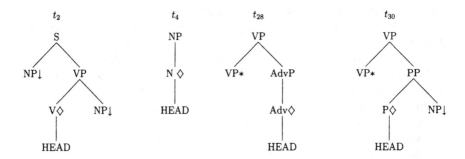

Fig. 5. Sample small grammar: trees for a transitive verb, a nominal argument, and two VP adjuncts from the right

symbol HEAD in the case of a tree schema. Finally, internal nodes of the elementary tree give rise to adjunction sites in the automaton. In the basic model in which adjunctions are modeled as independent events, we proceed as follows. To each non-leaf state, we add one self loop transition for each tree in the grammar that can adjoin at that state from the specified direction (e.g., for a state representing a node on the downward traversal, the auxiliary tree must adjoin from the left), labeled with the tree name. In Section 5, we discussed two other models that treat non-leaf nodes in a more complex manner. We omit a dull discussion of their construction, which is straightforward.

The result of this phase of the conversion is a set of FSMs, one per elementary tree of the grammar, whose transitions refer to other FSMs. We give a sample grammar in 5 and the result of converting one of its trees to an FSM in Figure 6[3].

6.2   Parameter Estimation

During the extraction of the TAGfrom the corpus, three kinds of counts are collected for each elementary tree schema T of the grammar: the number of times T has been selected as a root of a derivation tree, the number of substitutions of another elementary tree schema at the different substitution nodes of T, and the number of adjunctions of other elementary tree schemas at the internal nodes of T. Along with the last type of counts, the direction of the adjunction (left or right) is specified, as well as the order of the adjunction and the n preceding adjunctions of the same direction at this node.

These counts are used to estimate the root selection probabilities of the automata (the probability that an elementary tree schema constitues the root of a derivation tree) as well as the probabilities of their transitions. The initial probabilities, as well as the substitution and the adjunction probabilities in the positional models are estimated using simple add-one smoothing (actually, add-X smoothing with X tuned to 0.00001 on a development corpus), with the

---

[3] Due to space scarseness, we do not label the arcs of the automata of figure 6 with both probabilities and (function, supertag) pairs.

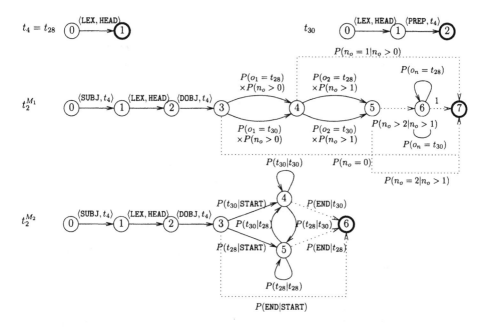

Fig. 6. FSMs derived from the grammar in figure 5. Two versions of tree t_2 has been built, corresponding to models 1 and 2.

quantities added to the counts optimized on a developpment corpus. The adjunction probabilities in the N-gram models are smoothed using linear interpolation with lower order N-grams.

7   Conclusion

We have presented a probabilistic generative formalism for dependency grammars which can be seen as a probabilistic lexicalized version of Recursive Transition Networks. The topology of the automata that constitue the grammars can be modified in order to account for different probabilistic models. Two such models have been discussed. We showed how PGDG can be extracted from a treebank. Empirical results using GDG on the Penn Treebank have been presented in [8] and results on a French treebank can be found in [16].

Further work on this topic will focus on the coupling of a supertagger with the parser and the developpment of other probabilistic models.

References

1. Rambow, O., Bangalore, S., Butt, T., Nasr, A., Sproat, R.: Creating a finite-state parser with application semantics. In: Proceedings of the 19th International Conference on Computational Linguistics (COLING 2002), Taipei, Republic of China (2002)

2. Woods, W.A.: Transition network grammars for natural language analysis. Commun. ACM **3** (1970) 591–606
3. Hays, D.G.: Dependency theory: A formalism and some observations. Language **40** (1964) 511–525
4. Gaifman, H.: Dependency systems and phrase-structure systems. Information and Control **8** (1965) 304–337
5. Abney, S.: A grammar of projections. Unpublished manuscript, Universität Tübingen (1996)
6. Madsen, O., Kristensen, B.: *LR*-parsing of extended context-free grammars. Acta Informatica **7** (1976) 61–73
7. Lombardo, V.: An Earley-style parser for dependency grammars. In: Proceedings of the 16th International Conference on Computational Linguistics (COLING'96), Copenhagen (1996)
8. Nasr, A., Rambow, O.: Supertagging and full parsing. In: Proceedings of the Workshop on Tree Adjoining Grammar and Related Formalisms (TAG+7), Vancouver, BC, Canada (2004)
9. Alshawi, H., Bangalore, S., Douglas, S.: Learning dependency translation models as collections of finite-state head transducers. cl **26** (2000) 45–60
10. Eisner, J.M.: Three new probabilistic models for dependency parsing: An exploration. In: Proceedings of the 16th International Conference on Computational Linguistics (COLING'96), Copenhagen (1996)
11. Bangalore, S., Joshi, A.: Supertagging: An approach to almost parsing. Computational Linguistics **25** (1999) 237–266
12. Chen, J.: Towards Efficient Statistical Parsing Using Lexicalized Grammatical Information. PhD thesis, University of Delaware (2001)
13. Xia, F., Palmer, M., Joshi, A.: A uniform method of grammar extraction and its applications. In: Proc. of the EMNLP 2000, Hong Kong (2000)
14. Chiang, D.: Statistical parsing with an automatically-extracted tree adjoining grammar. In: 38th Meeting of the Association for Computational Linguistics (ACL'00), Hong Kong, China (2000) 456–463
15. Schabes, Y., Waters, R.C.: Tree Insertion Grammar: A cubic-time, parsable formalism that lexicalizes Context-Free Grammar without changing the trees produced. Computational Linguistics **21** (1995) 479–514
16. Nasr, A.: Analyse syntaxique probabiliste pour grammaires de dTpendances extraites automatiquement. Habilitation a diriger des recherches, UniversitT Paris 7 (2004)

Integrating a POS Tagger and a Chunker Implemented as Weighted Finite State Machines

Alexis Nasr and Alexandra Volanschi*

Lattice-CNRS (UMR 8094)
Université Paris 7
{alexis.nasr, alexandra.volanschi}@linguist.jussieu.fr

Abstract. This paper presents a method of integrating a probabilistic part-of-speech tagger and a chunker. This integration lead to the correction of a number of errors made by the tagger when used alone. Both tagger and chunker are implemented as weighted finite state machines. Experiments on a French corpus showed a decrease of the word error rate of about 12%.

Keywords: Part-of-speech tagging, chunking, weighted finite state machines

1 Introduction

POS Tagging is often a prerequisite for more elaborate linguistic processing such as full or partial parsing. Probabilistic taggers implementing Hidden Markov Models (HMMs) are based on the hypothesis that the tag associated to a word depends on a local context, usually limited to the category(ies) of the preceding word(s). This hypothesis is generally verified and taggers implementing this model are known to be efficient and accurate (about 95% precision). The approximation is nevertheless responsible for the majority of tagging errors, which in turn lead to errors in subsequent processing stages. This situation is particularly frustrating since, at subsequent syntactic processing stages, the knowledge which could prevent the errors might be available. The present work is an attempt to deal with this problem by coupling the tagging and partial parsing stages. In this configuration, the choice of the tag is dictated by knowledge associated both to the tagger and the chunker. The model constitutes an alternative to the classical sequential model, in which the chunker input is the most probable solution of the tagger. In this configuration, choices made by the tagger can no longer be altered.

The type of error the present work tries to deal with is illustrated by the French sentence: *La démission n'est pas indispensable* (*the resignation is not indispensable*). Tagging the adjective *indispensable* might prove difficult as it may be masculine or feminine and the noun it agrees with (*démission*) is too

---

* This work was partly funded by the Technolangue Project of the French Ministry of Culture .

A. Yli-Jyrä, L. Karttunen, and J. Karhumäki (Eds.): FSMNLP 2005, LNAI 4002, pp. 167–178, 2006.
© Springer-Verlag Berlin Heidelberg 2006

remote from it (at least for an HMM tagger). In exchange, a chunker would group the sequences *la démission, n'est pas*, and *indispensable* into larger units called *chunks*. This would bring the two units agreeing in number and gender, namely (*la démission* and *indispensable*) closer to each other, thus making it possible for an HMM to capture agreement.

This article also aims to point out the advantages of using weighted finite state machines and operations defined on them for the whole processing. In this framework, all data (sentences to be analyzed, lexicons, grammars, n-grams) are represented as finite state automata and (almost) all treatments were implemented as standard operations on automata. This homogeneity has several advantages, the most significant of which being the possibility to easily combine different modules using automata combining operations, combinations which would be more difficult to achieve between modules based on different formal models. Another advantage of this homogeneity is the simplicity of the implementation: one no longer has to define specific formats for different types of data, to implement, adapt or optimize existing algorithms. Software libraries for automata manipulation are essential for such treatments; in the present work we have used the utilities FSM and GRM developed by ATT [1].

The paper is organized as follows: section 2 is a brief reminder of definitions concerning weighted finite state automata, introducing a number of notations used in the remainder of the article. Sections 3 and 4 describe respectively the principles of a probabilistic POS tagger and of a chunker as well as their implementation using weighted finite state machines. The method of integrating the two modules is presented in the section 4.3.

2   Definitions and Notations

In this article two types of finite state machines are manipulated: on the one hand automata, which recognize words u built on an alphabet Σ ($u \in \Sigma^*$), and on the other transducers, which recognize word pairs built on two alphabets Σ_1 and Σ_2 ($(u, v) \in \Sigma_1^* \times \Sigma_2^*$). In addition to standard regular operations (union, concatenation and iteration) defined on both types of machines, certain operations are specific for transducers, in particular *composition*, which plays an essential role in the present work. Given two transducers, A and B which recognize respectively the word pairs (u, v) and (v, w), the composition of A and B ($A \circ B$) is a transducer which recognizes the couple (u, w).

In addition, we use the notion of semiring, which is defined as a 5-tuple $(\mathbb{K}, \oplus, \otimes, \bar{0}, \bar{1})$ such that $\mathbb{K}$ is a set equipped with two operations defined on it, generally called addition (denoted by $\oplus$) and multiplication ($\otimes$), each having its neutral element denoted respectively by $\bar{0}$ and $\bar{1}$. By associating to every transition in an automaton a weight from the set $\mathbb{K}$, we obtain a weighted automaton built over the semiring $\mathbb{K}$. A weighted automaton together with a semiring $\mathbb{K}$ generates a partial function which associates values from $\mathbb{K}$ to every word recognized. Given an automaton R and a word u, the value associated to u by R, denoted by $[\![R]\!](u)$, is the multiplication ($\otimes$) of weights on transitions along the path in R corresponding to u. If several paths in R recognize u, then $[\![R]\!](u)$ equals the addition ($\oplus$) of weights of the different paths corresponding to u.

In the experiments described in the present work we systematically use the *tropical semiring* on $\mathbb{R}^+$: the weights used on transitions are opposites of the logarithms of probabilities[1]. With the tropical semiring the operation $\otimes$ corresponds to arithmetic addition (to compute the weight of a path in the automaton, weights on individual transitions constituting a path are added), while the $\oplus$ operation is the minimum (the weight associated by an automaton to a word recognized is the minimum weight of all paths corresponding to the word, i.e. the most probable path). Given a weighted automaton R over the tropical semiring, one can define the *n-best paths* operator, denoted by $bp(R, n)$, which yields the automaton made of the union of the n most likely paths in R.

3   Standard POS Tagging

In the present work, part of speech tagging follows the principles of Hidden Markov Models, introduced by [3]. The states in the HMM correspond to parts of speech and the observable symbols to words in the lexicon. The latter constitute the alphabet Σ_L and categories in the tagset constitute the alphabet Σ_C. POS tagging in such a framework consists in finding the most probable sequence of states through which the HMM passes, given a sequence of observable symbols produced by the model (the sentence).

The parameters of a HMM may be divided into emission probabilities and transition probabilities. An emission probability is the probability of a word given a category $(P(m|c))$ while the transition probability is the probability that a given category x immediately follow a category y $(P(x|y))$. The joint probability of a sequence of categories $c_{1,n}$ (a sequence of states the model goes through) and of a sequence of words $m_{1,n}$ (a sequence of observable symbols) is computed on the basis of the emission and transition probabilities:

$$P(c_{1,n}, m_{1,n}) = P(c_1)P(m_1|c_1) \prod_{i=2}^{n} P(m_i|c_i)P(c_i|c_{i-1})$$

Such a model, called a *bigram* model, relies on the Markov hypothesis, according to which a category only depends on the preceding category. This restraining hypothesis may be rendered more supple without changing the theoretical framework by making the hypothesis that a category depends on the two preceding categories; this type of model (*trigram*) is the one most commonly used for the POS assignment task. In a trigram model, a state no longer corresponds to a category, but to a pair of categories.

Such a HMM may be represented by two weighted transducers. The first one, E, represented on the left-hand side of figure 1 (in this example $\Sigma_L = \{a, b\}$ and $\Sigma_C = \{A, B\}$), encodes the emission probabilities. Its input alphabet

---

[1] Logarithms of probabilities are preferred to probabilities for reasons of numerical stability (as probabilities may be very small real numbers, by multiplying probabilities one may be not able to represent these values on computer).

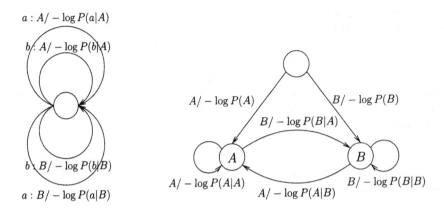

Fig. 1. The transducers E and T

is Σ_L and its output alphabet Σ_C. The transducer has a single state and as many transitions (from this state to itself) as there are pairs (m, c) where m is a word from the lexicon and c a category ($c \in \Sigma_C$) such that the emission probability $P(m|c)$ is non-null. The opposite of the logarithm of this probability $(-\log P(m|c))$ constitutes the weight of the transition tagged (m, c). In figure 1 such a transition is labeled $m : c/-\log P(m|c)$.

The second transducer, T, which has Σ_C as input and output alphabets, encodes transition probabilities. Its structure is isomorphic to that of the HMM: as many states as there are state pairs (x, y) (oriented from x to y) such that $P(y|x)$ is non null. Weights on transitions equal $-\log P(y|x)^2$. With a trigram model the structure of the automaton T is more complex: a state corresponds to a sequence of two categories and the transition weights are trigram probabilities.

The composition of E and T ($E \circ T$) allows to combine the emission and transition probabilities; the input alphabet of the transducer obtained is Σ_L and the output alphabet is Σ_C. Such a transducer associates to every couple $(m_{1,n}, c_{1,n})$ the weight $[\![E \circ T]\!](c_{1,n}, m_{1,n}) = -\sum_{i=1}^{n} \log P(m_i|c_i) - \log P(c_1) - \sum_{i=2}^{n} \log P(c_i|c_{i-1})$ which is in fact the opposite of the logarithm of the probability $P(c_{1,n}, m_{1,n})$, such as defined above.

Tagging a given sequence of words M is achieved by representing M as a linear automaton also called M (with one transition for every word in M) and subsequently composing M with $E \circ T$. The most probable sequence of categories given M is identified by looking for the best path of the transducer $M \circ E \circ T$. The POS tagger could then be formally defined as: $bp(M \circ E \circ T, 1)$.

The trigram probabilities encoded in the automaton T are not, as a rule, estimated by maximum likelihood on a training corpus, as trigrams appearing

---

[2] Strictly speaking, the machine described is an automaton, but it can be viewed as a transducer whose transitions output the same symbol as the one they read in the input. Such a transducer represents the identity relation restricted to the language recognized by the automaton.

in the texts to be tagged may never have occurred in the training corpus. It is therefore essential to use a probability smoothing technique, such as back-off [4]; the method consists in *backing-off* on the probability of bigram b c when trigram a b c is not observed in the training corpus, and on to the probability of the unigram c when bigram b c is never encountered. A back-off model may be directly represented by using *failure transitions* as described in [5]. Given a symbol α, a failure transition coming out of a state q is taken when there is no transition labeled by α. In the case of a back-off model, a failure or default transition is taken when a trigram or bigram was never observed. For more details, the reader is referred to the article cited above.

Several approaches in the literature [6, 7, 8] use finite state machines in order to simulate the functioning of HMMs. In all approaches, n-grams are represented by finite-state automata in a manner similar to ours. They are nevertheless different from our work in that they don't directly manipulate emission probabilities $(P(m|c))$ estimated on a training corpus, but resort to ambiguity classes, which are sets of categories associated to a word.

Preliminary Results. All the experiments described in the present work are conducted on the tagged and hand-validated corpus produced at the University of Paris 7[9]. The corpus consists of $900K$ words tagged with 222 tags indicating the category and morphological features. $760K$ words were used for training (*Train*). Tests are done on a $66K$ words fragment (*Test*). All experiments are achieved using the libraries FSM and GRM made available by AT&T. The error rate of the trigram model (denoted by $\mathcal{M}_1$) such as described above on *Test* is of $2, 18\%$[3]. This figure is our reference.

4   Language Models Derived from Probabilistic Chunking

The models of finite-state-based POS Tagging mentioned in section 3, agree on the necessity of integrating syntactic constraints. Kempe [7] anticipates the possibility of composing the tagger output with transducers encoding correction rules for the most frequent errors, Tzoukerman [6] uses negative constraints in order to drastically diminish the weight of paths containing unlikely sequences of tags (such as a determiner immediately followed by a verb). Basically, our work is different from the others in that it integrates two distinct, complete modules (a tagger and a chunker) within a single module which accomplishes both tasks at the same time. The approach does not consist in integrating a number of local grammars to the tagger, but in combining statistical information with the linguistic knowledge encoded by the chunker with a view to improving the

---

[3] The result is better than the one reported by [6] (4% error rate) on the same corpus, using the same tagset. The difference comes mainly from the fact that we excluded unknown words: all words in *Test* appear in the dictionary. We have made this choice because the purpose of the present work is to study the interaction of the chunker and HMM tagger, and we assume that the influence of unknown words would basically be the same on the different models we have tested.

quality of the tagger and, additionally producing a likely sequence of chunks. Before going into the details of the various integration models we conceived, let us briefly remind the principles of chunking, present a way of implementing a chunker as a finite state machine and explain the necessity of converting it into a probabilistic chunker which is also represented as a finite state machine.

4.1   Chunking as Finite State Machine Manipulations

Chunking designates a series of techniques whose purpose is to uncover the syntactic structure of a sentence, or more precisely the structure associated to the fragments which may only have one analysis. For instance, even if for a traditional grammar a sequence like *maison des sciences de l'homme* (*house of the science of the man* (*center for human sciences*)) constitutes a noun phrase, having a complex structure with several intermediate levels, a chunker would split it into 3 units called *chunks* : [maison]$_{NC}$ [des sciences]$_{PC}$ [de l'homme]$_{PC}$ as the prepositional attachment is potentially ambiguous. The technique, also known as *chunking*, was introduced by [10] in answer to the difficulties that robust analysis of raw text encountered.

Several approaches among which [11] have implemented chunking by finite state machines, or more precisely as cascaded finite state transducers. A cascade of finite state transducers is a sequence of transducers, each recognizing a type of chunk. The input of every transducer is constituted by the output of the previous one. Our solution consists in the simultaneous, rather than sequential, application of all the chunk automata which are integrated into a single transducer.

A chunk is the non-recursive core of a phrase, irrespective of its category. As opposed to [12], chunking embedding is not allowed in the present approach; in exchange, the longest string matching the definition of a chunk is selected: we prefer an analysis like [*le nouveau batiment*]$_{NC}$ (*the new building*) rather than [*le* [*nouveau*]$_{AC}$ *batiment*$_{NC}$].

Given their non-recursive character, chunks may be represented by finite state automata built on the alphabet Σ_C. 28 chunk grammars corresponding to nominal, adjectival, adverbial and prepositional chunks are constructed manually. These grammars belong to a class of context-free grammars which represent regular languages and which may, consequently, be compiled as finite-state machines ([13]) and integrated to the chunker. For every type of chunk K, an automaton also called K is built to recognize well-formed chunks of type K. Moreover, two symbols marking the chunk beginning (<K>), and the end (</K>) are associated to every chunk of type K. The whole set of chunk beginning and chunk end marks constitute a new alphabet called Σ_K. Chunk automata are grouped within a single transducer called A, i.e. the chunker, whose structure is represented in figure 2.

A's input alphabet is Σ_C and its output alphabet is $\Sigma_C \cup \Sigma_K$. It accepts sequences of categories and outputs sequences of categories and chunk beginning or end marks. Given a sequence of categories C, A outputs the same sequence in which every occurrence of a K chunk is delimited by the two symbols <K>

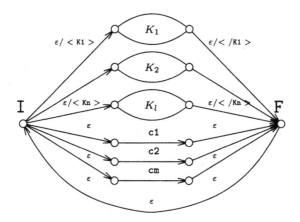

Fig. 2. Chunker structure

and `</K>`. As represented in figure 2, A is composed of two parts: the upper side is the union of the different chunk automata, K_i, while the lower side is made of as many transitions as there are POS categories in the input alphabet. Transitions linking A's initial state to the initial states of the chunk automata K_i introduce the chunk beginning marks, while transitions linking chunk automata K_i acceptance state to the state F of automaton A insert chunk ending symbols. Finally, an ε transition linking F to I builds a loop, thus making it possible to recognize several chunk occurrences in the same sequence of categories.

The automaton A recognizes any word C built on Σ_C. The analysis of C is achieved by representing it as a linear automaton, C, and then making the composition $C \circ A$. The product of this composition is most likely ambiguous, since for every sub-string s of C corresponding to a chunk K_i, two results are produced: one recognizes s as a chunk (passage through the automaton K_i), the other doesn't (passage through the lower part of A). Of these results the only one which is of interest to us is the one in which all chunk occurrences are marked by beginning and end tags. It is easy to limit the composition product to this result alone by associating a weight of 0 to intra-chunk transitions and a weight of 1 to extra-chunk transitions and selecting from the resulting transducer the minimal weight path. An additional penalty score is associated to transitions introducing chunk boundaries marks to ensure that the longest match would be chosen (i.e. the preferred analysis of a sentence would be one containing chunks, but as few boundaries marks as possible). This ensures that an analysis like [le livre rouge]$_{NC}$ (the red book) would be preferred to [le livre]$_{NC}$ [rouge]$_{AC}$. The analysis may thus be expressed by: $bp(C \circ A, 1)$.

The tagger and chunker integration could now be accomplished by a simple composition of the two models previously described, which may be expressed by: $bp(bp(M \circ E \circ T, 1) \circ A, 1)$. However, this model is an instance of the sequential architecture which was introduced and criticized in section 1: the selection of a particular POS tag is done independently of the chunking stage (in the present work, this stage being a mere chunk segmentation), and may not be altered to take into account the information available to the chunker. It is possible to provide the chunker not only with the best tagging solution but with the set of all tagging solutions represented by the automaton: $bp(M \circ E \circ T \circ A, 1)$. This goes to prove the flexibility of finite state processing. Nevertheless, such a model is not very interesting either since the chunker has no discriminating power: it cannot favor any of the tagger solutions. Indeed, unlike a CFG parser, which only associates structure to sequences belonging to the grammar language, our chunker accepts any sequence of categories in the tagger output, its role being limited to identifying certain sub-strings as chunks.

This is the reason which led us to build a probabilistic version of the chunker, that not only recognizes chunks, but associates them a probability according to a Markov model, the parameters of which are estimated on a corpus. Before going into the details of the ways in which such a probabilistic chunking model could be integrated with a part-of-speech tagger (section 4.3), we describe the construction of the chunker.

4.2   The Construction of a Probabilistic Chunker

The purpose of this model is not to favor a particular segmentation of a sequence of categories into chunks, but to provide a way to rank the different possible sequences of categories corresponding to the same sentence. To this effect, the chunker associates every sequence of categories a probability which increases function of the following factors:

(1) the sequence of categories corresponds to a sequence of well formed chunks
(2) these chunks appear in a linear order that has frequently been observed in a training corpus. In this respect, the chunker is (functionally) very similar to an n-gram of categories.

This approach has a lot in common with [14] which also employs weighted finite state transducers in order to build a probabilistic chunker. Nevertheless, in their work there are several ways of segmenting a sentence into chunks and their chunker is meant to find the most probable one among them. Moreover, the input of their chunker is a linear sequence of part-of-speech tags. Whereas our chunker takes as input a set of possible part-of-speech tags sequences represented as an automaton.

The probability of a sequence of categories segmented into chunks is computed function of two types of probabilities: intra- and extra-chunk probabilities. An intra-chunk probability is the probability of a sequence of categories $c_{1,k}$ making up a chunk of type K_i, probability denoted by $P_I(c_{1,k}|K_i)$. An inter-chunk probability is the conditional probability of the occurrence of a particular type of chunk given the $n - 1$ preceding chunks or categories (as this is a partial parse, certain categories in the sequence being analyzed are not integrated into chunks). The probability associated by the chunker to a sequence of categories is the product of internal probabilities of the chunks composing it and of the external probabilities of the sequence of chunks recognized.

Given the sequence of categories `<s> D N V D N P D A N </s>`[4], the segmentation proposed by the chunker is:

`C = <s> <NC> D N </NC> V <NC> D N </NC> <PC> P D A N </PC> </s>`

The probability associated to this sequence is the product of the external probabilities of the chunks recognized ($P_E(\cdot)$), and of internal probabilities of all chunks in the sequence:

$$P(C) = P_E(\texttt{<s> <NC> V <NC> <PC> </s>}) \times P_I(\texttt{D N|<NC>})^2 \times P_I(\texttt{P D A N| <PC>})$$

Internal probabilities are estimated by maximum likelihood on a training corpus, as will be shown in section 4.2. The probability of a sequence of chunks and categories is computed using an n-gram model, called external model, which encodes the probability of a chunk given the $n-1$ preceding chunks. In the case of a bigram model the external, inter-chunk probability of C is computed as follows:

$$P_E(C) = P_E(\texttt{<NC>|<s>}) \times P_E(\texttt{V|<NC>}) \times P_E(\texttt{<NC>|V}) \times P_E(\texttt{<PC>|<NC>}) \times P_E(\texttt{</s>|<PC>})$$

Model Construction and Parameter Estimation. The parameters of the external model and of the internal chunk models are estimated in two stages on a tagged corpus as illustrated in figure 3. First the corpus is analyzed using the non-probabilistic version of the chunker, **A**. The result of this analysis is a new corpus in which chunk beginning and end symbols are inserted. Two objects are derived from this corpus: on the one hand, all sequences of categories corresponding to a type of chunk K_i (which we call patterns) and on the other hand a *hybrid* corpus in which every chunk occurrence is replaced by a symbol representing the category of the chunk. This corpus is made of sequences of categories and chunk symbols replacing sequences of categories grouped into chunks. The first object is used to compute intra-chunk probabilities (by converting the chunk grammars written for the non-probabilistic version of the chunker described in section 4.1 into probabilistic context-free grammars) while the second one is used for estimating inter-chunks probabilities.

The estimation of inter-chunk probabilities starting from the hybrid corpus is identical to the estimation of n-gram probabilities described in section 3. These probabilities are represented by a transducer (the external model) whose structure is similar to that of T in figure 1 and whose transitions are labeled with categories or chunk symbols. Intra-chunk probabilities are estimated by maximum-likelihood. Given a chunk C_k and n different sequences of categories $(s_1, s_2, \ldots s_n)$ representing all possible patterns for this type of chunk, observed in a training corpus, n_i denotes the number of occurrences of the sequence c_i. The probability of the sequence s_i is estimated by its relative frequency: $P(s_i) = \frac{n_i}{\sum_{k=1}^{n} n_k}$. This probability is that of the path corresponding to s_i in the automaton K_i.

---

[4] Where D, N, V, P and A are the tags corresponding to the categories *determiner*, *noun*, *verb*, *preposition* and *adjective* respectively.

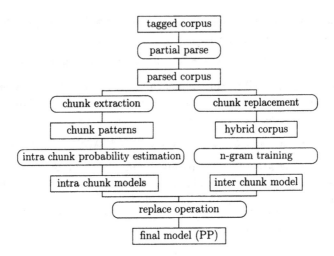

Fig. 3. The model construction stages

Intra-chunk models and the external model are combined within a single transducer using the *replacement* operation described in [1]. This operation substitutes the automaton K_i for each transition <Ki> in the external model. The resulting transducer is called PC (for probabilistic chunker) and has about 10 times more states and transitions than T, the transducer encoding trigram probabilities, however, we assumed that it encodes longer-distance dependencies for the estimation of which our training data would have been sparse. Therefore we conducted a series of experiments in which we replaced the transducer T with PC, using the tagging model $bp(M \circ E \circ PC, 1)$.

Probabilistic Chunker Performance. Intra- and inter-chunk probabilities are estimated on *Train* and the new tagging model $bp(M \circ E \circ PC, 1)$ ($\mathcal{M}_2$) was applied to *Test*. Disappointingly, we found that ($\mathcal{M}_2$) performs only slightly better than $\mathcal{M}_1$ (an error rate decrease of 6% relative). Nevertheless, the model is interesting in that it functions as a tagger and a chunker at the same time.

More interestingly, the two models don't make the same mistakes. $\mathcal{M}_2$ corrects 30% of the errors made by $\mathcal{M}_1$ but makes almost as many of its own. The new type of errors have various causes, most of which are related to the hypothesis we made that the form of a chunk (the sequence of categories which constitute a chunk) is independent of the context in which the given chunk occurs. This hypothesis is an approximation just like the Markov hypothesis. The sentence 'la discussion a été ouverte par l'article ...' (*the discussion was initiated by the paper ...*) is a good case in point. In this case, *ouverte* is rightly tagged past participle by model $\mathcal{M}_1$, while $\mathcal{M}_2$ tags it adjective. The reason is that $\mathcal{M}_2$ grouped *a été ouverte* as a verb chunk, but chose the category of *ouverte* without taking into account the context where the chunk occurred. On the other hand the model $\mathcal{M}_1$ probably takes advantage of the fact that *ouverte* is followed by the preposition *par* and attributes the right category.

4.3   Integration of the POS Tagger and the Probabilistic Chunker

In order to deal with the limitations of models $\mathcal{M}_1$ and $\mathcal{M}_2$ we have combined the two within a single complex model: $bp((M \circ E \circ PC) \cap (M \circ E \circ T), 1)$, denoted by $\mathcal{M}_3$. This automaton is the union of solutions common to $\mathcal{M}_1$ et $\mathcal{M}_2$ to which it associates the sum of weights attributed by $\mathcal{M}_1$ and $\mathcal{M}_2$ ($[\![\mathcal{M}_3]\!](x) = [\![\mathcal{M}_1]\!](x) + [\![\mathcal{M}_2]\!](x)^5$). This combination is a way of partially attenuating the effect of the independence hypothesis mentioned above. The dependency between the form of a chunk and the context where it occurs is partially modelled by $\mathcal{M}_1$. The error rate obtained by the model $\mathcal{M}_3$ on *Test* is of $1,92\%$, which is $11,9\%$ less than our reference model $\mathcal{M}_1$. Error analysis showed that $\mathcal{M}_3$ corrects $15,5\%$ of the errors $\mathcal{M}_1$ makes but makes $7,9\%$ new errors. The errors specific to $\mathcal{M}_3$ may be explained by a number of causes: some are still due to the independence hypothesis mentioned above, others (about 10%) are due to the method of estimating intra-chunk probabilities (the probability that a given sequence of categories constitutes a chunk). These probabilities are estimated by maximum likelihood and therefore attribute a null probability to chunk patterns which, although encoded in the chunk grammar, have never been seen in *Train*. A technique for smoothing these probabilities is necessary for the method to be more robust. Other errors are due to the theoretical limitations of the model and would probably only be corrected by using full syntactic analysis.

5   Conclusion

The work presented in this paper has shown that taking into account the syntactic knowledge encoded in a chunker may improve the result of a part-of-speech tagger. It has also shown how to represent these two modules as weighted finite-state machines and how to combine them using standard operations defined on automata. Two limits of the chunker probabilistic model have been brought to light : the estimation of the intra-chunk probabilities as well as the independence assumption between the form of a chunk and its context. This assumption can be partially relieved by combining a standard n-gram model and the chunker.

References

1. Mohri, M.: Weighted Grammars Tools: the GRM Library. In: Robustness in Language and Speech Technology. Jean-Claude Junqua and Gertjan Van Noord (eds) Kluwer Academic Publishers (2000) 19–40
2. Mohri, M.: Finite-state transducers in language and speech processing. Computational Linguistics **23** (1997)
3. Bahl, L.R., Mercer, R.L.: Part of speech assignment by a statistical decision algorithm. In: Proceedings IEEE International Symposium on Information Theory. (1976) 88–89

---

^{5} Unlike the models $\mathcal{M}_1$ and $\mathcal{M}_2$, the weight associated to a sequence of categories by $\mathcal{M}_3$ does no longer represent probabilities.

4. Katz, S.M.: Estimation of probabilities from sparse data for the language model component of a speech recogniser. IEEE Transactions on Acoustics, Speech, and Signal Processing **35** (1987) 400–401

5. Allauzen, C., Mohri, M., Roark, B.: Generalized algorithms for constructing statistical language models. In: 41st Meeting of the Association for Computational Linguistics, Sapporo, Japon (2003) 40–47

6. Tzoukermann, E., Radev, D.R.: Use of weighted finite state trasducers in part of speech tagging. Natural Language Engineering (1997)

7. Kempe, A.: Finite state transducers approximating hidden markov models. In: 35th Meeting of the Association for Computational Linguistics (ACL'97), Madrid, Spain (1997) 460–467

8. Jurish, B.: A hybrid approach to part-of-speech tagging. Technical report, Berlin-Brandenburgishe Akademie der Wissenschaften (2003)

9. Abeillé, A., Clément, L., Toussenel, F.: Building a treebank for french. In Abeillé, A., ed.: Treebanks. Kluwer, Dordrecht (2003)

10. Abney, S.P.: Parsing by chunks. In Berwick, R.C., Abney, S.P., Tenny, C., eds.: Principle-Based Parsing: Computation and Psycholinguistics. Kluwer, Dordrecht (1991) 257–278

11. Abney, S.: Partial parsing via finite-state cascades. In Workshop on Robust Parsing, 8th European Summer School in Logic, Language and Information, Prague, Czech Republic, pages 8–15. (1996)

12. Abney, S.: Chunk stylebook. http://www.vinartus.com/spa/publications.html (1996)

13. Mohri, M., Pereira, F.C.N.: Dynamic compilation of weighted context-free grammars. In: 36th Meeting of the Association for Computational Linguistics (ACL'98). (1998)

14. Chen, K.H., Chen, H.H.: Extracting noun phrases from large-scale texts: A hybrid approach and its automatic evaluation. In: Meeting of the Association for Computational Linguistics. (1994) 234–241

Modelling the Semantics of Calendar Expressions as Extended Regular Expressions

Jyrki Niemi and Lauri Carlson

University of Helsinki, Department of General Linguistics,
P.O. Box 9, FI–00014 University of Helsinki, Finland
{jyrki.niemi, lauri.carlson}@helsinki.fi

Abstract. This paper proposes modelling the semantics of natural-language calendar expressions as extended regular expressions (XREs). The approach covers expressions ranging from plain dates and times of the day to more complex ones, such as *the second Tuesday following Easter*. Expressions denoting disconnected periods of time are also covered. The paper presents an underlying string-based temporal model, sample calendar expressions with their XRE representations, and possible applications in temporal reasoning and natural-language generation.

1 Introduction

Temporal information and calendar expressions are essential in various applications, for example, in event calendars, appointment scheduling and timetables. Calendar expressions can be simple dates, times of the day, days of the week or combinations of them, or they can be more complex, such as *the second Tuesday following Easter*. The information should often be both processed by software and presented in a human-readable form.

Following Carlson [1], we propose in this paper an approach that models the semantics of natural-language calendar expressions as extended regular expressions (XREs), called calendar XREs. The well-known semantics of regular languages and regular expressions can be used in reasoning with temporal information represented as calendar XREs. We also believe that calendar XREs are structurally so close to the corresponding natural-language expressions that the latter can be generated from the former fairly straightforwardly.

A calendar expression is a temporal expression denoting a period or moment of time that does not depend on the time of use of the expression, such as *1 September 2005*. However, the denotation may be underspecified or ambiguous without context, as in the expression *September*. In addition to connected periods (convex intervals) of time, the present approach can model disconnected (non-convex) ones, such as *two Sundays*. It can also be extended to cover a number of deictic and anaphoric temporal expressions, such as *today* and *the following week*. We are mainly interested in the language-independent semantics of calendar expressions, abstracted from different syntactic variants and disambiguated.

To provide a denotation to calendar XREs, we model time as a long string of consecutive basic periods of time, such as minutes or seconds, each represented

A. Yli-Jyrä, L. Karttunen, and J. Karhumäki (Eds.): FSMNLP 2005, LNAI 4002, pp. 179–190, 2006.
© Springer-Verlag Berlin Heidelberg 2006

by a unique symbol. Basic calendar periods, for example days and months, are then represented as sets of substrings of this timeline string. The basic calendar periods are further combined with XRE operations to represent more complex calendar expressions, such as *1–2 September 2005* and *every second Wednesday of the year*. This requires operations that not only combine or select existing strings from operand languages but also extract parts of the strings.

The rest of the paper is organized as follows. Section 2 presents the notations and extended regular expression operations used. Section 3 outlines a string-based model of time. Section 4 presents a number of natural-language calendar expression constructs together with their corresponding XREs. Section 5 briefly describes application experiments: temporal reasoning using calendar XREs and natural-language generation from them. Section 6 presents some related work in temporal expression research. Section 7 concludes the paper with discussion and some directions for further research.

2 Regular Expression Operations and Notations

In addition to the basic regular expression operations of concatenation, union and Kleene star, we use a number of other operations. The usual XRE operations are intersection, complement and difference. We also use several operations defined using regular relations (finite transducers), for example substring, quotient and affix operations. Concatenation power and its generalized form are notational shorthands that help in making calendar XREs structurally closer to the corresponding natural-language calendar expressions.

Table 1 lists the operations referred to in this paper, our notation for them, and their definitions by means of sets. The notation $L(R)$ denotes the regular language specified by the XRE R; we abbreviate $L(\Sigma^*)$ as Σ^*. In the table, capital-letter variables denote XREs, the variable a denotes a single symbol of the alphabet Σ, and the variables x, y and z with possible subscripts denote strings over Σ. We use the same operation symbols for XREs and for the languages they denote. We include 0 in the set $\mathbb{N}$ of natural numbers. The exponent of a generalized concatenation power may consist of enumerated set expressions, intervals and unions of them. Intervals may either be closed or have ∞ as the upper limit.

The precedence of operations follows [2] (p. 119): unary prefix operations have the highest precedence, followed by unary postfix operations, then concatenation, with binary operations lowest. Otherwise evaluation proceeds from left to right. Parentheses are used to override precedence rules.

We also use parametrized macros to simplify XREs containing repeating subexpressions and to make calendar XREs structurally closer to natural language. For example, we could define a macro symmdiff(x,y) for symmetric difference as $(x - y) \cup (y - x)$; the expression symmdiff(a,b) would then denote the symmetric difference of a and b. The arguments to a macro may be either XREs or concatenation power exponents, depending on their use in the macro. The macros have no recursion or other means of control.

Table 1. XRE operations and notations

Notation	Name	Denoted language
Σ	any symbol	$L(\Sigma) = \{a \mid a \in \Sigma\}$
ε	empty string	$L(\varepsilon) = \{\varepsilon\}$
$A \cdot B$	concatenation	$L(A \cdot B) = \{xy \mid x \in L(A),\, y \in L(B)\}$
$A \cup B$	union	$L(A \cup B) = L(A) \cup L(B)$
$A \cap B$	intersection	$L(A \cap B) = L(A) \cap L(B)$
$A - B$	difference	$L(A - B) = L(A) - L(B)$
A^n	concatenation power	$n \in \mathbb{N},\, L(A^0) = \{\varepsilon\},\, L(A^n) = L(A \cdot A^{n-1})$
A^N	generalized concat. power	$N \subseteq \mathbb{N},\, L(A^N) = \bigcup_{n \in N} L(A^n)$
A^*	Kleene star	$L(A^*) = L(A^{\mathbb{N}})$
$\neg A$	complement	$L(\neg A) = L(\Sigma^* - A)$
$\text{in}_+ A$	non-empty substring	$L(\text{in}_+ A) = \{y \mid xyz \in L(A),\, x, y, z \in \Sigma^*\} - \{\varepsilon\}$
$\text{in}_+^* A$	non-empty subword	$L(\text{in}_+^* A) = \{y_1 \ldots y_n \mid x_1 y_1 x_2 \ldots x_n y_n x_{n+1} \in L(A),$
		$\quad x_1, \ldots, x_{n+1}, y_1, \ldots, y_n \in \Sigma^*,\, n \geq 1\} - \{\varepsilon\}$
$P \mathbin{/\!/} A$	prefix	$L(P \mathbin{/\!/} A) = \{x \mid xy \in L(A),\, x \in L(P),\, y \in \Sigma^*\}$
$A \mathbin{\backslash\!\backslash} S$	suffix	$L(A \mathbin{\backslash\!\backslash} S) = \{y \mid xy \in L(A),\, x \in \Sigma^*,\, y \in L(S)\}$
$\text{pref}_+ A$	non-empty untyped prefix	$L(\text{pref}_+ A) = L((\Sigma^* \mathbin{/\!/} A) - \varepsilon)$
$B \setminus A$	left quotient	$L(B \setminus A) = \{y \mid xy \in L(A),\, x \in L(B),\, y \in \Sigma^*\}$
A / B	right quotient	$L(A / B) = \{x \mid xy \in L(A),\, x \in \Sigma^*,\, y \in L(B)\}$
$\triangleleft A$	left closure	$L(\triangleleft A) = L(\neg(\Sigma^* . A . \Sigma^*) . A)$
$A \triangleright$	right closure	$L(A \triangleright) = L(A . \neg(\Sigma^* . A . \Sigma^*))$

3   A String-Based Model of Time

In order to be able to represent calendar expressions as XREs, we model periods of time as strings of symbols. The model presented here is not the only possible one. It may also be feasible to regard and process calendar XREs purely syntactically, without being committed to a specific semantic model.

Let the time domain $\mathcal{T}_\infty$ be an infinite set with a total order. Let us partition $\mathcal{T}_\infty$ to half-open intervals $t_k = [\tau_k, \tau_{k+1}[$, $k \in \mathbb{Z}$, where each $\tau_k \in \mathcal{T}_\infty$ represents a point of time. The intervals represent basic periods, the base granularity of calendar XREs. The sequence $T_\infty = (t_k)$ represents an infinite timeline.

Since regular expressions can specify only strings over a finite alphabet,[1] we choose an application-specific finite timeline $T_{m,n} = (t_{m+1}, \ldots, t_{m+n})$ (where $m \in \mathbb{Z}$ and $n \geq 1$) that is a connected subsequence of T_∞. For each basic period t_{m+i}, let a_i denote the corresponding symbol. These symbols form the alphabet $\Sigma_T = \{a_i \mid 1 \leq i \leq n\}$. The string $a_1 \ldots a_n$ corresponds to the timeline $T_{m,n}$; we denote this timeline string as T.

A single calendar XRE R specifies a regular language consisting of non-empty subwords (that is, possibly disconnected substrings) of the timeline

---

[1] Büchi automata could be used to represent infinite strings. However, representing infinite strings in the model presented here would require an infinite alphabet, which cannot be represented by Büchi automata. We also believe that, in general, finite periods of time should suffice for calendar applications.

string T: $L(R) \subseteq L(\mathbf{in}_+^* T)$. A calendar XRE R represents a period of time $T = (t_{m+i_1}, \ldots, t_{m+i_k})$ if and only if $L(R)$ contains the string $a_{i_1} \ldots a_{i_k}$, where $1 \leq i_j \leq n$ for $1 \leq j \leq k$, and $i_j < i_{j+1}$ for $1 \leq j < k$. (The period T is a subsequence of the timeline $T_{m,n}$.) For example, if the timeline begins from a Monday and the basic period is an hour, all Mondays are specified by the set $\{a_i \ldots a_{i+23} \mid i = 1 + 168k, 0 \leq k \leq \frac{n}{168}\} = \{a_1 \ldots a_{24}, a_{169} \ldots a_{192}, \ldots\}$.

A calendar XRE representing an inconsistent temporal expression, such as *30 February*, denotes the empty set.

The language of an XRE may contain strings that are not subwords of the timeline string T. They typically result from the use of concatenation or complement. Such a string contains a symbol a_i followed by an a_j with $i \geq j$. It is not meaningful as a representation of time, as a period of time may not be followed by the same or a preceding period. We limit the languages of calendar XREs to representing meaningful periods by intersecting them with $L(\mathbf{in}_+^* T)$.

The model of time described above cannot represent points of time, as each basic period of time t_i corresponds to an interval between points of time. In practice, even a moment regarded as a point of time usually covers a short period of time [1] (pp. 194–195).

4   Calendar Expressions and Their Regular Expressions

4.1   General Features

In this section we demonstrate key features of calendar XREs by presenting a number of constructs appearing in natural-language calendar expressions, and their representations as calendar XREs. Table 2 lists the constructs that we have treated, including those omitted here. They were originally found in a corpus of Web pages. A more detailed description of all the constructs can be found in [3].

The meaning of a natural-language calendar expression can be vague or underspecified, such as *Monday* or *in the morning*, or ambiguous, such as *a week*, which may denote either a calendar period or a duration. We do not model the natural-language expressions as such but instead their disambiguated meanings, while trying to retain underspecification wherever possible.

In the examples we leave implicit the intersection with the set $L(\mathbf{in}_+^* T)$. We generally present the expressions in a simple form, disregarding special cases that may require more complicated XREs. We also assume connected periods of time unless otherwise mentioned. We mention a macro defined for a calendar XRE construct only if it is referred to later or if it better illustrates an expression.

We have tried to make calendar XRE constructs compositional as far as possible: they should combine with each other analogously to the corresponding constructs of natural-language calendar expressions. However, a number of constructs are compositional only to a limited extent or not at all.

4.2   Basic Calendar Expressions

The basic expressions of calendar XREs denote sets of calendar periods. An unqualified natural-language calendar expression, such as *Monday* or *January*,

Table 2. Types and examples of natural-language calendar expressions

Expression type	Examples
calendar period	*12.00; September; year; Easter*
duration	*an hour; 4 to 10 hours; at least 8 days; 3 weeks short of 2 years*
list	*Mondays and Wednesdays; Mon and Wed or Tue and Thu*
subperiod	*on Friday; in September*
refinement	*Christmas Eve falling on a Friday; 22 May; in 2005 by April*
containment	*weekend containing Christmas Day*
interval	*Monday to Friday; from September on; before 15 May;*
	from 10 am on Sunday to 6 pm on Friday
exception	*8 am, except Mondays 9 am; every day except Monday*
anchored	*the second Tuesday following Easter;*
	the second and fourth Tuesday following Easter;
	four weeks before Christmas;
	the weekend preceding a mid-week Christmas Day
consecutive	*two consecutive Sundays; six consecutive months from May 2002*
ordinal	*the third and fourth Wednesday of the month;*
	every second Wednesday of the year
parity	*even Tuesdays of the month*
relative frequency	*four weeks a year; two Saturdays a month during the school year*
deictic	*today; next week*
anaphoric	*the following week*
time zone	*9.00–16.00 Central European time*

typically refers to the nearest past or future period relevant in the context. In this work, however, we interpret such expressions as underspecified, for example, referring to any Monday. The calendar XRE corresponding to *Monday* is *Mon*, which denotes the set of all Mondays. We regard the basic expressions as predefined constants that specify sets of substrings of the timeline string *T*.

The basic expressions corresponding to the basic periods of the Gregorian calendar include both generic periods, such as day, month and year (*min* to *year*), and specific ones, such as each hour (*h00* to *h23*), day of week (*Mon* to *Sun*), day of month (*1st* to *31st*), month (*Jan* to *Dec*) and year (*ynnnn*). Hours and shorter units of time are also treated as periods; for example, hour 10 is the hour beginning at 10 am. We also assume appropriately predefined sets for seasons and holidays, for example, *Easter* and *Christmas_Day*. Many of them could also be defined compositionally; for instance, Christmas Day is 25 December every year. Some of them are culture-specific; for example, Easter is often celebrated at different times in Eastern Orthodox churches and in Western churches.

The generic calendar periods are unions of the corresponding specific calendar periods. For example, a week is any connected seven-day period from a Monday to the following Sunday.[2] However, a week may also be a duration or a measurement unit consisting of any seven days or 168 hours. A week as a duration is not

---

[2] We could equally well define a week beginning from a Sunday.

necessarily aligned to calendar days or even hours, and it can be disconnected, spreading over a longer period of time. Such calendar-based measurement units are represented by the constant sets min_{dur} to $year_{dur}$, each of which contains all possible connected and disconnected periods of time of the duration in question. A variable-length duration, such as a month, is represented as the union of the durations of the possible lengths.

4.3   Duration Expressions

Basic durations can be combined to form more complex ones. Multiples of durations are formed using concatenation power; for example, the duration expression *five days* is represented as the calendar XRE $day_{dur}{}^5$. With the generalized concatenation power we can also express in a natural manner duration intervals, possibly with one endpoint omitted: *4 to 10 hours* can be represented as $hour_{dur}{}^{[4,10]}$ and *at least 8 days* as $day_{dur}{}^{[8,\infty[}$.

However, the denotation of the XRE $hour_{dur}{}^{[4,10]}$ only includes multiples of an hour and not for example the duration 4.5 hours. To cover all durations within the interval, we intersect the XRE for the minimum, with any number of basic periods added, and the XRE for the maximum, with any number of basic periods removed: $(hour_{dur}{}^4 \cdot \Sigma^*) \cap (hour_{dur}{}^{10} / \Sigma^*)$. This corresponds directly to the expression *at least 4 hours and at most 10 hours*.

A duration consisting of more than one basic duration is formed with concatenation; for example, *two years and three months* is represented as the XRE $year_{dur}{}^2 \cdot month_{dur}{}^3$. A duration with a subtraction, such as *three weeks short of two years*, is expressed by removing the shorter duration from the longer one using a quotient operation: $year_{dur}{}^2 / week_{dur}{}^3$.

4.4   Basic Combining Constructs

Four basic constructs combining calendar XREs are lists, concatenation, refinement and containment.

Lists of calendar expressions are in general represented using union. For example, the expression *Mondays and Wednesdays* can be interpreted as "any single Monday or Wednesday", and thus we represent the expression as the calendar XRE $Mon \cup Wed$. However, sometimes an expression contains both *and*s and *or*s: for example, *Mon and Wed or Tue and Thu*. In such a case, we use concatenation for *and* and union for *or*: $(Mon \cdot Wed) \cup (Tue \cdot Thu)$.

More generally, concatenation juxtaposes periods of time. Concatenating nonadjacent periods results in a disconnected period. For example, the above calendar XRE represents periods of time that contain a Monday followed by a Wednesday, or a Tuesday followed by a Thursday. The XRE does not guarantee that the second day of a period is the closest following suitable day; that would require a somewhat more complex XRE.

Refinement uses intersection to combine multiple subexpressions, each of which refines or restricts the period of time denoted by the whole expression. For example, the expression *Christmas Eve falling on a Friday* is represented as *Christmas_Eve* ∩ *Fri*. Refinement often combines expressions denoting periods of different lengths, in which case we need to apply a substring (subperiod) operation to at least the longer period; for example, *22 May* is represented as *22nd* ∩ **in**$_+$*May*. Here **in**$_+$*May* denotes the set of substrings of the strings representing all Mays. Intersecting it with the set corresponding to all the 22nd days of all months results in a set denoting the 22nd days of Mays.

A calendar expression may denote a period of time that contains another period, for example, *the week containing Christmas Eve*. This is expressed simply as *week* ∩ (*Σ**.*Christmas_Eve*.*Σ**).

4.5   Intervals

An interval *Monday to Friday* begins from a Monday and almost always ends in the closest following Friday. This interval can be expressed as the calendar XRE *Mon* . ¬ (*Σ**.*Mon*.*Σ**) . *Fri*, meaning "a Monday followed by anything not containing a Monday, followed by a Friday".[3] To simplify such XREs, we have defined a macro with which the above XRE can be written as interval(*Mon*,*Fri*). The same denotation can also be obtained with a closure operation: *Mon*▷. *Fri*.[4]

If either of the endpoints of an interval expression is omitted, we assume that the interval does not contain the previous or next period of the same kind as the endpoint that is present. For example, the expression *from September on* would denote a period extending from a September to the following August. This is the broadest denotation with which the expression is unambiguous.

Hour intervals require mapping the point-like hour expressions of natural language to the periods used in calendar XREs. We achieve this by removing the last hour of the interval with a quotient operation: *from 8 to 11 (am)* is represented as interval(*h08*,*h11*) / *hour*. If the end of the interval is expressed to the minute, as in *from 8.00 to 11.00*, only the last minute is removed.

4.6   More Complex Calendar Expressions

In this subsection we present examples of exception expressions, anchored expressions, ordinal expressions and relative frequency expressions.

The expression *8 am, except Mondays 9 am* is an exception expression. Such an expression consists of two or three parts: a default time, an exception scope and an optional exception time (cf. [1], pp. 194–195). In the above expression, *8 am* is the default time, *Mondays* the exception scope and *9 am* the exception time. In calendar XREs this can be expressed with union, difference and intersection: (*h08* − **in**$_+$*Mon*) ∪ (*h09* ∩ **in**$_+$*Mon*). If the exception time is omitted, the difference alone suffices.

---

[3] To obtain connected periods of time with the correct denotation, the XRE must be further intersected with **in**$_+$ *T* instead of **in**$_+^*$ *T*.

[4] The closure operations bear resemblance to the shortest-match directed replacement operator of Karttunen [4], and to the non-greedy variants of regular expression matching operators in the Perl programming language (http://www.perl.org/).

An anchored expression denotes a time relative to an anchor time. For example, the expression *the second Tuesday following Easter* refers to a time relative to Easter. To find a calendar XRE for the expression, we note that it denotes the last day in a string of days beginning from Easter, containing exactly two Tuesdays and ending in a Tuesday. Using a closure and a suffix operation, this can be expressed as the XRE *Easter* . $(\triangleleft Tue)^2 \setminus\setminus Tue$. Using a macro defined for this construct, the XRE would be nth_following(2, *Tue*, *Easter*). Similar *preceding*-expressions can be represented analogously by changing the order of the subexpressions and the direction of the closure and affix operations. By using the generalized concatenation power, we can represent such expressions as *the second and fourth Tuesday following Easter* and *two Tuesdays following Easter*.

The ordinal expression *the third and fourth Wednesday of the month* is similar to an anchored one, but counting takes place within a longer period. The expression denotes the last day in a string of days that begins from the beginning of a month, that contains three or four Wednesdays, and that ends in a Wednesday. We can represent the expression as $((\triangleleft Wed)^{\{3,4\}} \cap \mathbf{pref}_+ month) \setminus\setminus Wed$. By changing the order of the subexpressions and the directions of the operations, we can represent expressions counting from the end of a period, such as *the last Monday of the month*.

The expression *every second Wednesday of the year* is an example of another ordinal expression type. We interpret it to denote the first, third, fifth and so on Wednesday of the year, represented as $(((\triangleleft Wed)^2)^* . \triangleleft Wed \cap \mathbf{pref}_+ year) \setminus\setminus Wed$. Since this calendar XRE construct contains a concatenation power inside a Kleene star, it counts multiples of a natural number larger than one, and thus it is not star-free [5] (pp. 5–6). The only other non-star-free type of calendar expressions that we have encountered are parity expressions, such as *even Tuesdays of the month*. Parity expressions can be represented in a manner very similar to the above XRE.

A relative frequency expression, such as *two Saturdays a month*, denotes a certain number of shorter periods of time, not necessarily consecutive, within a longer one (cf. [1], p. 190). The above expression can be represented as the calendar XRE $Sat^2 \cap \mathbf{in}_+^* month$, which specifies disconnected periods of time.

4.7   Extensions

In addition to calendar expressions, many deictic and anaphoric temporal expressions can also be represented as calendar XREs. Following [1] (p. 173), we represent the current time as *now* and the reference time of an anaphoric expression as *then*. Using these variables, we can express *today* as $day \cap (\Sigma^*.now.\Sigma^*)$ ("the day containing the current time") and *the following week* as following(*week*, *then*).[5]

While we have treated calendar expressions independent of time zones, it is possible to represent periods of time in another time zone as calendar XREs by shifting the denoted strings by the appropriate amount relative to the timeline string.

---

[5] Macro following is defined as following$(x, y) = $ nth_following$(1, x, y)$.

5   Application Experiments

We have briefly experimented with temporal reasoning using calendar XREs, and with generating corresponding natural-language expressions from them.

5.1   Temporal Reasoning with Calendar XREs

We have mainly considered a form of temporal reasoning that finds the common periods of time denoted by two calendar XREs. Such reasoning could be used in querying temporal data; for example, a query to an event database could be used to find out at what time certain museums are open on Mondays in December, or which museums are open on Mondays in December. For the former query, we should find for each target XRE in the database the set of periods of time denoted by both the query and the target XRE, and for the latter, whether the query and target XREs denote some common periods or not. Both basically require computing the intersection of the query and target XREs.

In principle, such reasoning could be implemented straightforwardly as model checking, by constructing finite-state automata from the XREs and intersecting them, and by either enumerating the strings of each intersection or checking if the intersection is empty. In practice, however, constructing the automata would often require too much space or time or both to be tractable. Moreover, the enumerated language as such is seldom desirable as the result, as it may be very large and incomprehensible to a human.

We have used the Xerox Finite-State Tool (XFST) [6] to experiment with calendar XREs and with reasoning based on model-checking. Despite its efficiency, XFST was not able to complete in two gigabytes of virtual memory the construction of an automaton representing all the substrings of a timeline string of 2880 symbols, corresponding to the minutes in 48 hours. Constructing a subword automaton is even more demanding, as a string of n symbols has 2^n subwords. The set of substrings or subwords is needed to restrict the language of a calendar XRE to denoting only meaningful periods of time.

5.2   Natural-Language Generation from Calendar XREs

Calendar XREs could be used as a language-independent representation of calendar expressions in a possibly multilingual natural-language generation system. Our hypothesis was that calendar XREs should be structurally very close to the corresponding natural-language expressions, which should allow fairly straightforward generation following the structure of a calendar XRE.

In our experiments we encountered more complexities than we had expected, but they were at the surface-syntactic and morphological level, not in higher-level structures. The use of XRE macros was essential; without them, the natural-language expressions generated from complex XREs would have been cumbersome and their intended meaning probably impossible to understand.

We simplified the generation component proper by assuming it to be preceded by a separate transformation phase that could be used to make changes to the structure of a calendar XRE while preserving its meaning. This phase could, for example, normalize the order of subexpressions of an XRE or regroup them, doing the equivalent of transforming, for instance, *on Mondays in December* to *in December on Mondays*, or *1 May to 25 May* to *1–25 May*.

6   Related Work

Temporal expressions in general have been much studied, including modelling the semantics of calendar expressions and reasoning with them. Our main inspiration has been Carlson's [1] event calculus, which includes modelling calendar expressions as XREs.

The Verbmobil project [7] had a formalism of its own to represent and reason with temporal expressions occurring in appointment negotiation dialogues [8]. Its coverage of calendar expressions was similar to that of calendar XREs, but it did not cover disconnected periods of time.

The calendar logic of Ohlbach and Gabbay [9, 10] and in particular its time term specification language can represent calendar expressions of various kinds. However, calendar logic expressions are not structurally as close to natural-language expressions as calendar XREs. Han and Lavie [11] use their own formalism in conjunction with reasoning using temporal constraint propagation. They explicitly cover more types of expressions than we do, including underspecified expressions and quantified ones, such as *every week in May*.

Regular expressions are used in conjunction with temporal expressions by Karttunen et al. [12], who express the syntax of dates as regular expressions to check their validity. They limit themselves to rather simple dates, however. Fernando [13, 14] uses regular expressions to represent events with optional temporal information. Focusing on events, his examples feature only simple temporal expressions, such as *(for) an hour*.

7   Discussion and Further Work

In our view, extended regular expressions would in general seem to be fairly well suited to modelling the semantics of calendar expressions. Calendar XREs are structurally relatively close to natural-language calendar expressions, and the semantics of regular expressions is well known. The former property can be of use in natural-language generation, the latter in reasoning. However, to be useful in practice, the formalism should have a tractable reasoning method.

While calendar XREs cover many different types of calendar expressions, they cannot naturally represent fuzzy or inexact expressions, such as *about 8 o'clock*, or internally anaphoric expressions, such as *9.00 to 17.00, an hour later in winter*. Furthermore, fractional expressions, such as *the second quarter of the year*, seem to be impossible to represent compositionally as XREs, since regular expressions have no notion of fractions.

There are a number of limitations in the compositionality of the calendar XRE constructs that we have devised, and the XREs of some types of calendar expressions are rather complex. In particular, adding support for disconnected periods of time often significantly complicates a calendar XRE. Although some of the complexity can be hidden with macros, complex constructs make computation slower and may also weaken compositionality.

We have applied XREs only to calendar expressions of the Gregorian calendar system, but we expect the representation to work with any calendar system based on similar principles of hierarchical calendar periods, provided that appropriate basic expressions are defined for the periods.

Our main future research goal is to find a tractable and practical reasoning method for calendar XREs. One option would be to process XREs syntactically using term rewriting, with which we have already made some elementary experiments. Term rewriting would probably also allow representing a query result in a more user-friendly manner as another XRE. A major drawback of term rewriting is that each XRE operator and possibly each macro should be separately taken into account in the rewriting rules. Keeping the rewriting system terminating and confluent would also pose a challenge. Reasoning could also be made more efficient by representing basic calendar periods as regular relations (finite-state transducers) instead of sets of substrings of the timeline string (Nathan Vaillette, personal communication). Depending on the application, it might be possible to operate on the relations alone and dispose of the timeline string. In general, we could combine several different approaches, using each one where it is best.

Another major goal would be to extend the formalism to cover more expression types, in particular fuzzy expressions, and preferably also internally anaphoric and fractional expressions. The representation of fuzzy temporal expressions has been researched, for example, by Ohlbach [15]. Extending the coverage may require introducing some non-finite-state elements to the formalism, which would make it much less clean than at present. Another approach might be to have a higher-level representation with these features, translated to finite-state constructs. We would also like to try to improve the compositionality of current calendar XRE constructs and possibly to find simpler constructs for some expression types.

Since regular languages correspond to monadic second-order logic (MSOL), we could also represent calendar expressions using MSOL instead of XREs (or as a complement to them), in the spirit of the MONA system [16]. Some types of calendar expressions would probably be easier to express in MSOL, others perhaps as XREs.

Lastly, it might be worthwhile to explore options of representing events combined with calendar expressions, or at least to examine calendar expressions in their context. Such approaches might sometimes help to resolve the meaning of a single fuzzy or underspecified calendar expression.

Acknowledgements

We are grateful to the anonymous reviewers and Nathan Vaillette for their valuable comments and suggestions.

References

1. Carlson, L.: Tense, mood, aspect, diathesis: Their logic and typology. Unpublished manuscript (2003)
2. Karttunen, L.: The replace operator. In Roche, E., Schabes, Y., eds.: Finite-State Language Processing. Language, Speech, and Communication. MIT Press, Cambridge, Massachusetts (1997) 117–147
3. Niemi, J.: Kalenteriajanilmausten semantiikka ja generointi: semantiikan mallintaminen laajennettuina säännöllisinä lausekkeina ja lausekkeiden luonnolliskielisten vastineiden XSLT-pohjainen generointi [The semantics and generation of calendar expressions: Modelling the semantics as extended regular expressions and generating the corresponding natural-language expressions using XSLT]. Master's thesis, University of Helsinki, Department of General Linguistics, Helsinki (2004)
4. Karttunen, L.: Directed replacement. In: 34th Meeting of the Association for Computational Linguistics (ACL '96), Proceedings of the Conference, Santa Cruz, California. (1996) 108–115
5. McNaughton, R., Papert, S.: Counter-Free Automata. Number 65 in Research Monographs. M.I.T. Press, Cambridge, Massachusetts (1971)
6. Karttunen, L., Gaál, T., Kempe, A.: Xerox finite-state tool. Technical report, Xerox Research Centre Europe, Grenoble, France (1997) http://www.xrce.xerox.com/competencies/content-analysis/fssoft/docs/fst-97/xfst97.html.
7. Wahlster, W., ed.: Verbmobil: Foundations of Speech-to-Speech Translation. Artificial Intelligence. Springer, Berlin (2000)
8. Endriss, U.: Semantik zeitlicher Ausdrücke in Terminvereinbarungsdialogen. Verbmobil Report 227, Technische Universität Berlin, Fachbereich Informatik, Berlin (1998)
9. Ohlbach, H.J., Gabbay, D.: Calendar logic. Journal of Applied Non-classical Logics 8 (1998) 291–324
10. Ohlbach, H.J.: Calendar logic. In Gabbay, D.M., Finger, M., Reynolds, M., eds.: Temporal Logic: Mathematical Foundations and Computational Aspects. Volume 2. Oxford University Press, Oxford (2000) 477–573
11. Han, B., Lavie, A.: A framework for resolution of time in natural language. ACM Transactions on Asian Language Information Processing (TALIP) 3 (2004) 11–32
12. Karttunen, L., Chanod, J.P., Grefenstette, G., Schiller, A.: Regular expressions for language engineering. Natural Language Engineering 2 (1996) 305–328
13. Fernando, T.: A finite-state approach to event semantics. In: Proceedings of the 9th International Symposium on Temporal Representation and Reasoning (TIME-02), Manchester, IEEE Computer Society Press (2002) 124–131
14. Fernando, T.: A finite-state approach to events in natural language semantics. Journal of Logic and Computation 14 (2004) 79–92
15. Ohlbach, H.J.: Relations between fuzzy time intervals. In: Proc. 11th International Symposium on Temporal Representation and Reasoning (TIME 2004). (2004) 44–50
16. Henriksen, J.G., Jensen, J.L., Jørgensen, M.E., Klarlund, N., Paige, R., Rauhe, T., Sandholm, A.: MONA: Monadic second-order logic in practice. In Brinksma, E., Cleaveland, R., Larsen, K.G., Margaria, T., Steffen, B., eds.: Tools and Algorithms for the Construction and Analysis of Systems, First International Workshop, TACAS '95, Aarhus, Denmark, May 19–20, 1995, Proceedings. Number 1019 in Lecture Notes in Computer Science, Springer (1995) 89–110

Using Finite State Technology in a Tool for Linguistic Exploration

Kemal Oflazer, Mehmet Dinçer Erbaş, and Müge Erdoğmuş

Faculty of Engineering and Natural Sciences
Sabancı University
Tuzla, Istanbul, Turkey 34956
oflazer@sabanciuniv.edu,
{derbas, mugeerdogmus}@su.sabanciuniv.edu

Abstract. Intelligent, interactive and pervasively accessible tools for providing information about elements of a language are crucial in learning a language, especially in an advanced secondary language learning setting and learning for linguistic exploration. The paper describes a prototype implementation of a tool that provides intelligent, active and interactive tools for helping linguistics students inquire and learn about lexical and syntactic properties of words and phrases in Turkish text. The tool called LINGBROWSER uses extensive finite state language processing technology to provide instantaneous information about morphological, segmental, pronunciation properties about the words in any real text. Additional resources also provide access to semantic properties of (root) words.

1 Introduction

Linguistics students wishing to embark upon understanding linguistics properties of a language and conduct research on that language, need to have access to various resources. The need for such resources is much more acute for languages such as Turkish whose complex morphology makes linguistic exploration for non-native speakers all the more difficult. One can however employ language processing tools and resources to alleviate some of these difficulties.

This paper describes LINGBROWSER, an intelligent text browser that employs finite state language processing technology to provide an active and interactive environment for accessing all kinds of linguistic information about the elements of a text. LINGBROWSER provides information about morphological segmentation and features of a word, alignments of surface and lexical morphemes including explanations about any morphophonological phenomena, segmental structure, pronunciation and any relevant explanations about pronunciation phenomena such as the position of stress. Such information is pervasively available for all words in a text, *and* in any of the windows that display results of queries. Words are also linked to aligned concept ontology databases such as WordNet [1, 2], so that meanings can be accessed and semantic properties and neighbors of a word

A. Yli-Jyrä, L. Karttunen, and J. Karhumäki (Eds.): FSMNLP 2005, LNAI 4002, pp. 191–202, 2006.
© Springer-Verlag Berlin Heidelberg 2006

can be investigated. LINGBROWSER also provides lexical and morphological concordances, and will in the future provide morphological analysis, and synthesis
drills. LINGBROWSER has been implemented on a PC environment.

Although there has been much prior work in the use of computers in language
learning, dubbed Computer Assisted Language Learning (CALL), many CALL
systems have made very little use of advanced language technology. Borin, in
a recent paper reviewing the relationship between natural language processing
and CALL [3] essentially concludes that, "... in the eye of the casual beholder
– the two disciplines seem to live incompletely different worlds." Borin states
from the vantage point of NLP, CALL does not seem to have a place in natural
language processing, despite some fledging applications, though there have been
applications of AI in the broader field of intelligent tutoring systems. Similarly,
practitioners of CALL do not make use substantial and broad use of NLP (for
a survey of NLP in CALL, see Nerbonne [4]). There have been a number recent
of projects that have made use of language engineering technology to varying
extents in language learning. The GLOSSER Project [5] has developed a system
that aids readers of foreign language text, by providing access to a dictionary,
after performing a morphological analysis and part-of-speech disambiguation of
a word selected by the reader. In the context of Turkish, we can cite earlier work
by Güvenir [6], and Güvenir and Oflazer [7]. None of these however use any substantial language processing technology or address the concerns of sophisticated
learners of a language such as students of linguistics.

2   Turkish

Turkish has agglutinative word structures with productive inflectional and derivational processes. Turkish word forms consist of morphemes concatenated
to a root morpheme or to other morphemes, much like "beads on a string".
Except for a very few exceptional cases, the surface realizations of the morphemes
are conditioned by various regular morphophonemic processes such as vowel
harmony, consonant assimilation and elisions. The morphotactics of word forms
can be quite complex when multiple derivations are involved. For instance, the
derived modifier **sağlamlaştırdığımızdaki**[1] would be down as

   sağlamlaş+tır+dığ+ımız+da+ki

Starting from an adjectival root *sağlam*, this word form first derives a verbal stem
sağlamlaş, meaning "to become strong". A second suffix, the causative surface
morpheme *+tır* which we treat as a verbal derivation, forms yet another verbal
stem meaning "to cause to become strong" or "to make strong (fortify)". The
immediately following participle suffix *+dığ*, produces a nominal, which inflects
in the normal pattern for nouns (here for 1st person plural possessor which marks
agreement with the subject of the verb (*+ımız*), and locative case(*+da*). The

---

[1] Literally, "(the thing existing) at the time we caused (something) to become strong".
   Obviously this is not a word that one would use everyday.

final suffix, +*ki*, is a relativizer, producing a word which functions as a modifier in a sentence, modifying a noun somewhere to the right. For the word above, this segmented lexical morphographemic representation would be

```
sağlam+1Aş+DHr+DHk+HmHz+DA+ki
```

In this representation, lexical morphemes except the lexical root utilize meta-symbols that stand for a set of graphemes which are selected on the surface by a series of morphographemic processes, rooted in morphophonological processes some of which are discussed below. For instance, A stands for back and unrounded vowels *a* and *e*, in orthography, H stands for high vowels *ı, i, u* and *ü*, and D stands for *d* and *t*, representing alveolar consonants. Thus a lexical morpheme represented as +DHr actually represents 8 possible allomorphs, which appear as one of +*dır*, +*dir*, +*dur*, +*dür*, +*tır*, +*tir*, +*tur*, +*tür*, on the surface, depending on the local morphophonemic context.

Once the lexical structure of a word is obtained, one can then map the morphemes to the relevant morphosyntactic features and/or obtain further information about the word such as the location of the primary stress in its pronunciation.

3 LingBrowser Functionality

The current version of the LINGBROWSER prototype is designed to interactively provide linguistically relevant information about words in Turkish text. In this section, we review some of the functionality provided by the prototype implementation.

The main window of LINGBROWSER is shown in Figure 1, where one can load either a HTML or a text file. All functionality is available with a right-click menu in the main window *and* in all the information windows that pop up, as a result of user queries. The right-click menu provides the following functionality described in the following sections.

– **Morphological Analysis:** When the *Morphological Analysis* functionality is selected, a morphological analysis is performed and all morphological analyses of the selected word are displayed.[2] The morphological analysis (accessed from a database populated with output from a finite state morphological analyzer, [9]) includes the root word, the root part-of-speech and all relevant inflectional and derivational features encoded by any suffixes. In Figure 2, we see the analyses of the word *evinde*. The first analysis corresponds to the interpretation 'in your house', while the second one corresponds to the interpretation 'in his house'. Further, when mouse hovers on feature names such as +Loc, etc, a tool tip appears indicating what that feature means – locative case in this instance.

---

[2] In the very near future, we will highlight the contextually correct analysis using statistical morphological disambiguation techniques [8].

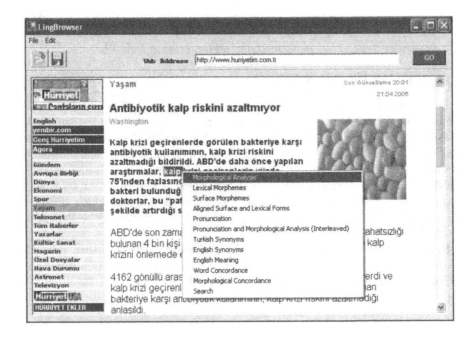

Fig. 1. LINGBROWSER main window with both HTML and text content

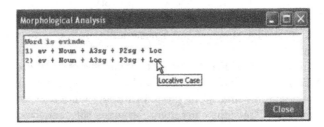

Fig. 2. Morphological analyses of a selected word

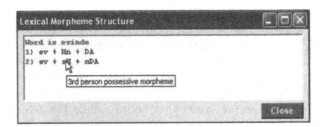

Fig. 3. Looking up the lexical morpheme structure

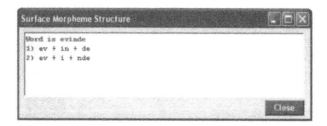

Fig. 4. Looking up the surface morpheme structure

- **Lexical Morpheme Structure:** The lexical morpheme structure of a word is the representation of the morphemes of a word where any allomorphy due to any morphographemic phenomena are abstracted away. For instance, although the words *masanda* and *evinde* in Turkish look quite different, the lexical morphemes except for the root are the same: *masanda* has the lexical structure `masa+Hn+DA`, while *evinde* has two possible lexical structures `ev+Hn+DA` and `ev+sH+nDA` corresponding to the interpretations 'in your house' and 'in his house' above.[3] Figure 3 shows the response of the system when *Lexical Structure* functionality is selected.

- **Surface Morpheme Structure:** LINGBROWSER provides access to the surface morpheme structure of the word in a text. The surface morpheme structure is like the lexical morpheme structure but the meta-symbols are resolved to their surface versions (along with possible deletions and insertions of symbols) by appropriate morphological rules. Thus, if the surface morpheme structure of the *evinde* is queried, one would get the result in Figure 4, where we see the meta-symbols resolved to their surface counterparts, H to i, A to e and D to d, and the symbol s in the second lexical morpheme in the second analysis is elided on the surface since the previous morpheme ends in a consonant.

- **Lexical Surface Alignment:** Understanding the morphological processes of a language involves an understanding the relationships between the lexical and surface structures, and the rules mediating those relationships, [10, 11], Thus, for instance one would like to select a word like *evinde* in LING-BROWSER and observe the following correspondence:[4]

  ev+Hn+DA   ev+sH+nDA
  ev0in0de   ev00i0nde

Looking at these aligned sequences of pairs of symbols, one can see that certain morphographemic rules are in effect. For instance, A is paired with

---

[3] For Turkish lexical morpheme representations we employ meta-symbols that represent classes of phonemes: here H represents a high-vowel (one of *ı*, *i*, *u* and *ü*) A represents a non-round low vowel (one of *a* and *e*), and D represents dental consonants *d* and *t*.

[4] The symbol 0 denotes the epsilon symbol of zero length, as used in two-level morphology.

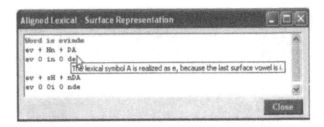

Fig. 5. Displaying the aligned feasible-pairs for a word

an **e**, since the vowel harmony rules in Turkish require that pairing if the
closest surface vowel on the left side of the pairing is one of *i, e, ö* or *ü*.
A sample output of LINGBROWSER for this functionality is depicted in
Figure 5. On this output, one can point to one of the feasible-pairs and
have a verbal explanation of the rule giving rise to that feasible-pair based
on the original two-level grammar [9], as a tooltip.

- **Pronunciation:** The problem of grapheme-to-morpheme mapping for Turkish is considerably simpler than for languages such as English or French.
Orthography more or less maps one-to-one to pronunciation. While all ho-
mophones are homographs, homographs can be morphologically interpreted
in different ways may give rise to different pronunciations. Such cases usually
stem from the fact that a loan word (usually from Arabic, Persian or French)
is a homograph of another Turkish word but has a different pronunciation -
either there is change in consonant quality or vowel length, none of which are
(usually) reflected to orthography. The other major source of pronunciation
ambiguity is the position of primary stress in the word. Turkish lexical stress
is determined by an interplay of any exceptional stress in root words and the
stress marking properties of morphemes [12].

LINGBROWSER provides access to possible pronunciations of a selected
word along with the morphological interpretation that gives rise to the associated pronunciation. In Figure 6, we see two examples:[5] In the first example,
we see the two possible pronunciations of the word *ajanda* (meaning either
'agenda' or 'on the agent'). The two pronunciations differ in the location of
the primary stress: in the first interpretation, the root word has exceptional
stress on the second syllable, while in the second interpretation where the
word is morphological segmented differently, the root word does not have
any exceptional stress properties and the primary stress surfaces on the final
syllable. The second example shows a case where in the first two interpretations, the senses of the root word **hal** are 'state' and 'wholesale fruit-
market' respectively. But in certain inflected forms with the first sense of
the word, the root vowel will lengthen. In Figure 7, we see the pronunciation
of the word *getiremiyorduk* ('we were not able to bring (it)') where now the
surface morphemes are interleaved with the features, and one can see the

---

[5] – indicates syllable boundary, " denotes the position of the primary stress, and :
indicates a long vowel.

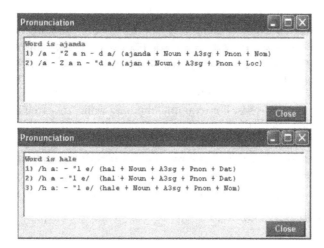

Fig. 6. Aligned pronunciation and morphological analysis lookup

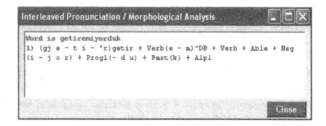

Fig. 7. Interleaved pronunciation representation

pronunciations of the surface morphemes and the morphological features they give rise to. Note that syllable and morpheme boundaries do not necessarily coincide and syllables may span multiple morphemes and a morpheme may be split over to multiple syllables.

In a future version of LINGBROWSER, we plan to add further functionality that will have an "explanation" feature that explains the reason why the stress is on a certain syllable or why a certain vowel is long, etc., based on the analyses described in Oflazer and Inkelas [12].

- **Lexicon Access:** Whenever there is an analysis of a word displayed after a query (except of surface morpheme lookup), the user can look up the the root word in various lexical databases such as the Turkish WordNet [2] or link to the English WordNet [1] that is aligned with the Turkish WordNet using interlingual-index number and then access the English meanings by accessing the glosses in the English WordNet.
- **Word and Morphological Concordances:** A concordance is a "word-in-context" view of a text in which all occurrences of a selected word is displayed along with some amount of context on the left and on the right. Such

concordance views are helpful for people to see how words are used and perhaps in what kinds collocations they are involved in. In addition to standard word form based-concordances, LINGBROWSER, also provides a morphological concordances for all morphological variants of a selected root word.

– **Search:** LINGBROWSER can currently also search the text based on various criteria such as root words, root part-of-speech, inflectional and derivational features of words. For example one may want to search for verbs with causative voice and then see their surface and lexical morphemes. This is done by maintaining a separate in-core database of all unique word forms annotated and indexed with all relevant search criteria so that rapid search can be performed.

4   Implementation

The prototype version of the LINGBROWSER described here has been implemented in Microsoft's .NET environment. All lexical lookup functionality has been implemented via a number of database interfaces to representations of morphological structure and pronunciation data. Although LINGBROWSER makes extensive use of finite state technology, it does so in an indirect way. We do not have access to a runtime library that would let us use the transducers directly at run time. Instead, we have created databases of word structure and features for a large set of words that we have extracted from a very large corpus, using the finite state transducers that we have developed. Even though Turkish has a very large word form vocabulary – infinite for all practical purposes, we use a limited vocabulary of a few hundred thousand word forms whose coverage is over 97% for the corpus we collected them from. This approach is quite feasible for a proof of concept demonstration system and full-fledged finite state technology can be incorporated trivially when the appropriate run-time libraries are available.

All our finite state transducers used for populating the lexical databases are derived from a core morphological analyzer [9] developed using Xerox finite state technology [13, 14, 15, 11]. The basic morphological analyzer has been amended with various additional finite state transducers to extract all the relevant representations such as the surface morpheme segmentations, the representations of the pronunciations, etc. The details of how these are described in detail by Oflazer and Inkelas [12].

We have however developed one of the transducers – the transducer for generating the aligned surface-lexical representations – separately, as it is not directly derivable from the basic morphological analysis transducer as the others used. To generate aligned pairs of symbols, we need a finite state transducer that maps from surface strings to (aligned) pairs of feasible pairs of lexical-surface symbols, *taking into account not just the morphographemic constraints but also the lexicon constraints*, since two-level rule transducer is wildly overgenerating without being composed with a lexicon transducer and it can not be directly used. Instead, we have created a modified version of the two-level rule transducer with a different set of feasible pairs as depicted in Figure 8. First, for every

e-e v-v +-0 s-0 H-i +-0 n-n D-d A-e

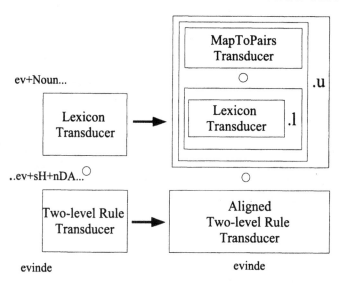

Fig. 8. The structure of the aligned feasible-pair transducer

feasible-pair `a:b` in the original two-level grammar[6] (for the transducer of the left), we have a feasible pair of the sort `"a-b":b` in the new two-level grammar (for the transducer on the right), where the lexical symbol `"a-b"` on the upper side also encodes the surface symbol. Then for a two-level rule like

`a:b => LC _ RC`

in the original rule grammar, where `LC` and `RC` are regular expressions over the set of feasible-pairs, denoting the left and right contexts, we have a rule in the new grammar

`"a-b":b => LC' _ RC'`

in which the lexical side of the feasible pair encodes the surface symbol and the context regular expressions are rewritten in terms of the new set of feasible pairs.[7]

To combine this transducer (that we denote as `AlignedTwoLevelRuleTransducer`) with the lexicon, we proceed as follows:

1. Create a transducer `MapToPairs` that maps every lexical symbol of the original lexicon representation, to the lexical side of the new feasible pairs that lexical symbol is involved in. For example, let's assume that our original

---

[6] Where `a` is a lexical symbol, `b` is a surface symbol.

[7] This transformation technically goes away with surface coercion rules ($<=$ +) rules, since each (new) lexical symbol now has only one surface symbol corresponding to it. We have not explored the full ramifications of this, at least in the case of converting our two-level grammar, we have not encountered any problems.

two-level grammar has the feasible pairs `A:a`, `A:e` and `A:0`.[8] The regular expression for `MapToPairs` then is a set of parallel upward replace operators, and for these 3 pairs, it will have the replace rules[9]

```
..., "A-a" <- A, "A-e" <- A, "A-0" <- A, ...
```

2. Assuming that the original lexicon transducer `LexiconTransducer` maps from lexical symbol sequences to feature symbol sequences for morphological analysis, the lower side of lexicon transducer, `LexiconTransducer.1`, contains all possible valid lexical symbol sequences encoding the morphotactical restrictions of the original grammar.

3. When `MapToPairs` is composed with `LexiconTransducer.1`, and the upper side of that composition is extracted, `[MapToPairs .o. Lexicon.1].u`, one gets a recognizer of all possible sequences of the upper sides of the new set of feasible pairs, constrained by morphotactics.

4. A final composition,

```
[[MapToPairs .o.  LexiconTransducer.1].u]
              .o.
      AlignedTwoLevelRuleTransducer
```

produces the transducer that we want, mapping from surface symbols to representations of the original feasible pairs.

5   Future Functionality

Subsequent development on LINGBROWSER will go beyond the lexical realm and will incorporate querying on multi-word and phrasal structures. The following is a short list of the functionality we intend to provide in the very near future:

- Disambiguation of the various kinds of morphological information that is provided using a recently developed morphological disambiguator [8].
- On-demand explanation of pronunciation phenomena observed (e.g. how morphemes interact to determine the primary stress location),
- Integration of multi-word constructs processors to identify lexicalized, semi-lexicalized and non-lexicalized collocations [16].
- Recognition of various simple noun phrases.
- English paraphrasing of Turkish word forms e.g., *evimdekiler* paraphrased as *those (things) in my home*.
- Morphological analysis and generation drills using feature and lexical morpheme representations.

---

[8] These are used to implement a certain kind of vowel harmony in Turkish.

[9] Using XRCE Regular Expression Syntax.

6   Conclusions

We have presented the functionality of the prototype implementation of LING-BROWSER, a tool for helping students Turkish linguistics explore linguistic properties of Turkish words and phrases. LINGBROWSER makes extensive use of finite state language processing technology to pervasively provide all kinds of information about the Turkish words in a Turkish text.

Acknowledgements

The work on LINGBROWSER is being supported by a joint grant from TÜBİTAK (Turkish National Science Foundation) and US NSF to Sabancı University and University of California, Berkeley, Department of Linguistics.

References

1. Fellbaum, C., ed.: WordNet, An Electronic Lexical Database. MIT Press (1998)
2. Bilgin, O., Çetinoğlu, O., Oflazer, K.: Building a Wordnet for Turkish. Romanian Journal of Information Science and Technology **7** (2004) 163–172
3. Borin, L.: What have you done for me lately? The fickle alignment of NLP and CALL. In: Proceedings of EuroCALL 2002 pre-conference workshop on NLP in CALL (2002), Jyvaskyla, Finland (2002)
4. Nerbonne, J.: Computer-assisted language learning and natural language processing. In Mitkov, R., ed.: Handbook of Computational Linguistics. Oxford University Press (2002)
5. Nerbonne, J., Karttunen, L., Paskaleva, E., Proszeky, G., Roosmaa, T.: Reading more into foreign languages. In: Proceedings of the Fifth Conference on Applied natural language processing, Washington, DC (1997) 135–138
6. Güvenir, H.A.: Drill and practice for Turkish grammar. In Swartz, M.L., Yazdani, M., eds.: Intelligent Tutoring Systems for Foreign Language Learning. Volume F80 of NATO ASI Series. Springer Verlag (1992) 275–291
7. Güvenir, H.A., Oflazer, K.: Using a corpus to teach Turkish morphology. In: Proceedings of the Seventh Twente Workshop on Language Technology, Enschede, The Netherlands (1994)
8. Külekçi, O.: Morphological disambiguation with distinguishing tags and its application to disambiguation of pronunciation. Ph.D Thesis Proposal, Sabancı University, Istanbul, Turkey (2004)
9. Oflazer, K.: Two-level description of Turkish morphology. Literary and Linguistic Computing **9** (1994) 137–148
10. Koskenniemi, K.: Two-level morphology: A general computational model for word form recognition and production. Publication No: 11, Department of General Linguistics, University of Helsinki (1983)
11. Beesley, K.R., Karttunen, L.: Finite State Morphology. CSLI Publications, Stanford University (2003)
12. Oflazer, K., Inkelas, S.: The architecture and the implementation of a finite state pronunciation lexicon for Turkish. Computer Speech and Language **20** (2006)
13. Karttunen, L., Beesley, K.R.: Two-level rule compiler. Technical Report, XEROX Palo Alto Research Center (1992)

14. Karttunen, L.: Finite-state lexicon compiler. XEROX, Palo Alto Research Center–Technical Report (1993)
15. Karttunen, L., Chanod, J.P., Grefenstette, G., Schiller, A.: Regular expressions for language engineering. Natural Language Engineering **2** (1996) 305–328
16. Oflazer, K., Çetinoğlu, O., Say, B.: Integrating morphology with multi-word expression processing in Turkish. In: Proceedings of the ACL 2004 Workshop on Multiword Expressions:Integrating Processing, Barcelona, Spain (2004)

Applying a Finite Automata Acquisition Algorithm to Named Entity Recognition

Muntsa Padró and Lluís Padró

TALP Research Center
Universitat Politècnica de Catalunya
{mpadro, padro}@lsi.upc.edu

Abstract. In this work, Causal-State Splitting Reconstruction algorithm, originally conceived to model stationary processes by learning finite state automata from data sequences, is for the first time applied to NLP tasks, namely Named Entity Recognition. The obtained results are slightly below the best systems presented in CoNLL 2002 shared task, though given the simplicity of the used features, they are really promising.

Once the viability of using this algorithm for NLP tasks is stated, we plan to improve the results obtained at NER task, as well as to apply it to other NLP sequence recognition tasks such as PoS tagging, chunking, subcategorization patterns acquisition, etc.

1 Introduction

Some Natural Language Processing (NLP) tasks may be naturally approached using finite state automata and machine learning algorithms. These automata can be hand built with linguistic knowledge or can be statistical models, such as Hidden Markov Models (HMM). In the case of statistical automata, usually their structure must be previously defined. For HMM, for example, it is necessary to define what the states represent, and the statistics are only applied to learn the transition and emission probabilities. Nevertheless there are algorithms that learn automata given some data [1, 2, 3, 4, 5, 6]. One of these kind of algorithms is CSSR (Causal State Splitting Reconstruction) which is based on inferring the causal states of a process given sequential data.

In this work a first approach to applying this algorithm to NLP tasks is presented. The task chosen to start applying this algorithm was Named Entity Recognition (NER). The results presented in this paper are preliminary, since the performed experiments take into account few features. Nevertheless, the obtained results are quite promising since they are not far from those of the state of the art systems and there is still a large margin for improvement to the presented preliminary experiments. At the sight of current results, it can be said that this algorithm can be reliably applied to NER and we expect to obtain good results in the future applying it to other NLP tasks.

The Named Entity Recognition (NER) task consists of detecting names referring to entities such as persons, locations, organizations, etc. in a text. This

A. Yli-Jyrä, L. Karttunen, and J. Karhumäki (Eds.): FSMNLP 2005, LNAI 4002, pp. 203–214, 2006.
© Springer-Verlag Berlin Heidelberg 2006

is used in many NLP applications such as Question Answering, Information Retrieval, Sumarization, etc. Furthermore, some Named Entity Classification (NEC) systems need to have the Named Entities (NE) previously detected. Other systems perform both tasks (detection and classification) at the same time. We only applied CSSR to the detection step, not to classification.

The rest of the paper is organized as follows: section 2 presents the CSSR algorithm and its theoretical basis. Section 3 defines our approach to apply the algorithm to NER task. In section 4 the performed experiments with the obtained results are discussed. Section 5 states some conclusions and future work.

2   CSSR Algorithm

The CSSR algorithm [7] performs the blind construction of asymptotically optimal nonlinear predictors of discrete sequences. It inferres the causal states from data, searching for optimal predictors for discrete random processes, in the form of Markov Models.

2.1   Causal States

Given a discrete alphabet Σ, consider a sequence x^- drawn from Σ (history) and a random variable for future sequences Z^+. Z^+ can be observed after x^- with a probability $P(Z^+|x^-)$. Two histories, x^- and y^-, are equivalent when $P(Z^+|x^-) = P(Z^+|y^-)$, i.e. when they have the same probability distribution for the future.

The different future distributions build the equivalence classes which are named *causal states* of the process. Each causal state is a set of history suffixes, up to a preestablished maximum length, with the same probability distribution for the future. The causal states of a process form a deterministic machine and are recursively calculable.

2.2   The Algorithm

Causal-State Splitting Reconstruction (CSSR) estimates an HMM inferring the causal states from sequence data. The main parameter of this algorithm is the maximum length (l_{max}) the suffixes can reach. That is, the maximum length of the considered histories. In terms of HMMs, l_{max} would be the potential maximum order of the model (the HMM would have l_{max} order if all the suffixes belonged to different states).

The algorithm starts by assuming the process is an identically-distributed and independent sequence with a single causal state, and then iteratively adds new states when it is shown by statistical tests that the current states set is not sufficient. The causal state machine is built in three phases (see [7] for details):

1. **Initialize**
   Create a state set with only one state containing only the null suffix. Set $l = 0$ (length of the longest suffix so far).

2. **Sufficiency**
   Iteratively build new states depending on the future probability distribution
   of each possible suffix extension (suffix sons). Before doing so it is necessary
   to estimate the probability distribution $\hat{P}(X_t|S = s)$ (where X_t is the ran-
   dom variable for the next alphabet symbol in the sequence) for each state s.
   This is necessary because this probability can change at each iteration when
   the new suffixes are added to a given state. This probability distribution is
   estimated (via maximum likelihood, for instance) using the data.

   At this phase, the suffix sons (ax) for each longest suffix (x) are created
   adding each alphabet symbol (a) at the beginning of each suffix. The future
   distribution $P(X_t|X_{t-l}^{t-1})$ (probability of each alphabet symbol given the last
   l symbols) for each son is computed and a hypothesis test with the following
   null hypothesis is performed,

$$P(X_t|X_{t-l}^{t-1} = ax) = P(X_t|S = s); \quad \forall a \in \Sigma$$

   This hypothesis is true if the new distribution is equal (with a certain con-
   fidence degree) to the distribution of an existing state (s). In this case, the
   suffix son is added to this state. If the hypothesis is rejected for all states, a
   new state for the suffix son is created. To check the null hypothesis we can
   use a statistical test such as χ^2 or Kolmogorov-Smirnov.

   As the suffix length grows, l is increased by one at each iteration. This
   phase goes on until l reaches some fixed maximum value l_{max}, the maximum
   length to be considered for a suffix, which represents the longest histories
   taken into account. The results of the system will be significantly different
   depending on the chosen l_{max} value, since the larger this value is, the more
   training data will be necessary to learn a correct automaton with statistical
   reliability. Also, the time needed to learn the automaton grows linearly with
   l_{max}. So it is necessary to tune the best maximum length for the amount of
   available data (or viceversa, the amount of necessary data for the required
   suffix length).

3. **Recursion**
   Since CSSR models stationary processes, first of all the transient states
   are removed. Then the states are splitted until a deterministic machine is
   reached. To do so, the transitions for each suffix in each state are computed
   and if two suffixes in one state have different transitions for the same symbol,
   they are splitted into two different states.

   At the end of this recursion phase, a deterministic automaton is obtained.

In figure 4 the pseudo code for this algorithm is presented. See [7] for extended
details and algorithm analysis.

3   Applying CSSR to Named Entity Recognition

In this work an approach to apply CSSR algorithm to Named Entity Recognition
is presented. We only worked on recognizing Named Entities, not in classifying
them.

Following CoNLL 2002 and 2003 shared task, we worked with the "B-I-O" approach [8]. Each word has a B, I or O tag, being B the tag for a word where a NE begins, I the tag if the word is part of a NE but not the beginning, and O the tag for the words not belonging to any NE. There are other possible approaches to tagging NEs [9] but this is one of the most widely used.

The general idea of our approach is to use CSSR to learn an automaton for NE structure. Once the automaton is learnt, it can be applied to detect NEs in untagged text.

3.1   Learning the Automaton

To learn the automaton that must reproduce NE structure, different information about the words is used. This information can be orthographic, morphosyntactic, about the position in the sentence, etc. Using this features, the words in a sentence are translated to a closed set of symbols, that will be the alphabet of the automaton. The sentence translated in such a way will be the sequence that we use to learn the automaton via CSSR.

A problem of using that algorithm for this task is that it is conceived to model stationary processes, but NE patterns are not in this category. So, what we did was to regard a text sequence as a stationary process in which NEs occur once a while. Doing so implies the automaton is modelling the pattern of the sequence (the text), not the pattern of a NE.

To allow CSSR to learn the pattern of the NEs, we introduce in the alphabet the information of the NE-tag (B, I or O) available in the supervised training corpus. So the correct NE-tag is taken into account for each kind of word when building the automaton.

To allow CSSR to learn the pattern of the NEs, we introduce in the alphabet the information of the NE-tag (B, I or O) available in the supervised training corpus. Thus, the hidden information (the tags) is taken into account when building the automaton.

In this way, although we obtain an automaton modelling the entire text sequence as an stationary process, we have information encoded in the transitions about B-I-O tags for NEs in the text. Thus, we can later use this information to compute the best path for a sequence and use it to tag NEs in a new text.

3.2   An Example

For instance, let's suppose an approach where the only feature taken into account is whether a word is capitalized or not. Let's say that a capitalized word will have the feature "A" and a non-capitalized word the feature "a". In this case, the alphabet will consist of six symbols, which are the possible combinations of a capitalization value and a B-I-O tag (A_B, A_I, A_O, a_B, a_I, a_O). Each word will be translated into sequences of these symbols depending on whether it is capitalized and on its NE-tag.

Figure 1 shows an example of a possible training sentence and its translation to this alphabet. The first two columns would be the sentences as they are in the training corpus: a word and its right B-I-O tag. The last column is their translation into the alphabet, which will be used as input for the CSSR algorithm. In this example it becomes clear that this alphabet would be too poor to capture appropiate NE patterns. It would be necessary, for example, to introduce information about the beginning of sentences (where all words appear capitalized and may not be a NE), or to introduce special words that may appear uncapitalized inside a NE (prepositions, articles...).

Word	Correct Tag	Alphabet Symbol
Yesterday	O	A_O
the	O	a_O
President	B	A_B
of	I	a_I
France	I	A_I
spoke	O	a_O
with	O	a_O
George	B	A_B
Bush	I	A_I
about	O	a_O
the	O	a_O
situation	O	a_O
in	O	a_O
Iraq	B	A_B
.	O	a_O
Bush	B	A_B
said	O	a_O
...		

Fig. 1. Example of a training sentence and its translation to a simple alphabet

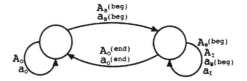

Fig. 2. Example of an automaton that models simple NEs

Once the data are properly translated into the alphabet, the automaton is built using CSSR. Figure 2 shows a possible (not real) automaton learned with CSSR with the alphabet { A_B, A_I, A_O, a_B, a_I, a_O }.

3.3   Using the Learned Automaton to Tag NEs

When a sentence has to be tagged, the information about the correct NE tag is not available, so there are several possible alphabet symbols for that word. It is only possible to know the part of the translation that depends on the word or sentence features. In our example, it would be possible to translate each word to an "*A*" or to an "*a*", but not to know the part of the symbol that depends on the NE-tag, which is, in fact, what we want to know.

To find this most likely tag for each word in a sentence –that is, to find the most likely symbol of the alphabet (e.g. G_B, G_I, G_O for a G word), a Viterbi algorithm is applied. That is, for each word in a sentence, the possible states the automaton could reach if the current word had the tag B, I, or O, and the probabilities of these paths are computed. Then, only the highest probability for each tag is recorded. That means that for each word, the best path for this word having each tag is stored. At the end of the sentence, the best probability is chosen and the optimal path is backwards recovered. In this way, the most likely sequence of B-I-O tags for each word in the sentence is obtained. There are some forbidden paths, which are those that lead to the OI tag-combination. The paths including this combination are pruned out.

3.4   Managing Unseen Transitions

When performing the tagging of NEs given a text, it is possible to find symbol sequences that haven't been seen in the training corpus. This will cause the automaton to fall in a *sink* state, which receives all the unseen transitions. This state can be seen as the state that contains all the unseen suffixes. All unseen transitions probabilities are smoothed to have a small probability of arriving to the sink state. Actually, the only sequences that have zero probability are those that have a forbidden combination of tags or of states being the beginning or the end of a NE.

When the automaton falls in the *sink* state, it can not follow the input sequence using transition information because, as the transitions weren't seen, they are not defined. To allow the system to continue tagging the text, when the automaton falls into *sink* state, the suffix of length l_{max} is built using the last $l_{max} - 1$ symbols and the next symbol from the input. A state containing this new suffix is searched over the automaton and, if found, the automaton goes to this state and continues its normal functioning. If not, the process is repeated, getting more symbols from the input sequence, until a state containing the new suffix is found.

This may cause skipping some part of the input, and is caused by the fact that the text sequence is considered as an stationary process, and so, when the CSSR-acquired automaton fails, we have to resynchronize it with the input data.

4   Experiments and Results

In this work, the data for the CoNLL-2002 shared task [10] for Spanish were used. These data contain three corpora: one for the train and two for the test: one for the development of the system and the other one for the final test. The amount of data in each corpus is shown in table 1.

With these data, two different kind of experiments were performed: one to validate the method, and the other one to evaluate it over real data.

Table 1. Number of words and NEs in each corpus

Corpus	Number of words	Number of NEs
Train	264,715	18,797
Test a	52,923	4,351
Test b	51,533	3,558

4.1 Validating the Method

The experiments to validate the method consist of tagging the training and test corpora using a simple hand-built automaton, and checking whether CSSR is able to learn and reproduce its behaviour. FreeLing analyzer [11] has a NER system that uses a simple hand-built automaton of four states, and was used to re-annotate all CoNLL datasets, obtaining training and test corpora tagged with a simple and systematic annotation criteria. These corpora were used to train and test CSSR at the NER task.

The used alphabet was the same –and encoded the same features– than the one used by FreeLing NE detection module, in which the following feature-sets are mapped to the alphabet symbols:

- **G:** Beginning of the sentence, capitalized, not containing numbers, not in the dictionary[1].
- **S:** Beginning of the sentence, capitalized, not containing numbers, one of its possible analysis being a common noun.
- **M:** Not at the beginning of the sentence, capitalized.
- **a:** Not at the beginning of the sentence, non-capitalized, functional word[2].
- **w:** Other.

In this way, the alphabet for CSSR will be the combination of these four features with the three possible NE tags (G_B, G_I, G_O, S_B, S_I, S_O, M_B, M_I, etc.).

Using the training corpus tagged with FreeLing an automaton was learned using CSSR algorithm. Then, this automaton was evaluated over the test corpora (also tagged with FreeLing). The system obtained $F_1 = 100\%$ when using $l_{max} = 2$ for both test sets, and using $l_{max} = 3$, $F_1 = 99,83\%$ for the development corpus (test a) and $F_1 = 99,98\%$ for the test corpus (test b) were obtained. For $l_{max} = 3$, the lost in F_1 is due to some missed NEs. In fact the system obtained a 100% precision in both cases, but the recall fell a little bit. This lose in the recall, could be due to the fact that if l_{max} rises, more training data are necessary to generate a correct automaton.

These results prove that CSSR is able to perfectly acquire the behaviour of the FreeLing annotation schema underlying the data. Although this is an easy task, since that schema is simple and systematic, it validates the viability of our adaptation of CSSR from stationary-process acquisition to pattern recognition.

---

[1] The used dictionary is the one provided by FreeLing [11].

[2] Functional words are articles or preposition that are often found inside a NE.

4.2 Applying CSSR over the Real Corpora

Next step was testing the method on a real NE task, over the corpora used in CoNLL-2002. In this case, the annotation was hand made, and thus, it will include cases much more complex than the naive FreeLing annotation, and also present noise and inconsistencies due to different annotator criteria or simply to human mistakes.

CSSR algorithm has three important parameters. One is the chosen maximum length (l_{max}), which is the most significant parameter. The other two are the test used to check the null hypothesis and the parameter α, controlling the test significance degree. We made several experiments (using the same alphabet presented in 4.1) for different l_{max} values and with two different statistical test: χ^2 and Kolmogorov-Smirnov. For each test, the experiments were performed with several α values. Figure 3 shows the obtained results with the different automata built using Kolmogorov-Smirnov test. The results obtained with χ^2 test have a similar behaviour but are slightly worse.

In this figure it can be seen that the significance degree value is not as influent as the l_{max} value. In fact, there is a range of α values for which the reached results are similar.

About the influence of l_{max}, the results show that best performance is obtained with small l_{max}, likely caused by the limited size of the training corpus, which seems not to allow statistically reliable acquisition of automata with too long histories. In fact, since our alphabet has 16 symbols, the number of suffixes of length 5 is 16^5 (over one million), which is approximately the size of the training corpus, so most of the possible suffixes wouldn't have been seen in the corpus.

The best performance is obtained with $l_{max} = 3$ and $\alpha = 1e - 5$. With these values, the system reaches a precision of 89.81%, a recall of 88.22% and $F_1 = 89.01\%$ for the development corpus (test a) and a 90.03% precision, 88.81% recall and $F_1 = 89.42\%$ for the test corpus (test b).

These results can be compared with the winner system of CoNLL-2002 shared task [12]. This system was developed with the same training and testing data and performs the NE recognition and classification separately , so it is possible to compare our system with the part that performs the NE recognition.

That system obtained a F_1 of 91.66% for the Spanish development corpus and a 92.91% for the test corpus. These results are higher than the results presented in this work, which was expected since the feature set used by that system is much richer (bag of words, disambiguated PoS tag, many orthographic features, etc.) than the used in our experiments.

Furthermore, it is possible to apply the NEC system used by [12] to the output of our NE detector. Doing so over our best results yields to a $F_1 = 76.30\%$, which would situate our system in the fifth position in CoNLL-2002 ranking table for complete NER systems in Spanish.

Another factor that is interesting to study is the number of generated states for each configuration. As it is expected, l_{max} and α values not only affect the performance of the system, but also change the number of states of the generated automata. The larger l_{max} and α are, the greater the number of states will be.

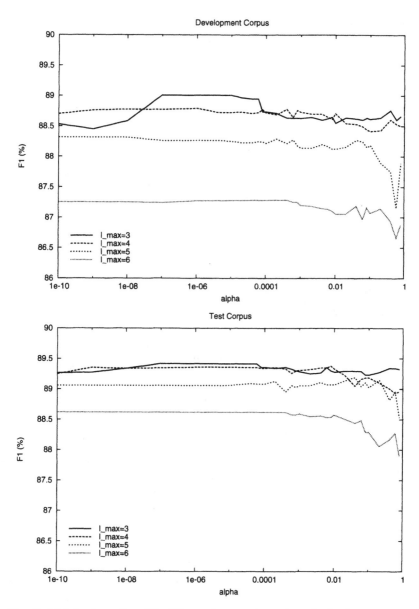

Fig. 3. Obtained results with different l_{max} and α values for both test corpora

As in the case of the system performance, the most influent parameter in the automata size is l_{max}, while the influence of α is important only for values over 0.01. Using values under this threshold, the number of generated states varies from 100 states for $l_{max} = 3$ to 2000 states for $l_{max} = 6$. For α bigger than 0.01 the number of states rises until these values are duplicated.

Algorithm CSSR $(\Sigma, \bar{x}, l_{max}, \alpha)$

$\qquad$ // **Initialization:** *init. the machine with a state with*
$l \leftarrow 0$ $\qquad$ // *only the null suffix.*
$q_0 \leftarrow \{\lambda\}; Q \leftarrow q_0$

$\qquad$ // **Sufficiency:** *build causal states.*
while $l < l_{max}$
$\quad$ **for** each $s \in Q$
$\qquad$ estimate $\hat{P}(X_t|S = s)$ $\qquad$ // *Estimate the prob. distr. for next symbol given the*
$\qquad$ **for** each $x \in s$ $\qquad$ // *curr. st. since it may have changed in the last iter.*
$\qquad\quad$ **for** each $a \in \Sigma$
$\qquad\qquad$ estimate $p \leftarrow \hat{P}(X_t|X_{t-l}^{t-1} = ax)$ // *Estimate the probability distribution for this*
$\qquad\qquad$ Reorganize_States(Q, p, ax, s, α) // *suffix son and perform the hypothesis test.*
$l \leftarrow l + 1$

$\qquad$ // **Recursion:** *rem. transient states, makes the mach.*
Remove transient states from Q $\qquad$ // *determ. and fills transition table ($T[state, symbol]$)*
repeat
$\quad$ $recursive \leftarrow True$
$\quad$ **for** each $s \in Q$
$\qquad$ **for** each $b \in \Sigma$
$\qquad\quad$ $x_0 \leftarrow$ first $x \in s$
$\qquad\quad$ $T[s, b] \leftarrow$ Class$(x_0 b, Q)$ $\qquad$ // *Look for the trans. for this suffix with this symbol.*
$\qquad\quad$ **for** each $x \in s,\ x \neq x_0$
$\qquad\qquad$ **if** Class$(xb, Q) \neq T[s, b]$ $\qquad$ // *If the trans. for another suffix goes to a different*
$\qquad\qquad\quad$ create new state $s' \in Q$ $\qquad$ // *state, creates a new state with this suffix and move*
$\qquad\qquad\quad$ $T[s', b] \leftarrow$ Class(xb, Q) $\qquad$ // *to this state all the suffix with the same transition.*
$\qquad\qquad\quad$ **for** each $y \in s \mid$ Class$(yb, Q) =$ Class(xb, Q)
$\qquad\qquad\qquad$ Move_Suffix(y, s, s')
$\qquad\qquad\quad$ $recursive \leftarrow False$
until $recursive$

function Reorganize_States(Q, p, y, s, α) // **Reorganize_States:** *test the null hypothesis and*
$\qquad$ // *decide to which state a suffix must be added*
$\qquad$ // *or create a new state.*
if null hypothesis passes a test $\qquad$ // *If the probability distribution for y is equal to*
of size α for s $\qquad$ // *the s distribution add y to this state.*
$\quad$ $s \leftarrow y \cup s$
else
$\quad$ **if** null hyp. passes a test of size α $\qquad$ // *If the prob. distr. for y is equal to the $s* \neq s$*
$\qquad$ for $s^* \in Q,\ s^* \neq s$ $\qquad$ // *distribution, add y to this state s^*.*
$\qquad$ $s' = s^*$
$\quad$ **else** $\qquad$ // *If the prob. distr. for y is different from that*
$\qquad$ $Q \leftarrow s'$ $\qquad$ // *of all states, create a new state and add y to it.*
$\quad$ Add_Suffix(y, s')

function Add_Suffix(y, s) $\qquad$ // **Add_Suffix:** *add a suffix to a state.*
$\quad$ $s \leftarrow s \cup y$
$\quad$ re-estimate $\hat{P}(X_t|\hat{S} = s)$

function Class(y, Q) $\qquad$ // **Class:** *return the causal state (equivalence class)*
$\quad$ **return** $(s \in Q|y \in s)$ $\qquad$ // *a suffix belongs to.*

function Move_Suffix(y, s_1, s_2) $\qquad$ // **Move_Suffix:** *move a suffix from one st. to another.*
$\quad$ $s_1 \leftarrow s_1 \setminus y$
$\quad$ re-estimate $\hat{P}(X_t|\hat{S} = s_1)$
$\quad$ $s_2 \leftarrow s_2 \cup y$
$\quad$ re-estimate $\hat{P}(X_t|\hat{S} = s_2)$

Fig. 4. Pseudo code for the CSSR algorithm

5   Conclusions and Further Work

In this work a finite automata acquisition algorithm has been applied to Named
Entity Recognition. The algorithm learns automata for stationary processes, so,

some arrangements have had to be done in the tagging step to fit a non-stationary pattern recognition NLP task such as NE recognition.

Firstly, the method has been validated by applying it to learn sentence patterns from a corpus annotated with a simple hand-made automaton, and checking that CSSR is able to exactly reproduce its behaviour.

Secondly, it has been shown that this algorithm can build automata that give pretty good results when applied to recognize the NEs of a text. In fact, the system results are not too far from those obtained by the winner system on CoNLL 2002 shared task and they may be expected to improve by introducing more information in the system, since we use a much simpler knowledge than all CoNLL 2002 participants.

The main conclusion of this work, is that CSSR algorithm can be satisfactorily applied to NER tasks, which opens a door to applying it to other basic NLP tasks which need to learn sequential pattern information from data (PoS tagging, chunking, etc.).

The future work to be developed is focused on improving this NER system and on applying CSSR algorithm to other NLP tasks. To improve NER, more orthographic and morpho-syntactic information will be introduced in the alphabet in order to build more accurate automata. Similarly, external information such as trigger word lists or gazetteers could be also used. Other NLP tasks where this algorithm can be applied are chunking, PoS tagging or subcategorization pattern acquisition.

Acknowledgements

This research is being funded by the Catalan Government Research Department (DURSI), by the Spanish Ministry of Science and Technology (ALIADO TIC2002-04447-C02) and by the European Commission projects: Meaning (IST-2001-34460) and CHIL (IST-2004-506909). Our research group, TALP Research Center, is recognized as a Quality Research Group (2001 SGR 00254) by DURSI.

References

1. Segarra, E., Sanchis, E., García, F., Hurtado, L.F., Galiano, I.: Achieving full coverage of automatically learnt finite-state language models. In: Workshop on Finite-State Methods in Natural Language Processing. 10th Conference of the European Chapter of the Association for Computational Linguistics (EACL2003), Budapest, Hungary (2003) 135–142
2. Pla, F.: Etiquetado Léxico y Análisis Sintáctico Superficial basado en Modelos Estadísticos. PhD thesis, Departament de Sistemes Informàtics i Computació, Universitat Politècnica de València (2000)
3. Lang, K.J.: Random dfa's can be approximately learned from sparse uniform examples. In: COLT '92: Proceedings of the fifth annual workshop on Computational learning theory, ACM Press (1992) 45–52
4. Oncina, J.M.: Aprendizaje de lenguajes regulares y funciones subsecuenciales. PhD thesis, Departamento de Sistemas Informáticos y Computación, Universidad Politécnica de Valencia (1991)

5. Rulot, H., Vidal, E.: Modelling (sub)string-length based constraints through a grammatical inference method. In: Pattern recognition theory and applications. Springer-Verlag (1987) 451–459
6. Trakhtenbrot, B., Barzdin, Y.: Finite Automata: Behaviour and Synthesis. North Holland Publishing Company (1973)
7. Shalizi, C., Shalizi, K.: Blind construction of optimal nonlinear recursive predictors for discrete sequences. In: Uncertainty in Artificial Intelligence: Proceedings of the Twentieth Conference. (2004)
8. Ramshaw, L., Marcus, M.P.: Text chunking using transformation-based learning. In: Proceedings of the Third ACL Workshop on Very Large Corpora. (1995)
9. Tjong Kim Sang, E.F., Veenstra, J.: Representing text chunks. In: Proceedings of EACL'99, Bergen, Norway (1999) 173–179
10. Tjong Kim Sang, E.F.: Introduction to the conll-2002 shared task: Language-independent named entity recognition. In: Proceedings of CoNLL-2002, Taipei, Taiwan (2002) 155–158
11. Carreras, X., Chao, I., Padró, L., Padró, M.: Freeling: An open-source suite of language analyzers. In: Proceedings of the 4th International Conference on Language Resources and Evaluation (LREC'04), Lisbon, Portugal (2004)
12. Carreras, X., Màrquez, L., Padró, L.: Named entity extraction using adaboost. In: Proceedings of CoNLL Shared Task, Taipei, Taiwan (2002) 167–170

Principles, Implementation Strategies, and Evaluation of a Corpus Query System

Ulrik Petersen

University of Aalborg
Department of Communication and Psychology
Kroghstræde 3, DK — 9220 Aalborg East, Denmark
ulrikp@hum.aau.dk
http://emdros.org/

Abstract. The last decade has seen an increase in the number of available corpus query systems. These systems generally implement a query language as well as a database model. We report on one such corpus query system, and evaluate its query language against a range of queries and criteria quoted from the literature. We show some important principles of the design of the query language, and argue for the strategy of separating what is retrieved by a linguistic query from the data retrieved in order to display or otherwise process the results, stating the needs for generality, simplicity, and modularity as reasons to prefer this strategy.

1 Introduction

The last decade has seen a growth in the number of available corpus query systems. Newcomers since the mid-1990ies include MATE Q4M [1], the Emu query language [2], the Annotation Graph query language [3], TIGERSearch [4], NXT Search [5], TGrep2 [6], and LPath [7].

Our own corpus query system, Emdros [8, 9], has been in development since 1999. It is based on ideas from the PhD thesis by Crist-Jan Doedens [10]. It implements a database model and a query language which are very general in their applicability: Our system can be applied to almost any linguistic theory, almost any linguistic domain (e.g., syntax, phonology, discourse) and almost any method of linguistic tagging. Thus our system can be used as a basis for implementing a variety of linguistic applications. We have implemented a number of linguistic applications such as a generic query tool, a HAL[1] space, and a number of import tools for existing corpus formats. As the system is Open Source, others are free to implement applications for their linguistic problem domains using our system, just as we plan to continue to extend the range of available applications.

The rest of the paper is laid out as follows: First, we briefly describe the EMdF database model underlying Emdros, and give an example of a database expressed in EMdF. Second, we describe the MQL query language of Emdros and its principles. Third, we argue for the strategy of separating the process of

---

[1] HAL here stands for "Hyperspace Analogue to Language," and is a statistical method based on lexical co-occurrence invented by Dr. Curt Burgess and his colleagues [11].

A. Yli-Jyrä, L. Karttunen, and J. Karhumäki (Eds.): FSMNLP 2005, LNAI 4002, pp. 215–226, 2006.
© Springer-Verlag Berlin Heidelberg 2006

retrieving linguistic query results from the process of retrieving linguistic objects based on such results for application-specific purposes. Fourth, we evaluate MQL against a set of standard queries and criteria for corpus query languages culled from the literature. Finally, we conclude the paper.

2   The EMdF Database Model

To illustrate how data can be stored in Emdros, consider Fig. 1. It shows an example of a discontiguous clause, taken from [12, p. 95], represented both as a tree and as a database expressed in the EMdF database model.

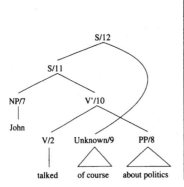

	1	2	3	4	5	6
Word	id: 1 surf.: John pos: NProp parent: 7	id: 2 surf.: talked pos: V parent: 10	id: 3 surf.: of pos: P parent: 9	id: 4 surf.: course pos: N parent: 9	id: 5 surf.: about pos: P parent: 8	id: 6 surf.: politics pos: N parent: 8
Phrase	id: 7 type: NP parent: 11		id: 9 type: Unknown parent: 12		id: 8 type: PP parent: 10	
Phrase		id: 10 type: V' parent: 11			id: 10 type: V' parent: 11	
Clause	id: 11 type=S parent: 12				id: 11 type=S parent: 12	
Clause	id: 12 type=S					

a. A tree with a discontiguous clause, adapted from [12, p. 95]

b. A EMdF representation of the tree

Fig. 1. Two representation of a tree with a discontiguous clause

At the top of Fig. 1.b. are the *monads*. A monad is simply an integer, and the sequence of the monads defines the logical reading order. An object is a (possibly discontiguous) set of monads belonging to an object type (such as "Word", "Phrase", "Clause"), and having a set of associated attribute-values. The object type of an object determines what attributes it has. For example, the "Word" object type in Fig. 1.b has attributes "id", "surface", "pos" (part of speech), and "parent". The id is a database-widely unique number that identifies that object. In the above database, this has been used by the "parent" attribute to point to the immediately dominating node in the tree.

In the EMdF database model, object attributes are strongly typed. The model supports strings, integers, ids, and enumerations as types for attributes, as well as lists of integers, ids, and enumeration labels. Enumerations are simply sets of labels, and have been used for the Word.pos, Phrase.type, and Clause.type attributes in the figure.[2] Real-number values are under implementation, and will be useful for, e.g., acoustic-signal timelines.

---

[2] The "dot-notation" used here is well known to programmers, and is basically a possessive: "Word.pos" means "the pos attribute **of** the Word object-type".

3   The MQL Query Language

The MQL query language of Emdros is a descendant of the QL query language described in [10]. Like QL, it is centered around the concept of "blocks", of which there are three kinds: "Object blocks", "gap blocks", and "power blocks".

An "Object block" finds objects in the database (such as phonemes, words, phrases, clauses, paragraphs, etc.) and is enclosed in [square brackets]. For example, the query [Word surface="saw"] will find Word objects whose surface attribute is "saw", whereas the query [Phrase type = NP and function = Subj] will find phrases whose phrase type is NP and whose function is Subject. Of course, this presupposes an appropriately tagged database. The attribute-restrictions on the object are arbitrary boolean expressions providing the primitives "AND", "OR", "NOT", and "grouping (parentheses)". A range of comparison-operators are also provided, including equality, inequality, greater-than (or equal to), less than (or equal to), regular expressions (optionally negated), and IN a disjoined list of values. For lists, the HAS operator looks for a specific value in the list.

A "gap block" finds "gaps" in a certain context, and can be used to look for (or ignore) things like embedded relative clauses, postpositive conjunctions, and other material which is not part of the surrounding element. A gap block is specified as [gap ...] when obligatory, and as [gap? ...] when optional.

A "power block" is denoted by two dots (".."), and signifies that there can be arbitrary space between the two surrounding blocks. However, this is always confined to be within the limits of any context block.

The power block can optionally have a restriction such as ".. <= 5" or ".. BETWEEN 3 AND 6" meaning respectively that the "space" can be between zero and five "least units" long, or that it must be between 3 and 6 "least units" long. Precisely what the "least unit" is, is database-dependent, but is usually "Word" or "Phoneme".[3]

The MQL query language implements the important principle of *topographic-ity* described in [10], meaning that there is an isomorphism between the structure of the query and the structure of the objects found. The principle of topographic-ity works with respect to two important textual principles, namely embedding and sequence.

As an example of topographicity with respect to embedding, consider the query Q1 in Fig. 3 on page 221. This query finds sentences within which there is at least one word whose surface is "saw". The "[Word surface="saw"]" object block is *embedded in* the "[Sentence ...]" object block. Because of the principle of topographicity, any Word objects found must also be *embedded in* the Sentence objects found.

Similarly, in Query Q5 in Fig. 3, the two inner [Syntax level=Phrase ...] object blocks find Syntax objects that immediately follow each other in sequential order, because the object blocks are adjacent. "Being adjacent" here means

---

[3] This is an example of the generality of the EMdF database model, in that it supports many different linguistic paradigms and methods of analysis.

"not being separated by other blocks" (including a power block). There is a caveat, however. The default behavior is to treat objects in the database as "being adjacent" even if they are separated by a gap in the surrounding context. For examle, in Query Q5, if the surrounding Sentence object has a gap between the NP and the VP[4], then that query will find such a sentence due to the default behavior. If this is not the desired behavior (i.e., gaps are not allowed), one can put the "!" (bang) operator in between the object blocks, as in Query Q4 in Fig. 3. This will require the objects found by the object blocks surrounding the bang to be strictly sequential.

An object block can be given the restriction that it must be first, last, or first and last in its surrounding context. An example using the last keyword can be seen in Query Q3 in Fig. 3.

The object retrieved by an object block can be given a name with the AS keyword. Subsequent object blocks can then refer back to the named object. An example can be seen in Query Q5 in Fig. 3, where the dominating Syntax object is named AS S1. The dominated phrase-level Syntax object blocks then refer back to the dominating object by means of the "possessive dot notation" mentioned previously. Obviously, this facility can be used to specify both agreement, (immediate) dominance, and other inter-object relationships.

The NOTEXIST operator operates on an object block to specify that it must not exist in a given context. An example can be seen in Query Q2 in Fig. 3, where the existence of a word with the surface "saw" is negated. That is, the query finds sentences in which the word "saw" does not occur.

Notice that this is different from finding sentences with words whose *surface* is not "saw", as the query [Sentence [Word surface<>"saw"]] would find. Relating this to First Order Logic, the NOTEXIST operator is a negated existential quantifier $\neg\exists$ at *object* level, whereas the <> operator is a negated equality operator $\neq$ at object *attribute* level. If the NOTEXIST operator is applied to an object block, the object block must be the only block in its context.

The Kleene Star operator also operates on an object block, and has the usual meaning of repeating the object block zero or more times, always restricted to being within the boundaries of any surrounding context block. For example, the query

```
[Sentence
   [Word pos=preposition]
   [Word pos IN (article,noun,adjective,conjunction)]*
]
```

would find the words of many prepositional phrases, and could be used in a stage of initial syntactic markup of a corpus. The Kleene Star also supports restricting the number of repetitions with an arbitrary set of integers. For example: [Phrase]*{0,1} means that the Phrase object may be repeated 0 or 1

---

[4] As argued by [12], the sentence "John, of course, talked about politics" is an example of an element with a gap, since "of course" is not part of the surrounding clause.

times;[5] [Clause]*{2-4} means that the Clause object may be repeated 2, 3, or 4 times; and any set of integers can be used, even discontiguous ones, such as [Phrase]*{0-3,7-9,20-}. The notation "20-" signifies "from 20 to infinity".

An OR operator operating on strings of blocks is available. It means that one or both strings may occur in a given context. An example is given in Query Q7 in Fig. 3.

MQL has some shortcomings, some of which will be detailed later. Here we will just mention four shortcomings which we are working to fix, but which time has not allowed us to fix yet. We have worked out an operational semantics for the following four constructs: AND between strings of blocks (meaning that both strings must occur, and that they must overlap);[6] Grouping of strings of blocks; and general Kleene Star on strings of blocks (the current Kleene Star is only applicable to one object block). A fourth operator can easily be derived from the existing OR construct on strings of blocks, namely permutations of objects.

4   Retrieval of Results

When querying linguistic data, there are often three distinct kinds of results involved:

1. The **"meat"**, or the particular linguistic construction of interest.
2. The **context**, which is not exactly what the user is interested in, but helps delimit, restrict, or facilitate the search in some way. For example, the user may be interested in subject inversion or agentless passives, but both require the context of a sentence. Similarly, the user may be interested in objects expressed by relative pronouns combined with a repeated pronoun in the next clause, which might require the presence of intervening, specified, but otherwise non-interesting material such as a complementizer.[7] In both cases, the user is interested in a specific construction, but a certain context (either surrounding or intervening) needs to be present. The context is thus necessary for the query to return the desired results, but is otherwise not a part of the desired results.
3. The **postprocessing** results which are necessary for purposes which are outside the scope of the search.

To illustrate, consider the query Q2 in Fig. 3. For display purposes, what should be retrieved for this query? The answer depends, among other things, on the linguistic domain under consideration (syntax, phonology, etc.), the linguistic categories stored in the database, the purposes for which the display is made, and the sophistication of the user. For the domain of syntax, trees might

---

[5] Notice that this supports optionality in the language; that the phrase object appears 0 or 1 times is equivalent to saying that it is optional.

[6] This is precisely what is needed for querying overlapping structures such as those found in speech data with more than one speaker, where the speaker turns overlap.

[7] E.g., "He gave me a ring, which, I really don't like that it is emerald."

be appropriate, which would require retrieval of all nodes dominated by the sentence. For the domain of phonology, intonational phrases, tones, pauses, etc. as well as the phonemes dominated by the sentence would probably have to be retrieved. As to purpose, if the user only needed a concordance, then only the words dominated by the sentence need be retrieved, whereas for purposes requiring a full-fledged tree, more elements would have to be retrieved. The level of sophistication of the user also has a role to play, since an untrained user might balk at trees, whereas keywords in context may be more understandable.

Similarly, for statistical purposes, it is often important to retrieve frequency counts over the entire corpus to compare against the current result set. These frequency counts have nothing to do with the answer to the original query, but instead are only needed after the results have been retrieved. They are, in a very real sense, outside the scope of the query itself: The user is looking for a particular linguistic construction, and the corpus query system should find those constructions. That the post-query purpose of running the query is statistical calculations is outside the scope of the query, and is very application-specific.

Thus what is asked for in a linguistic query is often very different from what needs to be retrieved eventually, given differences in linguistic domain, categories in the database, purpose of display, and sophistication of the user. Therefore, in our view, it is advantageous to split the two operations into separate query language constructs. The subset of the query language supporting linguistic querying would thus be concerned with returning results based on what is asked for in a linguistic query, whereas other subsets of the query language would be concerned with retrieving objects based on those results for display- or other purposes.

This separation, because it is general, supports a multiplicity of linguistic applications, since the concern of linguistic querying (which is common to all linguistic query applications) is separated from the concern of querying for display-, statistical, or other purposes (which are specific to a given application). Moreover, it shifts the burden of what to retrieve based on a given query (other than what is being asked for) off the user's mind, and onto the application, thus making the query language simpler both for the user and for the corpus query system implementor. Finally, this strategy lends itself well to modularization of the query language. That modularization is good, even necessary for correct software implementation has long been a credo of software engineering.[8]

5   Evaluation

Lai and Bird [13] formulate some requirements for query languages for treebanks. They do so on the backdrop of a survey of a number of query languages, including TGrep2, TIGERSearch, the Emu query language, CorpusSearch, NXT Search, and LPath. Lai and Bird set up a number of test queries (see Fig. 2) which are then expressed (or attempted expressed) in each of the surveyed query languages.

---

[8] Emdros adheres to this modular principle of separation of concerns between corpus query system and a particular linguistic application on top of it.

Q1. Find sentences that include the word 'saw'.
Q2. Find sentences that do not include the word 'saw'.
Q3. Find noun phrases whose rightmost child is a noun.
Q4. Find verb phrases that contain a verb immediately followed by a noun phrase that is immediately followed by a prepositional phrase.
Q5. Find the first common ancestor of sequences of a noun phrase followed by a verb phrase.
Q6. Find a noun phrase which dominates a word *dark* that is dominated by an intermediate phrase that bears an L-tone.
Q7. Find a noun phrase dominated by a verb phrase. Return the subtree dominated by that noun phrase.

Fig. 2. The test queries from [13], Fig. 1

```
Q1. [Sentence                        Q5.? [Syntax AS S1
        [Word surface="saw"]                 [Syntax level=Phrase AND type=NP
    ]                                             AND parent=S1.id]
Q2. [Sentence                                [Syntax level=Phrase AND type=VP
        NOTEXIST [Word                                AND parent=S1.id]
                surface="saw"]               ]
    ]                                  Q6.? [Intermediate tone="L-"
Q3. [Phrase type=NP                          [Phrase type=NP
        [Word last pos=noun]                     [Word surface="dark"]
    ]                                        ]
Q4. [Phrase type=VP                          ]
        [Word pos=verb]!               Q7.  [Phrase type=VP
        [Phrase type=NP]!                    [Phrase type=NP AS np1
        [Phrase type=PP]                         [Phrase parents HAS np1.id
    ]                                                [Word]
                                             ] OR
                                             [Word parent=np1.id]
                                         ]
                                     ]
```

Fig. 3. MQL queries for Q1-Q7

For all query languages surveyed, it is the case that at least one query cannot be correctly expressed.

The queries are attempted expressed in MQL as in Fig. 3. Query Q1 is trivial, and performs as expected. Query Q2 has already been explained above, and deserves no further comment. The constraint of query Q3 that the noun must be the rightmost child is elegantly expressed by the "last" operator on the noun.

In query Q4, the verb, the NP, and the PP are not separated by power blocks ("..") and so must immediately follow each other. As mentioned above, gaps are ignored unless the "bang" operator ("!") is applied in between the object blocks. Since the query specification explicitly mentions "immediately followed by", we have chosen to insert this operator. Of course, if the default behavior is desired, the bang operator can simply be left out.

Query Q5 fails to yield the correct results in some cases because it presupposes that the "first common ancestor" is the immediate parent, which it need not be. Had the "parent=S1.id" terms been left out of the conjunctions, the query would have found all ancestors, not just the immediate ancestor. It is a shortcoming of the current MQL that it is not easy to express other relationships than "general ancestry" and "immediate ancestry".

Query Q5 also presupposes a different database structure than the other queries: In the database behind Q5, all syntax-level objects have been lumped together into one "Syntax" type. This "Syntax" type has a "level" attribute specifying the linguistic level at which the element occurs (Phrase, Clause, etc.), as well as other attributes.

This reorganization of the database is necessary for Q5 because it does not specify what level the dominating node should be at (Phrase, Clause, or Sentence). It is a limitation in Emdros that it can only handle one, explicit type for each object block.

For some lingusitic databases, query Q6 would fail to retrieve all possible instances because it assumes that the NP is wholly contained in the Intermediate Phrase. But as [14, p. 176] reports, this is not always true.[9]

Query Q7 not only needs to specify context, but also to retrieve the subtree, presumably for display- or other purposes, since it is not part of what is being asked for (i.e., the "meat"). As mentioned in Sect. 4, Emdros adheres to a different philosophy of implementation. While it is possible in MQL to retrieve exactly whatever the user wants, the algorithm for doing so would in most cases be split between retrieving linguistic results and using other parts of the query language for retrieving objects for display-purposes.

The Q7 query nevertheless fulfills its purpose by retrieving all phrases dominated by the NP together with the words they contain, OR all words immediately dominated by the NP. Thus, Emdros is able to fulfill the purpose of the query even though Emdros was not designed for such use.

Lai and Bird go on from their survey to listing a number of requirements on linguistic query languages. The first requirement listed is "accurate specification of the query tree". Lai and Bird give eight subtree-matching queries, all of which can be expressed in MQL (see Fig. 4). Query number 5 would require the employment of the technique used for query Q5 in Fig. 3 of using a single object type for all syntax objects, using an attribute for the syntactic level, then leaving out the level from the query.

Another requirement specified by Lai and Bird is that of reverse navigation, i.e., the need to specify context in any direction. MQL handles this gracefully, in our opinion, by the principle of topographicity with respect to embedding and sequence. Using this principle, any context can be specified in both vertical directions, as well as along the horizontal axis.

---

[9] The example given there is an intermediate phrase boundary between adjectives and nouns in Japanese — presumably the adjective and the noun belong in the same NP, yet the intermediate phrase-boundary occurs in the middle of the NP.

1. Immediate dominance: A dominates B, A may dominate other nodes.   `[A AS a1 [B parent=A1.id]]`

2. Positional constraint: A dominates B, and B is the first (last) child of A.   `[A [B first] ]` or: `[A [B last] ]`

3. Positional constraint with respect to a label: A dominates B, and B is the last B child of A.   `[A [B last] ]`

4. Multiple Dominance: A dominates both B and C, but the order of B and C is unspecified.   `[A [B]..[C] OR [C]..[B]]`

5. Sibling precedence: A dominates both B and C, B precedes C; A dominates both B and C, B immediately precedes C, and C is unspecified.   precedes: `[A [B]..[C]]` immediately precedes: `[A [B][C]]` or `[A [B]![C]]`.

6. Complete description: A dominates B and C, in that order, and nothing else.   `[A as a1` `    [B first parent=a1.id]!` `    [B last parent=a1.id]` `]`

7. Multiple copies: A dominates B and B, and the two Bs are different instances.   `[A [B]..[B]]`

8. Negation: A does not dominate node with label B.   `[A NOTEXIST [B] ]`

Fig. 4. Subtree queries in the MQL query language, after Lai and Bird's Fig. 9

Lai and Bird then mention non-tree navigation as a requirement. They give the example of an NP being specified either as "[NP Adj Adj N]" or as "[NP Adj [NP Adj N]]", the latter with a Chomsky-adjoined NP inside the larger NP. MQL handles querying both structures with ease, as seen in Fig. 5. Note that the query in Fig. 5.a. would also find the tree in Fig. 5.b. Thus non-tree navigation is well supported.

Furthermore, Lai and Bird mention specification of precedence and immediate precedence as a requirement. MQL handles both with ease because of the principle of topographicity of sequence. General precedence is signified by the power block (".."), whereas immediate precedence is signified by the absence of the power block, optionally with the bang operator ("!").

Lai and Bird then discuss closures of various kinds. MQL is closed both under dominance (by means of topographicity of embedding) and under precedence

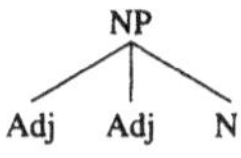

a. Flat structure

```
[Phrase type=NP
    [Word first
        pos=adjective]
    [Word pos=adjective]
    [Word last pos=noun]
]
```

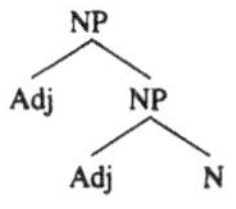

b. Chomsky-adjoined structure

```
[Phrase type=NP
    [Word first pos=adjective]
    [Phrase last type=NP
        [Word first pos=adjective]
        [Word last pos=noun]
    ]
]
```

Fig. 5. Queries on NP structure

and sibling precedence (by means of topographicity of sequence, as well as the power block and the AS keyword, which separately or in combination can be used to specify closures under both relationships). MQL is also closed under atomic queries involving one object (by means of the Kleene Star).[10]

Lai and Bird discuss the need for querying above sentence-level. Since the EMdF database model is abstract and general, the option exists of using ordered forests as mentioned by Lai and Bird. The MQL query language was designed to complement the EMdF model in its generality, and thus querying over ordered forests is well supported using the principle of topographicity of sequence combined with the AS construct. Thus the MQL language is not restricted to querying sentence-trees alone, but supports querying above sentence-level.

Another requirement mentioned by Lai and Bird is that of integration of several types of lingusitic data, in particular using intersecting hierarchies and lookup of data from other sources. The EMdF model supports intersecting hierarchies well. MQL, however, because of the principle of topographicity of embedding and the lack of an AND construct between strings of blocks, does not currently support querying of intersecting hierarchies very well, as illustrated by the failure of Query Q6 in Fig. 3 to be correct. Thus Emdros currently falls short on this account, though an AND construct is planned.

There is also currently a lack of support for querying data from other sources. However, this can be implemented by the application using Emdros, provided the data from other sources can be known before query-time and can thus be written into the query. This would, of course, presuppose that the application does some kind of rewriting of the query made by the user.

The final requirement mentioned by [13] is the need to query non-tree structure. For example, the TIGER Corpus [15] includes secondary, crossing edges, and the Penn Treebank includes edges for WH-movement and topicalization [16]. MQL handles querying these constructions by means of the AS keyword and referencing the ID of the thus named object, as in Query Q5 in Fig. 3.

6   Conclusion and Further Work

We have presented the EMdF database model and the MQL query language of our corpus query system, Emdros. We have shown how the data to be retrieved for display-, statistical, or other purposes can often be different from what is asked for in a linguistic query, differentiating between "meat", "context", and "postprocessing results". On the basis of this distinction, we have argued for the strategy of separating the process of lingusitic querying from the process of retrieval of data for display- or other purposes. This implementation strategy of separation of concerns gives rise to the benefits of generality of the language (and thus its applicability to a wide variety of linguistic applications), simplicity of the language (and thus ease of use for the user), and modularity (and thus ease

---

[10] Once we have implemented the general Kleene Star on strings of blocks, MQL will be closed under atomic queries involving more than one block.

of implementation, maintainability, and attainment of the goal of correctness for the system implementor). Finally, we have evaluated MQL against the queries and requirements of [13], and have shown MQL to be able to express most of the queries, and to meet most of the requirements that [13] puts forth.

However, Emdros falls short on a number of grounds. First, although its database model is able to handle intersecting hierarchies, its query language does not currently handle querying these intersecting hierarchies very well. This can be fixed by the inclusion of an AND operator between strings of object blocks. Second, a general Kleene Star is lacking that can operate on groups of (optionally embedded) objects. Third, the query language currently only supports one, explicit object type for any given object block. This can be fixed, e.g., by introducing true object orientation with inheritance between object types. Fourth, the system currently does not support real numbers as values of attributes of objects, which would be very useful for phonological databases. Fifth, it is currently not easy to express other, more specific dominance relationships than immediate dominance and general dominance. As has been described above, the removal of most of these shortcomings is planned.

Thus Emdros is able to meet most of the requirements being placed on today's linguistic query systems. We have not here fully explored its applicability to phonological or discourse-level databases, since [13] concentrated on treebanks, but that is a topic for a future paper.

References

1. Mengel, A.: MATE deliverable D3.1 – specification of coding workbench: 3.8 improved query language (Q4M). Technical report, Institut für Maschinelle Sprachverarbeitung, Stuttgart, 18. November (1999)
2. Cassidy, S., Bird, S.: Querying databases of annotated speech. In Orlowska, M., ed.: Database Technologies: Proceedings of the Eleventh Australasian Database Conference, volume 22 of Australian Computer Science Communications, Canberra, Australia. IEEE Computer Society (2000) 12–20
3. Bird, S., Buneman, P., Tan, W.C.: Towards a query language for annotation graphs. In: Proceedings of the Second International Conference on Language Resources and Evaluation. European Language Resources Association, Paris (2000) 807–814
4. Lezius, W.: TIGERSearch – ein Suchwerkzeug für Baumbanken. In Busemann, S., ed.: Proceedings der 6. Konferenz zur Verarbeitung natürlicher Sprache (KONVENS 2002), Saarbrücken. (2002) 107–114
5. Heid, U., Voormann, H., Milde, J.T., Gut, U., Erk, K., Pado, S.: Querying both time-aligned and hierarchical corpora with NXT Search. In: Fourth Language Resources and Evaluation Conference, Lisbon, Portugal, May 2004. (2004)
6. Rohde, D.L.T.: TGrep2 user manual, version 1.12. Available for download online http://tedlab.mit.edu/~dr/Tgrep2/tgrep2.pdf. Access Online April 2005 (2004)
7. Bird, S., Chen, Y., Davidson, S., Lee, H., Zheng, Y.: Extending XPath to support linguistic queries. In: Proceedings of Programming Language Technologies for XML (PLANX) Long Beach, California. January 2005. (2005) 35–46

8. Petersen, U.: Emdros — A text database engine for analyzed or annotated text. In: Proceedings of COLING 2004, 20th International Conference on Computational Linguistics, August 23rd to 27th, 2004, Geneva, International Commitee on Computational Linguistics (2004) 1190–1193 http://emdros.org/petersen-emdros-COLING-2004.pdf.

9. Petersen, U.: Evaluating corpus query systems on functionality and speed: Tigersearch and emdros. In Angelova, G., Bontcheva, K., Mitkov, R., Nicolov, N., Nikolov, N., eds.: International Conference Recent Advances in Natural Language Processing 2005, Proceedings, Borovets, Bulgaria, 21-23 September 2005, Shoumen, Bulgaria, INCOMA Ltd. (2005) 387–391 ISBN 954-91743-3-6.

10. Doedens, C.J.: Text Databases: One Database Model and Several Retrieval Languages. Number 14 in Language and Computers. Editions Rodopi, Amsterdam and Atlanta, GA. (1994)

11. Lund, K., Burgess, C.: Producing high-dimensional semantic spaces from lexical co-occurrence. Behavior Research Methods, Instruments and Computers **28** (1996) 203–208

12. McCawley, J.D.: Parentheticals and discontinuous constituent structure. Linguistic Inquiry **13** (1982) 91–106

13. Lai, C., Bird, S.: Querying and updating treebanks: A critical survey and requirements analysis. In: Proceedings of the Australasian Language Technology Workshop, December 2004. (2004) 139–146

14. Beckman, M.E., Pierrehumbert, J.B.: Japanese prosodic phrasing and intonation synthesis. In: Proceedings of the 24th Annual Meeting of the Association for Computational Linguistics. ACL (1986) 173–180

15. Brants, S., Hansen, S.: Developments in the TIGER annotation scheme and their realization in the corpus I. In: Proceedings of the Third International Conference on Language Resources and Evaluation (LREC 2002), Las Palmas, Spain, May 2002. (2002) 1643–1649

16. Taylor, A., Marcus, M., Santorini, B.: The Penn treebank: An overview. In Abeillé, A., ed.: Treebanks — Building and Using Parsed Corpora. Volume 20 of Text, Speech and Language Technology. Kluwer Academic Publishers, Dordrecht, Boston, London (2003) 5–22

On Compact Storage Models for Gazetteers

Jakub Piskorski

DFKI GmbH
German Research Center for Artificial Intelligence
Stuhlsatzenhausweg 3, 66123 Saarbrücken, Germany
Jakub.Piskorski@dfki.de

Abstract. This paper describes compact storage models for gazetteers using state-of-the-art finite-state technology. In particular, we compare the standard method based on numbered indexing automata associated with an auxiliary storage device, against a pure finite-state representation, the latter being superior in terms of space and time complexity, when applied to real-world test data. Further, we pinpoint some pros and cons for both approaches and provide results of empirical experiments, which form handy guidelines for selecting a suitable data structure for implementing a gazetteer.

1 Introduction

Traditionally, the term gazetteer refers to a dictionary that includes geographically related information on given places, e.g., data concerning the makeup of a country, region or location including social statistics, GDP, language, information on name variants, known abbreviations, full name, etc. In the NLP community, a gazetteer refers to a list of not only geographical references, but also names of people, organizations, months of the year, days, currency units, company designators and other similar keywords. Gazetteer look-up is usually seen as an independent process of linguistic analysis, in which the input stream of characters or tokens is matched against a gazetteer list, and an adequate annotation is produced. Typically, a gazetteer component is deployed in the process of named-entity recognition and plays a key role in solving other information extraction tasks.

There are several well-established techniques and data structures that can be used to implement a gazetteer, e.g., hashing, tries and finite-state automata. Some studies on real-world data reveal that finite-state automata seem to be a good choice, since they require less memory than alternative techniques and guarantee efficient access to the data [1, 2, 3, 4].

In this paper, we describe and discuss several state-of-the-art finite-state approaches to implementing a gazetteer look-up component. In particular, we investigate the standard technique involving numbered automata with multiple initial states combined with an external table [3]. Secondly, we examine another method, focused on converting the input data in such a way as to model the gazetteer solely as a single finite-state automaton without any auxiliary storage

A. Yli-Jyrä, L. Karttunen, and J. Karhumäki (Eds.): FSMNLP 2005, LNAI 4002, pp. 227–238, 2006.
© Springer-Verlag Berlin Heidelberg 2006

device tailored to it. Further, we explore how transition jamming — an equivalence transformation on finite-state devices [5] — impacts the size of the resulting automata. The main motivation for carrying out the aforementioned explorations was driven by the shortcomings of our first ad hoc implementation of a gazetteer look-up component, which turned to be inefficient in terms of space complexity with rapidly growing size and structure of the gazetteer resources employed in our NLP applications [6]. Interestingly, most of the gazetteer implementation descriptions report on deploying standard database systems for this purpose, which might appear suboptimal in the era of forthcoming content services for portable thin clients.

The rest of this paper is organized as follows. Firstly, in section 2, we introduce the basic definitions used throughout the paper. Section 3 presents the strategies for modeling and optimizing the data structure for a gazetteer look-up component. Subsequently, in section 4 we report on some empirical experiments, which were carried out on various real-world test data. We finish off with some conclusions in section 5.

2   Preliminaries

In this section we present the basic concepts, notions and techniques referred to in this paper, i.e., finite-state automata etc. A *deterministic finite-state automaton* (DFSA) is a quintuple $M = (Q, \Sigma, \delta, q_0, F)$, where Q is a finite *set of states*, Σ is the *alphabet* of M, $\delta : Q \times \Sigma \rightarrow Q$ is the *transition function*, q_0 is the *initial state* and $F \subseteq Q$ is the *set of final states*. $|Q|$ and $|\delta|$ denote the number of states and transitions in M respectively. The transition function can be extended to $\delta^* : Q \times \Sigma^* \rightarrow Q$ by defining $\delta(q, \epsilon) = q$, and $\delta(q, wa) = \delta(\delta^*(q, w), a)$ for $a \in \Sigma$ and $w \in \Sigma^*$. The *language accepted by an automaton* M is defined as $L(M) = \{w \in \Sigma^* | \delta^*(q_0, w) \in F\}$. Analogously, the *right language* of a state q is defined as $L(q) = \{w \in \Sigma^* | \delta^*(q, w) \in F\}$. A *path* in a DFSA M is a sequence of triples $\langle(p_0, a_0, p_1), \ldots, (p_{k-1}, a_{k-1}, p_k)\rangle$, where $(p_{i-1}, a_{i-1}, p_i) \in Q \times \Sigma \times Q$ and $\delta(p_i, a_i) = p_{i+1}$ for $1 \leq i < k$. The string $a_0 a_1 \ldots a_k$ is the *label* of the path. We denote the first and last state in a path π as $f(\pi)$ and $l(\pi)$ respectively. We call a path π a *cycle* if $f(\pi) = l(\pi)$. Further, we call a path π *sequential* if all intermediate states q on π, i.e., all states except $f(\pi)$ and $l(\pi)$, are not final and fulfill the property $|\{a : a \in \Sigma \wedge \delta(q, a) \text{ is defined}\}| = 1$ and $|\{p : \delta(p, a) = q \text{ for some } a \in \Sigma\}| = 1$. In other words, intermediate states on a sequential path have exactly one incoming and one outgoing transition. Among all DFSAs recognizing the same language, there is always one which has the minimal number of states. We call such an automaton *minimal*.

Minimal acyclic DFSA is the most compact data structure for storing and efficiently recognizing a finite set of words. It can be constructed in several ways. In particular, a space-efficient incremental algorithm for constructing a minimal acyclic DFSA from a list of strings in nearly linear time, presented recently by several authors [1, 7], can be used for this purpose. Another finite-state device we refer to in this paper is the so called *numbered minimal acyclic deterministic finite-state automaton*. Each state of such automata is associated with an integer representing the cardinality of the right language of this state. Figure 1 presents an example of such an automaton which accepts the words {*start, art, card, stunt, calk*}. Once a minimal acyclic DFSA has been constructed, state numbering can be computed in linear time by means of simple recursive traversal of the automaton. Numbered automata can be used for assigning each word they accept a unique numeric key, i.e., they implement *perfect hashing*. An index (hash key) $I(w)$ of a given word w can be computed in the following manner. We start with an index $I(w)$ equal to 0 and scan the input w with the automaton. While traversing the accepting path, in each state we increase the index by the sum of all integers associated with the target states of transitions lexicographically preceding the transition used. Additionally, for each final state in the accepting path we increase $I(w)$ by one. Once the input w has been consumed and a final state has been reached, $I(w)$ contains the unique index of the word. Alternatively, for a given index i the corresponding word w such that $I(w) = i$ can be computed in a somewhat similar way by deducing the transitions, i.e., the path which would lead to the index i. Instead of associating states with integers, each transition can be accompanied by the number of different routes to any final state outgoing from the same state as the current transition, whose label are lexicographically lower than the current one. In this case, computing the index of a given word consists solely of summing over the integers associated with traversed transitions, whereas memory requirements rise to about 30% (when dealing with natural language data). See [8, 9, 3] for details.

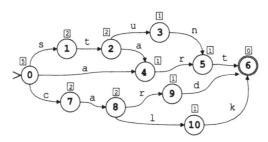

Fig. 1. Numbered minimal acyclic DFSA accepting {*start, art, card, stunt, calk*}

3   Modeling of a Gazetteer Look-Up Component

Before we start the discussion on modelling the gazetteer architecture please note that raw gazetteer resources are usually represented simply by a text file, where each line represents a single gazetteer entry in the following format: `keyword (attribute:value)+`. For each reading of an ambiguous keyword, a separate line is introduced. For the word *Washington* the gazetteer potentially includes the following entries:

```
Washington | type:city | variant:WASHINGTON | location:USA
           | full-name:Washington D.C. | subtype:cap_city
Washington | type:person | gender:m_f | surname:Washington
           | language:english
Washington | type:organization | subtype:commercial
           | full-name:Washington Ltd. | location:Canada
Washington | type:region | variant:WASHINGTON | location:USA
           | abbreviation: {W.A.,WA.} | subtype:state
```

We differentiate between open-class and closed-class attributes depending on their range of values, e.g., full-name is an open-class attribute, whereas gender is a closed-class attribute. As can be seen in the last reading for the word *Washington*, an attribute may be assigned a list of values (abbreviation).

3.1   Standard Approach

The standard approach to implementing dictionaries and thesauri presented in [9, 3] can be straightforwardly adapted to model the architecture of a gazetteer look-up component. The main idea is to encode the keywords and all attribute values in a single numbered minimal acyclic DFSA. In order to distinguish between keywords and different attribute values we extend the indexing automaton so that it has $n + 1$ initial states, where n is the number of attributes. The strings accepted by the automaton starting from the first initial state correspond directly to the set of the keywords, whereas the right language of the i-th initial state (for $i \geq 1$) corresponds to the range of values appropriate for i-th attribute. Further, the subautomaton starting in each initial state implements different perfect hashing function. Hence, the aforementioned automaton constitutes a word-to-index and index-to-word engine for keywords and attribute values. Once we know the index of a given keyword, we can access the indices of all associated attribute values in a row of an auxiliary table. Consequently, these indices can be used to extract the proper values from the indexing automaton. In the case of multiple readings an intermediate array for mapping the keyword indices to the absolute position of the block of rows containing all readings of a given keyword is indispensable. The overall architecture is sketched in figure 2. Note, that via introduction of multiple initial states $log_2(card(i))$ bits are sufficient for representing the indices for values of attribute i, where $card(i)$ is the size of the corresponding value set.

It is not necessarily convenient to index all attribute values and store the proper values in the numbered automaton, e.g., numerical data such as longitude or latitude could be stored directly in the attribute-value matrix since obviously automata are not a panacea in such situation. Alternatively, some attribute values could also be stored elsewhere (as depicted in figure 2). This procedure is reasonable if the range of the values is bounded and integer representation is more compact than anything else (e.g. long alphanumeric identifiers). Fortunately, the vast majority (but definitely not all) of attribute values in a gazetteer deployed in NLP happens to be natural language words or multi-word expressions. Therefore, one can intuitively expect the major part of the entries and attribute values to share suffixes, which leads to a better compression of the indexing automaton. The prevalent bottleneck of the presented approach is a potentially high redundancy of the information stored in the attribute-value matrix. However, this problem can be partially alleviated via automatic detection of column dependency, which might expose sources of information redundancy to gain better compression of the data [10]. Reccurring patterns consisting of raw fragments of the attribute-value index matrix could be indexed and represented only once.

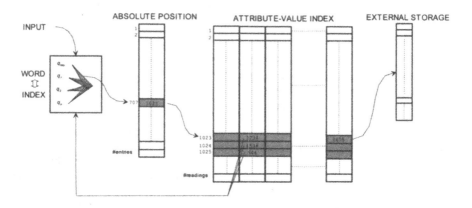

Fig. 2. Compact storage model for a gazetteer look-up component

3.2   Pure Finite-State Representation

One of the common techniques for squeezing finite-state devices in the context of implementing dictionaries is an appropriate coding of the input data. Converting a list of strings (word forms) into a minimal acyclic DFSA usually results in a good compression rate, since many words share prefixes and suffixes, which leads to transition sharing. If strings are associated with additional annotations representing certain categories, e.g., part-of-speech, inflection or stem information in a morphological lexicon, then an adequate encoding of such information is necessary in order to keep the corresponding automaton small. A simple solution is to reorder categories from the most specific to the most general ones, so that stem information would precede inflection and part-of-speech tag. Another technique is to precompute all possible annotation sequences for all entries and to replace them with an index. Nevertheless, the major part of a string that encodes the keyword and its tags might be unique and could potentially blow up the corresponding automaton enormously. Consider again the entry for the morphological lexicon consisting of an inflected word form and its tags, e.g. `striking:strike:v:a:p` (v - verb, a - present, p - participle). Obviously, the sequence `striking:strike` is unique. Through the exploitation of the word-specific information the inflected form and its base form share, one can introduce patterns describing how the lexeme can be reconstructed from the inflected word form, e.g., `3+e` - delete three terminal characters and append an *e* (*striking* → *strik* + *e*). Application of such patterns results in better suffix sharing, i.e., the suffix 3+e:v:a:p is certainly more frequently shared than strike:v:a:p. The encoding techniques like the one mentioned here are well studied and addressed elsewhere [2, 4].

The main idea behind transforming a gazetteer into a single automaton is to split each gazetteer entry into a disjunction of subentries, each representing some partial information. For each open-class attribute-value pair present in the entry a single subentry is created, whereas closed-class attribute-value pairs (or a subset of them) are merged into a single subentry and rearranged in order to fulfill the *first most specific, last most general* criterion. In our example, the entry for the word *Washington* (city) yields the following partition into subentries:

```
Washington #1 NAME(subtype) VAL(cap_city) NAME(type) VAL(city)
Washington #1 NAME(variant) WASHINGTON
Washington #1 NAME(location) USA
Washington #1 NAME(full-name) Washington D.C.
```

where NAME maps attribute names to single univocal characters not appearing elsewhere in the original gazetteer and VAL denotes a mapping which converts the values of the closed-class attributes into single characters representing them. The string #1, where # is again a unique symbol, denotes the reading index of the entry (first reading for the word *Washington*). Please note that, in the case of list-valued open-class attributes, we can simply add an appropriate subentry for each element in the list. Gazetteer resources converted in this manner are subsequently compiled into a minimal acyclic DFSA via application of any of the algorithms presented in [1, 7]. In order to gain better compression rate we utilized formation patterns for a subset of attribute values appearing in the gazetteer entries. These patterns resemble the ones for encoding morphological information, but they partially rely on other information. For instance, frequently, attribute values are just the capitalized form or the lowercase version of the corresponding keywords, as can be seen in our example. Such a pattern can be represented by a single character. Further, keywords and attribute values often share prefixes or suffixes, e.g., *Washington* vs. *Washington D.C.* Next, there are clearly several patterns for forming acronyms or abbreviations from the full form, e.g., *ACL* can be derived from *Association of Computational Linguistics*, by simply concatenating all capitals in the full name. We benefit from such formation rules and deploy other related patterns in a similar manner. Nevertheless, some part of the attribute values can not be replaced by patterns. Applying formation patterns to our sample entry would result in:

```
Washington #1 NAME(subtype) VAL(cap_city) NAME(type) VAL(city)
Washington #1 NAME(variant) PATTERN(AllCapital)
Washington #1 NAME(location) USA
Washington #1 NAME(full-name) PATTERN(Identity) D.C.
```

where PATTERN maps pattern names to unique characters not appearing elsewhere in the gazetteer. Some improvement in terms of space complexity may be obtained by reversing the attribute values not covered by any pattern, since prefix compression might be superior to suffix compression.

The outlined method of representing a gazetteer is an elegant solution and exhibits three major assets. First of all, we do not need any external table for storing/accessing attribute values. Secondly, the automaton involved is not a numbered DFSA, which means less space requirement and reduced searching time in comparison to automaton described in 3.1[1] Finally, as a consequence of the encoding strategy, there is only one single final state in the automaton. The states having outgoing transitions labeled with the unique symbols in the range of NAME are implicit final states. The right languages of these states represent attribute-value pairs attached to the gazetteer entries. On the other hand, the information stored in the gazetteers and the fashion in which the automaton is built, intuitively, does not allow for obtaining the same compression rates as in the case of the indexing automaton described in the previous subsection. For instance, many gazetteer entries are multiword expressions, which increase the size of the automaton by an introduction of numerous sequential paths. Therefore, we have investigated the usefulness of applying the so called transition jamming to remedy this problem.

3.3 Transition Jamming

Transition jamming is an equivalence operation on automata, in which transitions on each sequential path are transformed into a single transition labeled with the label of the whole path [5]. Intermediate states on the path are removed. Obviously, such a transformation does not have an impact on the functionality of an automaton, i.e., the jammed automaton still accepts the same language. Since sequential paths can be computed in linear time, automata jamming can be performed efficiently as well.

We have applied transition jamming in a somewhat different way. Let π be a sequential path in the automaton and $a = a_0 a_1 \ldots a_k$ be the label of π. We remove all transitions of π and introduce a new transition from $f(\pi)$ to $l(\pi)$ labeled with a_0 , i.e., $\delta(f(\pi), a_0) = l(\pi)$ and store the remaining character sequence $a_1 \ldots a_k$ in a list of sequential path labels. Once all such sequences are collected, we introduce a new initial state in the automaton and consecutively, starting from this state, we add all sequential path labels to the minimized automaton, while maintaining its property of being minimal [7]. The subautomaton starting from the new initial state implements a perfect hashing function. Finally, the new 'jammed' transitions in the automaton are associated with the corresponding indices in order to reconstruct the full label on demand. Since the word-index automaton in the standard approach contains far more than one final state in opposition to the pure FSA approach with a single final state, a better result of automata jamming is expected in the latter case. There are several ways of selecting sequential paths for jamming. Maximum-length sequential paths constitute the first choice and point of departure for further experiments. Jamming paths of bounded length might yield better or at least different

---

[1] Please note that we can deploy the formation patterns in the indexing automaton presented in 3.1 as well.

results. For instance, a sequential path whose label is a long fragment of a multiword expression could be decomposed into subpaths that either do not include whitespaces or consist solely of whitespaces. In turn, we could jam only the subpaths of the first type.

Storing sequential path labels in a new branch of the automaton obviously leads to the introduction of new sequential paths. Consider again in this context the numerous multi-word expressions in gazetteers, which potentially consist of more than four words. Therefore, we have investigated the impact of *repetitive transition jamming* on the size of the automaton. In each phase of repetitive transition jamming, we introduce a new initial state to the automaton from which the labels of the jammed paths identified in this phase are stored.

4   Experiments

4.1   Data

For the evaluation purposes of the presented strategies we have selected the following gazetteer data: (a) UK–Postal — a list of city names in the UK associated with county and postal code information, (b) LT–World[2] — a gazetteer of key players and events in the language technology community including persons, organizations, facilities, conferences, etc., (c) PL–NE — a gazetteer of Polish named-entities, including person names, geographical places, organizations, frequently used acronyms and all kinds of designators, (d) Mixed — a combination of the LT–World and PL–NE, (e) GeoNames[3] — an excerpt of the huge gazetteer of geographic names information covering countries and geopolitical areas, including complex information on name variants, acronyms, language, administrative divisions, different codes, etc. We have excluded some 10 digit-valued attributes from the gazetteer (e). Table 1 gives an overview of our test data, where the size is given in kilobytes. The last column gives the ratio of open-class attribute values for which formation patterns described in 3.2 could be applied to the total number of open-class attribute values in a given gazetteer.

Table 1. Parameters of test gazetteers

Gazetteer name	size	#entries	#attributes	#open-class attributes	average entry length	pattern applicability
UK–Postal	1,209	27 217	2	2	43	-
LT–World	4,154	96 837	19	14	40	99,1%
PL–NE	2,809	51 631	8	3	52	96,3%
Mixed	6,957	148 468	27	17	44	97,8%
GeoNames I	13,590	80 001	17	6	166	89,2%
GeonNames II	33,500	20 001	17	6	164	92,0%

---

[2] Extracted from http://www.lt-world.org.
[3] Taken from http://earth-info.nga.mil/gns/html/

4.2   Evaluation

We have conducted several experiments with different set-ups. Firstly, we compared the standard and pure-FSA approach as described in section 3.1 and 3.2. Secondly, we repeated the experiments enhanced by integration of single transition jamming. The size of the resulting automata are given in table 2. The numbers in the columns concerning the experiments with jamming correspond to transition jamming of maximum-length sequential paths and jamming of paths whose labels do not include any whitespaces (given in brackets) respectively.

Table 2. Size of the four types of automata

Gazetteer	Standard		Pure-FSA		Standard & Jamming		Pure-FSA & Jamming	
	$|Q|$	$|\delta|$	$|Q|$	$|\delta|$	$|Q|$	$|\delta|$	$|Q|$	$|\delta|$
UK–Postal	28 596	53 041	101 145	132 008	15 008 (15 251)	40 828 (40 903)	32 072 (32 146)	67 831 (67 248)
LT–World	191 767	266 465	259 666	341 015	86 613 (67 891)	172 583 (152 571)	110 409 (81 479)	207 950 (178 396)
PL–NE	37 935	70 773	60 119	97 035	21 106 (19 979)	55 839 (54 639)	27 919 (26 274)	67 435 (65 722)
Mixed	206 802	295 416	299 540	399 286	94 440 (75 755)	194 815 (174 817)	242 512 (96 038)	242 512 (212 265)
GeoNames I	280 550	410 609	803 390	1 110 668	104 857 (107 631)	258 680 (254 130)	231 887 (226 335)	603 320 (595 122)
GeoNames II	491 744	784 001	1 655 790	2 396 984	198 630 (204 188)	514 595 (517 081)	474 572 (469 678)	1 322 058 (1 311 564)

The increase in physical storage in the case of numbered automata has been reported to be in range of 30-40% (states are numbered) and 60-70% (transition numbering) [1]. Note at this point that automata are usually stored as a sequence of transitions, where states are represented only implicitly [1, 11]. Considering additionally the space requirement for the auxiliary attribute-value table in the standard approach for storing the indices for open-class attribute values, it turns out that this number oscillates around $m \cdot n \cdot log_{256}n$ bytes, in the case of our test data, where m denotes the number of open-class attributes and n is the number of entries in the gazetteer. Summing up these observations and taking a quick look at the table 2, we conclude without naming the absolute size of the physical storage required, that the pure-FSA approach turns out to be superior when applied to our test gazetteers. However, some results, in particular for the GeoNames, where $|\delta|$ is about three time as big as in the indexing automaton in the standard approach, indicate some pitfalls. The main reason for this was the fact that some open-class attributes in the GeoNames are alphanumeric strings of different lengths (even up to 12) which do not compress well with the other data. Further, some investigation reveals the necessity of additional formation patterns, which could work better with this particular gazetteer. Finally, the GeoNames gazetteer exhibits highly multilingual character and the size of the alphabet is significantly larger than elsewhere. Nevertheless, even in the case of these somewhat more problematic gazetteers, a better results were obtained via

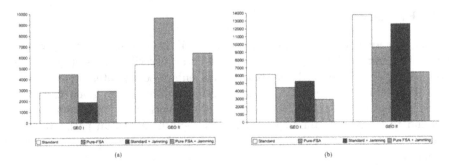

Fig. 3. Comparison of physical storage of the compiled GeoNames I and GeoNames II gazetteers given in KBs, where (a) gives the size of the automata, and (b) gives the total size of the gazetteers (automaton + space for the auxilliary table)

application of the pure-FSA approach. Figure 3 gives information on the physical storage of these gazetteers and the underlying automata.[4]

As expected, transition jamming works better with the Pure-FSA approach, i.e., it reduces the size of $|\delta|$ by a factor of 1.35 to 1.9, whereas in the other case the gain is less significant. Furthermore, transition jamming constrained to maximal whitespace-free paths turns out to allow for better compression rates, in particular when the gazetteer data does not include numerical or alphanumerical data (see table 2). Obviously, transition jamming is penalized through the introduction of state numbering in some part of the automaton and associating certain edges with indices, but the overall size of the automaton is still smaller than the original one. In the case of the LT–World gazetteer, there were circa 20000 sequential paths in the automaton. Consequently, we removed circa 134 000 transitions. Next, we studied the profitability of repetitive transition jamming. Figure 4 presents two diagrams which depict how this operation impacts the size of the automaton for the LT–World gazetteer. As can be observed, a more than 2-stage repetitive jamming does not significantly improve the compression rate. Interestingly, we can notice in the left diagram that for both approaches the repetitive jamming of maximum-length sequential paths leads (after stage 3) to a greater reduction of the size of $|Q|$ than jamming of whitespace-free paths. The corresponding numbers for other gazetteers in our test pool with respect to repetitive jamming were of similar nature.

Finally, we have tried out how reversing labels of sequential paths and reversing open-class attribute values not covered by any formation pattern influences the compression rate. Only an insignificant difference of 1-2% could be observed.

---

[4] In our automata implementation, we deploy the transition-list representation, where each transition is represented solely as quintuple consisting of a transition label, three bits marking: (a) whether the transition is final, (b) whether it is the last transition of the current state and (c) whether the first transition of the target state is the next one in the transition list, and a (possibly) empty pointer to the first outgoing transition of the target state. See [11] for details.

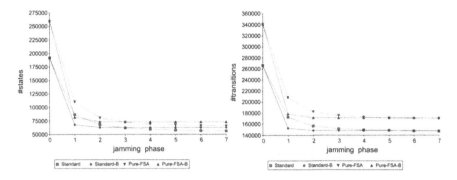

Fig. 4. Impact of repetitive transition jamming on the size of states and transitions of the automata implementing the LT–World gazetteer (Standard–B and Pure–FSA-B stands for repetitive jamming on paths whose labels do not include whitespaces)

5 Conclusions and Future Work

In this paper, we have studied various ways of modeling a gazetteer look-up component. In particular, we focused on finite-state methods in order to construct a time and space efficient data structure for storing gazetteer lists including attribute-value pairs of different kinds. Empirical experiments on gazetteers used reveal that a pure-FSA approach, in which all data is converted into a single minimal acyclic DFSA, turns out to outperform the standard approach based on an indexing numbered automaton accompanied by an auxiliary attribute-value matrix. At least in the case of data we are dealing with in the NLP context benefits are observable, since most, but not all, of the attribute values are contemporary word forms. A further investigation revealed the usefulness of transition jamming which reduces the size of the automata significantly. However, we pinpointed some risks when applying a single DFSA which is not a magic bullet for tackling all problems. Intuitively, for storing gazetteers containing a significant number of numerical and alphanumerical data the standard approach might be a better choice. Therefore, the numbers presented in section 4 are only meant to constitute a guideline, which might come in handy when selecting a compact data structure for storing a gazetteer. Ideally, a gazetteer look-up component should analyze the nature of attribute values in the input data and automatically select a suitable data structure based on some ranking heuristics.

There are a number of interesting questions and issues that can be researched in the future. We only considered jamming maximal-length sequential paths and whitespace-free paths, whereas jamming paths of bounded length might yield different and possibly better results. Furthermore, through finding more complex repeating substructures in the underlying automata, one could possibly obtain some additional space savings. The proximate activities could also address the deployment of finite-state transducers for handling the same task, especially due to the recent advances in this field, e.g., recently a generalized version of the algorithm for incremental construction of minimal acyclic DFSAs from unsorted data has been adapted to the case of transducers [12, 13]. Finally, for gazetteers containing mainly numerical data, the storage models presented in [8] could be considered for utilization.

Acknowledgements

I am indebted to Jan Daciuk for sharing ideas and to Wojciech Skut for some additional comments. The presented work was supported by the German BMBF-funded project COLLATE II under grant no. 01 IN C02.

References

1. Ciura, M.G., Deorowicz, S.: How to Squeeze a Lexicon. Software - Practice and Experience **31(11)** (2001) 1077–1090
2. Daciuk, J.: Incremental Construction of Finite-State Automata and Transducers. PhD Thesis. Technical University Gdańsk. (1998)
3. Kowaltowski, T., Lucchesi, C.L.: Applications of Finite Automata Representing Large Vocabularies. TR DCC-01/92, University of Campinas, Brazil (1992)
4. Kowaltowski, T., Lucchesi, C.L., Stolfi, J.: Finite Automata and Efficient Lexicon Implementation. TR IC-98-02, University of Campinas, Brazil (1998)
5. Beijer, N.D., Watson, B.W., Kourie, D.G.: Stretching and Jamming of Automata. In: Proceedings of SAICSIT 2003, Rep. South Africa (2003) 198–207
6. Drożdżyński, W., Krieger, H.U., Piskorski, J., Schäfer, U., Xu, F.: Shallow Processing with Unification and Typed Feature Structures — Foundations and Applications. Künstliche Intelligenz **2004(1)** (2004) 17–23
7. Daciuk, J., Mihov, S., Watson, B., Watson, R.: Incremental Construction of Minimal Acyclic Finite State Automata. Comp.Rep Linguistics **26(1)** (2000) 3–16
8. Daciuk, J., van Noord, G.: Finite Automata for Compact Representation of Language Models in NLP. Theoretical Computer Science **313(1)** (2004)
9. Graña, J., Barcala, F.M., Alonso, M.A.: Compilation Methods of Minimal Acyclic Automata for Large Dictionaries. Lecture Notes in Computer Scuence - Implementation and Application of Automata **2494** (2002) 135–148
10. Vo, B., Vo, K.P.: Using Column Dependency to Compress Tables. In: Proceedings of the 2004 IEEE Data Compression Conference, Los Alamitos, California, IEEE Computer Society Press (2004) 92–101
11. Daciuk, J.: Experiments with Automata Compression. In Yu, S., Paun, A., eds.: Proceedings of CIAA 2000 - Implementation and Application of Automata, London, Ontario, Canada, LNCS 2088, Springer (2000) 113–119
12. Mihov, S., Maurel, D.: Direct Construction of Minimal Acyclic Subsequential Transducers. In Yu, S., ed.: Implementation and Application of Automata. Volume 2088 of Lecture Notes in Computer Science. Springer (2001) 217–229
13. Skut, W.: Incremental Construction of Minimal Acyclic Sequential Transducers from Unsorted Lexical Data. In: Proceedings of COLING 2004, Geneva, Switzerland (2004)

German Compound Analysis with *wfsc*

Anne Schiller

Xerox Research Centre Europe,
6 chemin de Maupertuis,
38250 Meylan,
France
Anne.Schiller@xrce.xerox.com

Abstract. Compounding is a very productive process in German to form complex nouns and adjectives which represent about 7% of the words of a newspaper text. Unlike English, German compounds do not contain spaces or other word boundaries, and the automatic analysis is often ambiguous. A (non-weighted) finite-state morphological analyzer provides all potential segmentations for a compound without any filtering or prioritization of the results.

The paper presents an experiment in analyzing German compounds with the Xerox Weighted Finite-State Compiler (wfsc). The model is based on weights for compound segments and gives priority (a) to compounds with the minimal number of segments and (b) to compound segments with the highest frequency in a training list. The results with this rather simple model will show the advantage of using weighted finite-state transducers over simple FSTs.

1 Compound Construction

A very productive word formation process in German is compounding, which combines words to build more complex words, mainly nouns or adjectives. In a large newspaper corpus the Xerox German Morphological Analyzer [10] identified 5.5% of 9,3 million tokens and 43% of overall 420,000 types[1] as compounds. In other texts, such as technical manuals, the percentage of compound tokens may even increase (e.g. 12% in a short printer manual). This is comparable to the observations of Boroni et al. [1] who found in a 28 million newswire corpus that 7% of the tokens and 46% of the types were compounds.

Regarding the construction of compounds, any adjective or noun (including proper names) may, in principle, appear as head word[2], and any adjective, noun or verb may occur as the left-hand ("modifier") part of a compound.

- *Buchseite* (book page)
- *Großstadt* (big town)

---

[1] *Tokens* represent all words of the text, *types* count only different word forms.
[2] Verbal compounds (such as *spazierengehen*) exist, but are much less productive than nouns or adjectives. They are not taken into account in this experiment.

A. Yli-Jyrä, L. Karttunen, and J. Karhumäki (Eds.): FSMNLP 2005, LNAI 4002, pp. 239–246, 2006.
© Springer-Verlag Berlin Heidelberg 2006

- *grasgrün* (grass green)
- *Goethestück* (Goethe piece)

The Xerox finite-state tool [2] for German morphological analysis [10] implements this general principle without any semantic restrictions and with only a few morphosyntactic constraints concerning the so-called "linking" elements. The advantage of this very general approach is high and robust coverage. The inconvenience is potentially very ambiguous output due to "over-segmentation" of (long) words. A potential source of over-segmentation is the homonymy of compound parts with derivational affixes.

- derivational suffix *-ei* (ing) vs. noun *Ei* (egg), e.g.
  Spielerei (playing) – *Vogel#ei* (bird egg)
- prefix *ein-* (in-) vs. cardinal *ein* (one), e.g.
  Einwohner#zahl (inhabitant number) – *Ein#zimmer#wohnung* (one room apartment)

But other "accidental" homonymy may also lead to over-segmentation:

- *Verbraucher* (consumer) vs. *Verb#Raucher* (verb smoker)
- *Abteilungen* (departments) vs. *Abtei#Lungen* (abbey lungs)

While morphologically correct, most of these "over-segmentations" are semantically impossible—or at least very unlikely, i.e. they require a very special context to make sense. But there also exist some real ambiguities:

- *Hochzeit* (wedding) vs. *Hoch#Zeit* (high time)
- *Gründung* (foundation) vs. *grün#Dung* (green manure)

Another source for multiple analyses is the ambiguity of segments themselves, i.e. one surface form may be analyzed in different ways.

- noun *Alt* (alto) vs. adjective *alt* (old)
- prefix *auto-* (self) vs. noun *Auto* (car)
- masculine noun *Leiter* (leader) vs. feminine noun *Leiter* (ladder)

2 Finite-State Compound Analysis

A simple approach to modeling compound formation by a finite-state transducer can be described by a regular expression like TRUNC+ HEAD where TRUNC is a compound modifier (i.e. a left-hand side part), including a potential linking element (*"(e)s"* or *"en"*), and HEAD is the compound head word (i.e. its rightmost part).

Example 1. Compound Part Lexicon[3]:

---

[3] For the examples of regular expressions in this article we use the syntax of wfsc (Xerox Weighted Finite-State Compiler) [5].

```
((
V e r b r a u c h e r "+NmSg":0              # (consumer)
| V e r b r a u c h "+NmSg":0               # (consumption)
| V:v e r b r a u c h e:0 n:0 "+V":0        # (to consume)
| E:e r z "+NnSg":0                         # (ore)
| V e r b "+NnSg":0                         # (verb)
| r a u c h e:0 n:0 "+V":0                  # (to smoke)
| R:r a u c h "+NmSg":0                     # (smoke)
| R:r a u c h e r "+NmSg":0                 # (smoker)
)
"#":0 )*
(
A:a h l e 0:n "+NfPl":0                      # (awl)
| z a h l e n "+NnSg":0                      # (paying)
| Z:z a h l 0:e 0:n "+NfPl":0               # (numbers)
);
```

Assuming the sample definitions above and a set of rules to cope with upper/lower case restrictions for resulting nouns and adjectives, our compound analyzer would provide the following results for the input word *Verbraucherzahlen* (consumer numbers).

Example 2. Finite-State Compound Analysis

Verbraucher+NmSg#Zahl+NfPl	(consumer numbers)
Verbraucher+NmSg#zahlen+NnSg	(consumer paying)
Verbrauch+NmSg#Erz+NnSg#Ahle+NfPl	(consumption ore awls)
Verb+NnSg#Raucher+NmSg#Zahl+NfPl	(verb smoker numbers)
Verb+NnSg#Raucher+NmSg#zahlen+NnSg	...
Verb+NnSg#Rauch+NmSg#Erz+NnSg#Ahle+NfPl	
Verb+NnSg#rauchen+V#Erz+NnSg#Ahle+NfPl	

A human reader would probably only think of the first solution, while all others segmentations require a very special and artificial context to make sense.

The problem of over-segmentation may not affect applications such as part-of-speech tagging where only the category of the complex word is taken into account (which would be *noun* for all of the above decompositions. But a correct segmentation is crucial for applications like machine translation ([9], [6]) or information retrieval ([8]).

3   Weighted Finite-State Transducers

Weighted finite-state transducers (wFSTs) are like ordinary FSTs with input and output symbols on arcs, but they contain, in addition, a weight on every arc and every final state. These weights are combined during traversal of the automaton to compute a weight for each path [5]. To ensure that various operations on wFSTs are well defined, the weight set must correspond to the algebraic structure of a semiring:

semiring S = (K, $\oplus$, $\otimes$, $\bar{0}$, $\bar{1}$)
with

K = a set of weights
$\oplus$ = Collection operation
$\otimes$ = Extension operation
$\bar{0}$ = Identity element for collection
$\bar{1}$ = Identity element for extension

One example of a semiring is $(\Re^+, +, *, 0, 1)$, the *real semiring* (positive real weights with addition as the collection operator and multiplication as the extension operator. e.g. for modeling probability calculation, which will also be used for our experiment described in the sections below.

4   Adding Weights to the Lexicon

When looking at the results of the (unweighted) morphological analyzer we realized that the preferred reading for a human reader very often corresponds to the decomposition with the least number of segments. Section 4.1 describes how we can model this observation in a weighted finite-state analyzer that will output higher scores for analyses with lesser segments.

Furthermore we assume that we can use frequency information from a training corpus to obtain weights for segments with different lexical analyses in order to resolve ambiguities which remain after having chosen the "shortest" decomposition. This will be described in section 4.2.

4.1   Compound Segments with Equal Weights

The objective is to prioritize compounds with a minimal number of segments. Using the *real semiring* as shown above weights are multiplied along the path. If all segments have a weight less than 1, then a bigger number of segments leads to a lower overall weight.

With a segment weight of 0.5 our sample gives overall weights as follows:

Example 3. Finite-State Compound Analysis with Weights

```
Verbraucher+NmSg#zahlen+NnSg                    <0.25>
Verbraucher+NmSg#Zahl+NfPl                      <0.25>
Verbrauch+NmSg#Erz+NnSg#Ahle+NfPl              <0.125>
Verb+NnSg#Raucher+NmSg#zahlen+NnSg             <0.125>
Verb+NnSg#Raucher+NmSg#Zahl+NfPl               <0.125>
Verb+NnSg#Rauch+NmSg#Erz+NnSg#Ahle+NfPl       <0.0625>
Verb+NnSg#rauchen+V#Erz+NnSg#Ahle+NfPl        <0.0625>
```

4.2   Compound Segments with Weights from Training Corpus

When using weights for segments which are derived from compound analyses in a training list, we must provide a *default* weight for segments which do not occur in the training list. The overall goal is still to give preference to a minimal number of segments. Therefore the multiplication of 2 maximal weights should be less than the minimal (default) weight of a single segment.

With a default weight of 0.5 for unseen segments, the maximal weight for training segments should then be 0.7 in order to stay below 0.5 when multiplying the weights of 2 segments (as $0.7 * 0.7 = 0.49$). Therefore we choose the following formula for the weight of a segment which consists of a lexical form *lex* and a surface realization *srf*:

$$weight(lex : srf) = 0.5 + freq(lex : srf)/(freq(: srf) + 1)/5$$

where $freq(: srf)$ is the frequency of all segments with surface realization srf.

In regular expressions, weights are enclosed in angle brackets as shown in Example 4.

Example 4. Compound Part Lexicon with Weights

```
semiring  < realpos_sum_times > (
( V e r b r a u c h e r "+NmSg":0 <0.7>
| V e r b r a u c h "+NmSg":0 <0.65>
| V:v e r b r a u c h e:0 n:0 "+V":0 <0.55>
| E:e r z "+NnSg":0 <0.7>
| V e r b "+NnSg":0 <0.7>
| r a u c h e:0 n:0 "+V":0 <0.55>
| R:r a u c h "+NmSg":0 <0.65>
| R:r a u c h e r "+NmSg":0 <0.7>
)
"#":0 )*
(
A:a h l e 0:n "+NfPl":0 <0.7>
| z a h l e n "+NnSg":0 <0.55>
| Z:z a h l 0:e 0:n "+NfPl":0 <0.65>
);
```

Example 5. Finite-State Compound Analysis with Weights

```
Verbraucher+NmSg#Zahl+NfPl                    <0.455>
Verbraucher+NmSg#zahlen+NnSg                  <0.385>
Verbrauch+NmSg#Erz+NnSg#Ahle+NfPl            <0.3185>
Verb+NnSg#Raucher+NmSg#Zahl+NfPl             <0.3185>
Verb+NnSg#Raucher+NmSg#zahlen+NnSg           <0.2695>
Verb+NnSg#Rauch+NmSg#Erz+NnSg#Ahle+NfPl      <0.22295>
Verb+NnSg#rauchen+V#Erz+NnSg#Ahle+NfPl       <0.18865>
```

5 Training and Test Data

The experiment focuses on disambiguation of compound analysis. For training and testing we created manually disambiguated compound lists. We analyzed word lists built from large corpora and selected all words that were recognized as compounds, not taking into account hyphenated compounds (such as *US-Präsident* or *Olympia-Sieger*) which bypass the problem of segmentation.

- Corpus used for training:
  - **LNG:** 37,362 compounds (types) from various sources law, newspapers, manuals, ...)
  - **SPG:** 151,22 compounds from the weekly "Der Spiegel" (years 1994 and 1995)
- Corpus used for evaluation::
  - **NZZ:** 30,891 compounds from the daily "Neue Zürcher Zeitung" (year 1994)
  - **MED:** 26,196 compounds from medical texts (from European project "Muchmore")

The different texts are independent, but the extracted lists are not fully disjunctive, i.e. the test corpora share around 17% of the compounds with the training list SPG.

Corpus	compounds	nb. of chars			nb. of segments			ambiguity		
		min.	max.	avg.	min.	max.	avg.	1*	max.	avg.
LNG	37,362	6	46	22.9	2	6	2.5	39.0%	113	3.0
SPG	151,220	10	40	14.6	2	7	2.1	48.5%	55	2.1
NZZ	30,891	19	40	22.9	2	5	2.4	42.1%	120	2.8
MED	26,196	6	45	16.3	2	5	2.2	49.8%	80	2.0

(*) percentage of compounds with single analysis.

The longest compounds found in each compound list are

- **LNG:** Verkehrsinfrastrukturfinanzierungsgesellschaft
- **SPG:** Betäubungsmittelverschreibungsverordnung
- **NZZ:** Betäubungsmittelbeschaffungskriminalität
- **MED:** Normalgewebekomplikationswahrscheinlichkeiten

6   Tests and Results

The following process was applied for the evaluation:

- Take only "best scored" analysis results (i.e. all results for unweighted FSTs)
- Compare the FST result to the manually disambiguated lists:
  - *true positives* are the analyses which match the manual choice
  - *false positives* are all other results
  - Count a *false negative* if the manual choice is not among the results.
- The overall precision P is computed as
  $P = $ #(true positives) / #(true positives + false positives)
- The overall recall R for this experiment is
  $R = $ #(true positives) / #(true positives + false negatives)
- The F-score combines the two previous measures
  $F = (2*\text{precision}*\text{recall})/(\text{precision}+\text{recall})$

Test	NZZ			MED		
	P (%)	R (%)	F (%)	P (%)	R (%)	F (%)
baseline FST[4]	35.94	100.00	52.87	49.09	100.00	65.85
wFST with equal weights	66.24	99.91	79.67	63.28	99.90	77.48
wFST with weights from LNG	97.05	99.63	98.32	88.69	98.68	93.42
wFST with weights from SPG	97.73	99.06	98.39	95.90	98.32	97.09

7 Conclusion

Using weighted finite-state transducers for compound analysis with the suggested model provides different scores for different segmentations, and thus selecting results with best scores only filters out very unlikely readings. Most of the small number of remaining "real" ambiguities, however, may only be resolved with the full (semantic and syntactic) context of the compound, but a great majority of compounds were found to be unambiguous for a human reader even without context, and can also be disambiguated with a rather simple model of weights associated with compound parts.

We intend to conduct some additional experiments which include probabilities for segment pairs. This should improve the results for cases of high segment ambiguity (e.g. *Auto* (car) vs. *auto* (self)), but given the quite high precision with the simple model, we cannot expect a substantial increase of the overall precision.

Future work will show if similar results can be obtained for other compounding languages, such as Dutch, Swedish, Finnish, Hungarian, Greek, etc.

References

1. M. Baroni, J. Matiasek, and H. Trost. Predicting the Components of German Nominal Compounds. In *Proceedings of ECAI-2002*, pages 470–474, Amsterdam, 2002. IOS Press.
2. K. R. Beesley and L. Karttunen. *Finite State Morphology*. CSLI Studies in Computational Linguistics. CSLI Publications, 2003.
3. L. Karttunen. Applications of Finite-State Transducers in Natural Language Processing. In *Proceedings of CIAA-2000*. Springer Verlag, 2000.
4. A. Kempe. NLP Applications based on weighted multi tape automata. In *Proceedings of 11th Conference TALN*, Fes, Morocco, April 19–22 2004.
5. A. Kempe, C. Baeijs, T. Gaál, F. Guingne, and F. Nicart. WFSC - A new weighted finite state compiler. In *Proceedings of CIAA-03*, volume 2759 of *Lecture Notes in Computer Science*, pages 108–119, Santa Barbara, CA, USA, July 16–18 2003. Springer Verlag.
6. P. Koehn and K. Knight. Empirical Methods for Compound Splitting. In *Proceedings of ECAI-2003*, Budapest, Hungary, 2003.

---

[4] The 100% recall with the baseline FST results from the construction of the test and training data obtained by applying this FST on a word list and then disambiguated by hand.

7. M. Mohri, F. Pereira, and M. Riley. Weighted Automata in Text and Speech Processing. In *Proceedings ECAI-96, Workshop on Extended finite state models of language*, Budapest, Hungary, 1996.
8. C. Monz and M. de Rijk. Shallow Morphological Analysis in Monolingual Information Retrieval for Dutch, German and Italian. In C. Peters, editor, *Proceedings of CLEF 2001*, LNCS. Springer, 2002.
9. U. Rackow, I. Dagan, and U. Schwall. Automatic Translation of Noun Compounds. In *Proceedings of COLING-92*, Nantes, 1992.
10. A. Schiller. Xerox Finite-State Morphological Analyzer for German. on-line demo: http://www.xrce.xerox.com/competencies/content-analysis/demos/german, 2004.

Scaling an Irish FST Morphology Engine for Use on Unrestricted Text

Elaine Uí Dhonnchadha[1,2] and Josef Van Genabith[1]

[1]National Centre for Language Technology, School of Computing
Dublin City University, Dublin 9, Ireland
josef@computing.dcu.ie
[2]Centre for Language and Communication Studies
Trinity College Dublin, Ireland
uidhonne@tcd.ie

Abstract. This paper details the steps involved in scaling-up a lexicalised finite-state morphology transducer for use on unrestricted text. Our starting point was a base-line inflectional morphology engine [1], with 81% token coverage measured against a 15 million word corpus of Irish texts [2]. Manually scaling the FST lexicon component of a morphology transducer is time-consuming, expensive and rarely, if ever, complete. In order to scale up the engine we used a combination of strategies including semi-automatic population of the finite-state lexicon from machine-readable dictionary resources and from printed resources using optical character recognition, the addition of derivational morphology and the development of morphological guessers. This paper details the coverage increase contributed by each step. The full system achieves token coverage of 93% which is extended to 100% through the use of morphological guessers.

1 Introduction

The work in morphological analysis of Irish described here builds on an existing finite-state transducer implementation [1], using Xerox Finite-State Tools [3, 4]. This lexical transducer implemented all of the inflectional rules for Irish and contained a test lexicon of approximately 1,500 lemmas, including the lemmas associated with the 1,000 most frequently occurring word-forms in a corpus of approximately 15 million words [2]. Its token recognition rate was on average 81% on unrestricted text.

In order to improve recognition rates and obtain an analysis for all tokens in unrestricted text, semi-automatic population of the lexicon was carried out, derivational morphology rules were added and morphological guessers were implemented. The first two steps result in recognition rates of over 93% and when morphological guessers are included, an analysis is returned for 100% of tokens in unrestricted text [2].

A. Yli-Jyrä, L. Karttunen, and J. Karhumäki (Eds.): FSMNLP 2005, LNAI 4002, pp. 247–258, 2006.
© Springer-Verlag Berlin Heidelberg 2006

2   Semi-automatic Population of FST Lexicons

The finite-state transducer (FST) lexicon was increased by semi-automatically converting a machine-readable dictionary (MRD) [5] to Xerox lexc format. Lists of names and places in printed resources were scanned and incorporated into the lexicon, as newspaper and web texts in particular contain a high proportion of proper nouns. Some lists of personal names were found on the Internet [6]. After inclusion of these items, one or more analyses were returned for 93% of tokens in unrestricted text (up 12% from 81%).

2.1   Organisation of FST Lexicons

The lexicons in the Irish inflectional finite-state morphology engine [1], [7] are organised in a hierarchical manner whereby a stem is associated with a categorical class (called continuation classes in [3]) which in turn points to further continuation classes in order to produce the inflected surface forms and analyses associated with its particular inflectional paradigm. In order to add a new lexical item to the Irish FSM it is necessary to identify only its top-level continuation class. In the case of verbs and adjectives this is not particularly difficult, but nouns are far more challenging. Traditional Irish grammars [8] describe 5 paradigms (declensions) for nouns. However, within these paradigms there is considerable variation in the manner in which plurals can be formed (over 20 types of plural are encoded). Each of these 5 paradigms have been sub-divided ten times on average resulting in approximately 50 noun paradigms to choose from. Verbs and adjectives have 10 and 13 top-level continuation classes, respectively.

2.2   Automatic Population of FST Morphological Lexica from Machine Readable Dictionary Resources

Adding new words manually to the finite-state morphology (FSM) of an inflected language is a slow and labour intensive process. For example, in order to locate the correct lexical category (continuation class) for an Irish noun, it is necessary to know its gender, as well as details of case and number formation. It is therefore well worth making an effort to locate machine-readable and printed word-lists for the language. Preferably these lists should contain some grammatical information, which can be used to automate the process of FSM lexicon building. We were fortunate in obtaining permission to use a machine-readable version of a pocket Irish-English dictionary [5], with 15,000 Irish head-words. The following is an example of plain-text data from the dictionary:

```
cabhair1 kaur' f, gs -bhrach help, assistance
cabhair2 kaur' vt, pres -bhraíonn vn -bhradh emboss, chase
cabhán kaua:n m1, ~ abhann yellow water-lily
cabhlach kauləx m1 fleet; navy
cabhrach kaurəx a1 helpful
cabhraigh kauri: vi help, ~ liom help me
```

Table 1 shows that each entry provides up to four distinct types of information which can be used to automatically assign the headword to the appropriate FSM inflectional class.

Table 1. Sample of MRD Data

Headword	Phonetics	POS	Definition
cabhair1	kaur'	f	gs -bhrach help, assistance
cabhair2	kaur'	vt	pres -bhraíonn vn -bhradh emboss, chase
cabhán	kaua:n	m1	~ abhann yellow water-lily
cabhlach	kauləx	m1	fleet; navy
cabhrach	kaurəx	a1	helpful
cabhraigh	kauri:	vi	help, ~ liom help me

The table contains headwords which are either nouns, verbs or adjectives. The POS (part-of-speech) column provides the basic lexical classification for the headwords as well as gender in the case of nouns (f = feminine noun, m = masculine noun) and transitivity in the case of verbs (vt = transitive verb, vi = intransitive verb, vti = transitive and intransitive verb). Some nouns and adjectives contain a number indicating a declensional class (e.g. m1, a1).

Further valuable information can be found in the definition column. For instance, *gs -bhrach* indicates that the genitive singular of the noun *cabhair* 'help', is formed by syncopation, i.e. dropping of vowels in the final unstressed syllable, and addition of the suffix *-ach*. In the case of the verb *cabhair* 'help', *pres -bhraíonn vn –bhradh* states that the present tense is formed by syncopation of final syllable and addition of the suffix *-aíonn*, furthermore, the verbal noun (vn) derived from *cabhair* is formed by syncopation of the final syllable and addition of the *-adh* suffix.

This information, together with the structure of the headword in terms of number of constituent syllables and type of final syllable, can be used in the majority of cases to automatically determine which sub-category (continuation class) of verbs, nouns or adjectives a particular headword should be assigned to in the FSM lexicon. The phonetic description could also be used as a valuable aid to automatic assignment, although it was not necessary in this instance.

We implemented a Perl program to convert the machine-readable dictionary text to *lexc* format (Fig. 1). Each record is processed by first examining the POS field. In the case of verbs and adjectives, processing relies heavily on the structure of the headword, whereas processing for nouns, which have a far more complex (i.e. unpredictable) morphology, relies on the additional morphological information found in the definition field. For example, in Fig. 1, the headword *cabhair* 'help', points to continuation class **Nf5-2** which in turn points to other continuation classes that assign the appropriate morphological tags and inflectional triggers for this type of noun.

Despite the information available over a third of the 10,700 nouns could not be assigned a class with certainty due, in general, to a lack of information about plural formation in this MRD. In these cases the headword was assigned the

```
LEXICON Nouns
cabhair Nf5-2; ! Noun, feminine, class 5, sub-class 2
!!!!cabhán Nm1-1; ! Noun, masculine, class 1, sub-class 1
!!!!cabhlach Nm1-1; ! Noun, masculine, class 1, sub-class 1
LEXICON Verbs
cabhair V2-BR-sync; ! Verb, conj. 2, broad stem, syncopate
cabhraigh V2-BR; ! Verb, conjugation 2, broad stem
LEXICON Adjectives
cabhrach Adj1-3; ! Adjective, class 1, sub-class 3
```

Fig. 1. Sample of *lexc* compatible input derived from MRD

most likely subclass given the structure of the headword, and the output was prefixed with '!!!!' which served to highlight the fact that the item required manual checking. At the same time it also comments out the line causing the FST compiler *lexc* not to include it in the FSM. Overall, of the 15,000+ headwords in the MRD over 11,000 were automatically assigned to a FSM lexical class. On inspection of the remaining 4,000 headwords (mainly nouns), further patterns were detected and the conversion program was amended and re-run. Approximately 3,000 lemmas had to be assigned manually using a larger dictionary [9] (which we did not have in machine readable form).

2.3   Scanning and Optical Character Recognition (OCR)

When suitable data is not available in electronic format, scanning of printed material and the use of OCR software can be a viable alternative. This strategy was adopted in order to increase the number of proper nouns in the Irish FSM lexicons. Lists of towns and countries were scanned, as well as a book of Irish surnames [10], [11].

All scanned material was proof read and scanning accuracy proved to be high despite the fact that the OCR software was intended for Portuguese rather than Irish. Approximately 5% of names contained an OCR error. Due to the nature of the material it was possible to automatically correct almost all errors since the most common errors involved a number in place of a letter, (and no numbers were expected in the input), e.g. *0* (zero) instead of *O*, *1* (one) instead of *I*, *6* (six) instead of *ó* etc. Other common errors included *m* in place of *rn* and *oh* in place of *ch* but by searching for unusual letter combinations these were easily located, and automatically corrected.

In the sample of name data in Fig. 2 English surnames are followed by their Irish counterparts.

Abbott, *Abóid*

Acton, *Ó Gnímh*

Adair, *Ó Dáire*

Fig. 2. Sample of Scanned Data

As Irish texts, especially newspapers, are as likely to contain English names as Irish names, we created two lexicons, one containing Irish data and one English data

2.4 Internet

In a brief search, some personal names were located on the Internet and included [6]. The Internet is a resource which could be exploited (with relatively little effort) to increase the FSM lexicon, and this method merits further investigation.

2.5 Summary

Table 2 shows the total number of lexical items in the major part-of-speech categories after semi-automatic population had taken place. It also shows the number of surface (inflected) forms and morphological descriptions generated by inflectional rules from these headwords (lemma). Surface forms in general have more than one morphological analysis. The category 'Other' in Table 2 is the exception. This is made up of function words, most of which have one analysis per surface form, and in some cases, there are variant surface forms associated with the same morphological analysis.

As a result of the addition of these items, the token recognition rate on unrestricted text [2] rose from approximately 81% to 93% (see Table 3 for further details).

Table 2. FSM Lexicons including MRD, OCR

	Stems	Surface Forms	Morphological Descriptions
Verbs	1,630	105,000	305,100
Nouns: common (10,700) proper (4,200) proper (en) (7,200)	22,100	166,100	350,600
Adjectives	3,035	14,100	43,900
De-verbal Nouns/Adjs.	3,220	5,305	6,436
Other	555	640	630
Total	**30,540**	**291,145**	**706,666**

3 Derivational Morphology

Our base-line system [1] implements Irish inflectional morphology. Examination of the word-forms not recognized by the FSM showed that many contained a root that was already in the lexicons and that the addition of derivational morphology would improve recognition rates. Irish derivational morphology mainly involves prefixing of stems but there are also some derivational suffixes [8].

3.1   Derivational Suffixing

All nouns can accept a diminutive suffix -*ín*. If the final syllable of the noun is broad (i.e. ends in broad vowel *a, o, u, á, ó,* or *ú*) it must be slenderized by inserting a slender vowel i.e. *i* before attaching the slender suffix -*ín*. This is achieved by including a slenderisation trigger [1] in the surface form which when composed with the relevant replace-rule FST will result in slenderisation taking place.

Example 1.
a. *buachaill* 'boy', *buachaillín* 'little boy'
b. *rud* 'thing', *ruidín* 'little thing'

Similarly, all nouns and pronouns as well as verbs and prepositions which incorporate personal pronouns can accept an emphatic suffix. In this case, broad and slender forms of the suffix exist, therefore rather than changing the stem the appropriate suffix is chosen, e.g. in the case of the *sa/se* broad/slender pair, the *s* is added in the lexicon and either *a* or *e* is inserted by replace rule depending on the broad or slender nature of the previous syllable.

Example 2.
a. *mo theach* 'my house', *mo theachsa* '**my** house'
b. *mé* 'I', *mise* '**I**'
c. *déanaim é* 'I do it', *déanaimse é* '**I** do it'
d. *orm* 'on me', *ormsa* 'on **me**'

all verb stems and agentive nouns can accept one of a number of suffixes (and/or morphological processes) to create a (de)verbal noun. Likewise, a (de)verbal adjective is derived from each verb stem. For the 1,600+ verb stems (see Table 2) in the FSM, 20 new continuation classes were included to account for the various ways in which (de)verbal nouns are derived. For the same set of verb stems, 14 new continuation classes were included to accommodate the various ways in which (de)verbal adjectives are derived. The fact that verb stems were already assigned to verbal continuation classes based on number and type of syllables speeded up the task of assigning the appropriate continuation class for (de)verbal nouns and (de)verbal adjectives, since in all cases the stem structure is relevant.

3.2   Derivational Prefixing

Nouns, verbs and adjectives can all accept standard prefixes, which in general do not change the lexical class.

Example 3.
a. *déan* 'do/make', *athdhéan* 'redo/remake'
b. *maith* 'good', *sármhaith* 'excellent'
c. *féasta* 'feast', *an-fhéasta* 'great feast'

A regular relation containing over 250 common prefixes is defined. This is compiled and saved as a Prefix FST, which can be concatenated to the front of the noun FST. The boundary between the prefix and stem is marked by a boundary trigger in the pre-surface form which when composed with the relevant replace-rule FST will result in appropriate morphophonological processes taking place. In example 3 lenition takes place, i.e. when a prefix is joined to a stem, 'h' is inserted after the initial consonant of the stem, (i.e. *déan* -> *dhéan*, *maith* -> *mhaith*, *féasta* -> *fhéasta*). The verb and adjective FSTs are also prefixed in the same manner.

3.3 Compounding

New lexical items can also be created through compounding. In such cases, the new word inherits the lexical features of the right-most element. We re-use the finite-state lexicons to identify possible compounds for nouns, adjectives and verbs.

Example 4.
a. *domhain* 'deep' = adjective or *domhain* 'depth' = noun feminine
b. *comhrá* 'conversation' = noun masculine
c. *domhainchomhrá* 'deep conversation' = noun masculine

For example, in the case of nouns, we take all surface forms (without morpho-syntactic tags) recognised by the morphological analyser and concatenate this network to the front of the noun lexicon, marking the boundary with a compound boundary marker ^CB. This new FST of possible compounds is composed with the noun inflectional rules to produce all possible inflected forms, together with the morpho-syntactic tags associated with the noun.

As iterative compounding is unusual in Irish this method is sufficient for most cases, and any tokens with more than two elements will be handled by a more general noun guesser (see below).

3.4 Summary

The addition of derivational morphology increases recognition rates by less than 1.2%. De-verbal noun and adjective lexicons, which are important in terms of POS tagging and syntactical analysis, do not have much effect on recognition rates since these word-forms have in most cases the same form as an inflected verb or noun. In effect they provide an additional analysis to an already recognised word-form rather than providing a morphological analysis of a previously unrecognised word-form.

4 Morphological Guessers

A lexicon of approx 30K lemmas (Table 2) is still not very large, and since in addition a living language is constantly changing and acquiring new words, a method is needed for dealing with unrecognized words. We define a series of morphological guessers following [3] which make use of distinctive suffixes, syllable structure, initial capitals and foreign characters, to identify possible verbs, adjectives, nouns, proper nouns and foreign words. In addition to guessing the part-of-speech, we must also guess features such as gender, number and case (for nouns and adjectives), or tense, number and person (for verbs).

4.1   Verb Guesser

In Irish, verb inflectional suffixes are distinctive. Therefore if a token is not recognized by the main lexical transducer or one of the derivational transducers and it ends in one of these suffixes, we can confidently guess that it is a verb and has the features associated with that suffix. In (Fig. 3) a verb is defined in terms of a generic stem to which one of the defined suffixes is attached. 'VPresentSuf' shows some of the inflectional suffixes for present tense verbs (indicative mood) and their associated person and number feature tags.

```
define Stem [ Syl1 (Syl2) (Syl2) ];
define VPresentSuf [[%+Guess %+Verb %+PresInd .x. (e) a n n ] |
[%+Guess %+Verb %+PresInd %+1P %+Sg .x. (a) i m ] |
[%+Guess %+Verb %+PresInd %+1P %+Pl .x. (a) i m i d ] |
[%+Guess %+Verb %+PresInd %+Auto .x. t (e) a r ] ];
etc. etc. define Verb [ Stem [VPresentSuf | VPastSuf | VFutSuf |
VCondSuf | VImperSuf etc. ];
```

Fig. 3. Extract from Verb Guesser regular expression script

4.2   Noun Guessers

Nouns show far greater variability in their morphology than verbs. Two types of noun guessers have been implemented. The first one uses stem endings and suffixes that are usually (though not always) associated with a particular gender, number and case. The second type of guesser (Fig. 4) is a more general one. It guesses gender and number based on vowels in the last syllable in the word, and simply assigns nominative case.

In Fig. 4 we define a broad syllable 'BrSyl' and a slender syllable 'SlSyl' and use these to assign either feminine or masculine gender. We assume that singular nouns can have up to 3 syllables (e.g. *maireachtáil*, 'livlihood') and end in a consonant. We assume that plural nouns end in either *a* or *í* and we allow up to 5 syllables (e.g. *iompórtálacha* 'importations').

4.3   Lookup Strategy

The FSTs developed in this implementation are designed for use with the Xerox *lookup* tool [3]. This tool supports the specification of a lookup strategy whereby a sequence of finite-state transducers is tried until a morphological analysis is found. The lexical transducers are tried first followed by the guessers. The order

```
define BV [ a|o|u|á|ó|ú ] ; # Broad Vowels
define SV [ e|i|é|í ] ; # Slender Vowels
define BrSyl [ (C)(C)(C) (V)(V) BV (C) (C) (C) ];
define SlSyl [ (C)(C)(C) (V)(V) SV (C) (C) (C) ];
define NounsSg [(Syl) (Syl) SlSyl C ] "+Guess+Noun+Fem+Com+Sg:0"
| [ (Syl) (Syl) BrSyl C ] "+Guess+Noun+Masc+Com+Sg:0" ;
define FRoot [(Syl) (Syl) (Syl) SlSyl ];
define MRoot [(Syl) (Syl) (Syl) BrSyl ];
define NounsPl [FRoot [%+Guess %+Noun %+Fem %+Com %+Pl .x. [a|í]]]
| [MRoot [%+Guess %+Noun %+Masc %+Com %+Pl .x. [a|í]]] ;
```

Fig. 4. Extract from noun guesser regular expression script

in which the guesser transducers are applied is very important since the script terminates as soon as a match is found. In Irish, verbal endings are the most distinctive feature, followed by suffixed and prefixed word forms, verbal nouns and verbal adjectives. If none of these transducers is successful then the word is probably a noun. If the fairly unconstrained noun guesser were tried first, it would in almost all cases succeed even if the unknown word contained a distinctive verb ending. Therefore, the most specific transducer should be tried first (i.e. verb guesser) followed by the next most specific and so on ending with the most general transducer (i.e. foreign noun).

The *lookup* utility also enables 'virtual composition' whereby a transducer can be composed with another transducer on the fly where necessary. In the Irish FSM, all lexical items are defined in lowercase in the lexicons, except for proper nouns that are unlikely to be used without an initial uppercase character, e.g. *Dublin, London, Paris*. If the lexical transducer does not recognize a word, it may be because the word occurs at the start of a sentence and has been capitalized. A transducer, following [12], is defined which maps the initial letter of word forms (5a), or the second letter (5b) or third letter (5c), to a capital letter, or all letters to capitals (5d). These capitalizing transducers can be composed with the lexical transducer on the fly, and the resulting transducers are tried in the lookup script before going on to try the guesser transducers. The guessers can be composed with the capitalizers to gain maximum benefit.

Example 5.
a. *Uachtarán* 'President' – initial capital
b. *na hÉireann* 'of Ireland' – capital with initial mutation
c. *cúrsaí i bhFiontar* – 'courses in Fiontar' - capital with initial mutation
d. *TÁ* 'IS' - all capitals

5   Evaluation

A more fine-grained analysis of the effect of the additional FSTs on recognition rates is shown in Table 3. These results were obtained using a test corpus consisting of 3,000 sentences (76,000 tokens) randomly selected from a corpus of 30 million words of Irish text [13], including the original 15 million word corpus [2].

Table 3. Summary of Recognition Rates

	% of tokens recognised	% increase
FST LEXICONS		
Initial lexicons	**80.52**	
MRD Lexicons	90.74	10.22
OCR Lexicons	92.53	1.79
De-verbal Noun/Adj. Lexicons	93.10	0.57
Derivational Prefixes	93.69	0.59
Derivational Suffixes	**93.72**	0.03
FST GUESSERS		
Verb Guesser	93.99	0.27
De-verbal Noun/Adj Guesser	94.30	0.31
Noun Guesser 1	94.73	0.43
Noun Compound Guesser	95.55	0.82
Proper Noun Guesser	98.61	3.36
Noun Guesser 2, incl. abbreviations	98.88	0.27
Foreign Word Guesser	99.01	0.13
Other Guesser	100.0	0.99

Token analysis rates on the test corpus (i.e. 80.52% baseline and 93.10% using additional lexicons) are comparable to those obtained with [2], therefore we expect this test corpus to be representative to the overall corpus.

The first four entries in the table are composed as one lexical transducer, which provides morphological analyses for 93% of tokens encountered in unrestricted Irish texts. The remaining transducers are each tried in sequence. Table 3 shows that the single biggest increase in token recognition is due to the use of the machine-readable dictionary, followed by the proper noun guesser and the OCR scanned proper nouns.

Although the proper noun guesser makes a bigger impact on recognition rates, the analysis provided from the lexicons is more reliable in terms of morphologi-

Table 4. Analysis of Guessed Items (excl. compounds)

Guessed token	Overall %	Count	No. Correct	% Correct
Missing lexeme	55.0	1682	1485	88%
Misspelling	14.8	451	364	81%
Dialectal variant	11.7	356	202	57%
Foreign word	9.3	284	111	39%
Abbreviation	4.3	131	108	82%
Hyphenation error	2.8	85	33	39%
Neologism	2.1	64	57	89%
TOTAL	**100%**	**3053**	**2360**	**77%**

cal features (i.e. gender, number and case etc.). Therefore, further work should concentrate on improving the 93% recognition rate from the lexicons through further use of MRDs where possible and OCR where necessary.

We also evaluated the performance of the guessers by examining all of the lexical items in the test corpus which received a guessed analysis (i.e. lemma, part-of-speech and features). Compounds were excluded from this test as POS category and features of the head of a compound are inherited from a item found in the lexicon. The lexical items were classified according to the reasons why they were guessed and the results obtained are shown in Table 4. The results are encouraging in that 88% of guesses due to gaps in the lexicon (i.e. missing lexemes) received a correct analysis. Overall, taking into account other factors such as misspellings, foreign words, abbreviations etc. the average accuracy level was 77%.

6 Conclusion

In order to scale-up a finite-state morphology transducer for general use it is necessary to a) create as big a lexicon of stems as possible b) derive maximum use from these stems through the use of derivational morphology rules and c) to augment the lexicon with reliable guessers. We described two methods of semi-automatic population of the lexicon, namely population of FSM lexicons from machine-readable dictionaries and scanning of suitable printed material. Derivational morphology strategies for Irish were implemented, as well as a series of guessers and used with the Xerox *lookup* tool. As our evaluation results show, these are practical and effective ways of scaling up a FSM transducer for use on unrestricted text, with the use of MRDs being the single most effective method. Our approach maximises re-use of existing resources, an issue particularly pressing for minority languages where limited funding and lack of human resources are pressing issues. The methods reported in this paper resulted in an increased rate of morphological analysis from 81% to over 93% with the remaining tokens receiving a guesser-based analysis.

Acknowledgements

The authors wish to thank the anonymous reviewers for their valuable comments and suggestions which have improved the paper considerably.

References

1. Uí Dhonnchadha, E.: An analyser and generator for Irish inflectional morphology using finite state transducers. Master's thesis, School of Computing, Dublin City University, Dublin, Ireland (2002)
2. ITÉ: http://www.ite.ie/corpus/ (accessed Nov. 2005)
3. Beesley, K.R., Karttunen, L.: Finite State Morphology. CSLI Studies in Computational Linguistics. CSLI Publications (2003)

4. Karttunen, L., Beesley, K.R.: Two-level rule compiler. Technical report, Xerox PARC (1992)
5. An Roinn Oideachais, .: Foclóir Póca English-Irish/Irish-English Dictionary. An Gúm, Baile Átha Cliath (1986)
6. http://www.symbols.net/names/: Symbols (accessed Nov. 2005)
7. Uí Dhonnchadha, E., Nic Pháidín, C., Van Genabith, J.: Design, implementation and evaluation of an inflectional morphology finite-state transducer for Irish. MT - Machine Translation: Special Issue on Finite State Language Resources and Language Processing (in press)
8. Bráithre Críostaí, .: Graiméar Gaeilge na mBráithre Críostaí. An Gúm, Baile Átha Cliath (1999)
9. Ó Dónaill, N.: Foclóir Gaeilge Béarla. Oifig an tSoláthair, Baile Átha Cliath (1977)
10. Ó Droighneáin, M.: An Sloinnteoir Gaeilge agus an tAinmneoir. Coiscéim, Baile Átha Cliath (1991)
11. Ó Siochfhrada, N.: Foclóir Gaeilge/Béarla - Béarla/Gaeilge. An Comhlacht Oideachais, Baile Átha Cliath (1998)
12. Grefenstette, G., Schiller, A., Ait-Mokhtar, S.: Recognizing lexical patterns in text. In van Eynde, F., Gibbon, D., eds.: Lexicon Development for Speech and Language Processing. Kluwer Academic Publishers, Dordrecht (2000)
13. Kilgarriff, A., Rundell, M., Uí Dhonnchadha, E.: Efficient corpus creation for lexicography. Language Resources and Evaluation Journal (forthcoming)

Improving Inter-level Communication in Cascaded Finite-State Partial Parsers

Sebastian van Delden[1] and Fernando Gomez[2]

[1] Division of Mathematics and Computer Science
University of South Carolina Upstate
800 University Way, Spartanburg SC 29303, USA
svandelden@uscupstate.edu
[2] Department of Computer Science
University of Central Florida
Orlando FL 32816, USA
gomez@cs.ucf.edu

Abstract. An improved inter-level communication strategy that enhances the capabilities of cascaded finite-state partial parsing systems is presented. Cascaded automata are allowed to make forward calls to other automata in the cascade as well as backward references to previously identified groupings. The approach is more powerful than a design in which the output of the current level is simply passed to the next level in the cascade. The approach is evaluated on randomly extracted sentences from the Encarta encyclopedia. A discussion of related research is also presented.

1 Introduction

Cascaded finite-state partial parsing is the process of incrementally identifying syntactic relations in a natural language sentence with layers of regular expressions or their finite-state representations[1]. The output of $layer_i$ is the input to $layer_{i+1}$. An automaton on an arbitrary $level_n$ can use the information provided by automata on the preceding $levels_{1..n-1}$. We refer to this type of inter-level communication that is common to most cascaded partial parsing systems as *backward referencing*. As an initial step, part-of-speech tags are usually assigned to each token in the sentence by a part-of-speech tagger [3]. In this case, the automata also rely on the part-of-speech information provided by the tagger to group syntactic relations when creating the partial tree structure.

An easy-first approach [1] to cascaded finite-state partial parsing is one in which the first layers of automata identify smaller syntactic relations, like noun and verb phrases. These smaller relations are combined by automata later in the cascade to form larger syntactic relations, like prepositional phrases and relative and subordinate clauses. A larger-first approach [9] is opposite to the easy-first

---

[1] This work has been partially funded by the University of South Carolina Research and Productivity Scholarship fund.

A. Yli-Jyrä, L. Karttunen, and J. Karhumäki (Eds.): FSMNLP 2005, LNAI 4002, pp. 259–270, 2006.
© Springer-Verlag Berlin Heidelberg 2006

approach, identifying larger syntactic relations first and then the smaller relations within them. Both approaches are robust, producing a partial output even if the cascade fails to recognize every syntactic relation in the input sentence.

An easy-first approach is faster than a larger-first one because the smaller syntactic relations are simply grouped together to form larger ones. So the speed is dependant on the size of the input sentence and the number of layers of automata. In a larger-first approach, the larger relations that are identified earlier in the cascade must be re-examined to recognize the syntactic relations within them. Its speed is, therefore, dependant of the size of the input sentence, the number of layers of automata, and the number of groupings that are created during processing. A larger-first approach, however, is more powerful than an easy-first approach because it considers the larger context first and so is capable of: fully disambiguating clausal coordinate conjunctions and partially disambiguating phrasal coordinate conjunctions; disambiguating certain types of appositions from lists of noun phrases; and disambiguating prepositional phrases from subordinate clauses. An easy-first approach is not suited for accomplishing these tasks.

However, a common disadvantage to both approaches is their inability to recognize both instances of syntactic relations that can dominate each other. For example, a relative clause can dominate a list of noun phrases, but a list of noun phrases can also dominate a relative clause. For example: *[LIST Bill Turner, Ted Sanderson [REL who is our newest employee], and Susan Reilly] will all be at the meeting this afternoon.* versus *The new employee [REL who [LIST Bill, Ted, and Susan] hired] will be at the meeting this afternoon.* In one case, the relative clause is syntactically larger and in the other case the list of noun phrases is syntactically larger. Cascaded partial parsers cannot correctly identify both instances due to the one-way communication between the layers of automata. For example, if the automaton that recognizes a list of noun phrases is on a layer that precedes the automaton that recognizes a relative clause, then the cascade can recognize a relative clause that dominates a list of noun phrases, but not vice versa. Besides relative clauses and lists of noun phrases, such cross-dominating clauses are common in written texts containing commas:

- Comma Enclosed Prepositional Phrases versus Relative Clauses: *[PP After the meeting [REL which lasted three hours],] Bush finally made a decision. Bush finally made a decision [REL which [PP, despite strong criticism,] seemed the best choice at the time].*
- Comma Enclosed Appositions and Relative Clauses: *Mount Scenery on Saba [APOS , an island in the Caribbean [REL that is known for its scuba diving,]] is the tallest peak in the Dutch Kingdom. Saba is an island in the Caribbean [REL that Christopher Columbus [APOS , one of the greatest mariners in history,] spotted on his second voyage in 1493].*
- Infinitive Clauses and Comma Enclosed Appositions: *Jeffrey quickly agreed [INF to give Celeste [APOS , his beloved daughter,] more spending money]. Celeste bought "Harry Potter and the Prisoner of Azkaban" [APOS , a wonderful book [INF to read]].*

- Subordinate Clauses and Comma-Enclosed Relative Clauses: *The Prada purse [REL , which Elizabeth just bought [SUB because she received a large bonus,]] is now sold-out in every store. Elizabeth went shopping [SUB because Macys [REL , which only sells high quality clothing,] was having an incredible sale].*

- Comma Enclosed Subordinate Clauses and Relative Clauses: *The library refused to order the book [REL that the professor [SUB, because he was out of town for the last two weeks,] forgot to request in time]. The library refused to order the book [SUB , because the professor [REL who happened to be out of town for the last two weeks] didn't notify them soon enough].*

- Complement Clauses and Comma Enclosed Prepositional Phrases: *[PP Despite the excellent news [COMP that tomorrow's weather would be beautiful,]] we are still not going to hike. The news [COMP that tomorrow weather [PP, by late afternoon,] would be beautiful] convinced us that we should go hiking.*

This paper shows how a cascaded finite-state partial parser can be improved to overcome such problems by adding a new inter-level communication capability - a forward call. The next section describes the new inter-level communication in detail. Section 3 explains the partial parsing algorithm with this new communication mechanism. Section 4 presents some results of the approach when tested on randomly chosen sentences from the Encarta encyclopedia. Section 5 concludes the paper with a discussion of related research.

2   The Enhanced Inter-level Communication

At first thought one might suggest that the current cascaded framework does have this capability by simply adding separate automata on different levels which recognize the two versions of the cross-dominating clauses. For example, an automaton on a preceding level that recognizes relative clauses which do not contain a list of noun phrases (for example, called automaton REL-1), followed by a list of noun phrases automaton (LST-NPs), followed finally by another relative clause automaton (REL-2) which does consume an internal list of noun phrases. It may appear that this cascade would correctly identify both cases of the cross-dominating clauses. For example, ideally the clauses in the following sentence would be identified as follows:

We bought office supplies which include pencils, three-ring binders that can hold 500 sheets, and dry-erase markers.
We bought office supplies which include pencils, three-ring binders [REL-1 that can hold 500 sheets], and dry-erase markers.
We bought office supplies which include [LST-NPs pencils, three-ring binders [REL-1 that can hold 500 sheets], and dry-erase markers].
We need office supplies [REL-2 which include [LST-NPs pencils, three-ring binders [REL-1 that can hold 500 sheets], and dry-erase markers]].

H owever, this grouping will not occur with this setup because the REL-1 automaton will prevent the LST-NPs automaton from identifying the list of noun phrases, and subsequently REL-2 will also not be able to accept:

We bought office supplies which include pencils, three-ring binders that can hold 500 sheets, and dry-erase markers.
We bought office supplies [REL-1 which include pencils], three-ring binders [REL-1 that can hold 500 sheets], and dry-erase markers.

S ince *pencils* would be grouped with REL-1, the syntactic pattern *NP, NP, conjunction NP* can no longer be recognized as a list of noun phrases. An intuitive solution is to position the LST-NPs automaton before the REL-1 automaton and add a capability that allows the LST-NPs automaton to make a call to the REL-1 automaton to consume any internal relative clauses that may be present in the list. We refer to this new capability as a *forward call.* So for the preceding example, the LST-NPs automaton will make a forward call to the REL-1 automaton, making a correct grouping of the list of noun phrases:

We bought office supplies which include pencils, three-ring binders that can hold 500 sheets, and dry-erase markers.
We bought office supplies which include [LST-NPs pencils, three-ring binders [REL-1 that can hold 500 sheets], and dry-erase markers].

F urthermore, if we allow the REL-1 automaton to refer to the previous grouping (a backward reference) made by the LST-NPs automaton, then there is no need for a second REL-2 automaton, because REL-1 will group the list of noun phrases when it is processed later in the cascade: *We bought office supplies [REL-1 which include [LST-NPs pencils, three-ring binders [REL-1 that can hold 500 sheets], and dry-erase markers]].*

A forward call to another automaton is similar to how a Recursive Transition Network, or RTN ([12, 11]), has the ability to call another RTN. For example, a *sentence RTN* can call a *noun phrase RTN* to recognize a noun phrase in the sentence. However, there are several differences between RTNs and this work. The first being robustness. There is no single breaking point in this approach since it is a cascade of several automata. For example, if the relative clause automaton fails to recognize a relative clause, elements inside and surrounding that syntactic relation will still be identified and the output will still contain a partial tree structure. A second difference is that there is no need for either direct/indirect recursion in the automata of the cascade. Recursion is built into the RTNs so that each possible parse tree can be recovered. For example, a prepositional phrase RTN can call a noun phrase RTN which in turn can call the same prepositional phrase RTN. This (indirect) recursion is avoided since forward calls and backwards references will allow one level of recursion to be indirectly captured (see example below). A third difference is that only one possible (partial) parse is always created and attachment decisions are avoided wherever possible.

One level of recursion is indirectly captured by this approach. Consider the sentence: *Peter wants to go to the beach, the mall by Mary's house, and the restaurant later tonight.* Notice the prepositional phrase *by Mary's house* is inside a list of noun phrases which is inside another prepositional phrase. In order to recognize these groupings, it would appear that a prepositional phrase automaton would call a list of noun phrases automaton which in turn would have to call the prepositional phrase automaton again - requiring a recursive machine. However, in this approach, the prepositional phrase automaton cannot make a forward call to the list of noun phrases automaton because it occurs earlier in the cascade. Forward calls can only be made to automata later in the cascade. This prevents indirect recursion. But since the prepositional phrase automaton can make a backward reference to the list of noun phrases automaton (which may have already made a forward call to the prepositional phrase automaton earlier), one level of recursion can be captured.

If *larger* syntactic relations are identified first in a cascade of automata with forward calls, the list of noun phrases will have already been identified before the prepositional phrase automaton is processed on the sentence level. The list of noun phrases automaton will have made a forward call to the prepositional phrase automaton (as well as the noun phrase automaton) so that the following grouping will be made at that point: *Peter wants to go to [LST-NP [NP the beach] , [NP the mall] [PP by [NP Mary's house]], and [NP the club]] later tonight.* Later, when the prepositional phrase automaton is reached in the cascade, a backward reference would be made to the LST-NP grouping (made by the list of noun phrases automaton) so that the prepositional phrase can be recognized: *Peter wants to go [PP to [LST-NP [NP the beach] , [NP the mall] [PP by [NP Mary's house]], and [NP the club]]] later tonight.* The prepositional phrase (which contains a prepositional phrase within a list of noun phrases) has been recognized without the need for a recursive device.

To summarize: This approach to partial parsing is a larger-first cascade of finite-state automaton with improved inter-level communication capabilities that allow forward calls to automata later in the cascade.

3   The Algorithm

The partial parsing algorithm for a larger-first cascade of automata with forward call capabilities is shown below.

When an automaton is tried in the sentence at position m (line 3), the automaton attempts to consume tokens starting from its start state at position m in the sentence. The automaton simply consumes tokens that have been part-of-speech tagged or groupings that have already been made by previous automata (backward references). These tokens/groupings are simply grouped if the automaton eventually enters an accept state - similar to an ordinary easy- or larger-first cascade. However, allowing the automaton to consume tokens by making a forward call complicates the algorithm slightly. If a forward call is made to a new automaton on line 6, the algorithm would be recursively repeated with this new automaton at line 3. The extra conditions on lines 9 and 15 must be added to check if the algorithm is currently processing an automaton that has been forward called. To better illustrate how forward calls are made by this algorithm consider the partial cascade of simplified automata that were extracted from our system and are shown in Fig. 1. The complexity of these automata have been reduced considerably to illustrate how the algorithm works.

```
1 for each automaton i in cascade 1..n
2   for each position m in the sentence
3     try automaton i at position m
4       if automaton i makes a forward call to automaton j
5           in cascade i+1..n at position m+k
6       then recursively repeat this algorithm starting at line 3
7               with automaton j and starting position m+k.
8       if automaton i accepts at m + z
9       then if automaton i is a forward call
10          then group (LABEL i tokens m+k..m+z)
11                  return to calling automaton at position m+z
12          otherwise group (LABEL i tokens m..m+z)
13                  continue to position m+z+1
14      if automaton i halts
15      then if automaton i is a forward call
16          then return to calling automaton at position m+k
17          otherwise remove any groupings made by
18                  forward calls and continue to position m+1
```

The automata would be applied in the order they are listed - LST-NP first, REL second, PP third and NP last. Square brackets [ ] around an arc label indicate a forward call to an automaton located further down in the cascade. For example, arc DD in LST-NP makes forward calls to the NP, PP, and REL automata. If there are several forward calls on a single arc, then these forward calls should also be made in a larger-first order. For example, the [REL] automaton would be called before the [PP] and [NP] automata. Greater than and less than symbols <...> around an arc label indicate a grouping that has already been made by a previous automaton. An arc label starting with T: refers to a part-of-speech tag that was initially assigned. The Default label means that the associated arc is always taken if no other arc is possible. No tokens are consumed during a Default transition.

Now consider the following sentence that has been tokenized and part-of-speech tagged:

J ohn/NNP bought/VBD a/DT television/NN that/WDT includes/VBZ a/DT remote/NN controller/NN ,/, a/DT DvD/NNP connection/NN which/WDT is/VBP incompatible/JJ with/IN Susan/NNP 's/POS DvD/NNP player/NN ,/, and/CC HDTV/NNP capabilities/NNS ./.

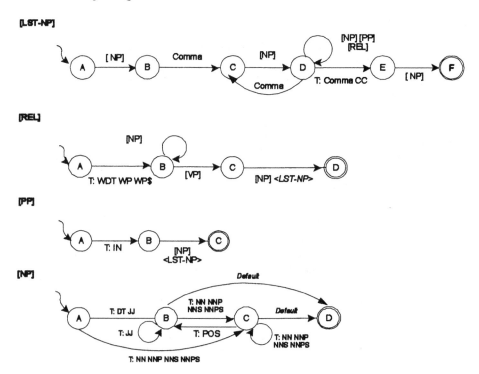

Fig. 1. A cascade of four simplified automata that were extracted from a handcrafted system of fifty three cascaded automata

T he LST-NP automaton is first tried at positions one through six (*John bought a television that includes*), each attempt resulting in a halting state. So processing continues and LST-NP is tried at position seven. LST-NP first makes a forward call to the noun phrases automaton (NP) on arc AB_{LST-NP} which consumes *a remote controller* with the path $AB_{NP}\ BC_{NP}\ CC_{NP}\ CD_{NP}$ and returns an NP grouping to the LST-NP automaton. Note that if LST-NP accepts, *a remote controller* will be grouped as an NP which will then also be grouped as part of the LST-NP. LST-NP then consumes the comma with arc BC_{LST-NP} and calls NP once again which consumes *a DvD connection* with the same path as before. LST-NP now makes a call to the relative clause automaton (REL). REL consumes *which* with arc AB_{REL} and accepts after making forward calls to the verb phrase (VP - not shown here) and noun phrase (NP) automata on arcs BC_{REL} and CD_{REL}, respectively. Note that the NP automaton has been generalized to recognize simple adjective phrases with the path AB_{NP} BD_{NP}. When REL accepts in state D_{REL}, it returns to state D_{LST-NP}. If LST-NP accepts, the following grouping would also be made inside of it: *(REL which (VP is) (NP incompatible))*. In an attempt to avoid explicit attachment decisions, no post verbal prepositional phrases are included in the relative clause. LST-NP now calls the prepositional phrase automaton (PP) which consumes *with* on arc AB_{PP} and makes a forward call to NP which consumes *Susan's*

DvD player with path AC_{NP} CB_{NP} BC_{NP} CC_{NP} CD_{NP}. Finally, LST-NP consumes the comma-conjunction bigram, and then calls NP which consumes the final noun phase *HDTV capabilities*. LST-NP now accepts in state F_{LST-NP} and groups everything it has consumed as a LST-NP. The sentence after LST-NP accepts becomes:

J ohn/NNP bought/VBD a/DT television/NN that/WDT includes/VBZ (LST-NP (NP a/DT remote/NN controller/NN) ,/, (NP a/DT DvD/NNP connection/NN) (REL which/WDT (VP is/VBP) (NP incompatible/JJ)) (PP with/IN (NP Susan/NNP 's/POS DvD/NNP player/NN)) ,/, and/CC (NP HDTV/NNP capabilities/NNS)) ./.

R EL is the next automaton in the cascade to be processed. REL comes into a halting state when it is tried at the first four positions in the sentence (*John bought a television*). When REL reaches the fifth position, it consumes *that* and calls the VP automaton which groups *includes*. Then a backward reference is made to LST-NP and the LST-NP grouping that was previously made is consumed. REL therefore adds the following grouping:

J ohn/NNP bought/VBD a/DT television/NN (REL that/WDT (VP includes/VBZ) (LST-NP (NP a/DT remote/NN controller/NN) ,/, (NP a/DT DvD/NNP connection/NN) (REL which/WDT (VP is/VBP) (NP incompatible/JJ)) (PP with/IN (NP Susan/NNP 's/POS DvD/NNP player/NN)) ,/, and/CC (NP HDTV/NNP capabilities/NNS)))./.

F inally, the remaining noun and verb phrases are identified by NP and VP in the final stages of the cascade, resulting in the final partial parse:

(NP John/NNP) (VP bought/VBD) (NP a/DT television/NN) (REL that/WDT (VP includes/VBZ) (LST-NP (NP a/DT remote/NN controller/NN) ,/, (NP a/DT DvD/NNP connection/NN) (REL which/WDT (VP is/VBP) (NP incompatible/JJ)) (PP with/IN (NP Susan/NNP 's/POS DvD/NNP player/NN))) ,/, and/CC (NP HDTV/NNP capabilities/NNS))./.

4   Results

The automata in our system were handcrafted while analyzing several sources such as the Penn Treebank III [6], the WorldBook and Britannica encyclopedias, and articles from the New York Times. A total of fifty three automata were created. One hundred new sentences were randomly taken from the 2001 Encarta encyclopedia for testing. This encyclopedia was chosen as a test bed because it is a well-written text containing fairly complex sentences. The sentences were first tagged with Brill's tagger [3]. However, if a sentence contained incorrect part-of-speech tags, they were corrected during the evaluation and the sentence was re-evaluated, to see how well the system performs on correct part-of-speech tags. On average, each sentence contained 22 words. Results were evaluated using precision and recall, and are shown in Table 1. There were ten other syntactic relations that the system identifies that did not appear in the test sentences and so are omitted here.

Table 1. Results of the Evaluation of the Encyclopedia Encarta

Syntactic Relation	Occur	Pre	Recall
Noun Phrase (NP)	358	98%	98%
Prep. Phrase	264	99%	99%
Verb Phrase	159	100%	100%
Coordinated NP (CNP)	38	100%	100%
Adverb Phrase	25	92%	88%
Relative Clause (RC)	22	100%	100%
Comma Enclosed RC	17	100%	100%
Apposition	15	92%	80%
Infinitive Clause (INF)	15	100%	100%
Lists of NPs INFs or Verb Clauses	12	85%	92%
Adjective Phrase	12	83%	83%
Coord Verb Clause	11	100%	100%
Two Coor. Verb Clauses	10	100%	100%
Comma Enclosed PP	8	89%	100%
Subordinate Clause	7	100%	86%
Phrasal Preposition	6	100%	100%
ING Clause	5	100%	100%
Comma Enclosed SC	4	100%	100%
Independent Clause	4	100%	100%
Comma Enclosed CNP	3	100%	100%
Comma Enclosed VC	3	100%	100%
Comma Enclosed Reduced SC	3	100%	67%
Time NP	2	100%	100%
Phrasal Subordinate Conjunct.	1	100%	100%
Transitional Phrase	1	100%	100%
Indirect Speech	1	0%	0%
Coordinated PP	1	100%	100%

Even though only one hundred sentences were randomly chosen, the power of this larger-first cascade with forward-call capabilities was observed several times. Consider the following three sentences taken from the test set:

(NP Other/JJ successful/JJ writers/NNS) (PP in/IN (NP this/DT school/ NN)) ,/, (**CO-REL1 including/VBG (LST-NP1 (NP Catherine/NNP Aird/NNP) ,/, (NP Reginald/NNP Hill/NNP) ,/, (NP Patricia/NNP Moyes/NNP) ,/, and/CC (NP June/NNP Thomson/NNP)))** ,/, (VP have/VBP) (PP at/IN (NP the/DT center/NN)) (PP of/IN (NP their/PRP$ works/NNS)) (NP an/DT imperfect/JJ) (PP though/IN

(NP sensitive/JJ sleuth/NN)) (**REL2 whose/WP$ (NP life/NN)** **(CC-NP and/CC (NP attitudes/NNS)) (VP are/VBP))** (PP of/IN (ADV almost/RB) (NP equal/JJ importance/NN)) (PP to/TO (NP the/DT mystery/NN)) ./.

(NP Other/JJ useful/JJ medical/JJ substances/NNS) (**REL1 now/RB** **manufactured/VBN**) (PP with/IN (NP the/DT aid/NN)) (PP of/IN (NP recombinant/JJ plasmids/NNS)) (VP include/VBP) (**LST-NP1 (NP** **human/JJ growth/NN hormone/NN**) ,/, (NP an/DT immune/JJ system/NN protein/NN) (**REL1 known/VBN**) (PP as/IN (NP interferon/NN)) ,/, (NP blood-clotting/JJ proteins/NNS) ,/, and/CC (NP proteins/NNS)) (**REL2 that/WDT (VP are/VBP** used/VBN)) (ING in/IN making/VBG (NP vaccines/NNS)) ./.

(**CO-PP (PP In/IN (NP large/JJ paintings/NNS)) (REL1 of-** ten/RB encrusted/VBN) (PP with/IN (**LST-NP1 (NP straw/NN** ,/, (NP dirt/NN) ,/, or/CC (NP scraps/NNS))) (PP of/IN (NP lead/NN))) ,/, (NP Kiefer/NNP) (VP depicted/VBD) (ING devastated/VBN (NP landscapes/NNS)) (CC-NP and/CC (NP colossal/JJ ,/, bombed-out/JJ interiors/NNS)) ./.

5   Related Research

More recently the focus in the research community has shifted to learning a partial parser from a corpus. The paragraphs below explain some of the methods that have been introduced. Automatically acquiring the rules of a partial parser have the benefit that minimal linguistic knowledge would be needed to construct the partial parser. However, unlike part-of-speech tagging paradigms, our research suggests that rules (or automata) that have been acquired from one or several sources (learned or hand-crafted) will not incur a dramatic decline in performance when applied to a new, unseen corpus. The primary benefit of training a part-of-speech tagger on a particular corpus is so that the likelihood of the part-of-speech tags for the words in the corpus can be compiled. If the tagger is applied to a different corpus without re-training, there is usually a noticeable different in performance primarily because the likelihood of the part-of-speech categories of words in the new corpus differ. Therefore, training the tagger on the new corpus will result in better performance on that new corpus. However, our handcrafted partial parsing automata did not experience a noticeable decline in performance when tested on new, unseen corpora, suggesting that re-training or re-learning a partial parser on a new corpus will not see the benefits that part-of-speech tagging learning approaches have had.

A study by [5] shows that learning a shallow parser has several advantages over learning a full parser, in particular: each layer of a shallow parser can be learned separately. The base phrases from a learned full parser were extracted and compared to that of a learned shallow parser. The results indicated that the learned partial parser had a higher accuracy in identifying the extracted phrases.

[7] presents a SNoW based learning approach to shallow parsing. The SNoW (Sparse Network of Winnows) learning architecture is a sparse network of linear functions over a pre-defined or incrementally learned feature space. Using Inside/Outside predictors are compared against using Open/Close predictors for determining noun phrases and subject-verb combinations. Inside/Outside predictors refer to using O to indicate the current word is outside the pattern; I to indicate the current word is inside the pattern; and B to indicate the current word marks the beginning of a pattern which directly follows another pattern. Open/Closed predictors refer to placing brackets [...] around the pattern. [7] found that both methods perform about the same for identifying noun phrases, but Open/Closed outperforms Inside/Outside for subject-verb patterns.

Several learning approaches to memory-based shallow parsing have also recently been developed [10, 8, 2, 4]. [2] use a novel learning method for recognizing local sequential patterns. Positive and negative evidence from a training corpus is used to recognize a sequence. For example, is the following sequence of part-of-speech tags a noun phrase: DT ADJ ADJ NN NNP? This long pattern may not be in the corpus, however, smaller noun phrases that cover sub-sections of this pattern may be present, like the prefix DT ADJ ADJ NN and suffix ADJ NN NNP. When combined, these sub-sections offer positive evidence that the sequence is a noun phrase. Negative evidence is generated from subparts in the raw data that do not have the right tag sequence.

[10] explore memory-based shallow parsing on the basis of words alone. Part-of-speech tags are used to overcome data sparseness, since a sequence of words is represented as a more general sequence of tags. However, with the abundance of training material currently available, [10] suggests that this material be used directly, avoiding an explicit part-of-tagging step. Their results show that attenuated words (descriptive tags that are given to low-frequency or unknown words to prevent data sparseness) along with gold-standard part-of-speech tags achieves better results than words, or part-of-speech tags alone.

References

1. S. Abney. Partial parsing via finite-state cascades. In *Proceedings of the ESSLLI'96 Robust Parsing Workshop*, 1996.
2. S. Argamon-Engelson, I. Dagan, and Y. Krymolowski. A memory-based approach to learning shallow natural language patterns. *Experimental and Theoretical AI*, 11:369–390, 1999.
3. E. Brill. Transformation-based error-driven learning and natural language processing: A case study in part of speech tagging. *Computational Linguistics*, 21(4): 543–565, 1995.
4. W. Daelemans, S. Buchholz, and J. Veenstra. Memory-based shallow parsing. In *Proceedings of the 3rd Conference on Natural Language Learning*, 1999.
5. X. Li and D. Roth. Exploring evidence for shallow parsing. In *Proceedings of the 5th Conference on Natural Language Learning*, pages 38–44, 2001.
6. M. Marcus, B. Santorini, and M. Marcinkiewicz. Building a large annotated corpus of english: the Penn Treebank. *Computational Linguistics*, 19(2):313–330, 1993.

7. M. Munoz, V. Punyakanok, D. Roth, and D. Zimak. A learning approach to shallow parsing. In *Proceedings of the Joint SIGDAT Conference on Empirical Methods in Natural Language Processing and Very Large Corpora*, pages 168–178, 1999.

8. E. T. K. Sang. Memory-based shallow parsing. *Machine Learning Research*, 2: 559–594, 2002.

9. S. van Delden and F. Gomez. A larger-first approach to partial parsing. In *Proceedings of the 2003 International Conference on Recent Advances in Natural Language Processing*, pages 124–131, 2003.

10. A. van den Bosch and S. Buchholz. Shallow parsing on the basis of words alone: A case study. In *Proceedings of the 40th Annual Meeting of the Association of Computation Linguistics*, pages 433–440, 2002.

11. T. Winograd. *Language as a cognitive process: Volume 1, Syntax.* Addison-Wesley Publishing Company, 1983.

12. W. Woods. Transition network grammars for natural language analysis. *Communications of the ACM*, 13:591–602, 1970.

Pivotal Synchronization Languages: A Framework for Alignments

Anssi Yli-Jyrä[1] and Jyrki Niemi[2]

[1] CSC - Scientific Computing Ltd.,
Finland
[2] Department of General Linguistics,
University of Helsinki, Finland
{aylijyra, janiemi}@ling.helsinki.fi

Abstract. We propose *pivotal synchronization languages* (PSLs) that represent alignments of parallel processes. PSLs are closely related to *synchronization languages* [10], but the strings in PSLs are partitioned into sequences of *pivots*. In the partitioned representation, each pivot gathers and aligns simultaneous process boundaries (starts and terminations). The paper demonstrates that PSLs (and new join operators) provide a unified framework for implementing some independent formalisms. In particular, we show that at least two existing formalisms, *generalized synchronization expressions* [10] and *interleave-disjunction-lock expressions* [8] have PSL-based counterparts. Furthermore, we sketch tentatively a new formalism that adapts the ideas of the operator of *generalized restriction* [11] to PSLs. All this suggests that the union of these formalisms might be implementable.

1 Introduction

In its simplest form, a *parallel execution* consists of two tiers whose elements are in one-to-one correspondence to each other. Such one-to-one correspondence pairs constitute the basis for phonological two-level rules used in finite-state morphology, where executions consist of lexical-surface string pairs such as

$$k\,a\,N\,p\,a\,n$$
$$\underline{k}\,\underline{a}\,\underline{m}\,\underline{m}\,\underline{a}\,\underline{n}.$$

Parallel executions are, however, seldom restricted to same-length and fully aligned relations: One tier may contain orphan elements that do not correspond to any element in some other tier. Alternatively, an element in one tier can correspond to a sequence of elements in another tier. In the original two-level morphology [7], copies of an auxiliary symbol '0' are inserted to the strings to make their lengths superficially equal. Parallel executions that contain complex correspondences require, however, a better representation, because the trick based on auxiliary zeros does not differentiate all cases.

Generalized synchronization expressions (GSEs) [10] define *generalized synchronization languages* (GSLs), which implement an expressive representation

A. Yli-Jyrä, L. Karttunen, and J. Karhumäki (Eds.): FSMNLP 2005, LNAI 4002, pp. 271–282, 2006.
© Springer-Verlag Berlin Heidelberg 2006

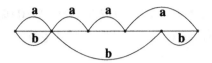

Fig. 1. A parallel execution

for parallel executions. The basic idea of GSLs is that their tiers contain start
and termination symbols (respectively a_s and a_t) of different symbols $a \in \Sigma$ in
the process symbol alphabet Σ. Because each process symbol has a start and
a termination symbol, the correspondences between the tiers can be indicated
more precisely. For example, the string $a_s b_s$ $b_t a_t$ $a_s b_s$ a_t $a_s a_t$ a_s b_t b_s $b_t a_t$
might encode the parallel execution that is shown in Figure 1. The figure indi-
cates, for example, that the second instance of process b starts after an instance
of process a, spans over two instances of a, and terminates properly inside the
last instance of a.

The strings in GSLs satisfy the start-termination condition (*st-condition* for
short) according to which the starts and terminations of each process are balanced, and no instance of a process is embedded inside another instance of the
same process. Moreover, we know [10] that GSLs are regular and that the set of
GSLs is closed under concatenation (sequencing), Kleene's closure (repetition),
and union (selection).

Synchronization languages (SLs) have, however, major problems. First, finding a complete characterization for the SLs [10] has turned out to be more
difficult than one would have expected. Secondly, SLs are designed to express
sequencing, iteration and selection of parallel processes, but it seems that they
cannot express that processes *must* overlap. This is related to the fact that every GSL is closed under a semi-commutativity relation [10] that reduces parallelism in the strings. For applications in natural language processing, e.g.
in auto-segmental phonology, it is necessary to express overlap and association between simultaneous processes. Thirdly, SLs do not seem to have any
way to express obligatory alignment of simultaneous starts or terminations of
processes.

To be able to express obligatory overlaps and alignments, we have to add
more structure to the representation of parallel processes. This article solves
the problem by introducing *pivotal synchronization languages* (PSLs), in which
special pivot processes implement alignment points inside strings. The set of
PSLs lends itself to the definition of special formalisms that specify families of
PSLs. Three such formalisms are defined in this paper.

The paper is structured as follows. Section 2.1 contains some formal prerequisites and definitions. In Section 2.2, we discuss some prior work on GSLs.
Section 3 presents the problem with GSLs. Section 4 defines the set of PSLs.
Section 5 develops new join operators. The new operators are used in Section 6 to
define PSL-based versions of three special-purpose formalisms. Section 7 closes
the paper with some general remarks.

2 Preliminaries

2.1 Basic Definitions

Let Γ be a finite alphabet. Each symbol $a \in \Gamma$ denotes both the symbol a and the set $\{a\}$. The empty string and the empty language are denoted respectively as ϵ and $\emptyset$.

Regular Operations. For languages $L_1 \subseteq \Gamma^*$ and $L_2 \subseteq \Gamma^*$, we have the following standard regular operations: *concatenation* $L_1 L_2$, *union* $L_1 \cup L_2$, *Kleene's closure* L_1^*, *positive closure* $L_1^+ = L_1 L_1^*$. *relative complement* $L_1 \backslash L_2$ and *intersection* $L_1 \cap L_2$. The *shuffle* of two strings $u, v \in \Gamma^*$ is $u \sqcup v = \{u_1 v_1 u_2 v_2 \ldots u_n v_n \mid u_i \in \Gamma^*, v_i \in \Gamma^*, u = u_1 u_2 \ldots u_n, v = v_1 \ldots v_n\}$. The shuffle of languages L_1 and L_2 is $\{u \sqcup v \mid u \in L_1, v \in L_2\}$. Inverse of a relation $R \subseteq \Gamma^* \times \Delta^*$ is denoted by R^{-1}.

   For any alphabet Γ and subset $\Delta \subseteq \Gamma$, define homomorphism $d_\Delta : \Gamma^* \rightarrow (\Gamma \backslash \Delta)^*$ in such a way that $d_\Delta(uv) = d_\Delta(u) d_\Delta(v)$ for all $u, v \in \Gamma^*$ and that $d_\Delta(a) = \epsilon$ for all $a \in \Delta$, and $d_\Delta(a) = a$ for all $a \in \Gamma \backslash \Delta$.

Starts and Terminations. For any process alphabet Γ, denote $\Gamma_s = \{a_s | a \in \Gamma\}$, $\Gamma_t = \{a_t | a \in \Gamma\}$ and $\Gamma_{st} = \Gamma_s \cup \Gamma_t$. Symbols a_s and a_t denote the start and the termination of process a, for any $a \in \Gamma$. For any language $L \subseteq \Gamma_{st}^*$ let $alpha(L)$ denote the smallest $\Omega \subseteq \Gamma$ such that $L \subseteq \Omega_{st}^*$.

The Total Process Alphabet. Let the *total process alphabet* be A. Symbols $\phi, \sigma \in A$ have special interpretations that will be presented later in the paper. The *external process alphabet* is $\Sigma = A \backslash \{\phi, \sigma\}$. Let $C_\Omega = \{c, [c, 1], [c, 2] \mid c \in \Omega\}$.

St-Condition. The st-condition for languages $L \subseteq \Sigma_{st}^*$ was defined in [10]. Intuitively, it means that, in strings, (i) every start a_s of process $a \in \Sigma$ is followed by a symbol a_t in such a way that there are no intervening instances of a_s, and that (ii) every termination a_t of process $a \in \Sigma$ is preceded by a symbol a_s in such a way that there are no intervening instances of a_t.

   Let $B = C_A$. The st-condition can be defined also for subsets of B_{st}^*. We say that string $w \in B_{st}^*$ satisfies the *st-condition over* $\Omega \subseteq B$, if and only if $w \notin \mathrm{NST}_\Omega$ where

$$\mathrm{NST}_\Omega = \bigcup_{a \in \Omega} \bigcup_{c \in C_{\{a\}}} B_{st}^* \, c_s \, (B_{st} \backslash \{c_t\})^* \, (((C_{\{a\}})_{st} \backslash \{c_t\}) \, B_{st}^*)^* \, \cup$$

$$(B_{st}^* \, ((C_{\{a\}})_{st} \backslash \{c_t\}))^* \, (B_{st} \backslash \{c_s\})^* \, c_t \, B_{st}^*$$

A language $L \subset A_{st}^*$ is said to satisfy the st-condition for subset $\Omega \subseteq A$, if, for every $w \in L$, $w \notin \mathrm{NST}_\Omega$. For every alphabet $\Omega \subseteq A$, define $W_\Omega = \Omega_{st}^* \backslash \mathrm{NST}_\Omega$.

2.2 Prior Work

Two types of synchronization languages have been defined [10] earlier: (1) restricted synchronization languages (RSLs) and (2) generalized synchronization languages (GSLs). The RSLs are a proper subfamily of GSLs. All these synchronization languages over Σ are regular subsets of W_Σ.

Synchronization languages were defined originally with synchronization expressions – restricted synchronization expressions (RSEs) and generalized synchronization expressions (GSEs). Both kinds of expressions are built from process symbols Σ under the operations of *sequencing* $\rightarrow$, *join* $\|$, *selection* $|$, *intersection* & and *repetition* $*$. The difference between RSEs and GSEs is that the join operator of RSEs requires disjoint alphabets for its operands. GSLs are obtained by generalizing the definition of join to allow shared alphabets while retaining the st-condition over Σ in the result. The semantics for both kinds of expressions reduces to regular operations.

Rewriting systems have helped to understand the properties of synchronization languages, and they provide a way to rewrite a string representing a parallel execution into a string with a lower or equal degree of parallelism.

Let Σ_{st} be the alphabet of strings. The rewriting system R_3 [10] consists of the rules

$$a_s b_s \leftrightarrow b_s a_s \text{ where } a \neq b \text{ and } a, b \in \Sigma, \tag{1}$$

$$a_t b_t \leftrightarrow b_t a_t \text{ where } a \neq b \text{ and } a, b \in \Sigma \tag{2}$$

$$b_s a_t \rightarrow a_t b_s \text{ where } a \neq b \text{ and } a, b \in \Sigma. \tag{3}$$

The rules of R_3 define a *semi-commutation relation* on Σ.

The rewriting system R_4 contains, in addition to the rules of R_3, other rules like $a_t a_s b_t b_s \leftrightarrow b_t b_s a_t a_s$ where $a \neq b$ and $a, b \in \Sigma_{st}$. Every RSL is closed under R_3 as well as under R_4, and every GSL is closed under R_3 [10].

It is difficult to characterize RSLs and GSLs with rewriting systems. For example, Ryl et. al [9] present the following result:

Proposition 1 ([9]). *There does not exist any rewriting system R such that each RSL is closed under R and that each regular st-language closed under R is a RSL.*

Nevertheless, it has been argued that R_3 and the set of *GSLs* are more natural than R_4 and the set of *RSL*. First, R_3 preserves regularity of st-languages while R_4 does not preserve regularity of st-languages in general ([10], p. 74). Second, Salomaa and Yu ([10], p. 79) show that there is a regular st-language $(b_s(a_s a_t)^* c_s b_t (a_s a_t)^* c_t)$ whose closure under R_4 is not an st-language. Third, every *finite* st-language closed under R_3 is a synchronization language [10].

3   The Problem

From the perspective of natural language processing applications, there is an important argument against both prior types of SLs: the semi-commutation relation defined by R_3 reduces parallelism, neutralizing certain important structural distinctions. For example, R_3 can rewrite the string $a_s b_s a_t b_t$ as $b_s a_s a_t b_t$ (by rule 1),

$a_s b_s b_t a_t$ (by rule 2), $b_s a_s b_t a_t$ (by rules 1 and 2), $a_s a_t b_s b_t$ (by rule 3) or $b_s b_t a_s a_t$ (by rules 1, 2 and 3), which means that the intended representation of partially overlapping processes a and b is neutralized.

One could try to insert into the string $a_s b_s a_t b_t$ a third process c that would coincide with the overlap of a and b. As far as the authors can judge, this does not seem to work out in practice: the rewriting rules of R_3 would move also the symbols c_s and c_t. Consequently, b_s can undesirably flip over a_t:

$$a_s b_s c_s c_t a_t b_t \rightarrow a_s c_s b_s a_t c_t b_t \rightarrow a_s c_s a_t b_s c_t b_t$$

In natural language processing, there would be several possible uses for a class of regular languages that could encode alignments and mandatory parallelism. For example, if we want to model the phonological sub-theory called Feature Geometry, associations between overlapping phonological features and tiers must be expressible. If we want to model phrase structures, segmentation or phonological processes with multi-segment changes, we may want to use process symbols that align to their internal structure. These needs motivate adding more explicit expressibility of overlaps and alignments to SLs.

4   Pivotal Synchronization Languages

Our approach to the presented problem is to introduce a special process, called *pivot*, ϕ, whose starts and terminations are barriers for local reordering captured by rewriting systems R_3 or R_4.

Based on the idea of pivots, we propose a family of synchronization-like languages: *pivotal synchronization languages (PSLs)*. In contrast to proper synchronization languages, PSLs are not primarily defined using a class of synchronization expressions, but by a set of properties.

Definition 1. *The set of* pivotal synchronization languages (PSLs) *over an external process alphabet Σ consists of*

1. *subsets of $(\phi_s \Sigma_t^* \Sigma_s^* \phi_t)^*$ that*
2. *satisfy the st-condition over $\Sigma \cup \{\phi\}$,*
3. *are regular, and*
4. *are closed under the rewriting system R_2 comprising rules (1) and (2).*

For example, a string of a GSL would now correspond to a string in a PSL as follows

$$a_s b_s \quad b_t a_t \quad a_s b_s \quad a_t \quad a_s \quad a_t \quad a_s \quad b_t \quad b_s \quad b_t a_t$$
$$\phi_s a_s b_s \phi_t \phi_s b_t a_t \phi_t \phi_s a_s b_s \phi_t \phi_s a_t \phi_t \phi_s a_s \phi_t \phi_s a_t \phi_t \phi_s a_s \phi_t \phi_s b_t \phi_t \phi_s b_s \phi_t \phi_s b_t a_t \phi_t$$

Theorem 1. *Pivotal synchronization languages are closed under concatenation, union, intersection and Kleene's closure.* □

Observation 1. The constant factor $\phi_t\phi_s$ is repeated in strings. A more efficient representation would use a single symbol, but the current representation is motivated by clarity and the st-property of process symbol ϕ.

Observation 2. Simultaneous starts or simultaneous terminations can be permuted in the pivots. A canonical order for them could optimize the implementation.

Observation 3. An anonymous reviewer inquired whether PSLs could be useful in finding a better characterization for synchronization languages in general. In this paper, we do not explore this interesting question.

5   Defining Join Operators for PSLs

5.1   The Join for Synchronization Languages

In generalized synchronization expressions [10], the extended join $L_1 \parallel L_2$ was defined as $(L_1 \sqcup L_2) \cap W_\Sigma = (L_1 \sqcup L_2)\backslash\mathrm{NST}_{alpha(L_1)\cap alpha(L_2)}$.

5.2   Sharing of Pivots

Given two strings $u, v \in A_{st}^*$ whose extended join is nonempty, the length of the resulting strings are the sum of the lengths of u and v. Because the processes cannot be embedded, this means that the pivots of the strings are interleaved. For example, joining two copies of $\phi_s a_s \phi_t \ \phi_s a_t \phi_t$ gives the string $\phi_s a_s \phi_t \ \phi_s a_t \phi_t$ $\phi_s a_s \phi_t \ \phi_s a_t \phi_t$. The result would nullify the motivation to use pivots. Pivots were needed for the alignment of parallel processes and now they do not do it.

The correct definition of the join operator for PSLs requires

1. that the pivots of the strings u and v may be *shared* (for example, the join of sets $\{\phi_s a_s \phi_t \ \phi_s a_t \phi_t\}$ and $\{\phi_s b_s \phi_t \ \phi_s b_t \phi_t\}$ should include string $\phi_s a_s b_s \phi_t$ $\phi_s a_t b_t \phi_t$).
2. that the result allows also for *interleaving* of the pivots (for example, the join of sets $\{\phi_s a_s \phi_t \ \phi_s a_t \phi_t\}$ and $\{\phi_s b_s \phi_t \ \phi_s b_t \phi_t\}$ should include also strings $\phi_s a_s \phi_t \ \phi_s b_s \phi_t \ \phi_s a_t b_t \phi_t$, $\phi_s a_s \phi_t \ \phi_s a_t \phi_t \ \phi_s b_s \phi_t \ \phi_s b_t \phi_t$ and $\phi_s a_s \phi_t \ \phi_s b_s \phi_t$ $\phi_s a_t \phi_t \ \phi_s b_t \phi_t$).

The shuffle operator seems incapable of handling the resulting complex operation. The sharing can be implemented with an intersection-like operation and the interleaving can be implemented with latent pivots. Language $(\phi_s \phi_t)^*$ could be added freely in places where unknown pivots could be interleaved later. With latent pivots, the input string $\phi_s a_s \phi_t \phi_s a_t \phi_t$ expands to the language $(\phi_s \phi_t)^* \phi_s a_s \phi_t (\phi_s \phi_t)^* \phi_s a_t \phi_t (\phi_s \phi_t)^*$. The expanded strings allow for interleaving of pivots, by reducing the interleaving to sharing.

5.3   Merging the Contents of Pivots

While the pivot structure ϕ is shared under join, *the contents of the corresponding pivots should be always merged*. For example, the join of languages

$\{\phi_s a_s \phi_t \phi_s a_t \phi_t\}$ and $\{\phi_s b_s \phi_t \ \phi_s b_t \phi_t\}$ should contain the R_2 closure of $\phi_s a_s b_s \phi_t$ $\phi_s a_t b_t \phi_t$. Moreover, the join of languages $\{\phi_s \phi_t \ \phi_s \phi_t\}$ and $\{\phi_s a_s \phi_t \ \phi_s a_t \phi_t\}$ should include string $\phi_s a_s \phi_t \ \phi_s a_t \phi_t$. Merging is more than intersection, but it can be implemented easily by combining intersection, substitutions and inverse substitutions. This approach will be used in Formula (4) where some further ideas, called 'reservations' and 'aligned processes' are also implemented.

Reservations. We want to have control over the merging. In the so-called IDL-expressions, we will need to implement an operator that locks the string so that further merges and interleaves inside the string are no more possible. To implement this, we will add, by default, *reservations* σ_s and σ_t for possible merges in the strings. For example, the sets of pivots $\phi_s \sigma_s^* a_s \sigma_s^* \phi_t$ and $\phi_s \sigma_s^* b_s \sigma_s^* \phi_t$ are merged by replacing σ_s once with b_s in the strings of the first set and with a_s in the strings of the second set, resulting into the set of pivots $\phi_s \sigma_s^* (a_s \sigma_s^* b_s \cup b_s \sigma_s^* a_s) \sigma_s^* \phi_t$.

For any subset $\Omega \subseteq A \backslash \{\phi\}$, let $P_\Omega = (\phi_s \Omega_t^* \Omega_s^* \phi_t)^*$. By Definition 1, PSLs are subsets of P_Σ. PSLs with reservations are subsets of $P_{\Sigma \cup \{\sigma\}}$. The reservations need to be removed in the completion of the construction of PSLs. We will do this by *discarding* the strings that contain symbols σ_s and σ_t.

Aligned Processes. In section 6.3, we will define a formalism with a so-called alignment operator that resembles the join when the alphabets of the operand languages are disjoint, but intersection if the alphabets of the operand languages are equivalent. The operator uses information on the shared symbols between the alphabet. In the result, the instances of the shared processes must coincide (they will be called *aligned processes*), while the rest correspond to reservations in one language and existing symbols in the other.

5.4   The New Join Operators

The Intersecting Join Operator. There is, indeed, a general operator that can be used both for defining the join with aligned processes as well as the normal join. This new operator, called *intersecting join*, is defined as

$$L_1 \|_\Omega L_2 = m_3^{-1}(m_{1,\Omega}(L_1) \cap m_{2,\Omega}(L_2) \backslash \mathrm{NST}_{C_\Sigma}) \tag{4}$$

where the parameter $\Omega \subseteq \Sigma$ is used to specify processes whose instances are interleaved, $\Sigma_1 = alpha(L1)$, $\Sigma_2 = alpha(L2)$, and the substitutions $m_{1,\Omega}$, $m_{2,\Omega}$, $m_3 : A_{st}^* \to 2^{B_{st}^*}$ are defined according to Table 1.

The Subtracting Join Operator. One more variant of the intersecting join operator is needed in section 6.3. This variant is called *subtracting join*, and is defined as

$$L_1 \backslash\!\backslash_\Omega L_2 = m_3^{-1}(m_{1,\Omega}(L_1) \backslash m_{2,\Omega}(L_2) \backslash \mathrm{NST}_{C_\Sigma})$$

where Ω, $m_{1,\Omega}$, $m_{2,\Omega}$, m_3, Σ_1 and Σ_2 are as in the definition of intersecting join. If $\Omega = \emptyset$, the operation reduces to subtraction. Otherwise, the result will contain any string $u \in L_1$, if, for all strings $v \in L_2$, $\{u\} \|_\Omega \{v\} = \emptyset$.

Table 1. The table contains definitions for the set-valued mappings $m_{1,\Omega}$, $m_{2,\Omega}$, m_3 : $A_{st} \to 2^{B^*_{st}}$ used in the definition of the join operators. These are extended to substitutions $A^*_{st} \to 2^{B^*_{st}}$ in the usual way.

w	$m_{1,\Omega}(w)$	$m_{2,\Omega}(w)$	$m_3(w)$
$a_x \in \{\phi_s, \phi_t\}$	$\{a_x\}$	$\{a_x\}$	$\{a_x\}$
$a_x \in \Sigma_{st}$	$\{[a,1]_x\}$	$\{[a,2]_x\}$	$\{[a,1]_x, [a,2]_x\}$
σ_x	$\{\sigma_x\} \cup \{[a,2]_x \mid a \in \Omega\}$	$\{\sigma_x\} \cup \{[a,1]_x \mid a \in \Omega\}$	$\{\sigma_x\}$

5.5 Putting It All Together

With the reservations for further merges inside pivots, sequences of latent pivots belong to the language $\phi_s \Lambda^* \phi_t$, where

$$\Lambda = \sigma_s^* \phi_t \phi_s \sigma_t^*.$$

Every process letter $a \in \Sigma$ corresponds to the language

$$\phi_s \sigma_s^* a_s \Lambda^+ a_t \sigma_t^* \phi_t.$$

A language with reservations can be locked by intersecting it with $\phi_s \mathrm{LockFilter} \phi_t$, where

$$\mathrm{LockFilter} = (\Sigma_s^+ \phi_t \phi_s \Sigma_t^+)^*.$$

In the following definitions for PSL-based formalisms, we have chosen to add the start ϕ_s of the initial pivot and the termination ϕ_t of the final pivot in the last step of the induction that returns the language denoted by an expression.

6   Applications: PSL-Based Formalisms

6.1 Synchronization Expressions

We can define synchronization expressions for pivotal synchronization languages. However, these expressions can specify only a subset of all possible PSLs.

Definition 2. *The set of basic synchronization expressions for PSLs over alphabet Σ, $\mathrm{SE}(\Sigma)$, is the smallest subset of $(\Sigma \cup \{\emptyset, \to, \&, |, \|, *, (,)\})^*$ defined inductively by the following set of rules. The PSL denoted by $\alpha \in \mathrm{SE}(\Sigma)$ is $\phi_s(\mathcal{L}(\alpha) \cap \mathrm{LockFilter})\phi_t$.*

1. *$\{\emptyset\} \cup \Sigma \subseteq \mathrm{SE}(\Sigma)$ and $\mathcal{L}(\emptyset) = \emptyset$.*
2. *if $a \in \Sigma$, then $a \in \mathrm{SE}$ and $\mathcal{L}(a) = \sigma_s^* a_s \Lambda^+ a_t \sigma_t^*$.*
3. *If $\alpha_1, \alpha_2 \in \mathrm{SE}(\Sigma)$, then $\{(\alpha_1 \to \alpha_2), (\alpha_1 \& \alpha_2), (\alpha_1 | \alpha_2), (\alpha_1 \| \alpha_2)\} \subseteq \mathrm{SE}(\Sigma)$ and*
   (a) *$\mathcal{L}(\alpha_1 \to \alpha_2) = \mathcal{L}(\alpha_1) \Lambda^* \mathcal{L}(\alpha_2)$*
   (b) *$\mathcal{L}(\alpha_1 \& \alpha_2) = \mathcal{L}(\alpha_1) \cap \mathcal{L}(\alpha_2)$*
   (c) *$\mathcal{L}(\alpha_1 | \alpha_2) = \mathcal{L}(\alpha_1) \cup \mathcal{L}(\alpha_2)$*
   (d) *$\mathcal{L}(\alpha_1 \| \alpha_2) = \Lambda^* \mathcal{L}(\alpha_1) \Lambda^* \|_\Sigma \Lambda^* \mathcal{L}(\alpha_2) \Lambda^*$.*
4. *If $\alpha \in \mathrm{SE}(\Sigma)$, then $(\alpha_1^*) \in \mathrm{SE}(\Sigma)$ and $\mathcal{L}(\alpha^*) = (\Lambda^* \mathcal{L}(\alpha) \Lambda^*)^*$.*

6.2   Interleave-Disjunction-Lock Expressions

Interleave-disjunction-lock (IDL) expressions [8] have been used to obtain compact representations for *finite* languages in natural language generation systems. IDL-expressions represent choices of phrases and their relative ordering by means of a *concatenation operator* ·, and three additional operators: *interleave* ||, *disjunction* ∨ and *lock* ×.

The interleave operator differs from shuffle by interacting with the lock operator. The lock operator is used to make a sequence of phrases look like a single unit when the two strings are interleaved. For example, the expression

$$(\times(\text{this\_bus} \cdot \text{stops}) \cdot \text{there})) \,\|\, \text{at\_5\_p.m.} \tag{5}$$

where $\Sigma = \{\text{this\_bus}, \text{stops}, \text{there}, \text{at\_5\_p.m.}\}$ defines a set that contains the strings *at_5_p.m. this_bus stops there*, *this_bus stops at_5_p.m. there*, and *this_bus stops there at_5_p.m.*, but not *this_bus at_5_p.m. stops there*. Figure 2 illustrates how the phrases correspond to processes.

PSLs can be used to implement expressions similar to IDL-expressions. The original compilation method for IDL-expressions was based on an algorithm that directly synthesized an automaton. When the string *it stops there now* is encoded as a string of a PSL, it will look like $\phi_s it_s \phi_t \ \phi_s it_t stops_s \phi_t \ \phi_s stops_t there_s \phi_t$ $\phi_s there_t now_s \phi_t \ \phi_s now_t \phi_t$. In the following, we will implement IDL-expressions on the basis of this correspondence.

Definition 3. *The set of* PSL-based IDL-expressions *over alphabet* Σ, IDL(Σ), *is the smallest subset of* $(\Sigma \cup \{[,], \cdot, \vee, \|, \times, (,)\})^*$ *defined inductively by the following set of rules. The PSL denoted by* $\alpha \in$ IDL(Σ) *is* $\phi_s \mathcal{L}(\times\alpha)\phi_t$.

1. *if* $a \in \Sigma$, *then* $[a] \in$ IDL(Σ) *and* $\mathcal{L}([a]) = (\sigma_s^* a_s \Lambda^+ a_t \sigma_t^*) \cap$ LockFilter.
2. *If* $\alpha \in$ IDL(Σ), *then* $(\times\alpha) \in$ IDL(Σ) *and* $\mathcal{L}(\times\alpha) = \mathcal{L}(\alpha) \cap$ LockFilter.
3. *If* $\alpha_1, \alpha_2 \in$ IDL(Σ), *then* $\{(\alpha_1 \cdot \alpha_2), (\alpha_1 \vee \alpha_2), (\alpha_1\|\alpha_2)\} \subseteq$ IDL(Σ), *and*

   (a) $\mathcal{L}(\alpha_1 \cdot \alpha_2) = \mathcal{L}(\alpha_1)\Lambda^*\mathcal{L}(\alpha_2)$
   (b) $\mathcal{L}(\alpha_1 \vee \alpha_2) = \mathcal{L}(\alpha_1) \cup \mathcal{L}(\alpha_2)$
   (c) $\mathcal{L}(\alpha_1\|\alpha_2) = \Lambda^*\mathcal{L}(\alpha_1)\Lambda^* \,\|_\Sigma\, \Lambda^*\mathcal{L}(\alpha_2)\Lambda^*$.

Observation 4. The iteration operator that is missing from the original IDL-expressions could be introduced to our PSL-based definition.

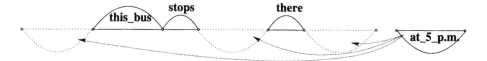

Fig. 2. Interpreting the interleave operator in terms of possible executions

6.3   Restriction Expressions

The Definition. Let Π be an alphabet such that $\Diamond \notin \Pi$. For each $g \in \mathbb{N}$, the operator of *generalized restriction* [11] involves (in addition to the universal language Π^*) two languages:

- set $L_1 \subseteq \Pi^*(\Diamond\Pi^*)^g$, called a *generalized precondition*
- set $L_2 \subseteq \Pi^*(\Diamond\Pi^*)^g$, called a *generalized postcondition*.

The operator maps these arguments to the subsets of Π^*, as follows

$$\text{generalized-restriction}(\Pi, \Diamond, L_1, L_2) = \Pi^* - d_{\{\Diamond\}}(L_1 - L_2). \qquad (6)$$

The operator has two equivalent syntactic forms, $L_1 \overset{g\Diamond}{\Rightarrow} L_2$ and $L_2 \overset{g\Diamond}{\Leftarrow} L_1$.

An Example Application. Generalized restrictions can be used to compile classical two-level rules [7] that have been a very successful formalism in computational morphology. Two-level rules — context restrictions (=> rules) and surface coercions (<= rules) — specify properties of strings over a pair-symbol alphabet $\Pi = \Sigma_1 \times \Sigma_2 = \{a : \underline{b} \mid a \in \Sigma_1, \underline{b} \in \Sigma_2\}$. Without loss of generality, we can assume $\Sigma_1 \cap \Sigma_2 = \emptyset$. For example, the two-level rule

$$\text{N:}\underline{m} \text{ <=> } \underline{} \text{ p:}\underline{p} \qquad (7)$$

specifies, by the convention [7], that symbol N pairs with $\underline{m}$ *if and only if* it is immediately followed by the pair p:$\underline{p}$. Rule (7) reduces to the following generalized restrictions

$$\Pi^* \ \Diamond \ \text{N:m} \ \Diamond \ \Pi^* \ \overset{2\Diamond}{\Rightarrow} \ \Pi^* \ \Diamond \ \{\text{N:}\underline{x} \mid \underline{x} \in \Sigma_2\} \ \Diamond \ \text{p:}\underline{p} \ \Pi^* \qquad (8)$$

$$\Pi^* \ \Diamond \ \text{N:m} \ \Diamond \ \Pi^* \ \overset{2\Diamond}{\Leftarrow} \ \Pi^* \ \Diamond \ \{\text{N:}\underline{x} \mid \underline{x} \in \Sigma_2\} \ \Diamond \ \text{p:}\underline{p} \ \Pi^*. \qquad (9)$$

The PSL-Based Reformulation

Definition 4. *The set of PSL-based restriction expressions over alphabet Σ, $\mathrm{RX}(\Sigma)$, is the smallest subset of $(\Sigma \cup \{..., \tilde{\ }, *, \mid, ::, :!, \Box, \nabla, \Rightarrow, (,)\})^*$ defined inductively by the following set of rules. The corresponding PSL denoted by $\alpha \in \mathrm{RX}(\Sigma)$ is $\phi_s(\mathcal{L}(\alpha) \cap \mathrm{LockFilter})\phi_t$.*

1. *$... \in \mathrm{RX}(\Sigma)$ and $\mathcal{L}(...) = \Lambda^*$.*
2. *$\Sigma \subseteq \mathrm{RX}(\Sigma)$ and $\mathcal{L}(a) = \sigma_s^* a_s \Lambda^+ a_t \sigma_t^*$.*
3. *If $\alpha \in \mathrm{RX}(\Sigma)$, then $\{(\alpha^*), (\tilde{\ }\alpha)\} \subseteq \mathrm{RX}(\Sigma)$ and*
   (a) $\mathcal{L}(\alpha^*) = \mathcal{L}(\alpha)^*$
   (b) $\mathcal{L}(\tilde{\ }\alpha) = (\sigma_s^* \Sigma_s^* \Lambda \Sigma_t^* \sigma_t^*)^* \backslash\!\backslash_{(\Sigma \backslash alpha(\mathcal{L}(\alpha)))} \mathcal{L}(\alpha)$.
4. *If $\alpha_1, \alpha_2 \in \mathrm{RX}(\Sigma)$, then $\{(\alpha_1\alpha_2), (\alpha_1 \mid \alpha_2), (\alpha_1 :: \alpha_2), (\alpha_1 :! \alpha_2)\} \subseteq \mathrm{RX}(\Sigma)$ and*
   (a) $\mathcal{L}(\alpha_1\alpha_2) = \mathcal{L}(\alpha_1)\mathcal{L}(\alpha_2)$
   (b) $\mathcal{L}(\alpha_1 \mid \alpha_2) = \mathcal{L}(\alpha_1) \cup \mathcal{L}(\alpha_2)$

(c) $\mathcal{L}(\alpha_1 :: \alpha_2) = \mathcal{L}(\alpha_1) \|_{\Sigma \setminus (alpha(\mathcal{L}(\alpha_1)) \cap alpha(\mathcal{L}(\alpha_2)))} \mathcal{L}(\alpha_2)$

(d) $\mathcal{L}(\alpha_1 :! \alpha_2) = \mathcal{L}(\alpha_1) \backslash\!\backslash_{\Sigma \setminus (alpha(\mathcal{L}(\alpha_1)) \cap alpha(\mathcal{L}(\alpha_2)))} \mathcal{L}(\alpha_2)$.

5. If $c \in \Sigma$ and $\alpha \in \mathrm{RX}(\Sigma)$ then $\{(\nabla c\alpha), (\Box c\alpha)\} \subseteq \mathrm{RX}(\Sigma)$ and

(a) $\mathcal{L}(\nabla c\alpha) = d_{\{c_s, c_t\}}(\mathcal{L}(\alpha))$.

(b) $\mathcal{L}(\Box c\alpha) = m_3^{-1}(m_{1, alpha(\mathcal{L}(\alpha)) \setminus \{c\}}(\mathcal{L}(\alpha)) \setminus NST_{C_\Sigma})$.

6. If $\alpha_1, \alpha_2 \in \mathrm{RX}(\Sigma)$ and $c \in \Sigma$, then $(\alpha_1 \overset{c}{\Rightarrow} \alpha_2) \in \mathrm{RX}(\Sigma)$ and
$\mathcal{L}(\alpha_1 \overset{c}{\Rightarrow} \alpha_2) = \mathcal{L}(\,\tilde{}\,(\nabla c\,(\alpha_1 :! \alpha_2)\,)\,)$.

The operator $\tilde{}$ presents one way to define the *complement* of a PSL. The current definition uses reservations to represent the symbols not in α.

The usual intersection operator is replaced here with *alignment* :: that is related to the : operator that creates correspondence pairs in [7]. When the alphabets of the arguments of :: are disjoint, the operator is similar to join of synchronization expressions, but if all the symbols in the alphabets are shared, the operator reduces to intersection. The *misalignment* operator :! is similar to :: but it returns the strings of the first operand if they cannot be aligned to any string in the second operand.

The $\Box$-operator is used to expand the reservations in partial descriptions of a set of parallel executions. Without it, the reservations would not match to the process symbols already in use in the language α. The start and the termination of an instance of c have the same function as the pair of $\Diamond$-symbols used in generalized conditions of (6). The process c is removed from the strings by operator ∇, which corresponds to homomorphism $d_{\{\Diamond\}}$ in (6). By combining the :!, ∇ and $\tilde{}$ operators, we formulate the *generalized restriction* operator $\overset{c}{\Rightarrow}$ for PSLs.

Example 1. The structure in Figure 1 can now be described very compactly with the following PSL-based restriction expression:

$$(a :: b) \nabla c (((a :: c)(a :: c)(a :: (cc))) :: ((b :: (ccc))(b :: c))).$$

Example 2. The expression in (8) corresponds to the following restriction expression:

$$(\Box c(...(c :: N :: \underline{m})...)) \overset{c}{\Rightarrow} \Box c(...(c :: N)(p :: \underline{p})...).$$

7   Concluding Words

In this paper, we introduced pivotal synchronization languages (PSLs) and provided PSL-based definitions for new types of join operators: intersecting join and subtracting join.

Several potential applications for PSLs suggest themselves, e.g. in natural language processing. We demonstrated that PSLs lend themselves for the reformulation of three special-purpose formalisms: (i) generalized synchronization expressions, (ii) IDL-expressions, and (iii) restriction expressions. The three PSL-based formalisms introduced here have already a lot in common and could be easily unified.

In fact, exploring different PSL-based formalisms may lead to a unified descriptional device for various alignment phenomena. PSLs may have applications in computational phonology [3] and multi-tiered morphology [6] as well as in speech annotation [4]. Some variant of the join operator could correspond to the operator used in describing non-concatenative processes in finite-state morphology [2]. Furthermore, PSLs may have relevance to related frameworks in computer science [1, 5].

The construction of IDL-expressions and extended two-level expressions has been initially tested with Xerox finite-state compiler (XFST). Comprehensive testing would, however, require using an extensible finite-state tool (such as FSA Utilities). Possible applications of PSLs would presumably have relatively large process alphabets. Therefore, without optimizations, the currently presented expressions might not be easy to evaluate.

We did not define expressions that would characterize PSLs. Discovering a complete set of expressions would help to understand the nature of PSLs better. Then, pivotal synchronization languages might contribute something to the general discussion on synchronization languages and expressions.

References

1. A. Amir, R. Cole, R. Hariharan, M. Lewenstein, and E. Porat. Overlap matching. *Information and Computation*, 181:57–74, 2003.
2. K. R. Beesley and L. Karttunen. *Finite State Morphology*. CSLI Studies in Computational Linguistics. CSLI Publications, Stanford, CA, USA, 2003.
3. S. Bird and T. M. Ellison. One-level phonology: Autosegmental representations and rules as finite automata. *Computational Linguistics*, 20(1):55–90, 1994.
4. S. Bird and M. Liberman. A formal framework for linguistic annotation. *Speech Communication*, 33:23–60, 2001.
5. J. M. Hélary, A. Mostefaoui, and M. Raynal. Interval consistency of asynchronous distributed computations. *Journal of Computer and System Sciences*, 64:329–349, 2002.
6. G. A. Kiraz. Multitiered nonlinear morphology using multitape finite automata: A case study on Syriac and Arabic. *Computational Linguistics*, 26(1):77–105, 2000.
7. K. Koskenniemi. *Two-level morphology: a general computational model for word-form recognition and production*. Number 11 in Publications of the Department of General Linguistics, University of Helsinki. Yliopistopaino, Helsinki, 1983.
8. M.-J. Nederhof. IDL-expressions: A formalism for representing and parsing finite languages in natural language processing. *Journal of Artificial Intelligence Research*, 21:287–317, 2004.
9. I. Ryl, Y. Roos, and M. Clerbot. About synchronization languages. In L. Brim et al., editors, *MCFS'98*, number 1450 in LNCS, pages 533–542. Springer-Verlag, Berlin Heidelberg, 1998.
10. K. Salomaa and S. Yu. Synchronization expressions with extended join operation. *Theoretical Computer Science*, 207:73–88, 1998.
11. A. M. Yli-Jyrä and K. Koskenniemi. Compiling contextual restrictions on strings into finite-state automata. In L. Cleophas and B. W. Watson, editors, *The Eindhoven FASTAR Days, Proceedings*, Computer Science Reports 04/40, Eindhoven, The Netherlands, September 3–4 2004. Technische Universiteit Eindhoven.

A Complete FS Model for Amharic Morphographemics

Saba Amsalu and Dafydd Gibbon

Universität Bielefeld, Germany

Our aim was to develop a complete morphographemic model for Amharic, the official language of Ethiopia, which urgently needs computational linguistic tools for information retrieval and natural language processing. Amharic is a Semitic language, with SOV word order and a complex morphology with consonantal roots and vowel intercalation, extensive agglutination, and both consonantal and vocalic stem modification. Previous computational models of Amharic lexemes are fragmentary, being restricted to affix stripping and radical extraction [2], [4], [3], [1]. The verb analysis by Fissaha and Haller [8] is the only previous FS based approach. FS and related approaches to other Semitic languages have also tended to concentrate on selected features of theoretical interest, such as the well–known analyses of Arabic intercalation [9], [5], [10].

In contrast, we have developed the first complete FS generator/analyser of Amharic morphology for all parts of speech (POS), including loan and native noun morphology, biradical, triradical and quadradical verb root generation, with vowel intercalation, conditioned internal vowel changes, agglutinative affixation of 13 affix classes, and full and partial reduplication. Phonological gemination is not represented in the Ethiopian Fidel orthography, and thus is not implemented.

Our development approach is linguistic rather than statistical, and includes novel features for modelling intercalation and reduplication. The analysis results are evaluated for precision and recall. The software used is XFST, with SERA (System for Ethiopian Representation in ASCII) romanisation. A port to Fidel Unicode is in progress.

Part of the system architecture is outlined in the activity diagram in Figure 1, which shows the FST verb cascade in generation direction, but is interpretable in both directions. Biradicals are generated from triradicals and quadradicals are independently generated; cf. [11], [6], [7], then vowels are intercalated, affixes are concatenated and phonological alternations processed.

Amharic has noun stem reduplication (with epenthetic vowel) (cf. Figure 2). A shell wrapper outside the FS system feeds XFST with a stream of words; the actual reduplication is then performed in the FS context using a novel bracketing 'diacritic' convention (not 'flag diacritic' [5]). Formally, this is a heuristic which treats the surface lexicon as the union of singleton sets of surface forms and applies the reduplication FST to the singleton sets individually.

For evaluation purposes we generate/analyse all POS separately. The FSTs for each POS are not unioned, because the individual FSTs are to be integrated into an FST chunk parser/tagger. Each POS is evaluated individually on a test corpus for standard recall and precision scores (ambiguity scores are currently implicit in the precision values). Recall/precision values for small finite

A. Yli-Jyrä, L. Karttunen, and J. Karhumäki (Eds.): FSMNLP 2005, LNAI 4002, pp. 283–284, 2006.
© Springer-Verlag Berlin Heidelberg 2006

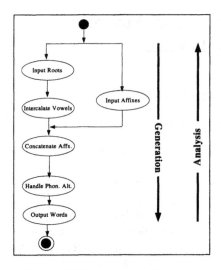

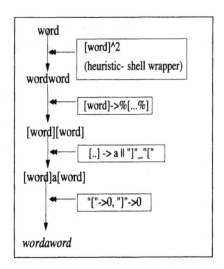

Fig. 1. FST cascade architecture   **Fig. 2.** Reduplication cascade

POS sets are, trivially, 1/1; verbs attain 0.94/0.54, nouns attain 0.85/0.94, and adjectives 0.88/0.81. The lower precision value for verbs is due to affix ambiguities (morphological syncretism).

References

1. N. Alemayehu and P. Willett. Stemming of Amharic words for information retrieval. *Literary and Linguistic computing*, 17(1):1–17, 2002.
2. L. A. Atalech Alemu and G. Eriksson. Building an Amharic lexicon from parallel texts. In *Proceedings of: First Steps for Language Documentation of Minority Languages: Computational Linguistic Tools for Morphology, Lexicon and Corpus Compilation, a workshop at LREC*, Lisbon, 2004.
3. A. Bayou. Developing automatic word parser for Amharic verbs and their derivation. Master's thesis, Addis Ababa University, Addis Ababa, 2000.
4. T. Bayu. Automatic morphological analyzer for Amharic: An experiment involving unsupervised learning and autosegmental analysis approaches. Master's thesis, Addis Ababa University, Addis Ababa, 2002.
5. K. Beesley and L. Karttunen. *Finite State Morphology*. CSLI, Stanford, 2003.
6. M. L. Bender, H. Fulas, and C. H. Dawkins. *Amharic Verb Morphology*. Michigan State University, African Studies Center, East Lansing, 1978.
7. C. H. Dawkins. *The Fundamentals of Amharic*. Sudan Interior Mission, Addis Ababa, Ethiopia, 1960.
8. S. Fissaha and J. Haller. Amharic verb lexicon in the context of machine translation. *TALN*, 2003.
9. M. Kay. Nonconcatenative finite–state morphology. In *EACL Proceedings*, pages 2–10, 1987.
10. S. Reinhard and D. Gibbon. Prosodic inheritance and morphological generalisations. In *Proceedings of EACL*, 1991.
11. B. Yimam. Root reductions and extensions in Amharic. *Ethiopian Journal of Languages and Literature*, 9:56–88, 1999.

Tagging with Delayed Disambiguation

José M. Castaño and James Pustejovsky

Department of Computer Science
Brandeis University, Waltham, MA, 02453
{jcastano, jamesp}@cs.brandeis.edu

Abstract. We discuss problems inherent in domain specific tagging (biomedical domain) and their relevance to tagging issues in general. We present a novel approach to this problem which we call *tagging with delayed disambiguation* (TDD). This approach uses a modified, statistically-driven lexicon together with a small set of morphological, heuristic, and chunking rules which are implemented using finite state machinery. They make use of both delayed disambiguation and the concept of tag underspecification as an ordered sequence of tags.

Current tagging techniques are very well established and there seems to be little room to improve the standard accuracy of 96%-97%. The availability of off-the-shelf taggers trained on significantly large corpora and their ability to be re-trained on any tagset and corpus are the determining factors for their extensive use and popularity. However when tagging a new domain, the performance drops significantly, e.g., TnT trained on the WSJ, has an accuracy of 85.19% on the GENIA Corpus.

Our approach to tagging and chunking within the bio-medical domain was motivated by practical concerns, namely targeted information extraction, in our MEDSTRACT project. This domain has been recognized as being particularly impervious to robust entity extraction [2], and our initial impression was that none of the off-the-shelf taggers we tried was performing well on this corpus. We present a novel approach called *Tagging with Delayed Disambiguation* (TDD), which uses a quantitatively derived lexicon and hand-crafted chunking rules, using finite state machinery. It has been a popular approach to address chunking as a tagging problem (e.g., CoNLL-2000 Shared Task on Chunking). The approach we have taken for tagging disambiguation is just the opposite, where disambiguation is delayed and done while chunking (if it is done at all). The key concepts in this approach are: (a) treating regular ambiguity in the language as underspecification; (b) delaying the disambiguation process, and resolving the ambiguities as chunking is performed.

Chunking rules (finite state patterns) refer to prefixes in an ordered sequence of tags (e.g., *"VBN VBD"*; past tense vs. past participle) which are interpreted as underspecified tags. They are implemented using 195 left handle rules. We also use a small set of 28 heuristic disambiguation rules *à la Brill* and a simple morphological module (33 suffixes and 44 prefixes). The system reflects common linguistic knowledge of English.

A. Yli-Jyrä, L. Karttunen, and J. Karhumäki (Eds.): FSMNLP 2005, LNAI 4002, pp. 285–287, 2006.
© Springer-Verlag Berlin Heidelberg 2006

The availability of GENIA [1] and the corpus of the UPenn Biomedical Information Extraction Project (*BioPenn*) [4] made it possible to train taggers in the Biological domain and allowed us to evaluate the performance of our approach against reference corpora. The first set of tests evaluated the TDD approach using the modified Brill lexicon (DD1) and the TnT tagger trained in the WSJ (as it comes with the distribution, TnT1). A second set of tests evaluated our approach compared with TnT trained on the WSJ and a set of approximately 1,000 abstracts from the GENIA corpus (TnT-2). The evaluation was performed on the whole set of the GENIA corpus, so there were 1,000 abstracts that were not used for training or deriving the lexicon of TnT. In TDD-2, we replaced Brill's Lexicon by the lexicon obtained from the training of TnT-2.

Table 1. Accuracy Results

Corpus	TDD-1	TnT-1	TDD-2	TnT-2
GENIA	95.18	85.19	97.92	97.62
WSJ	95.35	97.11	95.78	97.33
BioP	94.60	87.52	95.76	94.55

TDD-2 obtains state of the art accuracy (97.92%) on the GENIA corpus. The performance is lower on the WSJ, but it is remarkably good (95.78%) considering that, during the development we did not take into account any properties of this corpus. Our approach is similar to the one presented by [3], in the sense that it uses hand-crafted rules and keeps multiple tags. It is different however, because we use a statistically derived lexicon, and employ several disambiguation rules, and the evaluation is made against publicly available corpora (GENIA and WSJ), with the tagsets used in those corpora.

The rule-based, manually encoded tagger adapts itself and is easier to modify for specific purposes and domains. The annotated corpus can be seen as the desired output. It appears that a TDD approach provides a more stable result, with no need of retraining, while being less sensitive to the sparse data effect, guideline criteria and the lexicon employed .

Acknowledgements

This research has been funded by NLM grant 5R01 LM0006649-5.

References

1. N. Collier, H. Mima, S. Lee, T. Ohta, Y. Tateisi, A. Yakushiji, and J. Tsujii. The GENIA project: Knowledge acquisition from biology texts. *Genome Informatics*, 11:448–449, 2000.
2. L. Hirschman, J. C. Park, L. W. J. Tsujii, and C. H. Wu. Accomplishments and challenges in literature data mining for biology. *Bioinformatics Review*, 18(12), 2002.

3. C. Samuelsson and A. Voutilainen. Comparing a linguistic and a stochastic tagger. In P. R. Cohen and W. Wahlster, editors, *Proceedings of the ACL '97*, pages 246–253, Somerset, New Jersey, 1997. Association for Computational Linguistics.

4. S.Kulick, A.Bies, M.Liberman, M.Mandel, R.McDonald, M.Palmer, A.Schein, and L.Ungar.   Integrated annotation for biomedical information extraction.   In *NAACL/HLT Workshop on Linking Biological Literature, Ontologies and Databases: Tools for Users*, pages 61–68, 2004.

A New Algorithm for Unsupervised Induction of Concatenative Morphology

Harald Hammarström

Chalmers University of Technology
412 96 Gothenburg
Sweden
harald2@cs.chalmers.se

1   Introduction

This paper sketches a new algorithm for unsupervised induction of concatenative morphology. The algorithm differs markedly from previous approaches in both segmentation and paradigm induction. It is illustrated here with the respect to suffixes, using the following notation:

- W: the set (not bag) of words in the corpus
- $s \triangleleft w$: s is a suffix of the word w i.e there exists a (possibly empty) string x such that $w = xs$
- $Stems(s) = \{x | xs \in W\}$: the set of all strings ("stems") that make a word in the corpus if appended with s
- $f(s) = |\{w \in W | s \triangleleft w\}|$: the number of words with suffix s (equals $|Stems(s)|$)
- $s_i(w)$: the suffix of w that begins at position $0 \leq i \leq |w|$
- $Q(w) = \{s_i(w) | i < |w|\}$: the set of (non-empty) suffixes of s
- $S = \bigcup_{w \in W} Q(w)$: all suffixes in the corpus

2   Segmentation

The segmentation takes a corpus as input and output a ranked list of (all) suffixes. The ranking is meant to say how salient a suffix is for the language of the corpus, and is computed in three steps:

1. **Relative Frequency Increases:** Define $Z : S \times W \to \mathbf{Q}^+ \cup \{0\}$:

$$Z(s,w) = \begin{cases} 0 & \text{if not } s \triangleleft w \\ 1 & \text{if } s = s_0(w) \\ \frac{f(s_i)}{f(s_{i-1})} & \text{if } s = s_i(w) \text{ for some } 0 < i < |w| \end{cases} \qquad (1)$$

Note that f, and hence Z, depends on W.

2. **Accumulation:** Calculate $Z^W : S \to \mathbf{Q}^+$:

$$Z^W(s) = \sum_{w \in W} Z(s,w) \qquad (2)$$

3. **Re-scale:** Scale on suffix-length by a parametre $p = 2$: $\overline{Z^W}(s) = |s|^p \cdot Z^W(s)$

A. Yli-Jyrä, L. Karttunen, and J. Karhumäki (Eds.): FSMNLP 2005, LNAI 4002, pp. 288–289, 2006.
© Springer-Verlag Berlin Heidelberg 2006

3   Paradigm Induction

The paradigm induction phase outputs a ranked list of paradigms given a ranked list of segmented suffixes. By paradigm we simply mean a non-empty set of suffixes, and the ranking is meant to convey how salient a declension pattern is for the language in question. At first glance, the task of finding paradigms looks exceedingly difficult since the number of theoretically possible paradigms is exponential in the number of suffixes, and paradigms in real languages are often not mutually disjoint. Moreover, in a corpus of a real language we cannot expect to rely on there existing words that occur in all its forms.

1. **Testing Paradigm Heuristic:** Suppose we have a hypothesis of a paradigm P. We give a test metric using the idea that suffixes of P ought to show up on the "same stems". First, for each suffix $x \in S$, define its quotient function $H_x(y) : S \to [0,1]$ as:

$$H_x(y) = \frac{|\{z|\exists z(z \in Stems(x) \wedge zy \in W)\}|}{|Stems(x)|} \quad (3)$$

Construct a rank by summing the quotient functions of the members of P:

$$V_P(y) = \sum_{x \neq y \in P} H_x(y) \quad (4)$$

The $Rank_P(x) : S \to \mathbf{N}$ is then simply $|\{y|V_P(y) > V_P(x)\}|$.
Now, the test $VI(P)$ is a measure of how "high up" the sum of ranks of the members of P are, compared to the optimal sum (which depends on $|P|$ and is $0 + \ldots + |P| - 1$):

$$VI(P) = \frac{|P|(|P| - 1)}{2 \sum_{x \in P} rank_P(x)} \quad (5)$$

2. **Gradient Search:** It is intractable to list all hypotheses of paradigms P, thus we suggest a way to "grow" paradigms. Start with a one-member paradigm and greedily improve the VI-score, by successively adding or taking away one suffix at a time (until the score doesn't improve by a one-member change):

$$G(P) = argmax_{p \in \{P\} \cup \{P \text{ xor } s|s \in S\}} VI(p) \quad (6)$$

$$G^*(P) = \begin{cases} P & \text{if } G(P) = P \\ G^*(G(P)) & \text{if } G(P) \neq P \end{cases} \quad (7)$$

Where P xor s means $P \setminus \{s\}$ if $s \in P$ and $P \cup \{s\}$ if $s \notin P$.

Naturally, the induced paradigms $A = \{G(\{s\})|s \in S\}$ are all those that can be grown from (at least one) suffix in the corpus, and finally we rank them by their VI-score and average "suffixness" of its members:

$$R(P) : A \to \mathbf{Q}^+ \cup \mathbf{0}$$

$$R(P) = \frac{VI(P)}{|P|} \sum_{s \in P} \overline{ZW}(s) \quad (8)$$

Morphological Parsing of Tone: An Experiment with Two-Level Morphology on the Ha Language

Lotta Harjula

Institute for Asian and African Studies, University of Helsinki, Finland

Morphological parsers are typically developed for languages without contrastive tonal systems. Ha, a Bantu language of Western Tanzania, proposes a challenge to these parses with both lexical and grammatical pitch-accent [1] that would, in order to describe the tonal phenomena, seem to require an approach with a separate level for the tones. However, since the Two-Level Morphology [3] has proven successful with another Bantu language, Swahili [2], it is worth testing its possibilities with the tonally more challenging Bantu languages.

Lexical accents are naturally marked in the lexicon. The lexical accents of nouns and other word classes (except verbs) are lexically associated with certain vowels. Nominal lexical accents are only moved in restricted contexts which are easily defined in rules.

On the other hand, lexical accents of verbs are not underlyingly associated with any certain vowel but the association is determined by the complete verbal form. In addition to the lexical accents, verbal forms may have grammatical accents, realised either on the prefixes, or on the first or the second mora of the stem. The lexical accent or the absence of the accent, together with the grammatical accents, defines the grammatical forms of the verbs. Both lexical and grammatical accents are realised as high tones on certain tone-bearing units.

There are also some other grammatical tonal elements, called index forms that have floating accents, i.e. accents that are not underlyingly associated with any certain vowel. The accents of these forms are realised as a high tone either on the initial vowel or on the first vowel of the stem of the following word. When the possible lexical accent of the noun stem falls on the syllable following the accent of the index, the vowel of the augment is lengthened.

Thus, the morphological parser for Ha should be able to handle several different tonal phenomena: 1) the lexical accents, which are deleted or moved in some grammatical forms; 2) the grammatical accents and all their possible places of realisation; and 3) the floating accents of the index forms.

This experiment shows that it is indeed possible to morphologically parse a language with both lexical and grammatical accents with Two-Level Morphology rules. The basic idea is to mark the possible vowels on which the grammatical or moved lexical accents may fall in the lexicon, and write rules that allow the positions to be realised as surface accents when the appropriate tense marker or other segmental element is present. When there is no segmental but only tonal marking of a tense, the macrostem is lexically prefixed with a symbol that can be used as a context in the rules. Also, some of the grammatical accents may

A. Yli-Jyrä, L. Karttunen, and J. Karhumäki (Eds.): FSMNLP 2005, LNAI 4002, pp. 290–291, 2006.
© Springer-Verlag Berlin Heidelberg 2006

also be marked in the lexicon. For example, accents falling on verbal prefixes are lexically marked in a sublexicon which is only used with certain verbal forms.

However, the parsing formalism presented here does not always describe the tonal phenomena that are found in the Ha language. With some type of accents the lexical accents can be mapped directly to the surface realisations, but with others the interaction of the accents causes changes on the segmental level, or the morphophonemic changes of the segmental level affect the realisations of the accents. Thus, for proper description of the language, a formalism which would allow the tones or accents to be mapped with the segmental level only after certain rules have applied in the two levels separately, is required.

References

1. L. Harjula. *The Ha Language of Tanzania: Grammar, Texts, and Vocabulary*. Ruediger Koeppe Verlag, Cologne, 2004.
2. A. Hurskainen. Swahili Language Manager: A storehouse for developing multiple computational applications. *Nordic Journal of African Studies*, 13(3):363–397, 2004. Also in: www.njas.helsinki.fi.
3. K. Koskenniemi. *Two-level morphology: A general computational model for word form recognition and production*. Number 11 in Publications of the Department of General Linguistics. University of Helsinki, 1983.

Describing Verbs in Disjoining Writing Systems

Arvi Hurskainen, Louis Louwrens, and George Poulos

Institute for Asian and African Studies, University of Helsinki, Finland
University of South Africa, Pretoria, South Africa

Many Bantu languages, especially in Southern Africa, have a writing system, where most verb morphemes preceding the verb stem and some suffixes are written as separate words. These languages have also other writing conventions, which differ from the way they are written in other related languages. These two systems are conventionally called disjoining and conjoining writing systems. Disjoining writing can be considered simply as an under-specified way of writing, but for computational description it is a challenge, especially if the system allows only continuous sequences of characters to be recognised as units of analysis. In order to reduce unnecessary ambiguity, verb morphemes should be isolated from such strings of characters that are real words.

There are at least three approaches for handling disjoining writing. (a) Each continuous string of characters is considered a 'word' and ambiguity is resolved after morphological description. (b) Disjoining writing is first converted to conjoining writing, in other words, it is 'normalised', and morphological description is carried out on the basis of this new writing form [2]. (c) The verbs, together with disjoint prefixes and suffixes, are described directly as verb structures.

Here we are concerned with the third method.

The most efficient method of handling verbs in a disjoining writing system is to describe them directly without pre-processing. Below we shall discuss this method by using Northern Sotho language [3] as a test case. The aim is to construct a full scale implementation that includes all verb structures and all verb stems of the language.

In addition to disjoining writing, the description of the verb involves also such non-concatenative features as reduplication of the verb stem and the constraining of co-occurrence of such verb morphemes that are on different sides of the verb stem. All these phenomena are handled in the following implementation, which makes use of the finite state methods developed by Xerox [1]. A very brief skeleton lexicon of the verb **bona** (to see) is described below.

```
Multichar_Symbols
  ^[ ^]
  @P.PAST.ilE@   @R.PAST.ilE@
  @P.SBJN.a@     @R.SBJN.a@
  @P.SBJN.E@     @R.SBJN.E@
  @P.HABIT.e@    @R.HABIT.e@
  @P.NORM.a@     @R.NORM.a@
LEXICON Root
```

A. Yli-Jyrä, L. Karttunen, and J. Karhumäki (Eds.): FSMNLP 2005, LNAI 4002, pp. 292–294, 2006.
© Springer-Verlag Berlin Heidelberg 2006

```
    SubjPref;
LEXICON SubjPref
  ke=Sbjn+@P.NORM.a@:@P.NORM.a@ke%  FutPref;
  ke=Sbjn+@P.SBJN.E@:@P.SBJN.E@ke%  VStart;
  ke=Habit+@P.HABIT.e@:@P.HABIT.e@ke%  VStart;
  ke=Perf+@P.PAST.ilE@:@P.PAST.ilE@ke%  VStart;
LEXICON FutPref
  tla=Fut+:tla%  VStart;
LEXICON VStart
  0:^[{ VStem;
LEXICON VStem
  bon VFinV;
LEXICON VFinV
  +a@R.NORM.a@:@R.NORM.a@A VEnd;
  +a=Redup@R.NORM.a@:@R.NORM.a@A VEndRedup;
  +E@R.SBJN.E@:@R.SBJN.E@E VEnd;
  +E=Redup@R.SBJN.E@:@R.SBJN.E@E VEndRedup;
  +e@R.HABIT.e@:@R.HABIT.e@e VEnd;
  +e=Redup@R.HABIT.e@:@R.HABIT.e@e VEndRedup;
  +ilE@R.PAST.ilE@:@R.PAST.ilE@ilE VEnd;
  +ilE=Redup@R.PAST.ilE@:@R.PAST.ilE@ilE VEndRedup;
LEXICON VEnd
  0:}^1^] #;
LEXICON VEndRedup
  0:}^2^] #;
```

The full description of the verb in Northern Sotho contains a number of structures, where the verb-final vowel, or a suffix, constrains the co-occurrence of certain verb prefixes. In the above example we have four cases, where the marker of the correct word form is the verb final vowel or suffix. Because the marker is after the verb stem, it is not practical to construct the finite state lexicon separately for each case.

The Xerox tools offer a method for handling such cases. A set of flag diacritics can be used in the lexicon for controlling the co-occurrence of certain morphemes. In this implementation, we have used a pair of the P-type and R-type flag diacritics for controlling the morpheme sequences ([1], pp. 353-355).

Particularly important in the lower-side meta-language is the section of the string that is subject to reduplication. This section is delimited with special multi-character symbols ^[and ^]. We also see that the actual string to be defined as a regular expression is enclosed with curly brackets { and }. The multi-character symbol ^2 in the lower string triggers the reduplication of the preceding regular expression. The Xerox tool package contains a compile-replace algorithm, which makes it possible to include finite state operations other than concatenation into the morphotactic description ([1], pp. 379-380).

The full description of the Northern Sotho verb is much more complicated than what is described above. The morpheme slots, which mark agreement for each noun class, have a total of twenty alternative prefixes, including first and second person singular and plural. Morpheme slots of this type include the subject prefix, which can be repeated after tense-aspect marking in some forms, and the object prefix. Verb extensions also increase the number of possible forms.

Some amount of complexity is added also by the object prefix of the first person singular, which is a nasal. It causes several types of sound changes in the first phoneme of the verb stem, and such forms are written conjointly.

The normal compilation of the lexicon of this size and complexity into a transducer is no problem, although the verb structure produces more than 4 billion paths. The memory problem will be encountered when 'compile-replace lower' is applied to this initial network.[1]

It is possible to reduce the number of paths by merging identical morphemes in a morpheme slot into a single entry and return them to separate readings in the post-processing phase. By this method the maximum number of morphemes in a morpheme slot is reduced from twenty to eleven and the number of paths is reduced accordingly. Another, and more efficient, method for handling the memory problem is to cut the lexicon into parts, so that only the section requiring a regular expression notation, i.e. the verb stems, will be compiled with compile-replace lower, and then these partial lexicons are composed together as a single net. Because the verb reduplication concerns the verb stem only, the section of prefixes can be treated as a partial lexicon of its own. Using this method, it was possible to compile the full Northern Sotho verb lexicon with more than 4 billion paths. The total compilation time with Compac NX 7000 in Linux environment was less than two minutes.

References

1. K. Beęsley and L. Karttunen. *Finite State Morphology*. CSLI Studies in Computational Linguistics. Center for the Study of Language and Information, Stanford, CA, 2003.
2. A. Hurskainen and R. Halme. Mapping between disjoining and conjoining systems in Bantu languages: implementation on Kwanyama. *Nordic Journal of African Studies*, 10(3):399–414, 2001.
3. G. Poulos and L. J. Louwrens. *A linguistic analysis of Northern Sotho*. Via Afrika Ltd., Pretoria, 1994.

---

[1] For discussion on memory problems see [1], pp. 418-420.

An FST Grammar for Verb Chain Transfer in a Spanish-Basque MT System

Iñaki Alegria, Arantza Díaz de Ilarraza, Gorka Labaka, Mikel Lersundi,
Aingeru Mayor, and Kepa Sarasola

IXA Group, University of the Basque Country

We are developing an Spanish-Basque MT system using the traditional transfer model and based on shallow and dependency parsing. The project is based on the previous work of our group but integrated in OpenTrad initiative [2]. This abstract sumarizes the current status of development of an FST grammar for the structural transfer of verb chains. This task is quite complex due to the high distance between both languages. In the actual implementation we are using XRCE Finite States Tools [1].

We will focus on the translation of Spanish non-finite forms (21%), indicative forms (65%) and periphrases (6%) covering 92% of all possible cases.

Spanish finite verbs are composed by several morphemes giving information about voice, mood, aspect, tense, person and number. Verb conjugations have simple or compound tenses. The periphrases are composed by a finite auxiliary verb, an optional particle, and the main verb (non-finite form, infinitive or gerund, giving the meaning).

Basque finite verbs can be synthetic, consisting of a single word, or analytical, consisting of a participial form and an auxiliary. Participles carry information about meaning, aspect and tense, whereas auxiliaries convey information about argument structure, tense and mood.

Depending on the Spanish form of the verb, its translation into Basque should be obtained in a different way. For the non-finite forms we translate with a verbal noun or a participle. Simple and complex tense verbs can be translated as synthetic or as analytical depending on the verb and its tense and, in some cases, we need a dummy auxiliary and its aspect. For the periphrases the schemma for Basque is very different: the main verb, the translation of the periphrastic form (or a modal particle or an adverb) and in some cases a dummy verb (each one with a different aspect). In the last position another auxiliary verb which depends on the transitive feature of the main verb or of the auxiliary verb.

The FST grammar for verb chains we present takes as input the morphological information of the nodes of the Spanish verb chain, the Basque form corresponding to the Spanish main verb of the chain, agreement information about the objects (absolute and dative) and the type of subordination of the sentence. Its output is the list of the nodes of the corresponding Basque verb chain, each one with the information necessary to decide the order of the words, and to realize the morphological generation. The grammar contains three kinds of rules:

A. Yli-Jyrä, L. Karttunen, and J. Karhumäki (Eds.): FSMNLP 2005, LNAI 4002, pp. 295–296, 2006.
© Springer-Verlag Berlin Heidelberg 2006

Identification and markup rules identify the type of the Spanish verb chain, and add a different schema for the Basque verb chain depending on the type: non-finite forms, non-periphrastic verbs and four periphrasis type verbs.

```
[ esVerbChainType @-> ... "=>" euVerbChainSchema ]
```

Attributes replacement rules replace attributes in the Basque schema with their corresponding values, depending on the values of some attributes in the Spanish verb chain and/or in the Basque schema.

```
[ "euAttr" @-> "euVal" || ?* esVals ?* "=>" ?* euVals ?* _ ]
```

Cleaning rules remove the unnecessary information.

This example illustrates the process: *"porque no habré tenido que comer patatas" (because I won't have to eat potatoes).* The input for the sequence of transducers that will transfer the verb chain is the following:

```
haber[vaif1s]+tener[vmpp]+que[cs]+comer[vmn]/[tr][3p][caus]/jan
```

The first rule identifies the input of a Spanish verb chain that has a periphrastic of type 1, and adds the schema for the Basque verb for this type:

```
haber[vaif1s]+tener[vmpp]+que[cs]+comer[vmn]/[tr][3p][caus]/jan
=> P1> (main)Aspm/Per Aspp/Dum Aspd/Aux TenseM SubObjDat +RelM
```

The next rules replace one by one the attributes of the Basque verb schema. These are some of the replacements and contexts that constraint them:

Attribute	Value	Context
Per	behar(per)	?* 'tener' ?* 'que' ?* "=>" 'P1' ?*
Aspp	[partPerf]	?* VAIF ?* "=>" 'P1' ?*
Aux	edun(aux)	?* 'tener' ?* 'que' ?*
SubObjDat	[s1s][o3p]	?*'tr'?*'pl'?* '=>' ?*'edun(aux)'?*'1s'

The output after all these replacements is:

```
haber[vaif1s]+tener[vmpp]+que[cs]+comer[vmn]/[tr][3p][caus]/jan
=> P1> (main)[partPerf]/behar(per)[partPerf]/izan(dum)[partFut]
/edun(aux)[indPres][subj1s][obj3p]+lako[causal morpheme]
```

The last transducer eliminates the information of the input, and returns the desired output to the MT system. The information between parenthesis will be used to decide the order of the words in the syntactic generation phase and the information between brackets will be used in order to do the morphological generation. The translation obtained in the output of the system after the generation phase is the next sentence: *"ez ditudalako patatak jan behar izango"*

References

1. K. Beesley and L. Karttunen. *Finite-State Morphology.* CSLI Publications, Stanford, California, 2003.
2. A. M. Corbí-Bellot, M. L. Forcada, S. Ortiz-Rojas, J. A. Pérez-Ortiz, G. Ramírez-Sánchez, F. Sánchez-Martinez, I. Alegria, A. Mayor, and K. Sarasola. An open-source shallow-transfer MT engine for the Romance languages of Spain. In *EAMT 10th Annual Conference (EAMT 2005), 30-31 May 2005, Budapest, Hungary*, 2005.

Finite State Transducers Based on k-TSS Grammars for Speech Translation[*]

A. Pérez[1], F. Casacuberta[2], I. Torres[1], and V. Guijarrubia[1]

[1] Universidad del País Vasco
webperaa@lg.ehu.es, {manes, vgga}@we.lc.ehu.es
[2] Universidad Politécnica de Valencia
fcn@iti.upv.es

Abstract. Finite state transducers can be automatically learnt from bilingual corpus, and they can be easily integrated in an automatic speech recognition system for speech translation applications. In this work we explore the possibility of using k-testable language models to generate translations models. We report speech translation results for one easy and well known task, *EuTrans* (Spanish-English), and for other similar task, *Euskal Turista* (Spanish-Basque). Euskal Turista has proved to be a quite difficult task because of the distance between the languages involved.

1 Introduction

Finite state transducers (FST) can be automatically learnt from bilingual corpus using the GIATI [1] methodology. This technique combines both statistical alignments models [2] and classical n-gram models. Alternatively, in this work we propose the use of a syntactic approach to n-gram models: the *k-testable in the strict sense* language models (k-TSS) [3]. Another motivation behind this work, is to study the speech translation from Spanish into Basque.

Basque is a pre-Indoeuropean language of unknown origin. It is a minority, but official language (together with Spanish), in the Basque Autonomous Region. Both nominal and verbal morphology are strongly agglutinating. Regarding to the word ordering, contrary to Spanish, Basque has left recursion. These features are the basis of both the high vocabulary in the Basque application and the hard alignments between Basque and Spanish.

2 Two Architectures for Speech Translation

The goal of the statistical speech translation (summarized in eq. (1)) is to find the target language string ($\mathbf{t}$) with the highest probability, given the acoustic representation ($\mathbf{x}$) of any source language string ($\mathbf{s}$).

$$\widehat{\mathbf{t}} = \arg\max_{\mathbf{t}} P(\mathbf{t}|\mathbf{x}) = \arg\max_{\mathbf{t}} \sum_{s} P(\mathbf{t}, \mathbf{s}|\mathbf{x}) \tag{1}$$

[*] This work has been partially supported by the Universidad del País Vasco, under grant 9/UPV 00224.310-15900/2004 and by the Spanish CICYT under project TIN2005-08660-C04-03.

A. Yli-Jyrä, L. Karttunen, and J. Karhumäki (Eds.): FSMNLP 2005, LNAI 4002, pp. 297–299, 2006.
© Springer-Verlag Berlin Heidelberg 2006

Two architectures [1] can be used in order to build the speech translation system (Fig. 1): the serial and the integrated one.

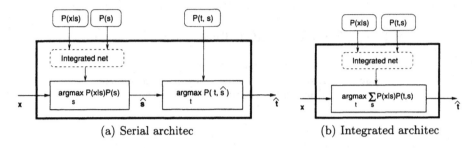

(a) Serial architec   (b) Integrated architec

Fig. 1. 1(a) A text translator after a speech decoder. 1(b) Integrated speech translator built on the basis of a text to text translator, expanding the source word on one edge by its phonetic transcription.

2.1 Serial Architecture

The speech is decoded in a conventional speech recognition system. In practice, $\hat{s}$ (the input sentence to the translator) is likely to be corrupted, since the speech recognition system is not an ideal device. Then, we can not expect the output translation to be as close to the reference as it could be in case of a perfect input. Moreover, the weakest device is the translator, therefore we should preserve it from errors as much as possible.

2.2 Integrated Architecture

In this approach, the acoustic knowledge is introduced in the whole FST. The main feature of this approach is it's ability to carry out both the recognition and the translation at the same time. In the integrated architecture, the speech recognizer and the translation system have been coupled into a unique automaton.

3 Experimental Results

Two series of experiments have been carried out on two synthetic bilingual corpora: EuTrans for Spanish to English translation [4], and Euskal Turista (ET) for Spanish to Basque translation. Spanish is the source language in both tasks. There are around 10.000 sentence pairs in the training set. The vocabulary size is around 650 word-forms in Spanish, 500 in English and 850 in Basque. In the text-test there are 3.000 pairs for Spanish to English translation, and 1.000 for Spanish into Basque. The speech corpora was recorded at 16 KHz in laboratory environment. It is composed of a training corpus of 1264 utterances by 16 speakers, and a test corpus of 336 utterances by 4 speakers [4].

The Spanish text-set perplexity is similar in both tasks (5.0), however, the speech perplexity is 6.9 for EuTrans and 13.5 for ET. Translation results are shown in table 1.

Table 1. Experimental results in means of recognition word error rate (WER) and translation word error rate (TWER)

Task	speech-WER	text-TWER	serial-TWER	integrated-TWER
EuTrans	4.4	8.1	8.9	9.1
ET	8.6	39.7	58.3	54.7

4 Concluding Remarks

A speech translation system supported on the grammatical structure provided by the k-TSS models is presented. It is a finite state transducer, learned on the basis of the so called GIATI algorithm. The finite state methods allow for an easy integration of both acoustic and translation models. Experimental results over two different corpora representing the same application task (EuTrans and ET) have been reported. In spite of the reduced vocabulary, ET has proved to be a quite difficult task (compared to EuTrans) because of great inflection and word reordering of the Basque language. Further work is needed in order to improve Basque translation models, both changing alignment methodology and including linguistic information.

References

1. Casacuberta, F., Vidal, E.: Machine translation with inferred stochastic finite-state transducers. Computational Linguistics **30** (2004) 205–225
2. Brown, P.F., Della Pietra, S.A., Della Pietra, V.J., Mercer, R.L.: The mathematics of statistical machine translation: Parameter estimation. Computational Linguistics **19** (1993) 263–311
3. Torres, I., Varona, A.: k-tss language models in a speech recognition systems. Computer Speech and Language **15** (2001) 127–149
4. Amengual, J., Benedí, J., Casacuberta, F., Castaño, M., Castellanos, A., Jiménez, V., Llorens, D., Marzal, A., Pastor, M., Prat, F., Vidal, E., Vilar, J.: The EuTrans-I speech translation system. Machine Translation **1** (2000)

Unsupervised Morphology Induction Using Morfessor

Mathias Creutz, Krista Lagus, and Sami Virpioja

Neural Networks Research Centre,
Helsinki University of Technology
P.O. Box 5400, FIN-02015 HUT, Finland
{mathias.creutz, krista.lagus, sami.virpioja}@hut.fi

Abstract. We present *Morfessor*, an unsupervised algorithm and software that induces a simple morphology of a natural language from a large corpus. Morfessor simultaneously builds a morph lexicon and represents the corpus with the induced lexicon using a probabilistic maximum a posteriori model.

The induced lexicon stores parameters related to both the "meaning" and "form" of the morphs it contains. The form of a morph consists of the string of letters, whereas the meaning corresponds to the typical context the morph appears in. The likelihood that a morph is assigned a particular grammatical category (prefix, stem, or suffix) is derived from the meaning of the morph. Depending on their categories, morphs are likely to occur in different positions with respect to each other; see [1] for details.

Morfessor has been designed to cope with languages having predominantly a concatenative morphology and where the number of morphemes per word can vary much. This distinguishes Morfessor from resembling unsupervised models, which assume a much more restricted word structure; e.g., [2].

Morph segmentations produced by Morfessor have been applied in language modeling for unlimited-vocabulary Finnish [3] and Turkish [4] speech recognition. In the experiments on Finnish, the word error rate was nearly halved compared to the traditional word-based approach. Furthermore, the use of Morfessor produced fewer recognition errors than the use of the manually designed Finnish two-level morphological analyzer, due to the better coverage of the word forms occurring in the data. Besides automatic speech recognition, further possible applications of Morfessor include information retrieval and machine translation.

Figure 1 shows some sample segmentations of Finnish, English, and Swedish word forms. An on-line demonstration and a software package implementing an earlier version of the method [5, 6] can be found at http://www.cis.hut.fi/projects/morpho/. Additionally, links to a number of related publications can be found on the web site.

A. Yli-Jyrä, L. Karttunen, and J. Karhumäki (Eds.): FSMNLP 2005, LNAI 4002, pp. 300–301, 2006
© Springer-Verlag Berlin Heidelberg 2006

aarre + kammio + i + ssa,   aarre + kammio + nsa,   bahama + saar + et,
bahama + saari + lla,   bahama + saar + ten,   edes + autta + isi + vat,
edes + autta + ma + ssa,   nais + auto + ili + ja + a,   pää + aihe + e + sta,
pää + aihe + i + sta,   pää + hän,   taka + penkki + lä + in+ en,   voi + mme + ko
abandon + ed,   abandon + ing,   abandon + ment,   beauti + ful,
beauty + 's,   calculat + ed,   calculat + ion + s,   express + ion + ist,
micro + organ + ism + s,   long + fellow + 's,   master + piece + s,
near + ly,   photograph + er + s,   phrase + d,   un + expect + ed + ly
ansvar + ade,   ansvar + ig,   ansvar + iga,   ansvar + s + för + säkring + ar,
blixt + ned + slag,   dröm + de,   dröm + des,   drömma + nde,   in + lopp + et + s,
in + lägg + n + ing + ar,   målar + e,   målar + yrke + t + s,   o + ut + nyttja + t,
poli + s + förening + ar + na + s,   trafik + säker + het,   över + fyll + d + a

Fig. 1. Examples of segmentations learned from data sets of Finnish, English, and Swedish text. Suggested prefixes are underlined, stems are rendered in **boldface**, and suffixes are *slanted*.

References

1. Creutz, M., Lagus, K.: Inducing the morphological lexicon of a natural language from unannotated text. In: Proceedings of the International and Interdisciplinary Conference on Adaptive Knowledge Representation and Reasoning (AKRR'05), Espoo, Finland (2005) 106–113
2. Goldsmith, J.: Unsupervised learning of the morphology of a natural language. Computational Linguistics **27** (2001) 153–198
3. Hirsimäki, T., Creutz, M., Siivola, V., Kurimo, M., Virpioja, S., Pylkkönen, J.: Unlimited vocabulary speech recognition with morph language models applied to finnish. Computer Speech and Language (2006) in press.
4. Hacioglu, K., Pellom, B., Ciloglu, T., Ozturk, O., Kurimo, M., Creutz, M.: On lexicon creation for Turkish LVCSR. In: Proc. Eurospeech'03, Geneva, Switzerland (2003) 1165–1168
5. Creutz, M., Lagus, K.: Unsupervised discovery of morphemes. In: Proc. Workshop on Morphological and Phonological Learning of ACL'02, Philadelphia, Pennsylvania, USA (2002) 21–30
6. Creutz, M., Lagus, K.: Unsupervised morpheme segmentation and morphology induction from text corpora using Morfessor 1.0. Technical Report A81, Publications in Computer and Information Science, Helsinki University of Technology (2005)

SProUT – A General-Purpose NLP Framework Integrating Finite-State and Unification-Based Grammar Formalisms

Witold Drożdżyński, Hans-Ulrich Krieger, Jakub Piskorski, and Ulrich Schäfer

German Research Center for Artificial Intelligence (DFKI), Language Technology Lab
Stuhlsatzenhausweg 3, D-66123 Saarbrücken, Germany
http://sprout.dfki.de

In these days, we are witnessing a growing trend of exploiting lightweight linguistic analysis for converting of the vast amount of raw textual data into structured knowledge. Although a considerable number of monolingual and task-oriented NLP systems have been presented, relatively few general-purpose architectures exist, e.g., GATE [1] or ELLOGON [2].

This presentation introduces SProUT – a novel general-purpose multilingual NLP platform [3][1]. The main motivation for its development comes from (i) the need of having one modular system for multilingual and domain-adaptive text processing, which is portable across different platforms and (ii) to find a balance between efficiency and expressiveness of the grammar formalism.

SProUT is equipped with a set of reusable online processing components for basic linguistic operations, ranging from tokenization, morphology, gazetteer etc. to text coreference resolution. They can be combined into a pipeline that produces several streams of linguistically annotated structures, which can serve as input for the grammar interpreter, applied at the next stage.

The grammar formalism in SProUT is a blend of efficient finite-state techniques and unification-based formalisms, guaranteeing expressiveness and transparency. To be more precise, a grammar in SProUT consists of pattern-action rules, where the LHS of a rule is a regular expression over typed feature structures (TFS) with functional operators and coreferences, representing the recognition pattern, and the RHS of a rule is a TFS specification of the output structure. Coreferences express structural identity, create dynamic value assignments, and serve as a means of information transport. Functional operators provide a gateway to the outside world and are utilized for introducing complex constraints in rules, for forming the output of a rule, and for integrating external processing components.

Grammars, consisting of such rules, are compiled into extended finite-state networks with rich label descriptions (TFSs). For their efficient processing, a handful of methods going beyond standard finite-state techniques have been introduced. Grammar rules can even be recursively embedded, which provides grammarians with a context-free formalism. The following rule for recognizing prepositional phrases gives an idea of the syntax of the grammar formalism.

---

[1] This publication is supported by a research grant COLLATE II 01 IN C02 from the German Federal Ministry of Education and Research.

```
pp :> morph & [POS Prep, SURFACE #prep, INFL infl & [CASE #c]]
      (morph & [POS  Adjective, INFL infl & [CASE #c, NUMBER #n, GENDER #g]]) *
      (morph & [POS  Noun, SURFACE #noun1, INFL infl & [CASE #c, NUMBER #n,
                                                        GENDER #g]])
      (morph & [POS  Noun, SURFACE #noun2, INFL infl & [CASE #c, NUMBER #n,
                                                        GENDER #g]]) ?
   -> phrase & [CAT pp, PREP #prep, CORE_NP #core_np,
                AGR agr & [CASE #c, NUMBER #n, GENDER #g]],
   where #core_np = Append(#noun1, " ", #noun2).
```

The first TFS matches a preposition. It is followed by zero or more adjectives. Finally, one or two noun items are consumed. The variables #c, #n, #g establish coreferences, expressing the agreement in case, number, and gender for all matched items (except for the initial preposition item which solely agrees in case with the other items). The RHS of the rule triggers the creation of a TFS of type phrase, where the surface form of the matched preposition is transported into the corresponding slot via the variable #prep. The value for the attribute core_np is created through a concatenation of the matched nouns (variables #noun1 and #noun2). This is realized via a call to the functional operator Append.

SProUT comes with an integrated graphical development and testing environment. The grammars can be either created in text or XML editing mode, and can be visualized in a graphical mode. The grammar GUI resembles state-of-the-art development environments for programming languages, e.g., errors and warnings listed in the error message window are linked to the corresponding piece of grammar in the editor. Several user interfaces for inspecting the output of the linguistic processing components and for testing the grammars are provided.

SProUT grammars can be cascaded in order to structure and combine different recognition strata. A declarative description of an architecture instance can be compiled to and encapsulated in a Java class and for example plugged into the Heart of Gold NLP middleware [4].

Currently SProUT has been adapted to processing 11 languages, including major Germanic, Romance, Slavonic, and Asian languages. It has been deployed as the core IE component in several industrial and research projects [3]. In our presentation we showcase the development of the SProUT named entity grammars.

References

1. Bontcheva, K., Tablan, V., Maynard, D., Cunningham, H.: Evolving GATE to Meet New Challenges in Language Engineering. In Natural Language Engineering, **12** No.(3/4), (2004) 349–373.
2. Petasis, G., Karkaletsis, V., Paliouras, G., Androutsopoulos, I. Spyropoulos, C.: Ellogon: A New Text Engineering Platform. In Proceedings of LREC 2002, Canary Island, (2002) 72–78.
3. Drożdżyński, W., Krieger, H.-U.,Piskorski J., Schäfer, U.: Shallow Processing with Unification and Typed Feature Structures – Foundations and Applications. In Künstliche Intelligenz, **1/04**, (2004) 17–23.
4. Schäfer, U.: Heart of Gold – An XML-based Middleware for the Integration of Deep and Shallow Natural Language Processing Components. User and Developer Documentation, DFKI Language Technology Lab, (2005) http://heartofgold.dfki.de.

Tool Demonstration: Functional Morphology

Markus Forsberg and Aarne Ranta

Department of Computing Science
Chalmers University of Technology and the University of Gothenburg
SE-412 96 Gothenburg, Sweden
{markus, aarne}@cs.chalmers.se

1 System Description

We will present *Functional Morphology*[1] [5], abbreviated *FM*, which is a tool that implements a methodology for constructing natural language morphologies in the functional language Haskell [8]. FM has its own runtime system that supports morphological analysis and synthesis. Moreover, a morphology implemented in FM can be compiled to many other source formats.

FM adopts a *word-and-paradigm* view of morphology: it represents a morphology as a set of inflection tables, *paradigms*, and the lexicon as a set of dictionary words each tagged with a pointer to an inflection table.

The basic idea behind FM is simple, instead of working with untyped regular expressions, which is the state of the art of morphology in computational linguistics, we use finite functions over hereditarily finite algebraic data types. These data types and functions constitute the language-dependent part of the morphology. The language-independent part consists of an untyped dictionary format which is used for synthesis of word forms, translations to other formats, and a decorated trie, which is used for analysis.

Functional Morphology builds on ideas introduced by Huet [6] in his computational linguistics toolkit Zen, which he has used to implement the morphology of Sanskrit. In particular, Huet's ideas about sandhi in Sanskrit have been adopted to a language independent description of compound analysis in FM.

The goal of FM has been to make it easy for linguists, who are not trained as functional programmers, to implement the morphology of a new language. In addition to the ease of programming, FM attempts to exploit the high level of abstraction provided by functional programming to make it possible to capture linguistic generalizations.

A morphology written in FM has a type system, which defines the inflectional and inherent parameters of the language described. By using algebraic data types, the type system can guarantee that no spurious parameter combinations appear in the morphology description, at the same time as all meaningful combinations are defined.

The use of the functional language Haskell provides, besides typing, many other language features that simplify the development of a morphology: *higher-order*

---

[1] FM homepage: http://www.cs.chalmers.se/~markus/FM/

A. Yli-Jyrä, L. Karttunen, and J. Karhumäki (Eds.): FSMNLP 2005, LNAI 4002, pp. 304–305, 2006.
© Springer-Verlag Berlin Heidelberg 2006

functions, functions as first class objects, give the possibility of defining a paradigm in terms of another paradigm; the *class system* is used for sharing code between morphologies of different languages.

The lifetime of a digital linguistic resource such as morphology depends on which system it has been developed in [3]. If the resource has been developed in a proprietary system with a binary-only format, and the system is no longer supported after some years, it may be impossible to access the resource. FM offers a solution to this problem by supporting translation to a multiple of different formats, such as XFST source code [2], GF [10] source code, SQL source code, full form lexicon, full form tables etc. This feature will hopefully prolong the lifetime of a morphology developed in FM. Furthermore, the system is completely open source, which should improve the situation even more.

2   Results

The following morphologies have been implemented in Functional Morphology: a Swedish inflection machinery and a lexicon of 20,000 words; a Spanish inflection machinery + lexicon of 10,000 words [1]; major parts of the inflection machinery + lexicon for Russian [4], Italian, Estonian [7], and Latin. Comprehensive inflection engines for Finnish, French, German, and Norwegian have been written following the same method but using GF as source language [9]. Since FM can generate GF source code, there exists a seamless connection between GF grammars and morphologies defined in FM.

References

1. I. Andersson and T. Söderberg. Spanish morphology – implemented in a functional programming language. Master's thesis in computational linguistics, Gothenburg University, May 2003. http://www.cling.gu.se/theses/finished.html.
2. K. R. Beesley and L. Karttunen. *Finite State Morphology*. CSLI Publications, Stanford, CA, 2003.
3. S. Bird and G. Simons. Seven dimensions of portability for language documentation and description. *Language*, 79:557–582, 2003.
4. L. Bogavac. Functional morphology for Russian. Master's thesis in computing science, Chalmers University of Technology, 2004.
5. M. Forsberg and A. Ranta. Functional morphology. In *Proceedings of the Ninth ACM SIGPLAN International Conference of Functional Programming*, pages 213–223, 2004.
6. G. Huet. The zen computational linguistics toolkit, 2002. http://pauillac.inria.fr/~huet/.
7. M. Pellauer. A functional morphology for estonian. Term Paper, 2005.
8. S. Peyton Jones and J. Hughes. Report on the programming language Haskell 98, a non-strict, purely functional language. Available from http://www.haskell.org, February 1999.
9. A. Ranta. Grammatical framework homepage. http://www.cs.chalmers.se/~aarne/GF/, 2000–2004.
10. A. Ranta. Grammatical framework: A type-theoretical grammar formalism. *The Journal of Functional Programming*, 14(2):145–189, 2004.

From Xerox to Aspell: A First Prototype of a North Sámi Speller Based on TWOL Technology

Børre Gaup[1], Sjur Moshagen[1], Thomas Omma[1], Maaren Palismaa[1], Tomi Pieski[1], and Trond Trosterud[2]

[1] The Saami Parliament, Norway
www.divvun.no
[2] Faculty of the Humanities, University of Tromsø
giellatekno.uit.no

Keywords: Sámi, transducers, language technology, spelling, proofing, minority languages.

1 Introduction

Our demo presents work from a joint project with a twofold goal: To build a parser and disambiguator for North and Lule Sámi, and to make a practical spell-checker for the same languages. The core analyser is written with the Xerox tools `twolc`, `lexc` and `fst` ([1]), and the disambiguator uses constraint grammar (`vislcg`). Cf. [2] for a presentation.

The spell-checker is intended to work on 3 platforms, for a wide range of programs. One of the speller engines we will have to cover is thus the `spell` family of spell-checkers (here represented by `Aspell`). This implies making a finite state automaton, rather than a transducer.

2 Aspell

Aspell (`http://aspell.net/`) is a simple list-based speller with its roots in the iSpell tradition (`http://fmg-www.cs.ucla.edu/fmg-members/geoff/ispell.html`), but with an improved spelling error detection and replacement algorithm. Its improved correction capability comes from merging Lawrence Philips Metaphone algorithm `http://aspell.net/metaphone/` with iSpell's near miss strategy of changing the input word within an editing distance of one. Aspell is nowadays recognised as a better speller than iSpell, but has several linguistic and technical limitations. It also has a reputation for being tuned for English, but our initial tests show good results for North Sámi as well. Aspell is interface compatible with iSpell, and is intended as a direct replacement.

Building on the iSpell code means that the linguistic expressive power is equally limited, and our challenge have been to find an automated way of transferring our FST to a simpler, one-level model.

A. Yli-Jyrä, L. Karttunen, and J. Karhumäki (Eds.): FSMNLP 2005, LNAI 4002, pp. 306–307, 2006.
© Springer-Verlag Berlin Heidelberg 2006

3 The Sámi Speller

Our present (alpha) version of the speller uses the Xerox tools to generate a fullform list of the whole lexicon (we exclude all circular entries), which initially created a whopping 580 Mb text file, corresponding to 150 million word forms. Aspell took that whole wordlist and could use it as it was, but it was hardly practical (it worked, though!). After some modifications our present transducer creates "only" 290 Mb of data. This list is then reduced to a set of inflection stems with the Aspell `munch-list` option. It works by passing the `munch-list` option a file of available inflection lexicons, and Aspell will then *munch* through the fullform wordlist and reduce all wordforms that fits an inflectional lexicon to one stem plus the identified inflection lexicon. Finally we compress the lexicon into an Aspell specific binary format. Its size is at the moment about 48 Mb.

This way of creating a finite state automaton is quite different from how the transducer itself works. Just like Finnish, Sámi has consonant gradation, but unlike in Finnish, the Sámi consonant gradation affects almost all consonant groups of the stressed syllable, in most stem classes (some stem classes are never altered). Moreover, in several word forms, the diphthong of the stressed syllable is altered as well. This gives us as much as 4 surface stems for one and the same lexeme. For the two-level transducer, this is not a problem, since these morphophonological processes are handled by our two-level rules, but it becomes a complicating factor when reverting to the single-level model of Aspell.

The Aspell munch-list way of creating stems and inflectional suffixes isn't very satisfying, for at least two reasons: we already have an excellent morphological description of North Sámi, and duplicating it in the form of the Aspell inflectional lexicon isn't very elegant and requires redoing the same work; and by having two parallel morphological descriptions the whole system requires more maintenance work and is more error-prone. But for the reasons cited above regarding Sámi morphophonology, we have at present not found an easy way to generate the correct inflectional stems directly from the Xerox tools.

Aspell is not the optimal speller architecture from a linguistic point of view, but it provides nice testing facilities (a command line interface with several options) and is one of the target spellers of the project. For some users the limited, word-list approach is even the preferred model over a linguistically more powerful one. It is also an interesting project in itself to make a decent Aspell, both academically and practically. Even though our alpha version shows the limitations of the simple automaton, it shows that it is powerful enough to represent even a morphophonologically complex language like Sámi.

For these reasons we targeted Aspell as our first application of our Sámi finite state transducer.

References

1. K. R. Beesley and L. Karttunen. *Finite State Morphology*. Studies in Computational Linguistics. CSLI Publications, Stanford, California, 2003.
2. T. Trosterud. Samisk språkteknologi. *Nordisk sprogteknologi - Årbog for Nordisk Sprogteknologisk Forskningsprogram 2000-2004*, 3:51–58, 2003.

A Programming Language
for Finite State Transducers

Helmut Schmid

Institute for Natural Language Processing (IMS)
University of Stuttgart, Germany
schmid@ims.uni-stuttgart.de

SFST-PL is a programming language for finite-state transducers which is based on extended regular expressions with variables. SFST-PL is used by the Stuttgart Finite-State-Transducer (SFST) tools which are available under the GNU public license. SFST-PL was designed as a general programming language for the development of tokenizers, pattern recognizers, computational morphologies and other FST applications. The first SFST application was the SMOR morphology [1], a large-scale German morphology which covers composition, derivation and inflection. An SFST program consists of a list of variable and alphabet assignments followed by a single regular expression which defines the resulting transducer. The following basic transducer expressions are available:

a:b	defines a transducer which maps the symbol **a** to **b**
a	abbreviation of **a:a**
a:.	maps the symbol **a** to any symbol that it occurs with in the alphabet (see below).
.	abbreviation of **.:.**, the union of all symbol-pairs in the alphabet.
[abc]:[de]	identical to **a:d | b:e | c:e** ("|" is the union operator.)
[a-c]:[A-C]	same as **[abc]:[ABC]**.
{abc}:{de}	identical to **a:d b:e c:<>** This expression maps the string **abc** to **de**.
var	the transducer stored in variable *var*.
"lex"	a transducer consisting of the union of the lines in the file *lex* (Apart from ":" and previously seen multi-character symbols, all symbols in the argument file are interpreted literally.)
"<file>"	is a pre-compiled transducer which is read from *file*

SFST-PL supports multi-character symbols (which are enclosed in angle brackets like **<Sg>**) and a wide range of operators including concatenation, union '\|', intersection '&', composition '\|\|', complement '!', optionality '?', Kleene star '*' and Kleene plus '+', range '^', domain '_', inversion '^_', and two-level rules (<=, =>, <=>). The special symbol <> represents the empty string.

Variables are surrounded by dollar signs. They are defined with a command **var = expression** (where **expression** is some transducer expression). The alphabet is defined with the command **ALPHABET = expression**. The definition

A. Yli-Jyrä, L. Karttunen, and J. Karhumäki (Eds.): FSMNLP 2005, LNAI 4002, pp. 308–309, 2006.
© Springer-Verlag Berlin Heidelberg 2006

of an alphabet is required for the interpretation of the wild-card symbol '.' and for the complement and replacement operators.

Comments start with a percent sign and extend up to the end of the line. Whitespace is ignored unless it is quoted by a backslash. Programs can be partitioned into several files which are combined with include commands (like #include "file") which insert the contents of the argument file at the current position. It is also possible to pre-compile component transducers in order to speed up the compilation.

A compiler translates SFST programs into minimized finite-state transducers. The compiler was implemented using a high-level C++ library and the YACC compiler generator, which makes it easy to change or extend the syntax of the programming language. The compiler generates three different transducer formats which are optimized for flexibility, speed or memory and startup efficiency, respectively. The SFST tools also include programs for analysis, printing, and comparison of transducers. The following simple SFST-PL program will correctly inflect adjectives like "easy" (easier, easiest) and late (later, latest).

```
% the set of valid character pairs
ALPHABET = [A-Za-z]:[A-Za-z] y:i [#e]:<>

% Read a list of adjectives from a lexicon file
$WORDS$ = "adj"

% rule replacing y with i if followed by # and e
$Rule1$ = y <=> i (#:<> e)

% rule eliminating e if followed by # and e
$Rule2$ = e <=> <> (#:<> e)

$Rules$ = $Rule1$ & $Rule2$

% add inflection to the words
$S$ = $WORDS$ <ADJ>:# ({<pos>}:{} | {<comp>}:{er} | {<sup>}:{est})

% apply the phonological rules to obtain the resulting transducer
$S$ || $Rules$
```

A more comprehensive morphology including mechanisms for dealing with derivation, compounding and inflection is available with the SFST tools. It is adaptable to other languages by changing the lexicon, the inflectional classes, and the phonological rules.

References

1. H. Schmid, A. Fitschen, and U. Heid. SMOR: A German computational morphology covering derivation, composition and inflection. In *Proceedings of the 4th International Conference on Language Resources and Evaluation*, volume 4, pages 1263–1266, Lisbon, Portugal, 2004.

FIRE Station

Bruce Watson

Technische Universiteit Eindhoven,
Department of Mathematics and Computer Science,
P.O. Box 513, NL-5600 MB Eindhoven, The Netherlands
bruce@bruce-watson.com

This demonstration will provide a quick introduction to the FIRE Station [1]. FIRE Station is a "workstation" environment for manipulating FInite automata/ transducers and Regular Expressions. It is built on top of the FIRE Works, a computational toolkit (with a programming interface only) for constructing, optimizing, manipulating, and using all sorts of regular language and regular relation objects. Both software systems are in a rather early stage, but the key insights are already apparent.

A key advantage over many other similar toolkits and environments is the close connection between the representation of an automaton (as a transition graph) and the representation of each state's accepted language (as a regular expression); indeed, these two concepts are simultaneously represented in a single abstract data-structure. This allows a unified view of regular languages, easing the way in which users interact with them. Perhaps more importantly, it can (in future versions) be used to allow for reversibility: from automaton back to regular expression/relation, and vice-versa. There are also significant performance advantages (in terms of memory and running time), and advantages in debugging/simulating automata. Finally, both systems are freely available, and we invite other implementors to work with us in creating new "skins" for various domains, such as computational linguistics, security systems, etc.

Reference

1. M. Frishert, L. Cleophas, and B. W. Watson. FIRE Station: an environment for manipulating finite automata and regular expression views. In M. Domaratzki, A. Okhotin, K. Salomaa, and S. Yu, editors, *CIAA 2004*, volume 3317 of *LNCS*, pages 125–133, Berlin and Heidelberg, 2005. Springer-Verlag.

A. Yli-Jyrä, L. Karttunen, and J. Karhumäki (Eds.): FSMNLP 2005, LNAI 4002, p. 310, 2006.
© Springer-Verlag Berlin Heidelberg 2006

Author Index

Printing: Mercedes-Druck, Berlin
Binding: Stein+Lehmann, Berlin

Lecture Notes in Artificial Intelligence (LNAI)